KU-681-236

Exam 70-058: Objectives

Exam 70-058: Objectives

OBJECTIVE	PAGE
PLANNING	
Select the appropriate connectivity devices for various token-ring and Ethernet networks. Connectivity devices include: • Repeaters • Bridges • Routers • Brouters • Gateways	390
List the characteristics, requirements, and appropriate situations for WAN connection services. WAN connection services include: • X.25 • ISDN • Frame relay • ATM	375, 420
IMPLEMENTATION	
Choose an administrative plan to meet specified needs, including performance management, account management, and security.	323
Choose a disaster recovery plan for various situations.	350, 471
Given the manufacturer's documentation for the network adapter, install, configure, and resolve hardware conflicts for multiple network adapters in a token-ring or Ethernet network.	111, 294
Implement a NetBIOS naming scheme for all computers on a given network.	251
Select the appropriate hardware and software tools to monitor trends in the network.	355, 484
TROUBLESHOOTING	
Identify common errors associated with components required for communications.	304, 467
Diagnose and resolve common connectivity problems with cards, cables, and related hardware.	305, 484
Resolve broadcast storms.	405
Identify and resolve network performance problems.	308, 459

Exam objectives are subject to change at any time without prior notice and at Microsoft's sole discretion. Please visit Microsoft's Training & Certification Web site (www.microsoft.com/Train_Cert) for the most current exam objectives listing.

MCSE: Networking Essentials Study Guide
Third Edition

James Chellis
Charles Perkins
Matthew Strebe

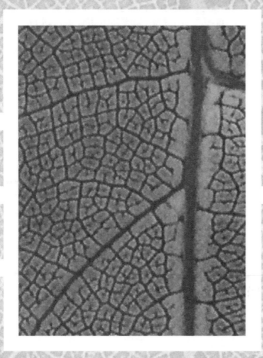

San Francisco • Paris • Düsseldorf • Soest • London

Associate Publisher: Neil Edde
Contracts and Licensing Manager: Kristine O'Callaghan
Acquisitions & Developmental Editor: Neil Edde
Associate Developmental Editor: Dann McDorman
Editors: Kelly Winquist, Ben Miller
Technical Editor: Maryann Brown
Book Designers: Bill Gibson, Patrick Dintino
Graphic Illustrator: Inbar Berman
Electronic Publishing Specialists: Cyndy Johnsen; Maureen
    Forys, Happenstance-Type-O-Rama; Bill Gibson
Project Team Leaders: Jennifer Durning, Eryn Osterhaus
Proofreader: Molly Glover
Indexer: Hugh Maddocks
CD Coordinator: Kara Schwartz
CD Technician: Keith McNeil
Cover Designer: Archer Design
Cover Illustrator/Photographer: The Image Bank

SYBEX®

To our valued readers:

From the start, Sybex has made every effort to publish high quality MCSE study guides, working closely with Microsoft, our authors, and technical reviewers to ensure the accuracy and relevance of our texts. We realize, however, that readers such as yourself require more than accurate text; you need software that offers you the opportunity to reinforce your understanding of the subject matter, test your knowledge, and gain hands-on experience with the NT computing environment. With Microsoft's recent introduction of adaptive and simulative exam formats, it's become even more critical that exam candidates possess a comprehensive understanding of NT and other Microsoft programs. It was with these points in mind that we decided to publish these new editions of our best-selling MCSE study guides.

Along with the highly acclaimed courseware on the pages that follow, you'll now find enhanced CD content that includes the following:

Program Simulators Not a mock-up, but a program that shows you how Windows NT really looks and operates. In addition to video walk-throughs of the exercises in the book, we also provide a number of hands-on simulation exercises that require your input, just as it will be required on a simulative format exam!

Electronic Flashcards for PCs and Palm Devices With each study guide, we now provide hundreds of flashcard-style questions that you can use to reinforce your understanding of key concepts. And we provide these flashcard questions in two formats—one that can be run off a standard PC and another that can be run off a Palm device. Now you can study anywhere, any time!

Sample Adaptive Exams Now a standard feature in our test engine, the adaptive testing component gives you an opportunity to experience the pressure of taking an adaptive test, one that will quickly determine if you're ready or not.

Bonus Exam-style Questions We've added hundreds of additional exam-style questions to our test engine, so you can test and re-test yourself before sitting for the actual exam.

We value your opinion and encourage you to e-mail us at Support@Sybex.com if you encounter any problems with the study guide you purchased. You can also e-mail me directly at JGold@Sybex.com with suggestions for improvements for future study guides.

Thank you for supporting Sybex and good luck in pursuit of your MCSE!

Sincerely,

Jordan Gold
Vice President/Publisher
Sybex, Inc.

SYBEX INC. 1151 MARINA VILLAGE PARKWAY, ALAMEDA, CA 94501
TEL: 510/523-8233   FAX: 510/523-2373   HTTP://WWW.SYBEX.COM

Acknowledgments

To Sibylla

Thank you to Sybilla for being there while I was busy working; Charles and Matthew for their expertise and fine writing; all of my friends and family for everything; and Neil, Ben, Ron, Guy, Dusty, Bonnie, and everyone else at Sybex for their professionalism and patience.

—*James Chellis*

To Mom and Dad

I would like to thank my family and friends for their support; James Chellis, EdgeTek, and Sybex for giving me the opportunity to write this book; Michael for pointing me in their direction; and Bonnie, Neil, Ben, and Dusty for their patience. Thanks especially to Christy for letting me steal so much of her husband Matthew's time.

—*Charles Perkins*

To my wife

I thank my wife for her support and patience; James for his support and patience; my family, especially daan for being daan; Mike and Laura; Dylan and Joan; Steve; Mike and Katy; Chuck; Farrell; Dawni; and the refugees from LL.

—*Matthew Strebe*

Contents At a Glance

Table of Contents

Introduction

T he Microsoft Certified Systems Engineer (MCSE) certification is *the* hottest ticket to career advancement in the computer industry today. Hundreds of thousands of corporations and organizations worldwide are choosing Microsoft products for their networks. This has created a tremendous need for qualified personnel and consultants to help implement and support these networks. The MCSE certification and the more advanced MCSE+Internet (or MCSE+I) certification are your ways to show these corporations and organizations that you have the professional abilities they need.

This book has been developed in alliance with Microsoft Corporation to give you the knowledge and skills you need to prepare for one of the core requirements of the MCSE certification program: Networking Essentials. Certified by Microsoft, this book presents the information you need to acquire a solid understanding of the fundamentals of networking, to prepare for the Networking Essentials exam, and to take a big step toward MCSE certification.

Computers and computer networks require increasingly well-trained network professionals to install and maintain them. As the computer network industry grows in both size and complexity, the need for proven ability is becoming more important. To address this need, certification programs for administrators have been designed to ensure that the people who manage and support computer networks are qualified to do so.

Whether you are just getting started or are ready to move ahead in the computer industry, the knowledge and skills you have are your most valuable assets. Microsoft, recognizing these assets, has developed its Microsoft Certified Professional (MCP) program to give you credentials that verify your ability to work with Microsoft products effectively and professionally. The MCP credential for professionals who work with Microsoft networks is the Microsoft Certified Systems Engineer (MCSE) certification.

Is This Book for You?

If you want to learn about the fundamentals of computer networking, this book is for you. You'll find clear explanations of the fundamental concepts you need to grasp. If you want to become certified as a Microsoft Certified Systems Engineer (MCSE), this book is definitely for you. This book will give you what you need to become truly prepared for the challenge of MCSE certification.

Microsoft Certified Professional Magazine's recent surveys reveal the average MCSE is earning a base salary of more than $65,000 (US) per year, while the average MCSE+I is earning a base salary of more than $74,000 per year. If you want to acquire the knowledge base you need to pass Microsoft's Networking Essentials exam, take a step closer to your MCSE, and boost your career efforts, this book will serve you well.

What Does This Book Cover?

Think of this book as Microsoft Networking Essentials 101. It covers all of the key topics covered in Microsoft Networking Essentials exam, and will provide you with the fundamental knowledge you need for your career as a computer network professional. This book begins with the most basic networking concepts, such as:

- What is a network?
- What does a network do?

Next, you will learn about the building blocks of networks:

- Network hardware and media
- Network topologies
- Standards and protocols

The discussion then moves on to more sophisticated concepts of network design, WANs, remote access to networks, the Internet, and a further examination of protocols.

How Do You Become an MCSE or MCSE+I?

Attaining MCSE or MCSE+I status is a serious challenge. The exams cover a wide range of topics, and require dedicated study and expertise. Many people who have achieved other computer industry credentials have had troubles with the MCSE. This challenge is, however, why the MCSE certification is so valuable. If achieving MCSE status were easy, the market would be quickly flooded by MCSEs and the certification would quickly become meaningless. Microsoft, keenly aware of this fact, has taken steps to ensure that the certification means its holder is truly knowledgeable and skilled.

Exam Requirements

Successful candidates have to pass a minimum set of exams that measure technical proficiency and expertise:

- Candidates for the MCSE must pass four core requirements and two electives.
- Candidates for the MCSE+Internet must pass seven core requirements and two electives.

Exam	Title	MCSE	MCSE+Internet
70-058	Networking Essentials	Required	Required
70-067	Windows NT Server 4.0	Required	Required
70-068	Windows NT Server 4.0 in the Enterprise	Required	Required
70-073 *or*	Windows NT Workstation 4.0	Required	Required
70-064 *or*	Windows 95		
70-098	Windows 98		
70-059	Internetworking with TCP/IP on Windows NT 4.0	Elective	Required
70-077 *or*	Internet Information Server 3.0 and Index Server 1.1	Elective	Required
70-087	Internet Information Server 4.0		
70-079	Internet Explorer Administration Kit	Elective	Required
70-076 *or*	Exchange Server 5.0	Elective	Elective
70-081	Exchange Server 5.5		

Exam	Title	MCSE	MCSE+Internet
70-026 *or* 70-028	System Administration for SQL Server 7.0 Administering Microsoft SQL Server 7.0	Elective	Elective
70-088	Proxy Server 2.0	Elective	Elective
70-085	SNA Server 4.0	Elective	Elective
70-018 or 70-086	Systems Management Server 1.2 Systems Management Server 2.0	Elective	Elective

For a more detailed description of the Microsoft certification programs, go to www.microsoft.com/train_cert.

This book is a part of a series of Network Press MCSE study guides, published by Sybex, that covers the four core requirements as well as the electives you need to complete your MCSE track.

What Types of Questions Are There?

Until recently, the formats of the MCSE exams were rather straightforward, consisting almost entirely of multiple-choice questions appearing in a few different sets. Prior to taking an exam, you knew how many questions you would see and what type of questions would appear. If you had purchased the right third-party exam preparation products, you could even be quite familiar with the pool of questions you would be asked. All of this is changing.

In an effort to both refine the testing process and protect the quality of its certifications, Microsoft has recently begun introducing adaptive testing as well as new exam elements. These innovations add new challenges for individuals taking the exams. Most importantly, they make it much more difficult for someone to pass an exam after simply "cramming" for it.

Real skills and in-depth knowledge are now needed much more than they were before. Because Microsoft has a policy of not stating in advance what type of format you will see, let's take a look at adaptive testing and the new exam question types so you can be aware of all the possibilities.

Adaptive Exams

Microsoft is in the process of converting exams to a new "adaptive" format. This format is radically different from the conventional format previously used for Microsoft certification exams. If you have never taken an adaptive test, there are a few things you should know.

Conventional tests and adaptive tests are different in that conventional tests are static, containing a fixed number of questions, while adaptive tests change or "adapt," depending on your answers to the questions presented. The number of questions presented in your adaptive test will depend on how long it takes the exam to "figure out" what your level of ability is (according to the statistical measurements upon which the exam questions are ranked).

To "figure out" a test-taker's level of ability, the exam will present questions in increasing or decreasing orders of difficulty. By presenting sequences of questions with determined levels of difficulty, the exam is supposed to be able to determine your level of understanding.

For example, we have three test-takers, Herman, Sally, and Rashad. Herman doesn't know much about the subject, Sally is moderately informed, while Rashad is an expert. Herman answers his first question incorrectly, so the exam gives him a second, easier question. He misses that, so the exam gives him a few more easy questions, all of which he misses. Shortly thereafter, the exam ends, and he receives his failure report. Sally, meanwhile, answers her first question correctly, so the exam gives her a more difficult question, which she answers correctly. She then receives an even more difficult question, which she answers incorrectly, so the exam gives her a somewhat easier question, as it tries to gauge her level of understanding. After numerous questions, of varying levels of difficulty, Sally's exam ends, perhaps with a passing score, perhaps not. Her exam included far more questions than Herman's included, because her level of understanding needed to be more carefully tested to determine whether or not it was at a passing level. When Rashad takes his exam, he answers his first question correctly, so he's given a more difficult question, which he also answers correctly. He's given an even more difficult question, which he also answers correctly. He then is given a few more very difficult questions, all of which he answers correctly. Shortly thereafter, his exam ends. He passes. His exam was short, about as long as Herman's.

Microsoft has begun moving to adaptive testing for several reasons:

- It saves time by focusing only on the questions needed to determine a test-taker's abilities. This way an exam that, in the conventional format, took $1\frac{1}{2}$ hours, can be completed in less than half that time. The number of questions presented can be far less than the number required by a conventional exam.

- It protects the integrity of the exams. By exposing a fewer number of questions at any one time, it makes it more difficult for individuals to collect the questions in the exam pools with the intent of facilitating exam "cramming."

- It saves Microsoft and/or the test delivery company money by cutting down on the amount of time it takes to deliver a test.

WARNING Unlike the previous test format, the adaptive format will not allow you to go back to see a question again. The exam only goes forward. Once you enter your answer, that's it; you cannot change it. Be very careful before entering your answer. There is no time limit for each individual question (only for the exam as a whole). As your exam may be shortened by correct answers (and lengthened by incorrect answers) there is no advantage to rushing through questions.

Select-and-Place Exam Questions

Select-and-place exam questions involve graphical elements that the test-taker must manipulate in order to successfully answer a question. For example, a question could present a diagram of a computer network, as shown in Figure 1.

FIGURE 1

A "Quick Drop" screen from a Select-and-Place exam question

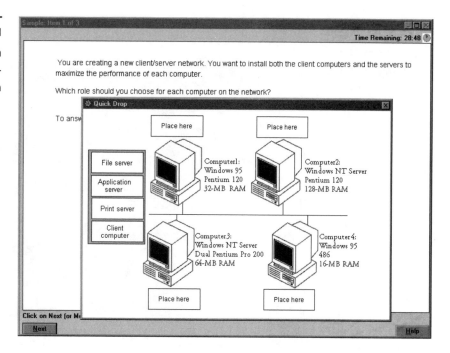

In the diagram are several computers next to boxes that read "Place Here." There are also several labels representing different computer roles on network, such as Print Server, File Server, etc. Based on information given for each computer, you are asked to drag and drop each label to the correct box.

You need to correctly drag the correct labels to *all* correct boxes in order to get credit for the question. No credit is given if you correctly label only some of the boxes.

Simulations

Simulations are the kinds of questions which most closely represent and test the actual skills you use while working with Microsoft software interfaces. These types of exam questions include a mock or imitation interface on which you must perform certain actions according to a given scenario. The simulated interfaces look nearly identical to what you see in the actual product, as shown in Figure 2.

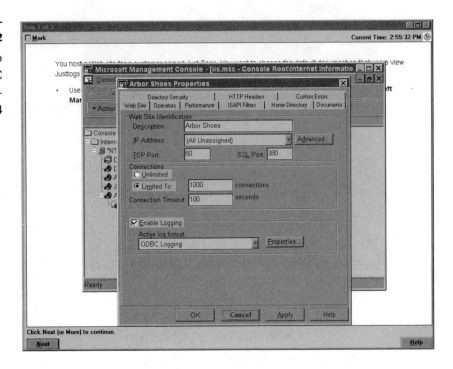

Simulations are, by far, the most complex element introduced into Microsoft exams to date. Because of the number of possible errors that can be made on simulations, it is worthwhile to consider the following recommendations from Microsoft:

- Do not change any simulation settings that don't directly pertain to the solution.

- Assume default settings when related information has not been provided because it is non-critical.

- Be sure entries are spelled correctly.

- Close all simulation application windows after completing the set of tasks in the simulation.

Most important, however, is that you spend time working with the operating system. You may also find it valuable to work with the WinSim product on the CD enclosed with this study guide.

Case Study-Based Questions

Case Study-based questions first appeared in the Microsoft Certified Solution Developer program (Microsoft's certification for programmers). The basic idea of the Case Study-based exam item is that you have a scenario with a range of requirements. Based on the information provided, you need to answer a series of multiple-choice questions. The interface for Case Study-based questions has a number of tabs with the information about the scenario appearing under each tab. The net result is that you have a rather lengthy description of a scenario, with several multiple-choice questions.

What Does the Networking Essentials Exam Measure?

The Networking Essentials exam is the most general of the MCSE core exams. It covers a broad range of network concepts and skills in the following areas:

- Standards and terminology
- Planning
- Implementation
- Troubleshooting

Because the exam is a largely conceptual, general survey exam, it is the least hands-on of the MCSE exams you will face. It can be quite challenging for people who don't have experience in the field. If you are lacking that experience, this book will be especially helpful.

Microsoft provides exam objectives to give you a very general overview of possible areas of coverage of the Microsoft exams. For your convenience, we have added in-text objectives listings at the points in the text where specific Microsoft exam objectives are covered.

Exam objectives are subject to change at any time without prior notice and at Microsoft's sole discretion. Please visit Microsoft's Training & Certification Web site (www.microsoft.com/Train_Cert) for the most current exam objectives listing.

How Does Microsoft Develop the Exam Questions?

Microsoft follows an exam development process consisting of eight mandatory phases. The process takes an average of seven months and contains more than 150 specific steps. The phases of Microsoft Certified Professional exam development are

1. Job analysis

2. Objective domain definition

3. Blueprint survey

4. Item development

5. Alpha review and item revision

6. Beta exam

7. Item selection and cut-score setting

8. Exam live

Microsoft describes each phase as follows.

Phase 1: Job Analysis

Phase 1 is an analysis of all the tasks that make up a specific job function, based on tasks performed by people who are currently performing that job function. This phase also identifies the knowledge, skills, and abilities that relate specifically to the performance area to be certified.

Phase 2: Objective Domain Definition

The results of the job analysis provide the framework used to develop objectives. The development of objectives involves translating the job function tasks into a comprehensive set of more specific and measurable knowledge, skills, and abilities. The resulting list of objectives—the *objective domain*—is the basis for the development of both the certification exams and the training materials.

Phase 3: Blueprint Survey

The final objective domain is transformed into a blueprint survey in which contributors—technology professionals who are performing the applicable job function—are asked to rate each objective. Contributors may be selected from lists of past Microsoft Certified Professional (MCP) candidates, from appropriately skilled exam development volunteers, and from within

Microsoft itself. Based on the contributors' input, the objectives are prioritized and weighted. The actual exam items are written according to the prioritized objectives. Contributors are queried about how they spend their time on the job, and if a contributor doesn't spend an adequate amount of time actually performing the specified job function, his or her data is eliminated from the analysis.

The blueprint survey phase helps determine which objectives to measure, as well as the appropriate number and types of items to include on the exam.

Phase 4: Item Development

A pool of items is developed to measure the blueprinted objective domain. The number and types of items to be written are based on the results of the blueprint survey. During this phase, items are reviewed and revised to ensure that they are

- Technically accurate

- Clear, unambiguous, and plausible

- Not biased for any population subgroup or culture

- Not misleading or tricky

- Testing at the correct level

- Testing for useful knowledge, not obscure or trivial facts

Items that meet these criteria are included in the initial item pool.

Phase 5: Alpha Review and Item Revision

During this phase, a panel of technical and job function experts reviews each item for technical accuracy, then answers each item, reaching consensus on all technical issues. Once the items have been verified as technically accurate, they are edited to ensure that they are expressed in the clearest language possible.

Phase 6: Beta Exam

The reviewed and edited items are collected into beta exams. During the beta exam, each participant has the opportunity to respond to all the items in this beta exam pool. Based on the responses of all beta participants, Microsoft performs a statistical analysis to verify the validity of the exam items and to determine which items will be used in the certification exam. Once the analysis has been completed, the items are distributed into multiple parallel forms, or versions, of the final certification exam.

Phase 7: Item Selection and Cut-Score Setting

The results of the beta exams are analyzed to determine which items should be included in the certification exam based on many factors, including item difficulty and relevance. During this phase, a panel of job function experts determines the *cut score* (minimum passing score) for the exams. The cut score differs from exam to exam because it is based on an item-by-item determination of the percentage of candidates who answered the item correctly and who would be expected to answer the item correctly. The cut score is set in a group session to increase the reliability among the experts.

Phase 8: Exam Live

The exams hit the street. Microsoft Certified Professional exams are administered by Sylvan Prometric and VUE (Virtual University Enterprises).

Tips for Taking the Networking Essentials Exam

Here are some general tips for taking the exams successfully:

- Arrive early at the exam center so you can relax and take one last review of your study materials, particularly tables and lists of exam-related information.

- Read the questions carefully. Don't be tempted to jump to an early conclusion. Make sure you know *exactly* what the question is asking.

- Answer all questions.

- On simulations, do not change settings that are not directly related to the question. Also, assume default settings if the question does not specify or imply what they might be.

- Use a process of elimination to get rid of the obviously incorrect answers first on questions that you're not sure about. This method will improve your odds of selecting the correct answer if you need to make an educated guess.

- A reminder: The adaptive format will *not* allow you to go back to see a question again. Be very careful before entering your answer. Because your exam may be shortened by correct answers (and lengthened by incorrect answers) there is no advantage to rushing through questions.

Where Do You Take the Exams?

You may take the exams at any of more than 1,000 Authorized Prometric Testing Centers (APTCs) and VUE Testing Centers available around the world. For the location of a testing center near you, call 800-755-EXAM (755-3926) or call VUE at 888-837-8616. Outside the United States and Canada, contact your local Sylvan Prometric or VUE registration center.

To register for a Microsoft Certified Professional exam,

1. Determine the number of the exam you want to take.

2. Register with the Sylvan Prometric or VUE registration center that is nearest to you. At this point you will be asked for advance payment for the exam—as of October 1999, the exams are $100 each. Exams must be taken within one year of payment. You can schedule exams up to six weeks in advance or as late as one working day prior to the date of the exam. You can cancel or reschedule your exam if you contact the center at least two working days prior to the exam. Same-day registration is available in some locations, subject to space availability. Where same-day registration is available, you must register a minimum of two hours before test time.

You may also register for your exams online at www.sylvanprometric.com/ or www.vue.com/ms/.

When you schedule the exam, you'll be provided with instructions regarding appointment and cancellation procedures, ID requirements, and information about the testing center location. In addition, you will receive a registration and payment confirmation letter from Sylvan Prometric or VUE.

Microsoft requires certification candidates to accept the terms of a Non-Disclosure Agreement before taking certification exams.

What Software Products Are on the CDs?

With this third edition of our best-selling MCSE Study Guides, we are dramatically expanding our array of training resources. On the first CD are numerous practice exams, flashcards, and even a few simulations to help you study for the exam. On the second CD is a training video from LearnKey. These are detailed in the following sections.

The Sybex WinSim NT

We developed WinSim NT to provide readers with multimedia and interactive experiences of Microsoft Windows products in operation. This product provides both audio/video files and hands-on experiences. Built around the discussions in this study guide, WinSim NT can give you knowledge and hands-on skills that are invaluable for understanding Windows NT and passing the exam. Note that the Networking Essentials exam is more theoretical than the other MCSE exams; for that reason, the WinSim product included with the other study guides includes many more hands-on exercises. Figure 3 shows a sample screen from WinSim NT.

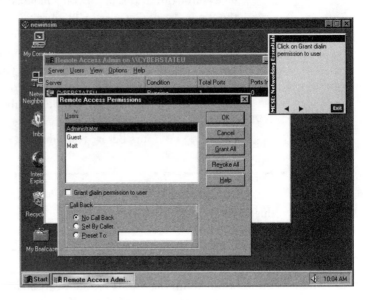

FIGURE 3

Interactive experiences based upon the exercises in the book help you understand Windows products

The Sybex MCSE EdgeTests

The EdgeTests are a collection of multiple-choice questions that can help you prepare for your exam. They consist of

- 150 questions specially prepared for this edition of the study guide.
- An adaptive test simulator that will give the feel for how adaptive testing works.
- All of the questions from the study guide presented in a test engine for your review.

Figure 4 is a screen capture from the Sybex MCSE EdgeTests.

The Sybex MCSE
EdgeTest for
Networking
Essentials

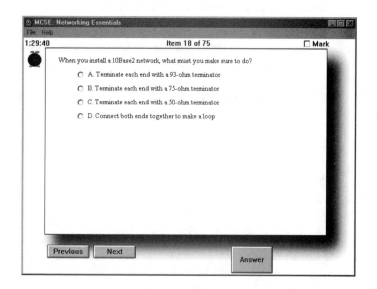

The Sybex MCSE Flashcards

The "flashcard" style of exam question offers an effective way to quickly and efficiently test your understanding of fundamental concepts covered in the Networking Essentials exam. The Sybex MCSE Flashcards consist of one hundred questions presented in a special engine developed specifically for this study guide series. Figure 5 shows the Sybex MCSE Flashcards interface.

The Sybex MCSE
Flashcards for
Networking
Essentials

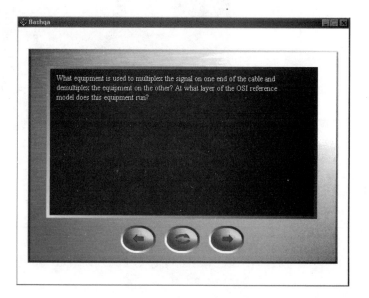

The Sybex MCSE Flashcards for the Palm

After receiving numerous requests for such a product, we developed, in conjunction with Land-J Technologies, a version of the flashcard questions that you can take with you on your 3COM Palm device.

Multimedia Windows Networking Essentials Training from LearnKey

Included on the second CD that accompanies the study guide is a Networking Essentials video from one of the leading video production companies, LearnKey. This LearnKey video covers important topics that can help you with your studies. This product, the first of three in LearnKey's Networking Essentials set, has a retail value of $99.95. The full set of Networking Essentials videos may be purchased directly from LearnKey. Figure 6 shows a screen capture from the LearnKey Networking Essentials video included with this study guide.

FIGURE 6

The LearnKey video

How to Use This Book

This book can provide a solid foundation for the serious effort of preparing for the Networking Essentials exam. To best benefit from this book, you may wish to use the following study method:

1. Study each chapter carefully. Do your best to fully understand the information.

2. Complete all hands-on exercises in the chapter, referring back to the text as necessary so that you understand each step you take. If you do not have access to a lab environment in which you can complete the exercises, install and work with the exercises available in the WinSim software included with this study guide.

3. Answer the review questions at the end of each chapter. (You will find the answers to these questions in Appendix A.) We've included the chapter questions in the EdgeTests on the CD. If you would prefer to answer the questions in a timed and graded format, install the EdgeTests and answer the chapter questions there instead of in the book.

4. Note which questions you did not understand and study the corresponding sections of the book again.

5. Make sure you complete the entire book.

6. Before taking the exam, go through the Sybex MCSE EdgeTests included on the CD that comes with this book. Be sure to try the adaptive version of the EdgeTests that is included with the CD. Lastly, review and sharpen your knowledge with the MCSE Flashcards.

To learn all the material covered in this book, you will need to study regularly and with discipline. Try to set aside the same time every day to study and select a comfortable and quiet place in which to do it. If you work hard, you will be surprised at how quickly you learn this material. Good luck!

If you prefer to use this book in conjunction with classroom or online training, you have many options. Both Microsoft-authorized training and independent training are widely available. CyberState University is a Microsoft Certified Technical Education Center offering excellent online MCSE programs across the Internet, using the Sybex materials. Their program also includes an online NT lab where you can practice many of the exercises in this book, as well as videos, exam preparation software, chat forums, and lectures, all centered around the Sybex MCSE Study Guide series. You can reach CyberState at 1-888-GET-EDUCated (888-438-3382) or www.cyberstateu.com.

Contact Information

To find out more about Microsoft Education and Certification materials and programs, to register with Sylvan Prometric, or to get other useful information, check the following resources.

Resource	Contact Information	Description
Microsoft Training and Certification Home Page	www.microsoft.com/ train_cert	Visit the MCP for information about the Microsoft Certified Professional program and exams, and to order the latest Microsoft Roadmap to Education and Certification.
Sylvan Prometric testing centers	(800) 755-EXAM or www.sylvanprometric .com	To register to take a Microsoft Certified Professional exam at any of more than 800 Sylvan Prometric testing centers around the world, contact Sylvan Prometric.
VUE testing centers	(888) 837-8616 or www.vue.com	To register to take a Microsoft Certified Professional exam at a VUE testing centers call the VUE registration center.
Microsoft Certification Development Team — Web	www.microsoft.com/ Train_Cert/mcp/ examinfo/certsd.htm	Contact the Microsoft Certification Development Team through their Web site to volunteer for one or more exam development phases or to report a problem with an exam. Address written correspondence to: Certification Development Team; Microsoft Education and Certification; One Microsoft Way; Redmond, WA 98052.

Resource	Contact Information	Description
Microsoft TechNet Technical Information Network	(800) 344-2121 or `www.microsoft.com/technet/subscription/about.htm`	Use this Web site or number to contact support professionals and system administrators. Outside the United States and Canada, instead of using the telephone number, contact your local Microsoft subsidiary for information.
Palm Training Product Development: Land-J	(407) 359-2217 or `www.land-j.com`	Land-J Technologies is a consulting and programming business currently specializing in application development for the 3Com Palm Personal Digital Assistant. Land-J developed the Palm version of the Edge Tests which is included with this study guide.
Training Resources: CyberState University	(888) 438-3382 or `www.cyberstateu.com`	CyberState University is a Microsoft Certified Technical Education Center that offers online MCSE certification training from virtually anywhere in the world, using a curriculum centered around the Sybex MCSE Study Guides.

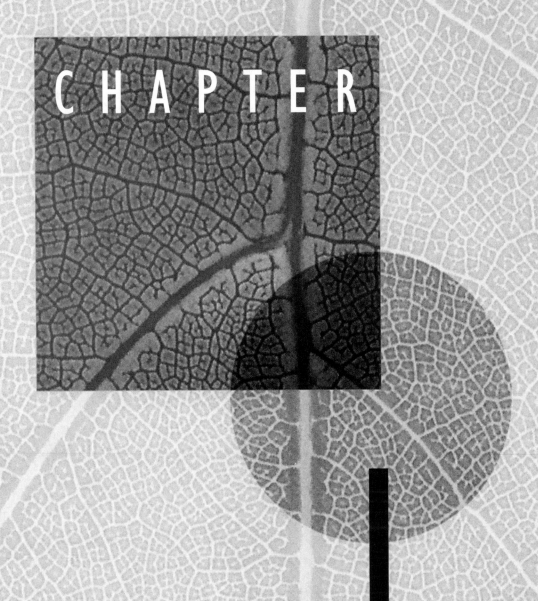

CHAPTER

1

An Introduction to Networks

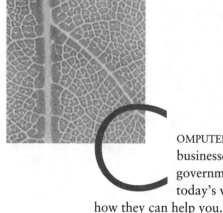

COMPUTER NETWORKS ARE everywhere. You find them in large businesses and small ones, schools and charitable institutions, government offices, and high-school students' bedrooms. In today's world it's important to know what networks are and how they can help you.

If you are responsible for a network, you need to understand how the network works and how you can most effectively tailor the network to the needs of your organization. Networks are sophisticated and complex tools, but they need not be difficult to understand and use. With a little study and some hands-on experience, you can make networks work for you.

What Is Networking?

N THIS SECTION you will learn what networks are and how networks can enhance the usefulness of your computers. This discussion introduces you to the computer as an information tool and then shows you how networks enhance the computer's ability to exchange, share, preserve, and protect information. You will also see how networks can make it easier to share expensive hardware and software.

Networking Is All about Information

Every business runs on information, whether the business is banking, dry-cleaning, aerospace, or computer chip manufacturing. Inventory and payroll, account balances, contact lists, and customer preferences are all types of information that are vital to a successful business.

The type of information changes from business to business and industry to industry, and the way that information is stored and worked with also varies:

- A sole proprietor of a small business may keep business information in his or her head.

- A bookstore may track the ebb and flow of sales on paper.

- A multinational corporation may have mainframe computers and an army of technicians to care for the corporate knowledge base.

- An engineering firm may store technical specifications on a network server and coordinate changes by e-mail.

More and more businesses, small and large, now rely on personal computers and networks to store their precious information.

Consider how you use information in your work. Look around and see the information flowing about you. Imagine how a network might make it flow more quickly or efficiently.

REAL WORLD PROBLEMS

An insurance agency matches clients' insurance needs with insurance companies' policies.

- What information does this agency maintain?

A bakery produces and delivers doughnuts and cakes to coffee shops around town.

- What information does this company maintain?

A software company develops sophisticated graphics packages for Windows and Macintosh computers. The company sells the software through regular software distribution channels and directly to the consumer through mail order. The company provides a generous upgrade path to registered users of the company's software.

- What information does this company maintain?

The Personal Computer as an Information Tool

The personal computer is a fantastic information tool. It gives you the ability to control the flow of information in your life. But it is shipped from the manufacturer with just enough software to make it run and be marginally useful; it is up to you to customize it for your own purpose. With the right software, your computer can meet nearly any information-processing need; for example, a dog-grooming shop can track animals and their owners with a specialized database, and a legal firm can search CD-ROM legal archives and prepare briefs with word processors. A graphics design house can manipulate images with graphics software, and an engineering firm can track numbers with spreadsheets. Figure 1.1 illustrates some of the benefits a computer can bring.

An entire industry—software publishing—exists to customize the personal computer for any use imaginable. Specialized software exists for almost any market niche, whether it is meat-packing or bookstore inventory management. There is even software available specifically to help carpenters design cabinets for houses.

FIGURE 1.1

A computer is a versatile tool that can perform many tasks when configured with the right software.

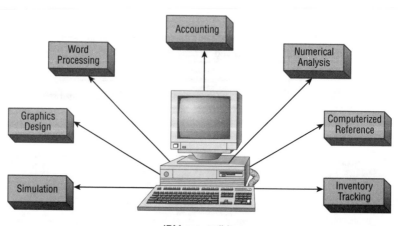

Exchanging Information

Information constantly flows through your business. Orders are taken in the sales department and passed through to shipping; research and development sends new device specifications to manufacturing; accounting collects statistics and passes them to management. A small design house distributes parts of a project to the various members of a team, who work together to prepare a final, integrated proposal. A publishing house collects market projections, receives manuscript drafts, delivers edited proofs, and requests corrections and elaboration, and finally a book is sent to be printed.

Once, all business information was transmitted verbally or on paper. Before networks, even with the computer, people had to personally move the information about, whether it was on paper, over the phone, or on floppy disk or magnetic tape.

When you use a computer not connected to a network, you are working in what is called a *stand-alone environment.* You can use software to produce data, graphics, spreadsheets, documents, and so on, but to share your information you must print it out or put it on floppy disk so that someone else can use it. You are moving the information about yourself rather than letting the computer do it for you. Figure 1.2 illustrates a stand-alone environment.

FIGURE 1.2

The stand-alone environment is an isolated computer.

The Network

Computers connected over a network can make that information exchange easier and faster. The information moves directly from computer to computer rather than through a human intermediary. People can concentrate on getting their work done rather than on moving information around the company.

The most elementary network consists of two computers communicating over a cable. When you link computers together, you can more swiftly and efficiently move information between them. The computers can also share resources, such as printers and fax modems, allowing you to better use your hardware. A group of computers and other devices connected together is called a *network*, and the concept of connected computers sharing resources is called *networking*.

A *local area network* (*LAN*) is a number of computers connected to each other by cable in a single location, usually a single floor of a building or all the computers in a small company. The most common cabling method in the 1980s allowed about 30 users on a maximum cable length of about 600 feet. Figure 1.3 shows a simple local area network.

FIGURE 1.3

A network is a number of computers linked together to share resources.

Laser printer

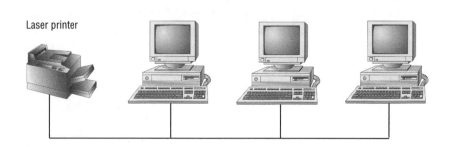

Often, businesses have offices throughout a large region. For instance, most banks have a headquarters site and offices throughout a city, state, or nation. While local area networks are perfect for sharing resources within a building or campus, they cannot be used to connect distant sites.

Wide area networks (*WANs*) fill this need. Stated simply, wide area networks are the set of connecting links between local area networks. These links are made over telephone lines leased from the various telephone companies. In rare instances, WANs can be created with satellite links, packet radio, or microwave transceivers. These options are generally far more expensive than leased telephone lines, but they can operate in areas where leased lines are not available. Figure 1.4 shows a simple wide area network.

FIGURE 1.4

A wide area network
links computers in
different locations.

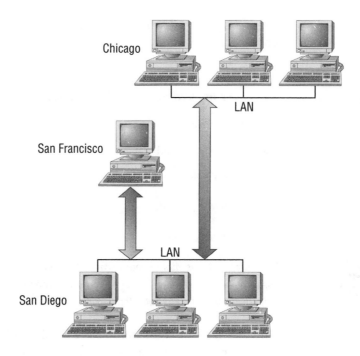

Most WANs are private and owned by the business that operates with
them. Recently, however, the Internet has emerged as both the largest and the
least expensive WAN in the world. Many companies are now forming private
WANs through encrypted communications over the Internet.

WANs suffer from extremely limited bandwidth. The fastest commercially
feasible wide area data links are many times slower than the slowest local area
links. This makes the sharing of resources over a WAN difficult. Generally,
WAN links are used only for interprocess communications to route short messages, such as e-mail or HTML (World Wide Web) traffic.

Sharing Information

Just as a lot of information is moved about a business, some information is
centrally controlled and shared. Most businesses have one set of financial
books, and not everyone is given access to them. The information must be
kept consistent and secure, and timely access must be given to those who need
the information to run the business.

Other types of information you might want to centrally locate and share or control include

- Inventory

- Company letterhead and letter styles

- Sales contact information

- Company procedures manuals

- Sensitive financial records

- Employee records

- Company memos

What information is vital to your organization? What information do you need to keep consistent, or restricted, or in one place for everyone to access? Consider how a network would help you manage that information.

If you select one computer to store the shared information and have all other computers reference the information on that computer over the network, the computer can help you centralize the information and maintain control over it. The central computer is often called a *server*, and special software and operating systems are often used in server computers. Figure 1.5 shows a server.

Sharing Hardware Resources

Computers that are not networked cannot effectively share resources. For instance, a small office with ten stand-alone computers and one printer allows only the user with the printer attached to his or her computer to print. Other users must put their data on a floppy disk, transfer it to the computer with the printer, and print it from there. This of course interrupts the user who would normally be using the computer with the printer attached. Figure 1.6 illustrates a stand-alone computer.

A network allows anyone connected to the network to use the printer, not just the individual sitting at the computer to which the printer is attached.

FIGURE 1.5

FIGURE 1.5

A server can hold data in a central place for better control over the information and for more efficient sharing.

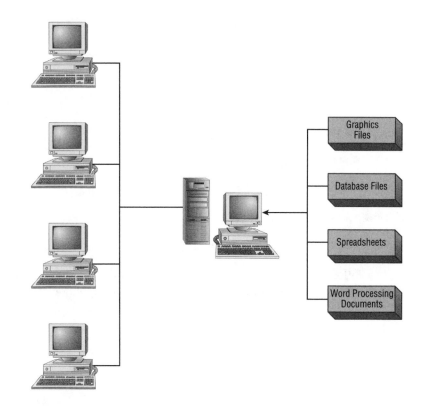

FIGURE 1.6

Only the person sitting at the computer can use a stand-alone printer.

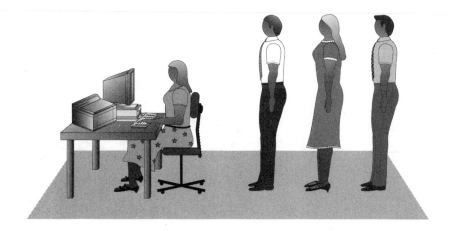

Networked computers can also share

- Fax modems

- Scanners

- Hard disks

- Floppy disks

- CD-ROMs

- Tape backup units

- Plotters

- Almost any other device that can be attached to a computer

You can attach some peripherals directly to the network; they do not need to be attached to a computer to be shared on the network. Figure 1.7 illustrates how anyone on a network can use a shared printer.

FIGURE 1.7

You can make a shared printer available to anyone on the network.

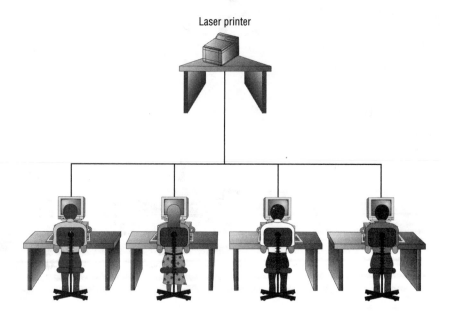

Laser printer

Sharing Software Resources

Software resources can also be used more effectively over a network. With stand-alone computers, the software used on the computer must be present on each computer's hard disk, whether or not that computer is used at that moment for that task. Software costs can become prohibitive for a large number of computers. It is also difficult and time consuming to install and configure the software individually on every one of the computers.

Not all software will use a network even if one is installed. You should check the software documentation to see what features, if any, the software provides in a network environment.

With a network you can centrally install and configure the software, vastly reducing the work required to make computer programs available to an organization. You can also restrict access to programs—for instance, to make sure the number of people using the word processor does not exceed the number of copies of the program you have licensed.

Different software packages have different restrictions on how the software can legally be used on a network. Some require that you have as many licenses as there are simultaneous users of the software; others require that a copy of the software be purchased for every user of the package, whether or not the user is using it at any particular time. Carefully read the documentation to be sure your network users can legally use the software you make available on the network.

Preserving Information

A network also allows for information to be backed up to a central location. Important information can be lost by mistake or accident when a stand-alone computer has no backup. It is difficult to maintain regular backups on a number of stand-alone computers. When you back up to a central location (often to a tape cartridge in the network server), you have one place to look for the lost information, and you can be assured that the information is being backed up.

Network backup is one of the most important actions a network administrator can per-form. Computers are complicated, and every computer user experiences a "crash" sooner or later, usually at the most inconvenient time. Network components can also fail. Your life, and those of other network users, will be a lot less frustrating when a failure occurs if you have regular backups.

Protecting Information

A network provides a more secure environment for a company's important information. With stand-alone computers, access to the computers often means access to the information on the computers. Networks provide an addi-tional layer of security by way of passwords. You can give each network user a different account name and password, allowing the network server to distin-guish among those who need access to have it and protecting the information from tampering by those who do not. Figure 1.8 shows the Windows 95 login screen, which requests both a name and a password.

FIGURE 1.8

The network login screen allows only authorized users to access your company's data.

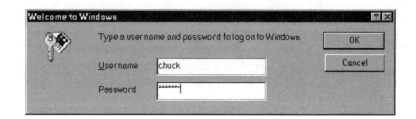

E-Mail

The computer network can also help people communicate. One of the greatest benefits to users of networks is electronic mail, or e-mail. Rather than exchanging memos and directives on paper, engaging printing costs and delays, network users can instantly send messages to others and even check to see whether their message has been received. You can attach electronic documents to mail messages, instantly duplicate and forward mail, and perform many more tasks that are cumbersome or impossible with paper messaging systems.

REAL WORLD PROBLEMS

You are an investment consultant. You have a personal computer in your home office. You have a printer, modem, fax machine, and scanner attached to your computer.

■ Do you need a network?

You maintain the computers in a graphics design studio. The computers all have large hard drives to store files and optical disk drives with removable cartridges. Someone who wants to print an image takes a cartridge with the image stored on it over to the computer with the printer.

■ How would a network help this studio?

You are explaining the advantages of networks to your firm's accountant. She wants to know which devices can be shared on a network.

■ Which devices can be shared on a network?

Your boss asks about sharing software on the network.

■ What are the advantages of sharing software, and why must you be careful about placing software on the network?

Your company is having a difficult time keeping information consistent because not all users have the most current version of the project reports on their computers' hard drives. Also, important information has been lost because one individual consistently fails to back up his hard drive.

■ How would you use a network to improve this situation?

Your company uses a lot of paper for inter-office memos because every morning the secretaries in your company must make hundreds of copies of the memos to distribute around the company.

■ How could you use a network to reduce these costs in paper and productivity?

Clients, Servers, and Peers

THERE ARE THREE roles for computers in a local area network:

- Clients, which use but do not provide network resources
- Peers, which both use and provide network resources
- Servers, which provide network resources

Microsoft ✓ *Exam Objective*

Compare a client/server network with a peer-to-peer network.

Each of these computer roles is determined by the type of operating system the computer uses. Servers run network operating systems such as Windows NT Server or Novell NetWare. Clients run client operating systems, such as MS-DOS or OS/2 2.0. Peers run peer network operating systems, such as Windows 95 or the Macintosh operating system. Each of these operating systems is optimized to provide service for the role it plays.

Many times the role of a computer is also determined simply by use. For instance, a computer running Windows 95 is not a peer unless it is actually sharing network resources. This means that it may be in use only as a client or that it may not be on a network at all. It is also possible to run Windows NT Server simply as a client operating system, although it does not make much sense to use a powerful operating system in that role.

Based on the roles of the computers attached to them, networks are divided into three types:

- Server-based (also called client-server), containing clients and the servers that support them.

- Peer (also called-peer-to-peer), which have no servers and use the network to share resources among independent peers.

- Hybrid network, which is a client-server network that also has peers sharing resources. Most networks are actually hybrid networks.

Server-Based Networks and Domains

Server-based networks are defined by the presence of servers on a network that provide security and administration of the network. Servers have many roles, as discussed later in this chapter.

Server-based (or client-server) networks divide processing tasks between clients and servers. Clients (often called the "front end") request services, such as file storage and printing, and servers (often called the "back end") deliver them. Server computers typically are more powerful than client computers, or are optimized to function as servers.

In Windows NT, server-based networks are organized into what are called *domains*. Domains are collections of networks and clients that share security trust information. Domain security and logon permission are controlled by special servers called domain controllers. There is one master domain controller, called the Primary Domain Controller (PDC), which may be assisted by secondary domain controllers called Backup Domain Controllers (BDC) during busy times or when the PDC is not available for some reason.

No computer users can access the resources of servers in a domain until they have been authenticated by a domain controller.

Advantages of Server-Based Networks

Server based networks have a great many advantages, including:

- Strong central security

- Central file storage, which allows all users to work from the same set of data and provides easy backup of critical data

- Ability of servers to pool available hardware and software, lowering overall costs

- Ability to share expensive equipment, such as laser printers

- Optimized dedicated servers, which are faster than peers at sharing network resources

- Less intrusive security, since a single password allows access to all shared resources on the network

- Freeing of users from the task of managing the sharing of resources

- Easy manageability of a large number of users

- Central organization, which keeps data from getting lost among computers

Disadvantages of Server-Based Networks

Server-based networks do have some disadvantages, although they are mostly related to the cost of server equipment, including:

- Expensive dedicated hardware

- Expensive network operating system software and client licenses

- A dedicated network administrator (usually required)

Peer Networks

Peer networks are defined by a lack of central control over the network. There are no servers in peer networks; users simply share disk space and resources, such as printers and faxes, as they see fit.

Peer networks are organized into workgroups. Workgroups have very little security control. There is no central login process. If you have logged in to one peer on the network, you will be able to use any resources on the network that are not controlled by a specific password.

Access to individual resources can be controlled if the user who shared the resource requires a password to access it. Because there is no central security trust, you will have to know the individual password for each secured shared resource you wish to access. This can be quite inconvenient.

Peers are also not optimized to share resources. Generally, when a number of users are accessing resources on a peer, the user of that peer will notice significantly degraded performance. Peers also generally have licensing limitations that prevent more than a small number of users from simultaneously accessing resources.

Advantages of Peer Networks

Peer computers have many advantages, especially for small businesses that cannot afford to invest in expensive server hardware and software:

- No extra investment in server hardware or software is required

- Easy setup

- No network administrator required

- Ability of users to control resources sharing

- No reliance on other computers for their operation

- Lower cost for small networks

Disadvantages of Peer Networks

Peer networks, too, have their disadvantages, including:

- Additional load on computers because of resource sharing

- Inability of peers to handle as many network connections as servers

- Lack of central organization, which can make data hard to find

- No central point of storage for file archiving

- Requirement that users administer their own computers

- Weak and intrusive security

- Lack of central management, which makes large peer networks hard to work with

Hybrid Networks

Hybrid networks have all three types of computers operating on them and generally have active domains and workgroups. This means that while most shared resources are located on servers, network users still have access to any resources being shared by peers in your workgroup. It also means network users do not have to log on to the domain controller to access workgroup resources being shared by peers.

Advantages of Hybrid Computing

Hybrid computing provides these advantages:

- The advantages of server-based networking

- Many of the advantages of peer-based networking

- Ability of users and network administrators to control security based on the importance of the shared resource

Disadvantages of Hybrid Computing

Hybrid computing shares the disadvantages of server-based networking.

Peer Security vs. Server Security

One large difference in the way peer-to-peer and server-based networks operate is in how they implement security. Peer-to-peer networks are usually less secure than are server-based networks, because peer-to-peer networks commonly use share-level security, while server-based networks commonly use file-level or access permission security.

Microsoft ✓ *Exam* *Objective*

Compare user-level security with access permission assigned to a shared directory on a server.

In Windows 95, for example, the user of the computer can allow any other computer on the network to access a shared directory or device. The user can assign a password to the shared resource if some degree of security is required.

However, the user cannot specify which users on the network can access the resource—any user on the network that knows the password can access the resource.

Another limitation of peer-to-peer shares implemented in this manner is that each shared resource that you wish to control access to must have its own password. The number of passwords to resources that you must remember can quickly grow unwieldy in a large network.

Most server-based networks implement security differently. Instead of requiring a password for every shared resource you wish to access, the server-based network only requires one password for you to access all resources on the network that you have permission to use.

The security advantage of peer-to-peer networking is that each user controls access to their own resources. The security disadvantage of peer-to-peer networks is that you cannot differentiate among network users when you allow access to a resource. The security advantage of server-based networking is that each user is allowed access to only those resources that the user has the privilege to access. A disadvantage is that someone must centrally administer the security on your network.

Selecting the Right Network Type

When deciding which type of network to use, your primary consideration will be whether you can afford a network file server, network operating system software, and the cost of an administrator. If you can, you should consider using a hybrid networking environment to get the advantages of both types of networking. If you cannot, you should use a peer-based network.

It is possible to organize a peer-based network in a fashion similar to a server-based network by using a single powerful peer computer to store network files and share such resources as printers. Then you will be able to administer shared resources centrally and back up your network in one location. This computer will be loaded down, though, so it should be reserved for light computer use only. Peers used this way are called nondedicated servers.

REAL WORLD PROBLEMS

You are installing a small network for a collections agency. There will be only five stations on the network. Cost is an issue, and the company would prefer not to dedicate an individual's time to maintaining a network. However, the agency is also concerned about keeping its data safe, and the users are not sophisticated computer users.

■ In what ways is a peer-to-peer network appropriate for this company? In what ways is it inappropriate?

■ In what ways is a server-based network appropriate for this company? In what ways is it inappropriate?

You are replacing the minicomputer and terminals in a travel agency with a network of 35 personal computers. The computers will be installed with Windows 95, which includes built-in peer-to-peer networking. You must justify the additional cost of a server and server software.

■ Why is it a good idea to make this a server-based network instead of or in addition to a peer-to-peer network?

Server Types

Not all servers are alike in a server-based network. A server in a network is dedicated to performing specific tasks in support of other computers on the network. One server may perform all these tasks, or a separate server may be dedicated to each task. A file server, for instance, is dedicated to the task of serving files. A print server provides print services to client computers on the network.

Microsoft ✓ *Exam Objective*

Compare a file-and-print server with an application server.

Common server types include

■ File servers

■ Print servers

- Application servers

- Message servers

- Database servers

Windows NT Server supports all of these capabilities. In fact, one Windows NT Server can, by itself, serve in all of these capacities simultaneously on a small network. On larger networks, however, you need to spread these roles among multiple servers. Let's take a look at what services each of these server types provides.

File Servers

File servers offer services that allow network users to share files. File services are the network applications that store, retrieve, and move data. This type of service is probably the most important reason companies invest in a network. With network file services, users can exchange, read, write, and manage shared files and the data contained in them. File servers are designed specifically to support the file services for a network. There are several popular types of file servers, such as Windows NT, NetWare, AppleShare, and Banyan Vines.

The following sections consider these types of file services:

- File transfer

- File storage and data migration

- File update synchronization

- File archiving

FILE TRANSFER Before networking computers became a popular way of sharing files, sneakernet was the dominant method. To transfer a file from one computer to another, you would save the file to a floppy disk, put on your sneakers, and walk it over to the other computer. Even in a small office this was an inconvenience, especially when files were too large for a single floppy. For longer distances, it was impossible. The most sophisticated option was to dial the other computer and transfer your files with a modem or across a direct serial connection. But this, too, is an impractical method of sharing files regularly. Fortunately, networks became more sophisticated and began to offer file transfer services. Users can typically transfer files between clients and servers and between multiple servers.

With all this file transferring taking place, the need for file security arises. Every network operating system has its own level of file security. Higher levels use passwords to control system access, file attributes to limit file usage, and encryption schemes to prevent data from being obtained by unauthorized individuals.

FILE STORAGE AND DATA MIGRATION   One by-product of the era of the "information explosion" is a huge amount of data that must be stored somewhere. Nowhere is this more evident than on the networks of the world.

Twenty years ago, the idea of gigabytes of data would make your average computer enthusiast's eyes roll. Now, there are teenage Internet surfers whose 1.6 gigabyte hard drives are completely full. On networks, terabyte storage systems may become fairly common before too long. As a network administrator, you must find the most affordable and efficient means of storing all this data.

A megabyte equals 1,048,576 bytes. A gigabyte equals 1,073,741,824 bytes. A terabyte equals 1,099,511,627,776 bytes!

Not long ago, most storage took place on hard drives. Hard drives can be accessed quickly, but, despite the fact that you can practically set your watch by the falling cost of gigabytes on hard drives, there are still more affordable network storage devices.

There are three main categories of file storage:

- Online storage
- Offline storage
- Near-line storage

Online storage consists, most notably, of hard drive storage. Information stored on a hard drive can be called up very quickly. For this reason, hard drives are used to store files that are accessed regularly. However, hard drive space is, as mentioned earlier, relatively expensive. There is also another limitation specific to internal hard drives (but not external hard drives): because they are a fairly permanent part of a computer, they cannot be conveniently removed, placed in storage, and replaced when needed.

Much of the heavy load of data most file servers take on is not urgent data. For example, financial records from previous years may be stored on a company's network, waiting only for the day when an audit is necessary.

This type of data can be stored just as well on less accessible, less expensive devices.

Offline storage devices include media such as data tapes and removable optical disks. This type of storage offers a high-capacity, low-price alternative to online storage. One disadvantage of this type of storage, however, is that it requires a person to retrieve the disk or tape and mount it on the server. In this age of convenience, that is enough to make a network administrator want to cry. This type of storage is best for data that is rarely used and for data backup.

Fortunately, there is a happy medium. Near-line storage devices offer fairly low costs and high storage capacities, without requiring the network administrator to wake up, go to the archive shelf, and mount the tape or disk on the server. Instead, a machine, such as a tape carousel or jukebox, automatically retrieves and mounts the tape or disk. These systems tend to offer faster, more efficient data access than offline systems, but they are still only fast enough for infrequently used data and applications.

The process by which data is moved from online to offline or near-line storage is called data migration. Network operating systems usually have some type of facility available as an option, possibly from a third party that automatically migrates files from hard drives to near-line or offline storage. Files are selected for migration based on factors such as the last time the file was accessed, the file owner, or the file size.

FILE UPDATE SYNCHRONIZATION File update synchronization has the lofty goal of ensuring that each user of a file has the latest version. By using time and date stamping and user tracking, file synchronization works to ensure that changes made to a file are organized in the chronological order in which they actually took place and that files are properly updated.

Imagine that you download some files from a network server onto a laptop. You then take the laptop on a trip to Africa. Meanwhile, back on the network, people are changing those same files left and right. You also make some changes to your copies of the files. When you log in to the network and begin to copy those files back to the network, all the changes will need to be synchronized in some way to make sure the server keeps them in order and your files are updated with the latest changes. Both your files and the server files need updates to put everything in order. This is where file update synchronization comes into play.

File synchronization is usually a third-party option or an upgrade package for most network operating systems. Also, a network operating system cannot synchronize data within files if it is not aware of the file format. For this reason, many database and other information management programs include their own data-synchronization mechanisms.

Ideally, update utilities would be able to solve any conflicts. However, at present, there are many cases in which update utilities cannot resolve problems. These utilities merely alert you by flagging files when there are conflicting updates.

FILE ARCHIVING File archiving is the process of backing up files on offline storage devices, such as tapes or optical disks. Because networks occasionally destroy files arbitrarily, without any concern for users' needs, it is best to use a file-archiving system as insurance.

Because you can back up all the servers on a network onto a single backup storage, archiving files is really not very difficult. Some backup systems even allow central backup for client workstations. In other words, you can back up files that reside on multiple client workstations without leaving your chair. This way, you may be able to store every file on a network on a single central storage device.

It's best not to procrastinate when it comes to file archiving. Do it now, or you'll later wish you had.

Print Servers

Another important factor in the genesis of computer networking was the demand for the ability to share printers. Before networks made this possible, there were few alternatives. You could employ sneakernet. You could use a manual switching device that hooked up a few computers to a single printer. Or you could keep your printer on a cart and wheel it from computer to computer.

The advent of networking represented a whole new level of computer printing, because a network can

- Allow users to share printers
- Allow you to place printers where convenient, not just near individual computers
- Achieve better workstation performance by using high-speed network data transfer, print queues, and spooling
- Allow users to share network fax services

Print services manage and control printing on a network, allowing multiple and simultaneous access to printing facilities. The network operating system achieves this by using print queues, which are special storage areas where print jobs are stored and then sent to the printer in an organized fashion. When a computer prints to a queue, it actually functions as though it were printing to the printer. The print job is simply stored in the queue and then forwarded to the printer when the printer has finished the jobs scheduled ahead of it.

Jobs in print queues may be forwarded in the order received, or they may be prioritized in accordance with other criteria (such as by the size of the egos of the users whose jobs are in the queue).

To keep everyone happy, you might consider setting up a separate printer for "important" users. Then other users won't need to wait for their lower-priority print jobs.

You can place printers anywhere on a network, and anyone on the network can use any one of those printers. For example, if you want to print on a special 11- by 17-inch network printer that resides five miles away, you can do that.

Printing on a network with queues can be a more efficient way for users to work. The print data is transferred to the queue at network speed. The user can then continue working in an application while the network takes care of the printing.

Network printing also cuts costs by allowing shared access to printing devices. This is especially important when it comes to the more expensive varieties of printers. High-quality color printers, high-speed printers, and large-format printers and plotters tend to cost a lot. It is seldom feasible for an organization to purchase one of these for every individual computer that should have access to one.

Another print service is fax services. Fax machines are now a fundamental communication device around the world. With network print services, you can fax straight from your workstation to a receiving fax machine. This way, you can eliminate the step of printing a hard copy and scanning it into a fax machine. From an application, you can send a document to a fax queue, which then takes care of the faxing. Furthermore, with a fax server, you can receive faxes directly on your workstation. Optical character recognition (OCR) software can even convert these faxes into editable text, thereby saving a lot of time and effort.

Application Servers

Application services allow client PCs to access and use extra computing power and expensive software applications that reside on a shared computer. You can add specialized servers to provide specific applications on a network. For example, if your organization needed a powerful database, you could add a server to provide this application.

Application servers are used when efficiency or security requires a program to stay close to the data, and the data stays in one place—for example, to handle large databases or transaction processing.

Application servers can be dedicated computers set up specifically for the purpose of providing application services, or they can serve multiple functions. A single server, for example, can provide file, print, communication, and database services.

An application server dedicated solely to the task of providing application services can be useful. An organization with such a server can accommodate growth simply by upgrading that server. Windows NT Server makes an excellent application server.

Although in the earlier days of networking, application services were not often found on networks, they have recently become more popular. In terms of network models, they reflect more directly the centralized processing model of the mainframe world. When they do appear on a network, application servers are usually dedicated machines, minimizing the drain on file servers' resources. For example, an accounting department of a large corporation might have an AS400 machine running OS 400 to handle its accounting database software.

Message Servers

Message servers provide message services in a wide variety of communication methods that go far beyond simple file services. With file services, data can pass between users only in file form. With message services, data can take the form of graphics, digitized video, or audio, as well as text and binary data. As hypertext links (electronic connections with other text, images, sounds, and so on) become more common in messages, message services are becoming an extremely flexible and popular means of transmitting data across a network.

Message services must coordinate the complex interactions between users, documents, and applications. For example, with message services, you can send an electronic note, attached to a voice-mail message, to a fellow user on a network.

There are four main types of message services:

- Electronic mail

- Workgroup applications

- Object-oriented applications

- Directory services

ELECTRONIC MAIL Electronic mail, or e-mail, is an increasingly popular reason for installing a network. With e-mail you can easily send a message to another user on the network or on other networks, including the Internet (once your network is connected to other networks, of course).

Originally, e-mail was text-based—it contained only text characters. Now e-mail systems can transfer video, audio, and graphics, as well. With e-mail, sending this data halfway around the world is usually much easier than by any other method. E-mail is much faster than traditional "snail mail" (regular postal mail delivery), much cheaper than courier services, and much simpler than dialing the recipient's computer and transferring the files to it.

E-mail systems are quickly becoming more complex. Integrated voice mail is one of the most popular of the recent developments, rapidly fusing computers and telephones into a single communication system.

Users can now call into the network from a distant telephone and, using a text-to-speech program, have their computer convert their e-mail messages to a synthesized voice that will deliver those messages. In the not-too-distant future, speech-to-text systems that allow you to talk to your computer and convert your speech to an e-mail message may be perfected.

WORKGROUP APPLICATIONS Workgroup applications produce more efficient processing of tasks among multiple users on a network. The two main workgroup applications are

- Workflow management applications

- Linked-object documents

Workflow management applications route documents, forms, and notices among network clients. Tasks that require the input of multiple network users are often much easier using this type of application. Scheduling programs are one application of this sort. More complex applications can take care of otherwise difficult paperwork processes. For example, for a supply clerk to complete a requisition at a military base, approval from several higher-ups may be needed. This process could be automated so that each person whose approval is routinely needed would receive the requisition form on the network. The application would send the form around from one person to the next, in the correct order, until all approvals had been granted (or refused).

Linked-object documents are documents containing multiple data objects. A variety of types of data objects can be linked to construct a document. For example, a single linked-object document could contain voice, video, text, and graphics linked together. Network message services can then act as an agent for each of these objects, passing messages between the object and its originating application or file.

OBJECT-ORIENTED APPLICATIONS Object-oriented applications are programs that can accomplish complex tasks by combining smaller applications, called objects. By using a combination of objects, object-oriented applications gain the ability to handle large tasks.

Message services facilitate communication between these objects by acting as a go-between. This way, objects do not need to communicate with other objects on the network. Instead, an object can simply pass data to the agent, which then passes the data to the destination object.

DIRECTORY SERVICES Directory services servers help users locate, store, and secure information on the network. The Windows NT Server organizes computers (servers and clients) into domains and maintains information about which resources are available to which users and clients in the domain.

You can configure a single server computer to perform any one or all of the above functions in a server-based network.

DATABASE SERVERS Database services can provide a network with powerful database capabilities that are available for use on relatively weak PCs. Most database systems are client-server based. This means that the database applications run on two separate components:

- The client-end portion of the application runs on the client, providing an interface and handling less intensive functions, such as data requests.

- The server-end portion of the application handles the intensive performance of database operations. It runs on the database server, managing the database, processing queries, and replying to clients.

For example, imagine a network with a 100-gigabyte database. This database could be managed by a centralized database application based on the client-server model. Clients could request information from the server, which would then perform a query and report the results to the client. The client could then access the data, process it on the client end, and return it to the server.

Database servers are becoming increasingly powerful, providing complex services including security, database optimization, and data distribution. Distributed databases, utilizing database management systems, are becoming increasingly popular.

Distributed databases maximize network efficiency by storing data near where it is needed. From the user end, the database appears as a single entity, even though the data might be stored across the network, close to the users who need those parts. This can boost performance by helping to ensure that users are using local resources to access data, rather than, for example, using WAN lines to access it.

REAL WORLD PROBLEMS

You have a 40-node network with a single server. You run a Microsoft Exchange Server on your server computer to route e-mail to and from the Internet and your corporate headquarters, and you run Microsoft SQL Server on it to keep track of organizational data. All three of your printers are attached to the server, and all organizational files are stored to the server's hard disk.

- What can you do to improve the performance of your network?

Your network installation company uses Microsoft Access to keep track of customers, potential customers, and the various aspects of running a network installation job. The database has grown rather large, and as your company expands and more people access the database, the response time lags.

- How can you improve the performance of the database system?

It is essential that your organization not lose data.

- What aspects of a dedicated file server will help keep your data safe?

Server Software

Network servers are computers, just like the personal computers used for more mundane tasks, such as word processing and spreadsheet calculations. It is the server operating system software that makes the server computer unique. A server operating system must meet a different and more stringent set of requirements than a network client operating system, such as Microsoft Windows 95 or the Macintosh operating system.

For example, several characteristics of the Windows NT server operating system set it apart from most client systems, as described in Table 1.1.

TABLE 1.1	CATEGORY	DESCRIPTION
Characteristics of the Windows NT Operating System	Symmetric Multiprocessing (SMP)	SMP allows the work of a server to be spread evenly over more than one processor in a single computer
	Multiple-platform support	Computer chip makers constantly produce faster and better chips, and they are not necessarily all compatible with each other. A server operating system should be able to adapt to the fastest chip available
	Log-based file system (NTFS)	A log-based file system is not corrupted by the failure of a disk operation to complete. This keeps data much safer in the face of hardware and software failures
	File name/directory length	255 characters
	File size	16EB (exabytes)
	Partition size	16EB (exabytes)

An exabyte is slightly larger than one billion gigabytes. This should be plenty for a while.

Server Hardware

Although the server computer is much like a personal computer, it is often considerably more powerful. With many clients requiring its services, a more powerful processor, more memory, a larger hard drive, and more powerful network adapter cards all help the network server keep the information flowing. A typical server computer has at least a Pentium processor and 16- to 32MB of RAM.

As computers get faster and network demands grow, you may find yourself replacing your server computer with a more powerful one. Often, you can recycle your old server as an excellent client computer.

Client Hardware

With the shared services concentrated in network servers, client computers do not need the extra RAM or hard drive storage that would be required if they were to serve the information themselves. A typical client computer now has at least a 486 processor and 8- to 16MB of RAM.

Network Topology

I N THE PRECEDING section you learned how computers are organized into networks to share information and hardware resources. In this section you will see the ways in which the wires (or other media) can be run to link those computers together.

Microsoft
Exam
Objective

Select the appropriate topology for various token-ring and Ethernet networks.

The way in which the connections are made is called the *topology* of the network. Network topology specifically refers to the physical layout of the network, especially the locations of the computers and how the cable is run between them. It is important to select the right topology for how the network will be used. Each topology has its own strengths and weaknesses.

The four most common topologies are the bus, the star, the ring, and the mesh.

Bus Topology

The bus topology is often used when a network installation is small, simple, or temporary.

How a Bus Network Works

On a typical bus network, the cable is just one or more wires, with no active electronics to amplify the signal or pass it along from computer to computer. This makes the bus a *passive* topology. When one computer sends a signal up (and down) the wire, all the computers on the network receive the information, but only one (the one with the address that matches the one encoded in the message) accepts the information. The rest disregard the message.

Only one computer at a time can send a message; therefore, the number of computers attached to a bus network can significantly affect the speed of the network. A computer must wait until the bus is free before it can transmit. These factors also affect star and ring networks.

Another important issue in bus networks is *termination*. Since the bus is a passive topology, the electrical signal from a transmitting computer is free to travel the entire length of the cable. Without termination, when the signal reaches the end of the wire, it bounces back and travels back up the wire. When a signal echoes back and forth along an unterminated bus, it is called *ringing*. To stop the signals from ringing, you attach *terminators* at either end of the segment. The terminators absorb the electrical energy and stop the reflections. Cables cannot be left unterminated in a bus network.

Ethernet 10Base2 (also known as thinnet) is an inexpensive network based on the bus topology.

If you are having trouble on a bus network, make sure it is terminated properly. Improperly terminated or unterminated bus networks can behave erratically.

Figure 1.9 illustrates computers connected in a bus topology network.

FIGURE 1.9

In a bus topology the computers are connected in a line.

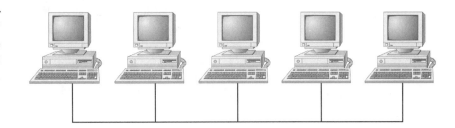

Advantages of the Bus

There are several advantages to a bus topology:

- The bus is simple, reliable in very small networks, easy to use, and easy to understand.

- The bus requires the least amount of cable to connect the computers together and is therefore less expensive than other cabling arrangements.

- It is easy to extend a bus. Two cables can be joined into one longer cable with a BNC barrel connector, making a longer cable and allowing more computers to join the network.

- A repeater can also be used to extend a bus; a repeater boosts the signal and allows it to travel a longer distance.

Disadvantages of the Bus

A bus topology is commonly subject to the following disadvantages:

- Heavy network traffic can slow a bus considerably. Because any computer can transmit at any time, and computers on most bus networks do not coordinate with each other to reserve times to transmit, a bus network with a lot of computers can spend a lot of its bandwidth (capacity for transmitting information) with the computers interrupting each other instead of communicating. The problem only gets worse as more computers are added to the network.

- Each barrel connector weakens the electrical signal, and too many may prevent the signal from being correctly received all along the bus.

- It is difficult to troubleshoot a bus. A cable break or malfunctioning computer anywhere between two computers can cause them not to be able to communicate with each other. A cable break or loose connector will also cause reflections and bring down the whole network, causing all network activity to stop.

Star Topology

In a *star* topology, all the cables run from the computers to a central location, where they are all connected by a device called a *hub*.
Figure 1.10 shows a star topology.

Stars are used in concentrated networks, where the endpoints are directly reachable from a central location; when network expansion is expected; and when the greater reliability of a star topology is needed.

How a Star Network Works

Each computer on a star network communicates with a central hub that resends the message either to all the computers (in a *broadcast star* network) or only to the destination computer (in a *switched star* network). The hub in a broadcast star network can be active or passive.

An *active hub* regenerates the electrical signal and sends it to all the computers connected to it. This type of hub is often called a *multiport repeater*. Active hubs and switches require electrical power to run. A passive hub, such as wiring panels or punch-down blocks, merely acts as a connection point and does not amplify or regenerate the signal. Passive hubs do not require electrical power to run.

You can use several types of cable to implement a star network. A hybrid hub can accommodate several types of cable in the same star network.

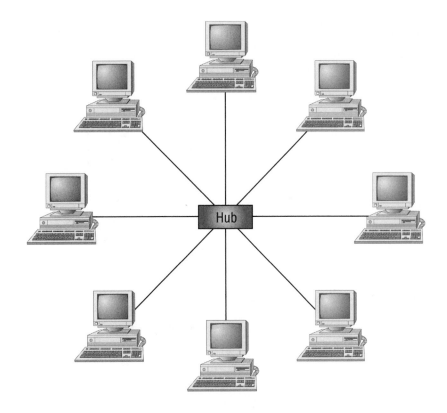

FIGURE 1.10

In a star topology the computers are all connected by cables to a central point.

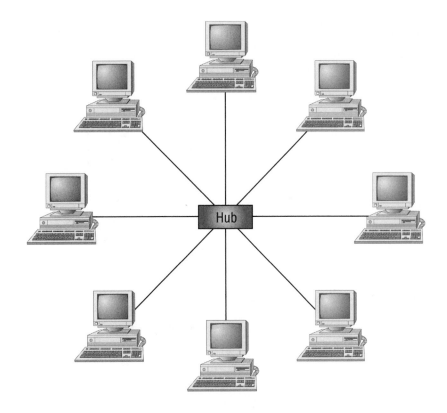

You can expand a star network by placing another star hub where a computer might otherwise go, allowing several more computers or hubs to be connected to that hub. This creates a *hybrid star* network, like the one shown in Figure 1.11.

Ethernet 10baseT is a popular network based on the star topology.

Advantages of the Star

There are several advantages to a star topology:

- It is easy to modify and add new computers to a star network without disturbing the rest of the network. You simply run a new line from the computer to the central location and plug it into the hub. When the capacity of the central hub is exceeded, you can replace it with one that has a larger number of ports to plug lines into.

FIGURE 1.11

The hybrid star network has several central star network points linked in a star.

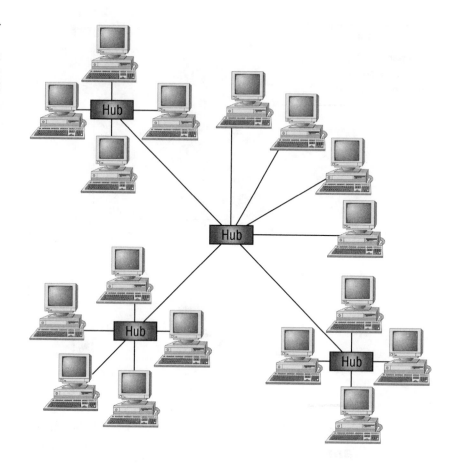

- The center of a star network is a good place to diagnose network faults. Intelligent hubs (hubs with microprocessors that implement features in addition to repeating network signals) also provide for centralized monitoring and management of the network.

- Single computer failures do not necessarily bring down the whole star network. The hub can detect a network fault and isolate the offending computer or network cable and allow the rest of the network to continue operating.

- You can use several cable types in the same network with a hub that can accommodate multiple cable types.

Of the four network types, the star is the most flexible and the easiest to diagnose when there is a network fault.

Disadvantages of the Star

The star topology has a few disadvantages:

- If the central hub fails, the whole network fails to operate.

- Many star networks require a device at the central point to rebroadcast or switch network traffic.

- It costs more to cable a star network because all network cables must be pulled to one central point, requiring more cable than other networking topologies.

Ring Networks

In a ring topology, each computer is connected to the next computer, with the last one connected to the first.

Microsoft Exam Objective

> **Describe the characteristics and purpose of the media used in IEEE 802.3 and IEEE 802.5 standards.**

Token Ring networks are defined by the IEEE 802.5 standard.

Figure 1.12 shows a network with a ring topology.

Rings are used in high-performance networks, networks requiring that bandwidth be reserved for time-sensitive features such as video and audio, or when even performance is needed when a large number of clients access the network.

FIGURE 1.12

In a ring topology
computers are connected
in a circle.

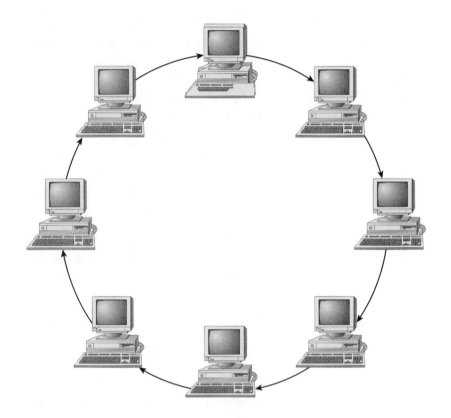

FIGURE 1.12
In a ring topology computers are connected in a circle.

Bandwidth is the capacity of a medium to convey data. (Media are discussed in the next section). One example of bandwidth is automobile traffic. A two-lane road with a speed limit can accommodate only so many cars before there are too many and a traffic jam results. You can increase the bandwidth of a road by making the cars travel more quickly (which corresponds to using a faster transmission method in networks) or by making the road wider (which corresponds to using more wires in networks).

How a Ring Network Works

Every computer is connected to the next computer in the ring, and each retransmits what it receives from the previous computer. The messages flow around the ring in one direction. Since each computer retransmits what it receives, a ring is an *active* network and is not subject to the signal loss problems a bus experiences. There is no termination because there is no end to the ring.

Some ring networks do *token passing*. A short message called a *token* is passed around the ring until a computer wishes to send information to another computer. That computer modifies the token, adds an electronic address and data, and sends it around the ring. Each computer in sequence receives the token and the information and passes them to the next computer until either the electronic address matches the address of a computer or the token returns to its origin. The receiving computer returns a message to the originator indicating that the message has been received. The sending computer then creates another token and places it on the network, allowing another station to capture the token and begin transmitting. The token circulates until a station is ready to send and captures the token.

This all happens very quickly: a token can circle a ring 200 meters in diameter at about 10,000 times a second. Some even faster networks circulate several tokens at once. Other ring networks have two counter-rotating rings that help them recover from network faults.

FDDI is a fast fiber-optic network based on the ring topology. We will discuss FDDI in detail in Chapter 4.

Advantages of the Ring

The ring topology offers the following advantages:

- Because every computer is given equal access to the token, no one computer can monopolize the network.

- The fair sharing of the network allows the network to degrade gracefully (continue to function in a useful, if slower, manner rather than fail once capacity is exceeded) as more users are added.

Disadvantages of the Ring

The ring topology has the following disadvantages:

- Failure of one computer on the ring can affect the whole network.

- It is difficult to troubleshoot a ring network.

- Adding or removing computers disrupts the network.

Star Bus and Star Ring

You will also see in networks today combinations of the topologies of bus, star, and ring. Figure 1.13 shows the two most common combination networks.

FIGURE 1.13

Star bus and star ring topologies combine aspects of the star, bus, and ring.

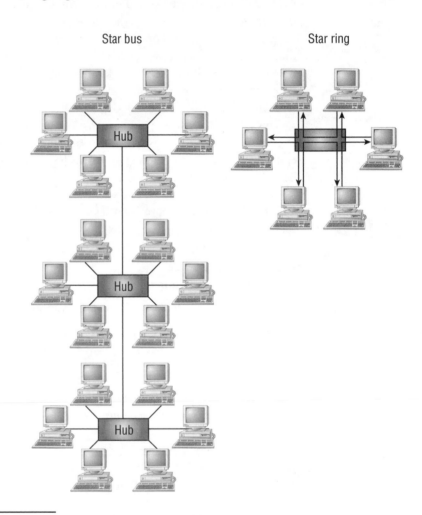

Star bus   Star ring

Star Bus

The *star bus* topology combines the bus and the star, linking several star hubs together with bus trunks. If one computer fails, the hub can detect the fault and isolate the computer. If a hub fails, computers connected to it will not be able to communicate, and the bus network will be broken into two segments that cannot reach each other.

Star Ring

In the *star ring*, also called the *star wired ring*, the network cables are laid out much like a star network, but a ring is implemented in the central hub. Outlying hubs can be connected to the inner hub, effectively extending a loop of the inner ring.

Token Ring is considered a star ring. Although its topology is physically a star, it functions logically in a ring. This is covered in greater detail in Chapter 4.

Physical Mesh Topology

The mesh topology is distinguished by having redundant links between devices. A true mesh configuration has a link between each device in the network. As you can imagine, this gets unmanageable beyond a very small number of devices. Most mesh topology networks are not true mesh networks. Rather, they are hybrid mesh networks, which contain some redundant links, but not all. Figure 1.14 illustrates both a true mesh and a hybrid mesh topology.

Mesh Installation

Mesh topology networks become more difficult to install as the number of devices increases because of the sheer quantity of connections that must be made. A true mesh of only six devices would require 15 connections (5+4+3+2+1). A true mesh topology of seven devices would require 21 connections (6+5+4+3+2+1), and so on.

Mesh Troubleshooting and Reconfiguration

Mesh networks are easy to troubleshoot and are very fault tolerant. Media failure has less impact on a mesh topology than on any other topology. The redundant links enable data to be sent over several different paths.

Reconfiguration, like installation, gets progressively more difficult as the number of devices increases.

Mesh Advantages and Disadvantages

The major advantage of the mesh topology is fault tolerance. Other advantages include guaranteed communication channel capacity and the fact that mesh networks are relatively easy to troubleshoot.

FIGURE 1.14

Physical mesh topology

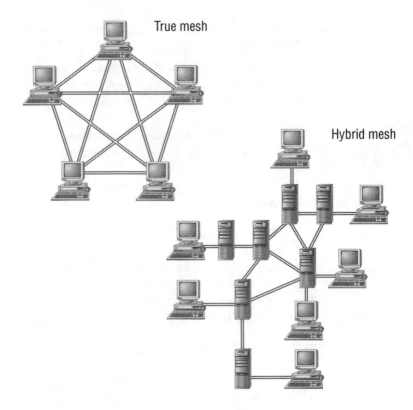

Disadvantages include the difficulty of installation and reconfiguration, as well as the cost of maintaining redundant links.

REAL WORLD PROBLEMS

You need to link a small number of computers in a room into a network for a training exercise. This will be a temporary network, and low cost is important.

■ Which network topology is appropriate for this situation?

You must install a network in an office building. The network must be reliable and easy to expand. Faults must be quickly diagnosed and solved. A single computer or network card failure must not bring down the whole network.

(continued)

REAL WORLD PROBLEMS (CONTINUED)

■ Which network topology is appropriate for this situation?

You are considering networking topologies for a network for a telemarketing firm.

■ Under what circumstances would a ring be more appropriate than a star?

■ Under what circumstances would a ring be less appropriate than a star?

■ Compare the star bus with the star ring.

■ What are the advantages and disadvantages of a mesh?

Network Media

N THE PRECEDING section you were introduced to several ways of physically linking computers. In this section we will briefly discuss what their connection media are made of and how that affects computer networking.

***Microsoft
Exam
Objective***

Select the appropriate media for various situations. Media choices include:

- Twisted-pair cable
- Coaxial cable
- Fiber-optic cable
- Wireless

Situational elements include:

- Cost
- Distance limitations
- Number of nodes.

What Are Media?

Media are what the message is transmitted over. Different media have different properties and are most effectively used in different environments for different purposes.

For example, television is a good medium for quick coverage and dramatic presentation of news events, whereas newspapers are better suited for a more in-depth presentation of issues. A scholarly journal or technical report might marshal facts more convincingly than television or newspapers. Figure 1.15 illustrates the concept of media.

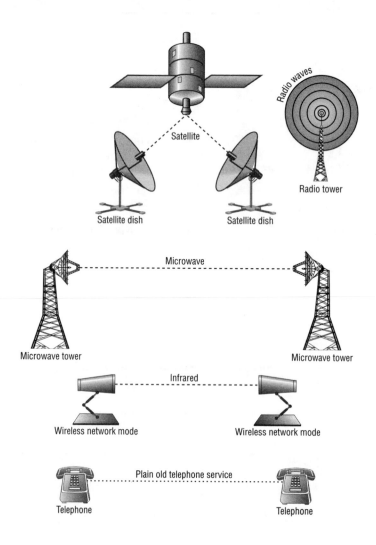

In computer networking, the medium affects nearly every aspect of communication. Most important, it determines how quickly and to whom a computer can talk and how expensive the process is.

Copper

The most common network medium is copper. This metal has served our communications needs for over a century and will most likely be widely used for another century. Engineers have become very good at sending electrical signals over copper wires and detecting them with a great deal of fidelity at the other end.

Fidelity is how precisely the signal that is received corresponds to the signal that was sent. High-fidelity audio equipment attempts to give the listener an experience as close to being there as is possible with electronics. Fidelity in networks means that the engineers try to get the signal from the source to the destination with the minimum amount of distortion from external sources, such as radio waves or magnetic fields from electric motors.

Electricity is the native language of computer circuitry. It is electricity, not photons or radio waves, that flows through the logic of personal computers, so it is convenient to send that electricity out over copper wires to be detected by other computers.

Electricity over copper wires loses energy the farther it gets from its source, and it requires a lot of energy to operate at the high speeds of today's computers.

Glass

Photons are the basic particles of light. (Photons can also act as waves, but that is not important to this text.) Photons are not affected by interference from electrical devices or radio waves, which is a major concern in high-speed copper networks. Fiber-optics is a networking technology developed to exploit the communications medium of light in long strands of glass.

Light can travel for several miles in the less expensive multi-mode fiber-optic cable without signal loss. The more expensive single-mode fiber-optic cable long-distance telephone companies use can carry a light signal for several hundred miles without signal degradation.

A single strand of fiber-optic cable can transmit data at over 2 gigabits per second. Two thousand novels of average length could be transmitted over fiber-optics in one second.

Unfortunately, properly installing fiber-optics requires more skill than installing copper wire, and an adapter card for a computer to send data at several gigabits is very expensive. Fiber-optics is used mainly in environments where copper will not work and where the faster speed is really needed—for instance, a machinery shop where interference would disturb signals on copper wire or an animation studio where the large animation files would take a long time to exchange over copper wire.

Air

Both fiber-optics and copper cabling have the drawback that you need a cable to connect the computers. Infrared technology can send the data right through the air—no cabling required! Infrared provides an effective solution for temporary or hard-to-cable environments, or where computers (such as laptops) are moved around a lot. For example, a worker equipped with a laptop or other mobile computer can connect to a network or print to a printer by lining up the computer's infrared port with an infrared port attached to the network or printer.

Infrared is a line-of-sight technology. The photons will not go through walls, which limits the usefulness of infrared in office environments. Figure 1.16 illustrates an infrared network in an office environment.

Infrared is not a very high-speed network when compared to copper and fiber-optic networks. Most local area networks today operate at a speed of 10Mbps, and networks that operate at 100Mbps are becoming affordable. Infrared adapters operate at speeds ranging from .3Mbps (adapters designed for serial printing) to 4Mbps (the new IRDA standard for infrared communication). Some infrared equipment, such as infrared laser bridges, operate at data rates of 100Mbps and beyond, but the cost and complexity of such specialized hardware make it impractical to use them in local area networks. The limited amount of infrared equipment produced for local area networks keeps costs high, but as infrared technology improves and gains wider acceptance, the prices will drop.

FIGURE 1.16

Infrared network interface
adapters connect
computers without wires.

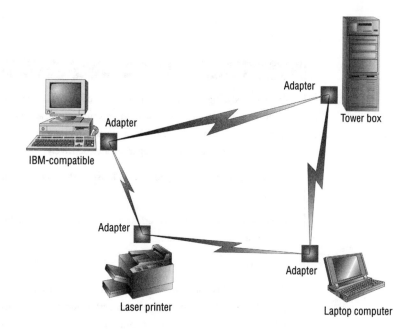

Radio

Another through-the-air method is via radio. Engineers have been sending information over electromagnetic waves for almost as long as they have over copper wires.

Radio waves will go through walls. Radio waves will also reach places it is difficult to get a network cable to. There is a very dynamic industry providing radio links to connect networks together.

Radio links can connect computers without regard to walls or line of sight. Radio is also immune to rain and snow, unlike external infrared installations.

Radio is a carefully regulated technology. Some radio communications equipment can be operated without a license, but your organization may need to have a license or permit to operate the higher-power or more sophisticated systems.

One problem with radio is that there is only so much electromagnetic spectrum to go around. Much of it is already occupied by television, radio, and important government and military communications systems, so there is little left for networking computers. This situation is changing, though, and as more sections of the spectrum become available and engineers learn to better exploit the areas left over, more and more exciting networking solutions will be in radio.

REAL WORLD PROBLEMS

You are designing a network for an office complex. Several buildings must be linked together with high-performance long-distance links, and servers within the buildings must be linked together with a high-speed backbone. Hundreds of client computers in each building must be linked together inexpensively.

■ Explain which media types you will use in this network and where you will use them.

You are considering an infrared laser link between two buildings on your company's campus in Aspen, Colorado.

■ What are the drawbacks of using a laser wireless link in this instance?

You need to link the computers on your marine research ship with the LAN on your shore facility. The research ship stays within line-of-sight of the shore facility (about 15 miles), exploring local ocean conditions.

■ How will you link the ship to the shore?

Network Protocols

THE PRECEDING SECTION covered what computers talk over (the medium), and the section before that described how the computers are linked together (the topology). Now we'll look at the languages or protocols computers speak.

What Are Protocols?

Protocols are the agreed-upon ways that computers exchange information. Networks are full of protocols. A computer needs to know exactly how messages will arrive from the network so it can make sure the message gets to the right place. It needs to know how the network expects the message to be formatted (for instance, which part of the message is the data and which part of the message identifies the recipient) so the network can convey the data to its destination. As a comparison, consider the road-traffic protocols employed at an intersection to allow cars to cross safely (see Figure 1.17).

Green – Go
Yellow – Slow Down
Red – Stop

It is green, I can go.

Green – Go
Yellow – Slow Down
Red – Stop

It is red, I must stop.

There are many levels of protocols in a network. (We'll examine several protocols in greater detail in Chapter 3.) Protocols can be broadly divided into hardware and software categories.

Hardware Protocols

Hardware protocols define how hardware devices operate and work together. The 10baseT Ethernet protocol is a hardware protocol specifying exactly how two 10baseT Ethernet devices will exchange information and what they will do if it is improperly transmitted or interrupted. It determines such things as voltage levels and which pairs of wires will be used for transmission and reception. There is no program involved; it is all done with circuitry.

The Hardware-Software Interface

Whenever a program in a computer needs to access hardware, such as when a message has arrived from the network and is now waiting in the adapter card's memory, ready to be received, the computer program uses a predefined hardware-software protocol. This basically means that the computer program can expect the data to always be in the same place; that certain registers on the card will indicate what is to be done with it; and that when other registers are accessed in the proper order, the card will do something logical, such as receive another message or send a message out.

Software Protocols

Programs communicate with each other via software protocols. Network client computers and network servers both have protocol packages that must be loaded to allow them to talk to other computers. These packages contain the protocols the computer needs to access a certain network device or service.

There are different protocol packages for different networks and even for different kinds of servers on the same network. Microsoft Windows NT Server and Microsoft Windows 95 come with a large number of network protocols so you can make the best use of your network.

All the computers on your network must have at least one set of protocols in common in order to communicate. To communicate with the Internet, your computers must have the TCP/IP set of protocols. TCP/IP (Transmission Control Protocol/Internet Protocol) will be explained in more detail in Chapter 3, and Chapters 6 and 7 will describe how to configure your client and server to use TCP/IP.

Planning a Network for Your Organization

USING THE KNOWLEDGE you have gained in this chapter, you can now begin to plan a network for your organization. Technical details such as the protocols used and the types of network adapters and cable will be covered in later chapters, but you now have enough information to determine the overall character of your network.

This discussion assumes you do not already have a network. If you do have a network, you can use this text as a guide to see how well your current network fits your organization's needs.

Peer or Server

The first step is to determine whether your network should be server based or peer-to-peer.

Microsoft ✓ *Exam Objective*

Compare a client/server network with a peer-to-peer network.

In the following situations, a peer-to-peer network would be appropriate for your organization:

- There are fewer than ten people in your organization.

- The people in your organization are sophisticated computer users.

- Security is not an issue or the users can be trusted to maintain good security.

- There is no one central administrator who sets network policies.

- The cost of an additional computer just to serve files exceeds available funds.

- Users can be relied upon to back up their own data.

- Users are physically close together and there are no plans for expansion of the network.

In the following situations, a server-based network would be appropriate for your organization:

- There are more than ten people in your organization.

- Many of the people are not sophisticated computer users.

- Your organization maintains information that must be centrally controlled.

- You have enough users that central file servers and application servers are less expensive than storing files and licensing applications on each client computer.

- A central administrator will set network policies and oversee network maintenance.

By using these criteria, you can now decide whether your network should be server based or peer-to-peer.

Server Issues

If a server-based network is appropriate for your organization, you will also wish to consider the following questions:

- How many client computers will be connected to your network?

If you have a large number of users (25 or more) you may wish to divide the load among several servers.

- Which of the following tasks will your servers perform?

  - Client-server applications

  - Backup

  - Communication

  - Database

  - E-mail

- Fax

- Mirroring

- Printing

- User directories

- Shared directories

You may wish to limit each server to one or two of the above items to maintain the best performance on your network.

- Is your organization built around several functional units?

If you have several departments in your organization, such as financing, sales, research and development, manufacturing, administration, personnel, and so on, you may wish to have your network match your organization with a server for each functional unit.

Topology

Now you should determine which topology is right for you.

Microsoft Exam Objective

Select the appropriate topology for various token-ring and Ethernet networks.

In the following situations, a bus topology will be best suited to your organization:

- The network is small.

- The network will not be frequently reconfigured.

- The least expensive solution is required.

- The network is not expected to grow much.

In the following situations, a star topology will be best suited to your organization:

- It must be easy to add or remove client computers.

- It must be easy to troubleshoot.

- The network is large.

- The network is expected to grow in the future.

In the following situations, a ring topology would be best suited to your organization:

- The network must operate reasonably under a heavy load.

- A higher-speed network is required.

- The network will not be frequently reconfigured.

You may wish to consider a star bus topology if your network requires an inexpensive solution that can be reconfigured and can grow in the future.

A star ring may be appropriate if you need a network that is large and must operate at high speeds or operate reasonably under a heavy load.

By using these criteria, you can now decide which network topology best fits your organization.

Media

You also need to determine the media on which your network will operate. The most common choice is copper, which is the least expensive. However, if you have a demanding network environment, fiber-optics will provide better performance. Whole networks are seldom implemented with infrared or radio technology, but you may choose to implement portions of your network with wireless links to overcome difficult obstacles, such as roads or gaps between buildings.

Review

COMPUTERS ARE INFORMATION tools, and networks are how the computers exchange that information.

Networked computers can share data and peripherals, allowing people in an organization to communicate better and more effectively use their hardware resources.

In peer-to-peer networks, every computer is both a client and a server. Server-based networks dedicate a computer to more effectively perform server functions. Some networks use a combination of both servers and peers.

Topology is the shape of the network:

- In a bus, the computers are connected in a line.

- In a star, the computers are linked together at a central point.

- In a ring, the computers form a circle.

- The star bus or star ring results when network topologies are combined.

Media are what the network cables are made of. Copper is the most common networking medium, while fiber-optics is used for high performance. Infrared and radio are used when cables are inappropriate for a certain network location.

Review Questions

1. You are installing a new network for a company that is growing rapidly. The current design calls for 40 computers, with expansion to 100 in the next six months. Because of the speed at which the network is expected to grow, you want to make sure that troubleshooting will be as easy as possible. Considering these factors, which of the following topologies should be used in the new network?

   A. Star

   B. Ring

   C. Mesh

   D. Bus

2. The Windows NT operating system provides many features that take advantage of advanced server hardware. Which of the following features are supported by Windows NT? Choose all that apply:

   A. Extremely large file size

   B. Intel and RISC microprocessors

   C. Symmetric Multiprocessing

   D. Plug-and-Play

3. You manage a small engineering firm that has 10 employees, all with their own computers. Sharing resources has become a necessity, but cost is an issue. You trust each of your employees to handle their computers responsibly. Which of the following network types would be best to install in your situation?

   A. Hybrid

   B. Mainframe/terminal

   C. Peer-to-peer

   D. Server-based

4. Which of the following network topologies degrades most gracefully in high network load situations?

   A. Star

   B. Ring

   C. Mesh

   D. Bus

5. The network that you support includes 14 separate offices nationwide, connected via T-1 lines. What kind of network do you have?

   A. Campus Area Network

   B. LAN

   C. MAN

   D. WAN

6. You are planning a network installation for a small design firm. The majority of the staff is not terribly computer savvy, so centralized administration and backups are important. However, the CAD/CAM team is very experienced and is able to handle much of their own networking needs. Which of the following network types is best suited to your situation?

A. Hybrid

B. Mainframe/terminal

C. Peer-to-peer

D. Server-based

7. You need to connect two buildings on your corporate campus with a high-speed link. Due to security concerns, it must be immune to electromagnetic interference and highly secure. Which of the following media types should you choose?

A. Air (wireless infra-red)

B. Copper

C. Glass

D. Radio

8. Which of the following best describes a network that connects computers in the same building?

A. Campus Area Network

B. LAN

C. MAN

D. WAN

9. Suppose the following situation exists: Your company has decided to network some of its existing computers. The manager would like to get the operations staff networked together first, then, if all goes well, move on to the rest of the company. There are 22 computers in operations, and 45 computers in the rest of the company.

Required result: You must have a highly reliable topology that tolerates problems with individual computers.

Optional desired results: The lowest setup costs of any topology. The network should be relatively easy to expand.

Proposed solution: Implement a ring topology network.

Which result does the proposed solution produce?

A. The proposed solution produces the required result and produces both of the optional desired results.

B. The proposed solution produces the required result and produces only one of the optional desired results.

C. The proposed solution produces the required result but does not produce any of the optional desired results.

D. The proposed solution does not produce the required result.

10. You have been asked to wire a conference room with six computers for a demonstration tomorrow. It needs be done quickly and with the lowest possible expense. What network topology is best suited to this situation?

A. Star

B. Ring

C. Mesh

D. Bus

11. You have been asked to put together a proposal for a new computer network for your company. Your boss has asked you to specifically list the advantages to networking. Of the following equipment your company owns, which devices can be shared on a network? Choose all that apply:

A. Keyboards

B. Scanners

C. CD-ROM drives

D. Printers

12. Your computer network must be fairly secure, but as transparent as possible. It is very important that you are able to control access to resources by user account. What type of security should you implement?

A. Physical

B. Peer-based

C. Server-based

D. Hybrid

13. You company has asked you to provide a plan to network an auditorium for a large presentation. Speed is not an issue, nor is cost. However, the presentation manager is concerned that attendees will trip over cables and take the whole network down. Which of the following media would be appropriate to implement this network? Choose all that apply:

A. Air (wireless infra-red)

B. Copper

C. Glass

D. Radio

14. As a consultant, you have been asked to design a network for a mid-sized accounting firm. Because of the data handled by the company, security is extremely important. The network must support 80 computers with easy expandability to more than 100 in the next few months. What type of network would be best for you to install at your client's office?

A. Internet

B. Mainframe/terminal

C. Peer-to-peer

D. Server-based

15. The Internet is a collection of redundant high-speed wide-area links. Which network topology does the Internet use?

A. Star

B. Ring

C. Mesh

D. Bus

16. You want to implement a network with the most readily available and widely supported media. Which of the following media types would you choose?

A. Air (wireless infra-red)

B. Copper

C. Glass

D. Radio

17. You are planning a small server-based network with requirements for file, print, e-mail, and database services. You are leaning toward using Windows NT as your server operating system. What is the minimum number of servers you will need?

A. One

B. Two

C. Three

D. Four

18. Your boss is considering implementing a bus topology network. Which of the following arguments could you use to dissuade him from this decision? Choose all that apply:

A. A loose connector can interfere with network communication.

B. Heavy network traffic can slow a bus network considerably.

C. Failure of one computer in the network interrupts communication throughout the network.

D. A cable break disrupts communication on the network

19. In a client/server networking environment, the processing (choose all that apply):

    A. Takes place only on the client side.

    B. Is shared between the client and the server.

    C. Of requests by the client is handled by the server.

    D. Takes place only on the server side.

20. Which of the following statements describe benefits of a ring topology network? Choose all that apply:

    A. It requires fiber-optic cable.

    B. It gracefully handles increased numbers of computers.

    C. A single computer failure does not affect network communication.

    D. It ensures equal access to the media for all computers.

21. A series of star networks connected together (hubs linked, but not in a loop) is what?

    A. A hybrid ring

    B. A hybrid mesh

    C. A star bus

    D. A hybrid star

22. What kind of topology is Token Ring? Choose the most correct answer:

    A. Star Ring

    B. Star Bus

    C. Hybrid Star

    D. Mesh

CHAPTER

2

Network Components

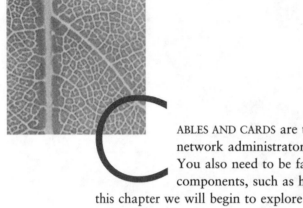

CABLES AND CARDS are the nuts and bolts of networks. As a network administrator, you need to understand them well. You also need to be familiar with other common network components, such as hubs, transceivers, jacks, and panels. In this chapter we will begin to explore these and other fundamental components that make up a network.

Signal Transmission

ignaling is the way data is transmitted across the medium. It uses electrical energy to communicate. Somehow the data, or the bits and bytes, must be represented in such a way that the sender can create a message and the receiver can understand it. This is done by means of *encoding* (also called *modulation*). The original signal is altered in a certain way to allow it to represent data.

The information to be communicated can exist in either of two forms: analog or digital. A characteristic of analog information is that it changes continuously. An example of this is an analog clock. It is always changing its representation of time because the second hand never stops (as long as it's working).

Digital data, on the other hand, consists of discrete states: On or Off, 1 or 0, and so on. A digital clock does not show the variations of time between minutes. It's either 12:01 or 12:02, not anything in between.

The two signaling methods correspond to the two types of data described above:

- Digital signaling

- Analog signaling

Figure 2.1 shows the difference between an analog signal and a digital signal.

Analog and digital signals

Analog signal

Digital signal

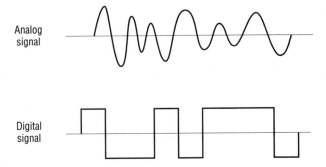

Note that the analog signal is constantly changing and represents all values in a range. It is actually an electromagnetic waveform. In contrast, the digital signal represents discrete states, and the state change is practically instantaneous.

These signaling methods are discussed in detail in the following sections.

Digital Signaling

Because computers are inherently digital, most computer networks use *digital signaling*. There are many methods of encoding data in a digital signal. These methods are called encoding schemes. They can be grouped into two general categories based on whether the recognition of a given state is triggered by a certain voltage level or by the transition from one level to another:

- Current-state encoding

- State-transition encoding

Current-State Encoding

In current-state encoding strategies, data is encoded by the presence or absence of a signal characteristic or state. For example, a voltage of +5 might represent a binary 0, while a voltage of −5 could represent a binary 1, as shown in Figure 2.2. The signal is monitored periodically by network devices in order to determine its current state. That state then indicates the data value encoded within it.

FIGURE 2.2

Current-state encoding

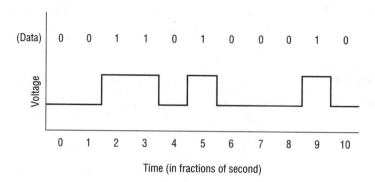

The following encoding schemes use current-state encoding:

- Unipolar

- Polar

- Return-to-Zero (RZ)

These encoding schemes are described in the section "Digital Encoding Schemes" a little later in this chapter.

State-Transition Encoding

State-transition encoding methods differ from current-state encoding in that they use transitions in the signal to represent data, as opposed to encoding data by means of a particular voltage level or state. For example, a transition occurring from high to low voltage could represent a 1, while a transition from low to high voltage could represent a 0.

Another variation might be that the presence of a transition represents a 1 and the absence of a transition indicates a 0. This type of state-transition encoding is illustrated in Figure 2.3.

The following encoding schemes use state-transition encoding:

- Bipolar-Alternate Mark Inversion (AMI)

- Non-Return-to-Zero (NRZ)

- Manchester

- Differential Manchester

- Biphase Space (FM-0)

These methods are described in the next section.

FIGURE 2.3

State-transition encoding

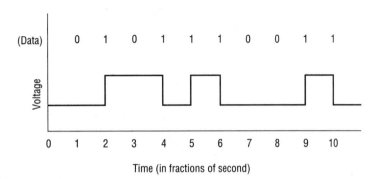

Time (in fractions of second)

Digital Encoding Schemes

Here are brief descriptions of some common digital encoding schemes:

- **Unipolar:** An encoding scheme that uses two levels for encoding data. One of the levels is zero, which could represent a binary 1, and the other level can be either positive or negative. If a particular implementation of Unipolar is using negative voltages, a −3 V, for example, would represent the other value: a binary 0.

- **Polar:** This is similar to unipolar, except that it can use both positive and negative voltages for encoding data. For example, a −3 V could represent a 1 and a +3 V could represent a 0.

- **Return-to-Zero (RZ):** An encoding scheme in which the signal transitions to zero in the middle of each bit interval. A positive voltage level transitioning to zero could represent a 0, and a negative voltage transitioning to zero could represent a 1. The mid-bit transition is included to make this strategy self-clocking.

- **Biphase:** This encoding scheme requires at least one mid-bit transition per bit interval. An example of a biphase encoding scheme is Manchester encoding.

- **Manchester:** In Manchester encoding, a low-to-high mid-bit transition represents one value, such as a binary 0, and a high-to-low transition represents the other, such as a binary 1. Manchester encoding is used in Ethernet LANs.

- **Differential Manchester:** This encoding scheme is also considered to be a biphase coding scheme because it uses a mid-bit transition. In this case, however, the mid-bit transition does not represent data; it is used for clocking. The actual data is represented by a transition at the beginning of the bit interval. The presence of a transition indicates one value, such as a 0. The absence of a transition indicates a 1. Differential Manchester is used in Token Ring LANs.

- **Non-Return-to-Zero (NRZ):** This encoding scheme is similar to Differential Manchester in that the presence or absence of transition at the beginning of the bit interval determines the bit value. For example, if a transition occurs, it could represent a 1, and no transition means a 0. NRZ is unlike Differential Manchester in that there is no mid-bit transition for clocking.

The details of these encoding methods are considered beyond the scope of this portion of the MCSE study program. The brief descriptions here are intended to give you a better understanding of digital signaling in general.

Analog Signaling

Analog signals consist of electromagnetic waves. An analog wave is constantly changing. A wave cycle is the change from high to low and back to high (or low to high and back to low). Three characteristics are used to measure or describe electromagnetic waveforms: amplitude, frequency, and phase. Characteristics of an analog signal are illustrated in Figure 2.4.

FIGURE 2.4

Characteristics of analog signals

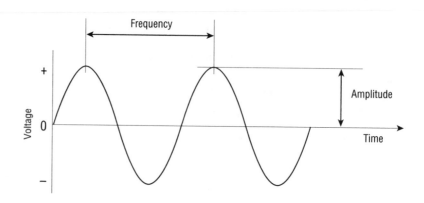

Amplitude measures the strength of the signal or the height of the wave. Amplitude is expressed in volts for electrical potential, amps for electrical current, watts for electrical power, and decibels to indicate the ratio between the power of two signals. Figure 2.5 illustrates a wave that is varying in amplitude.

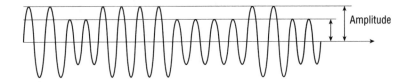

Frequency is the amount of time it takes for a wave to complete one cycle. For example, if a signal takes 1 second to go from high to low and back to high (in other words, to complete one cycle), the frequency of the wave is one. Frequency is measured in hertz (Hz), or cycles per second. Figure 2.6 shows a wave that is varying in frequency.

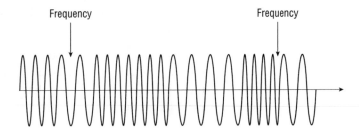

Phase is a different type of measurement than amplitude or frequency in that it requires more than one wave. Phase is the relative state of one wave when timing began; that is, relative to another, reference wave. An illustration is particularly helpful in this case. Figure 2.7 shows three waves or signals that differ from each other in phase. Phase is measured in degrees. The easiest phase shift to spot visually is that of 180 degrees. In our illustration, signal B and signal C differ from each other by 180 degrees; that is, signal B goes down when signal C goes up, and vice versa.

Analog Signal Modulation

All three of these characteristics—amplitude, frequency, and phase—can be used to encode data in an analog signal. For example, a higher amplitude could represent a 1 and a lower amplitude could represent a 0. Similarly, a higher frequency

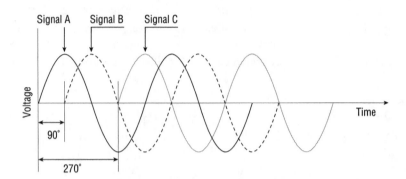

could represent a 0 and a lower frequency could represent a 1. Analog signals are periodically measured by network devices to determine the encoded value.

There are three main strategies for encoding data using analog signals. The first two, amplitude shift keying and frequency shift keying, are considered current-state encoding schemes because a measurement is made to detect a particular state or level.

The third strategy, phase shift keying, is a state-transition encoding scheme because it relies on the presence or absence of a transition from one phase to another to indicate the value.

AMPLITUDE SHIFT KEYING (ASK) You can use amplitude shift keying, or ASK, to encode binary data by varying the amplitude of the signal. In the example shown in Figure 2.8, a stronger voltage could represent a 1 and a weaker voltage could represent a 0.

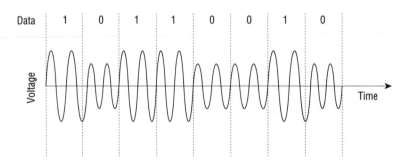

FREQUENCY SHIFT KEYING (FSK) Frequency shift keying, or FSK, is similar to ASK except that the frequency, not the amplitude, of the signal is varying. In the example shown in Figure 2.9, one frequency could represent a 1 and another could represent a 0.

FIGURE 2.9

Frequency shift keying

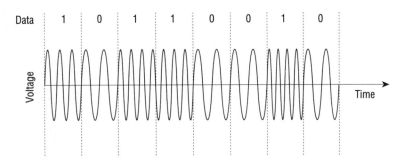

PHASE SHIFT KEYING (PSK)   Phase shift keying, or PSK, uses a transition or shift from one phase to another to encode data. As in other state-transition encoding schemes, the presence or absence of a transition can be used to encode data. Figure 2.10 shows an example of PSK in which a 1 is represented by the presence of a transition (in this case, a 180-degree phase shift), and a 0 is represented by the absence of a transition (as in no phase shift).

FIGURE 2.10

Phase shift keying

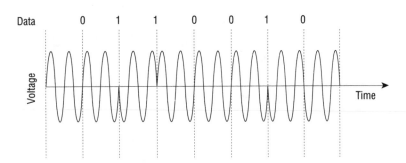

Comparing the Signaling Methods

In general, digital signaling provides the following advantages over analog signaling:

- Fewer errors from noise and interference

- Uses less expensive equipment

On the other hand, one disadvantage is that digital signals suffer from greater attenuation than analog signals over the same distance.

In general, analog signaling provides the following advantages:

- Less attenuation than digital signals over the same distance

- Can be multiplexed to increase bandwidth

One disadvantage is that analog signals are more prone to errors from noise and interference.

Bit Synchronization

In the previous sections, we described ways of encoding data in analog or digital signals. These encoding schemes rely on changes or modulations to a particular characteristic of the signal. The receiving network device must then interpret the signal by measuring that modulated or changed characteristic. Timing is important because the receiver needs to know when to measure the signal in order to extract the correct meaning from it.

The coordination of signal measurement timing is called bit synchronization. The two major methods of bit synchronization are asynchronous and synchronous.

Asynchronous Bit Synchronization

Asynchronous communication requires that messages begin with a start bit so that the receiving device can synchronize its internal clock with the timing of the message. When no data is being transmitted, the media is idle and the sender's and receiver's clocks are not synchronized.

Asynchronous transmissions are normally short, and the end of the message is signaled by a stop bit.

Synchronous Bit Synchronization

Synchronous communication requires that some kind of clocking mechanism be put into place to keep the clocks of the sender and receiver synchronized. The following three methods are used for synchronous timing coordination:

- Guaranteed state change

- Separate clock signal

- Oversampling

Each of these three methods implements a distinct clocking technique.

GUARANTEED STATE CHANGE Guaranteed state change describes a method in which the clocking information is embedded in the data signal. This way, the receiver is guaranteed that transitions will occur in the signal at predefined intervals. These transitions allow the receiver to continually adjust its internal clock.

The guaranteed state change is the most common method, and it is frequently used with digital signals. The digital encoding schemes described earlier as self-clocking use this method.

SEPARATE CLOCK SIGNALS In the separate clock signals method, a separate channel between the transmitter and receiver provides the clocking information. Since this method requires twice the channel capacity of embedding the clock in the data stream, it is inefficient. This method is most effective for shorter transmissions, such as those between a computer and a printer.

OVERSAMPLING Oversampling is a method in which the receiver samples the signal at a much faster rate than the data rate. This permits the use of an encoding method that does not add clocking transitions. If the receiver samples the signal ten times more quickly than the data rate, out of any ten measurements, one would provide the data information, and the other nine would determine whether the receiver's clock is synchronized.

Baseband and Broadband Transmissions

Bandwidth use refers to the ways of allocating the capacity of transmission media. The total media capacity or bandwidth can be divided into channels. A channel is simply a portion of the bandwidth that can be used for transmitting data.

The two ways of allocating the capacity of bounded transmission media are the following:

- **Baseband:** These transmissions use the entire media bandwidth for a single channel. Baseband is commonly used for digital signaling, although it can also be used for analog signals. Most LANs use baseband signaling.

- **Broadband:** These transmissions provide the ability to divide the entire media bandwidth into multiple channels. Since each channel can carry a different analog signal, broadband networks support multiple simultaneous conversations over a single transmission medium.

Figure 2.11 shows the difference between baseband and broadband transmission.

FIGURE 2.11

Baseband and broadband
transmission

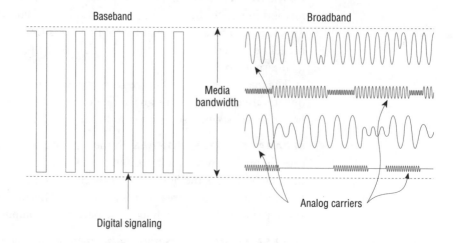

REAL WORLD PROBLEMS

You are asked to evaluate two new networking products for transmitting data over
special coaxial cable. One product uses analog signaling, the other digital signaling.

- Which product is more likely to cost less? Why?

- Which product is more likely to provide greater bandwidth? Why?

You wish to link two distant sites using a single cable. You need to combine digital and
analog information on the same cable.

- What kind of transmission is well-suited to this use?

A coworker is confused about the difference between analog and digital signals.
"They're both electrical, aren't they?" he says.

- Explain how analog and digital are different.

Network Media Types

N THE PRECEDING section you learned how signals are transmitted over a network link. In this section we discuss the specific types of cable and wireless networking:

- Coaxial

- Twisted-pair

- Fiber-optic

- Infrared

- Microwave

- Radio

Computers send electronic signals to each other using electric currents, radio waves, microwaves, or light-spectrum energy from the electromagnetic spectrum. These signals represent network data as binary impulses (0's and 1's). The physical path through which computers send and receive these signals is called the transmission media.

Microsoft ✓ *Exam* *Objective*

Select the appropriate media for various situations. Media choices include:

- Twisted-pair cable
- Coaxial cable
- Fiber-optic cable
- Wireless

Situational elements include:

- Cost
- Distance limitations
- Number of nodes

The electromagnetic spectrum provides a wide variety of ways in which signals may be passed through transmission media from one computer to another. The electromagnetic spectrum ranges from electric currents to infrared light and gamma rays. Figure 2.12 shows the electromagnetic spectrum divided into waveforms and their frequencies.

Transmission media are divided into two categories:

- Cable media have a central conductor enclosed in a plastic jacket. They are typically used for small LANs. Cable media normally transmit signals using the lower end of the electromagnetic spectrum, such as simple electricity and, sometimes, radio waves.

- Wireless media typically employ the higher electromagnetic frequencies, such as radio waves, microwaves, and infrared. Wireless media are necessary for networks with mobile computers or networks that transmit signals over large distances; they are especially prevalent in enterprise and global networks.

Cellular phone networks use microwaves to broadcast signals.

Networks that cover multiple sites frequently use combinations of cable and wireless media to link computers and devices.

Each media type has certain characteristics that make it suitable for particular networks. To choose the best type of media for your network, you should know how each medium's characteristics relate to the following factors:

- Cost

- Installation

- Capacity

- Attenuation

- Immunity from electromagnetic interference (EMI)

The following sections describe how these factors affect your network. The specifics of how each medium performs in these areas are covered later in this chapter.

FIGURE 2.12

The electromagnetic spectrum

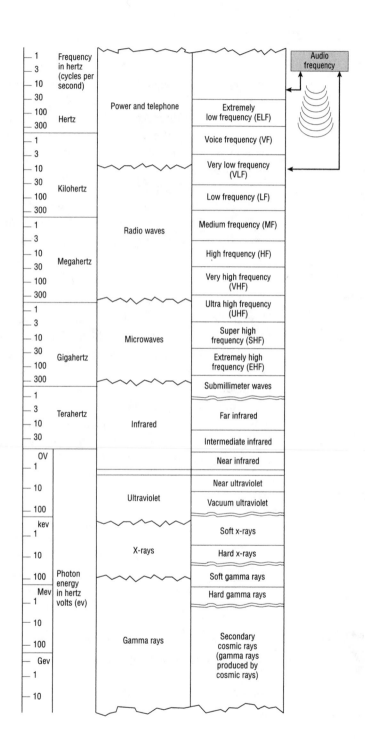

Cost

The cost of each media type should be weighed against the performance it provides, and the available resources. For example, it is common practice among network integrators to attempt to run a network across unused, left-over telephone cabling. Although this could reduce costs, in many cases it is not a viable solution—for example, when cable drops of greater than 100 meters are required.

Each network installation is different, and you must look for the most affordable viable solution. You should take into consideration your real needs. For example, fiber-optic cable is fast, but you may not need that much speed. It's easy to spend too much if you're not writing the checks.

Installation

How difficult installation is depends on the individual situation, but some general comparisons between the media are possible. Some types of media can be installed with simple tools and little training; others require more training and knowledge and may be better left to professionals. For example, unshielded twisted-pair cable is easy to install, but fiber-optic cable requires professional training. To connect two lengths of fiber together, you may need to use electric fusion or a chemical epoxy process. These are jobs you probably don't want to undertake unless you know how to do them. Later sections of this chapter discuss installation in detail.

Bandwidth Capacity

The capacity of a medium is usually measured in bandwidth. In the world of networking, bandwidth is measured in terms of megabits per second (Mbps). Ethernet, for example, has a bandwidth of 10Mbps. A medium with a high capacity has a high bandwidth; a medium with a low capacity has a low bandwidth.

In the field of communications, the term bandwidth refers to the range of frequencies a medium can accommodate. In networking, bandwidth is measured in terms of the number of bits that can be transmitted across a given medium per second.

A high bandwidth normally increases throughput and performance, but the cable length and signaling techniques affect the bandwidth a cable can accommodate.

Node Capacity

Also of vital importance on a network is how many computers you can attach easily to the network cables. Each network cabling system has a natural number of computers that can be attached to the network before expensive devices such as bridges, routers, repeaters, and hubs must be used to expand the network.

Attenuation

Electromagnetic signals tend to weaken during transmission. This is referred to as *attenuation*. As the signals pass through the transmission medium, part of their strength is absorbed or misdirected. This phenomenon imposes limits on the distance a signal can travel through a medium without unacceptable degradation. The farther you are from a person, the harder it is to hear what that person is saying. Part of this is attenuation, and part is interference.

When the signal gets weak, it becomes difficult to tell a 1 from a 0, and errors can creep into the communication link. Because of attenuation and dispersion, you must be careful that network cables do not exceed the maximum length recommended for that type of cable. Exceeding the limits may lead to intermittent errors or network failure.

Electromagnetic Interference

Electromagnetic interference (EMI) affects the signal that is sent through the transmission media. EMI is caused by outside electromagnetic waves affecting the desired signal, making it more difficult for the receiving computer to decode the signal. Some media are more influenced by EMI than others. EMI is often referred to as noise. If you are in a quiet room, it is easier to hear a person than if you are at a rock concert.

A related concern is eavesdropping, especially if your network data requires a high level of security. The same characteristics of a cable that allow an external signal to interfere with the signal on the cable also make it easy for someone to detect the signal on the cable externally, without piercing the cable. Therefore, if you need a cable that is relatively invulnerable to eavesdropping, look for a cable that is relatively invulnerable to EMI.

Cable Media

C ABLES HAVE A central conductor that consists of a wire or fiber surrounded by a plastic jacket. Three types of cable media are twisted-pair, coaxial, and fiber-optic cable. Two types of twisted-pair cable are used in networks: unshielded (UTP) and shielded (STP). Table 2.1 summarizes the characteristics of these types of cable media, which are discussed in the following sections.

TABLE 2.1 Characteristics of Cable Media	FACTOR	UTP	STP	COAXIAL	FIBER-OPTIC
	Cost	Lowest	Moderate	Moderate	Highest
	Installation	Easy	Fairly easy	Fairly easy	Difficult
	Bandwidth Capacity	1- to 155Mbps (typically 10Mbps)	1- to 155Mbps (typically 16Mbps)	Typically 10Mbps	2Gbps (typically 100Mbps)
	Node Capacity per Segment	2	2	30 (10base2) 100 (10base5)	2
	Attenuation	High (range of hundreds of meters)	High (range of hundreds of meters)	Lower (range of a few kilometers)	Lowest (range of tens of kilometers)
	EMI	Most vulnerable to EMI and eavesdropping	Less vulnerable than UTP but still vulnerable to EMI and eavesdropping	Less vulnerable than UTP but still vulnerable to EMI and eavesdropping	Not affected by EMI or eavesdropping

Twisted-Pair Cable

Twisted-pair cable uses one or more pairs of two twisted copper wires to transmit signals. It is commonly used as telecommunications cable.

When copper wires that are close together conduct electric signals, there is a tendency for each wire to produce interference in the other. One wire interfering with another in this way is called *crosstalk*. To decrease the amount of crosstalk and outside interference, the wires are twisted. Twisting the wires allows the emitted signals from one wire to cancel out the emitted signals from the other and protects them from outside noise.

Twisted pairs are two color-coded, insulated copper wires that are twisted around each other. A twisted-pair cable consists of one or more twisted pairs in a common jacket. Figure 2.13 shows a twisted-pair cable.

FIGURE 2.13

Twisted-pair cable has two twisted copper wires

Insulation

Copper wire conductor

Let's look at the two types of twisted-pair cable: unshielded and shielded.

Unshielded Twisted-Pair Cable

Unshielded twisted-pair (UTP) cable consists of a number of twisted pairs with a simple plastic casing. UTP is commonly used in telephone systems. Figure 2.14 shows a UTP cable.

FIGURE 2.14

Unshielded twisted-pair (UTP) cable

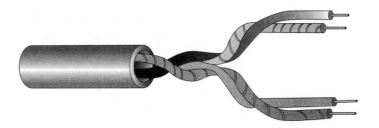

The Electrical Industries Association (EIA) divides UTP into different categories by quality grade. The rating for each category refers to conductor size, electrical characteristics, and twists per foot. The following categories are defined:

- Categories 1 and 2 were originally meant for voice communication and can support only low data rates, less than 4 megabits per second (Mbps). These cannot be used for high-speed data communications. Older telephone networks used Category 1 cable.

- Category 3 is suitable for most computer networks. Some innovations can allow data rates much higher, but generally Category 3 offers data rates up to 10MB. This category of cable is the kind currently used in most telephone installations.

- Category 4 offers data rates up to 20Mbps.

- Category 5 offers enhancements over Category 3, such as support for Fast Ethernet, more insulation, more twists per foot, and data rates of 100Mbps and higher, but Category 5 requires compatible equipment and more stringent installation. In a Category 5 installation, all media, connectors, and connecting equipment must support Category 5, or performance will be affected.

Data-grade UTP cable (Categories 3, 4, and 5) consists of either four or eight wires. A UTP cable with four wires is called a two-pair. Network topologies that use UTP require at least two-pair wire. You may want to include an extra pair for future expansion. Figure 2.15 shows a four-pair cable.

FIGURE 2.15

Unshielded four-pair cable

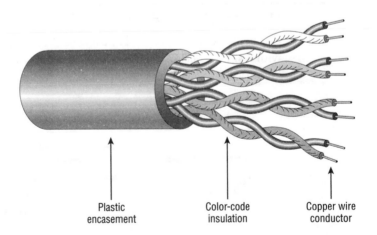

Plastic encasement

Color-code insulation

Copper wire conductor

Because UTP cable was originally used in telephone systems, UTP installations are often similar to telephone installations. For a four-pair cable, you need a modular RJ-45 telephone connector. For a two-pair cable, you need a modular RJ-11 telephone connector. These connectors are attached to both ends of a patch cable. One end of the patch cable is then inserted into a computer or other device, and the other end is inserted into a wall jack. The wall jack connects the UTP drop cable (another length of cable) to a punch-down block.

The other side of the punch-down block is wired to a patch panel. The patch panel provides connectivity through patch cables to other user devices and connectivity devices. Figure 2.16 shows how UTP might be installed.

FIGURE 2.16

A common UTP installation

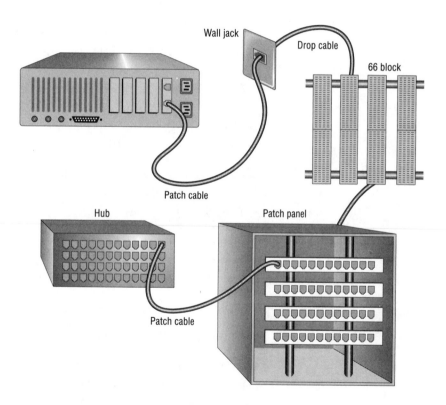

UTP's popularity is partly because UTP was first used in telephone systems. In many cases a network can be run over the already existing wires installed for the phone system, at a great savings in installation cost.

Before using existing telephone wiring for your data network, make sure the wiring can handle data transmission. A telephone is much more forgiving than a data network and will operate when the wiring lacks proper twisting and other electrical characteristics that a computer network needs.

UTP cable has the following characteristics:

- **Cost:** Except for professionally installed Category 5, the cost of UTP is very low when compared with other transmission media. It continues to be mass produced for telecommunications applications, such as computer and telephone networks.

- **Installation:** UTP cable is easy to install, so installation can be done with very little training. Because UTP uses equipment similar to telephone equipment, maintenance and network reconfiguration should be relatively simple.

- **Bandwidth capacity:** With current technologies, UTP may support data rates from 1- to 155Mbps at distances of up to 100 meters (328 feet). The most common rate is 10Mbps.

- **Node capacity:** Since only two computers can be connected together by a UTP cable, the number of computers in a UTP network is not limited by the cable. Rather, it is limited by the hub or hubs that connect the cables together. In an Ethernet network, which is the most common type of UTP network, the useful upper limit is around 75 nodes on a single collision domain, but it depends on the type of data traffic in your network. There is a specified upper limit of 1024, but you will probably never reach this limit.

- **Attenuation:** Transmissions across copper wire tend to attenuate rapidly. Because of this, UTP is normally restricted to distances of 100 meters.

- **EMI:** UTP is very susceptible to EMI. Twisting reduces crosstalk, but some interference still exists. Also, external devices that emit electromagnetic waves, such as electric motors and fluorescent lights, can cause problems. In addition, because copper wire emits signals, UTP is very susceptible to eavesdropping.

Shielded Twisted-Pair Cable

The only difference between shielded twisted-pair (STP) and UTP is that STP cable has a shield—usually aluminum/polyester—between the outer jacket or casing and the wires. Figure 2.17 shows STP cable.

FIGURE 2.17

Shielded twisted-pair (STP) cable

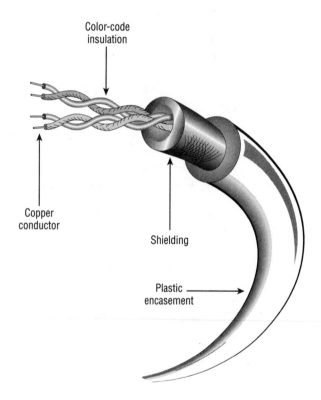

The shield makes STP less vulnerable to EMI because the shield is electrically grounded. If a shield is grounded correctly, it tends to prevent signals from getting into or out of the cable. It is a more reliable cable for LAN environments. STP was the first twisted-pair cable to be used in LANs. Although many LANs now use UTP, STP is still used.

Transmission media specifications from IBM and Apple Computer use STP cable. IBM's Token Ring network uses STP, and IBM has its own specifications for different qualities and configurations of STP. A completely different type of STP is the standard for Apple's AppleTalk networks. Networks that conform to each vendor's specifications have their own special requirements, including connector types and limits on cable length.

STP has the following characteristics:

- **Cost:** Bulk STP is fairly expensive. STP costs more than UTP and thin coaxial cable but less than thick coaxial or fiber-optic cabling.

- **Installation:** The requirement for special connectors can make STP more difficult to install than UTP. An electrical ground must be created with the connectors. To simplify installation, use standardized and prewired cables. Because STP is rigid and thick (up to 1.5 inches in diameter), it can be difficult to handle.

- **Bandwidth capacity:** With the outside interference reduced by the shielding, STP can theoretically run at 500Mbps for a 100-meter cable length. Few installations run at data rates higher than 155Mbps. Currently, most STP installations have data rates of 16Mbps.

- **Node capacity:** Since only two computers can be connected together by an STP cable, the number of computers in an STP network is not limited by the cable. Rather, it is limited by the hub or hubs that connect the cables together. In a Token Ring network, which is the most common type of STP network, the useful upper limit is around 200 nodes in a single ring, but it depends on the type of data traffic in your network. There is a specified maximum limit of 270, but you will probably never reach this limit.

- **Attenuation:** STP does not outperform UTP by much in terms of attenuation. The most common limit is 100 meters.

- **EMI:** The biggest difference between STP and UTP is the reduction of EMI. The shielding blocks a considerable amount of the interference. However, since it is copper wire, STP still suffers from EMI and is vulnerable to eavesdropping.

See Table 2.1 (shown earlier in this chapter) for a comparison of the characteristics of STP and UTP cable.

Your company recently renovated its telephone system, including cabling, and had installed excess cables for future growth. Now you would like to use the excess cabling to network the computers in your company.

■ What sort of network performance (data capacity and cable length) can you reasonably expect from these new telephone cables?

You would like to use the old telephone cables in your building to network your computers.

■ What sort of network performance (data capacity and cable length) can you reasonably expect from these old telephone cables?

You will install a new physical plant (network cabling system) for your network. You will use Category-5 unshielded twisted-pair cabling throughout.

■ What sort of network performance (data capacity and cable length) can you reasonably expect from this new physical plant?

Your company has offices and manufacturing facilities in the same building, and you must network computers throughout the building.

■ In what circumstances might you use shielded twisted-pair cabling in your network?

Coaxial Cable

Coaxial cable, commonly called coax, has two conductors that share the same axis. A solid copper wire or stranded wire runs down the center of the cable, and this wire is surrounded by plastic foam insulation. The foam is surrounded by a second conductor, a wire mesh tube, metallic foil, or both. The wire mesh protects the wire from EMI. It is often called the shield. A tough plastic jacket forms the cover of the cable, providing protection and insulation. Figure 2.18 shows a coaxial cable.

Coaxial cable comes in different sizes. It is classified by size (RG) and by the cable's resistance to direct or alternating electric currents (measured in ohms, also called impedance).

FIGURE 2.18

Coaxial cable

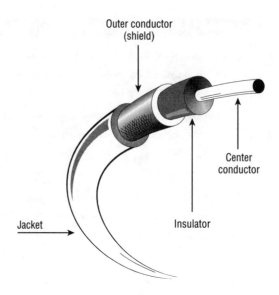

The following are some coaxial cables commonly used in networking:

- 50-ohm, RG-8, and 75-ohm, RG-11, used for Thick Ethernet

- 50-ohm, RG-58, used for Thin Ethernet

- 75-ohm, RG-59, used for cable TV

- 93-ohm, RG-62, used for ARCnet

Coaxial cable has the following characteristics:

- **Cost:** Coax is relatively inexpensive. The cost for thin coaxial cable is less than STP or Category 5 UTP. Thick coaxial is more expensive than STP or Category 5 UTP but less than fiber-optic cable.

- **Installation:** Installation is relatively simple. With a little practice, installing the connectors becomes easy, and the cable is resistant to damage. Coaxial cable is most often installed either in a device-to-device daisy-chain (Ethernet) or a star (ARCnet). The interface may involve T connectors or vampire clamps (or taps). Coaxial cable must be grounded and terminated. Grounding completes the electrical circuit. Terminating keeps the signals that reach the end of the cable from reflecting and causing interference.

- **Bandwidth capacity:** A typical data rate for today's coaxial networks is 10Mbps, although the potential is higher. Coaxial cable's bandwidth potential increases as the diameter of the inner conductor increases.

- **Node capacity:** The specified maximum number of nodes on a thinnet segment is 30 nodes; on a thicknet segment it is 100 nodes.

- **Attenuation:** Because it uses copper wire, coaxial cable suffers from attenuation, but much less so than twisted-pair cables. Coaxial cable runs are limited to a couple of thousand meters.

- **EMI:** Coaxial cabling is still copper wire and vulnerable to EMI and eavesdropping. However, the shielding provides a much better resistance to EMI's effects.

PVC and Plenum Cable

Polyvinyl chloride (PVC) is commonly used in coaxial cabling because it is a flexible, inexpensive plastic well suited for use as insulation and cable jacketing. PVC is often used in the exposed areas of an office.

A *plenum* is the space between the false ceiling of an office and the floor above. The air in the plenum circulates with the air in the rest of the building, and there are strict fire codes about what can be placed in a plenum environment.

Because PVC gives off poisonous gases when burned, you cannot use it in a plenum environment. You must use plenum-grade cable instead. Plenum-grade cable is certified to be fire resistant and to produce a minimum amount of smoke. Plenum cable is also used in vertical runs (walls) without conduit (a tube to hold the cable). Plenum cable is more expensive and less flexible than PVC.

Fire safety is a deadly serious issue. Consult your local fire and electrical regulations before running cable in your office.

Fiber-Optic Cable

Fiber-optic cable transmits light signals rather than electrical signals. It is enormously more efficient than the other network transmission media. As soon as it comes down in price (both in terms of the cable and installation costs), fiber-optic will be the choice for network cabling.

Each fiber has an inner core of glass or plastic that conducts light. The inner core is surrounded by cladding, a layer of glass that reflects the light back into the core. Each fiber is surrounded by a plastic sheath. The sheath can be either tight or loose. Figure 2.19 shows examples of these two types of fiber-optic cables.

FIGURE 2.19

Fiber-optic cables with tight and loose sheaths

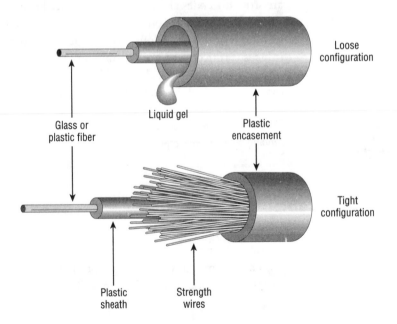

Tight configurations completely surround the fibers with a plastic sheath and sometimes include wires to strengthen the cable (although these wires are not required). Loose configurations leave a space between the sheath and the outer jacket, which is filled with a gel or other material. The sheath provides the strength necessary to protect against breaking or extreme heat or cold. The gel, strength wires, and outer jacket provide extra protection.

A cable may contain a single fiber, but often fibers are bundled together in the center of the cable. Optical fibers are smaller and lighter than copper wire. One optical fiber is approximately the same diameter as a human hair.

Optical fibers may be multimode or single-mode. Single-mode fibers allow a single light path and are typically used with laser signaling. Single-mode fiber can allow greater bandwidth and cable runs than multimode but is more expensive. Multimode fibers use multiple light paths. The physical characteristics of the multimode fiber make all parts of the signal (those from the various paths) arrive at the same time, appearing to the receiver as though they were one pulse. If you want to save money, look into multimode, since it can be used with LEDs (light-emitting diodes), which are a more affordable light source than lasers. Figure 2.20 shows single-mode and multimode fibers.

FIGURE 2.20

Single-mode and multimode optical fibers

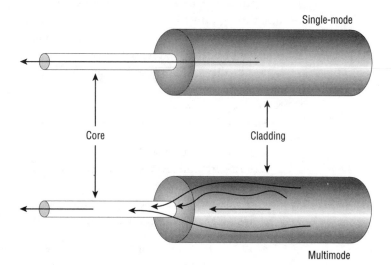

Optical fibers are differentiated by core/cladding size and mode. The size and purity of the core determine the amount of light that can be transmitted. The following are the common types of fiber-optic cable:

- 8.3-micron core/125- micron cladding, single-mode

- 62.5-micron core/125-micron cladding, multimode

- 50-micron core/125-micron cladding, multimode

- 100-micron core/140-micron cladding, multimode

A typical LAN installation starts at a computer or network device that has a fiber-optic network interface card (NIC). This NIC has an incoming interface and an outgoing interface. The interfaces are directly connected to fiber-optic cables with special fiber-optic connectors. The opposite ends of the cables are attached to a connectivity device or splice center.

Splicing fiber-optic cable can involve electric fusion, chemical epoxy, or mechanical connectors. Fiber-optic cables, with cores as thin as 8.3 microns, can be very difficult to line up precisely.

Optical interface devices convert computer signals into light for transmission through the fiber. Conversely, when light pulses come through the fiber, the optical interface converts them into computer signals. For single-mode fiber, light pulses are created by injection laser diodes (ILDs), which create a higher quality of light. For multimode fiber, LEDs are used. When the light pulse is received, it is converted back into electric signals by P-intrinsic N diodes or photodiodes.

Fiber-optic cable has the following characteristics:

- **Cost:** Fiber-optic cable is slightly more expensive than copper cable, but costs are falling. Associated equipment costs can be much higher than for copper cable, making fiber-optic networks much more expensive. Single-mode fiber devices are more expensive and more difficult to install than multimode devices.

- **Installation:** Fiber-optic cable is more difficult to install than copper cable. Every fiber connection and splice must be carefully made to avoid obstructing the light path. Also, the cables have a maximum bend radius, which makes cabling more difficult.

- **Bandwidth capacity:** Because it uses light, which has a much higher frequency than electricity, fiber-optic cabling can provide extremely high bandwidths. Current technologies allow data rates from 100Mbps to 2 gigabits per second (Gbps). The data rate depends on the fiber composition, the mode, and the wavelength (frequency) of the transmitted light. A common multimode installation can support 100Mbps over several kilometers.

- **Node capacity:** Since only two computers can be connected together by a fiber-optic cable, the number of computers in a fiber-optic network is not limited by the cable. Rather, it is limited by the hub or hubs that connect the cables together. In an Ethernet network the useful upper limit is around 75 nodes on a single collision domain. Fiber-optic networks using other protocols, such as FDDI, usually use the fiber cable as a backbone between slower LANs and therefore do not place many computers or other network devices on the fiber network.

- **Attenuation:** Fiber-optic cable has much lower attenuation than copper wires, mainly because the light is not radiated out in the way electricity is radiated from copper cables. Fiber-optic cables can carry signals over distances measured in kilometers. Fiber-optics suffers very little from attenuation but has instead a different problem: chromatic dispersion. Different wavelengths of light travel through glass differently, and the colors of a single pulse of light will spread apart slightly as they travel down a cable. This is the same effect you see when you look at a rainbow—white light is separated into its colorful components. At a distance of several miles, one bit may shift into the next bit, causing data to be lost. Single-mode fiber-optic cable conveys only one frequency of light down the cable, so it does not suffer from chromatic dispersion. Single-mode fiber is used to provide network links several hundred kilometers in length.

- **EMI:** Fiber-optic cable is not subject to electrical interference. In addition, it does not leak signals, so it is immune to eavesdropping. Because it does not require a ground, fiber-optic cable is not affected by potential shifts in the electrical ground, nor does it produce sparks. This type of cable is ideal for high-voltage areas or in installations where eavesdropping could be a problem.

> **REAL WORLD PROBLEMS**
>
> You must connect a research institution's main offices with the testing site 30 miles away. You will connect them with fiber-optic cable.
>
> - Which type of fiber cable will you use? Why will you not use the other type?
>
> You are replacing your thicknet backbone between your servers with a high-speed network cable. You are considering using Category 5 twisted-pair cable or multimode fiber cable.
>
> - Under what circumstances would you install the fiber?
>
> - Under what circumstances would you not install the fiber?

Wireless Media

WIRELESS MEDIA DO not use an electrical or optical conductor. In most cases, the earth's atmosphere is the physical path for the data. Wireless media is therefore useful when distance or obstructions make bounded media difficult. There are three main types of wireless media: radio wave, microwave, and infrared.

Radio Wave Transmission Systems

Radio waves have frequencies between 10 kilohertz (KHz) and 1 gigahertz (GHz). The range of the electromagnetic spectrum between 10KHz and 1GHz is called radio frequency (RF).

Radio waves include the following types:

- Short-wave

- Very-high-frequency (VHF) television and FM radio

- Ultra-high-frequency (UHF) radio and television

Most radio frequencies are regulated. To use a regulated frequency, you must receive a license from the regulatory body over that area (the FCC in the United States). Getting a license can take a long time, costs more, and makes it more difficult to move equipment. However, licensing guarantees that, within a determined area, you will have clear radio transmission.

The advantage of unregulated frequencies is that there are few restrictions placed on them. One regulation, however, does limit the usefulness of unregulated frequencies: unregulated frequency equipment must operate at less than 1 watt. The point of this regulation is to limit the range of influence a device can have, thereby limiting interference with other signals. In terms of networks, this makes unregulated radio communication bandwidths of limited use.

Because unregulated frequencies are available for use by others in your area, you cannot be guaranteed a clear communication channel.

In the United States, the following frequencies are available for unregulated use:

- 902- to 928MHz

- 2.4GHz (also internationally)

- 5.72- to 5.85GHz

Radio waves can be broadcast omnidirectionally or directionally. Various kinds of antennas can be used to broadcast radio signals. Typical antennas include the following:

- Omnidirectional towers

- Half-wave dipole

- Random-length wire

- Beam (such as the Yagi)

Figure 2.21 shows these common types of radio frequency antennas.

The power of the RF signal is determined by the antenna and transceiver (a device that TRANSmits and reCEIVEs a signal over a medium such as copper, radio waves, or fiber-optic cables). Each range has characteristics that affect

FIGURE 2.21

Typical radio frequency
antennas

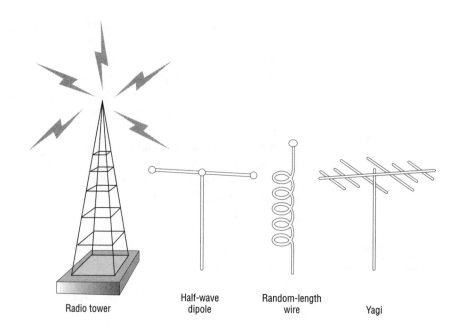

Radio tower

Half-wave
dipole

Random-length
wire

Yagi

its use in computer networks. For computer network applications, radio
waves fall into three categories:

- Low-power, single-frequency

- High-power, single-frequency

- Spread-spectrum

Table 2.2 summarizes the characteristics of the three types of radio wave
media, which are described in the following sections.

TABLE 2.2

Radio Wave Media

FACTOR	LOW-POWER, SINGLE-FREQUENCY	HIGH-POWER, SINGLE-FREQUENCY	SPREAD-SPECTRUM
Frequency Range	All radio frequencies (typically low GHz range)	All radio frequencies (typically low GHz range)	All radio frequencies (typically 902- to 928MHz in U.S.; 2.4 also used)

TABLE 2.2 Radio Wave Media (continued) FACTOR	LOW- POWER, SINGLE- FREQUENCY	HIGH- POWER, SINGLE- FREQUENCY	SPREAD- SPECTRUM
Cost	Moderate for wireless	Higher than low-power, single-frequency	Moderate
Installation	Simple	High	Moderate
Bandwidth Capacity	From below 1- to 10Mbps	From below 1- to 10Mbps	2- to 6Mbps
Attenuation	High (25 meters)	Low	High
EMI	Poor	Poor	Fair

Low-Power, Single-Frequency

As the name implies, single-frequency transceivers operate at only one frequency. Typical low-power devices are limited in range to around 20 to 30 meters. Although low-frequency radio waves can penetrate some materials, the low power limits them to the shorter, open environments.

Low-power, single-frequency transceivers have the following characteristics:

- **Frequency range:** Low-power, single-frequency products can use any radio frequency, but higher gigahertz ranges provide better throughput (data rates).

- **Cost:** Most systems are moderately priced compared with other wireless systems.

- **Installation:** Most systems are easy to install, if the antenna and equipment are preconfigured. Some systems may require expert advice or installation. Some troubleshooting may be involved to avoid other signals.

- **Bandwidth capacity:** Data rates range from 1- to 10Mbps.

- **Node capacity:** This type of network is usually implemented as a single collision domain, so it has the same limitations as an Ethernet network using regular cables. This capacity is scaled down for reduced bandwidth and communications overhead. (A 1Mbps low-power, single-frequency network could not support the number of nodes a 10Mbps network could.)

- **Attenuation:** Attenuation is determined by the radio frequency and power of the signal. Low-power, single-frequency transmissions suffer from attenuation because of their low power.

- **EMI:** Resistance to EMI is low, especially in the lower bandwidths, where electric motors and numerous devices produce noise. Susceptibility to eavesdropping is high, but with the limited transmission range, eavesdropping would generally be limited to within the building where the LAN is located.

High-Power, Single-Frequency

High-power, single-frequency transmissions are similar to low-power, single-frequency transmissions but can cover larger distances. They can be used in long-distance outdoor environments. Transmissions can be line-of-sight or can extend beyond the horizon as a result of being bounced off the earth's atmosphere. High-power, single-frequency can be ideal for mobile networking, providing transmission for land-based or marine-based vehicles as well as aircraft. Transmission rates are similar to low-power rates, but at much longer distances.

High-power, single-frequency transceivers have the following characteristics:

- **Frequency range:** As with low-power transmissions, high-power can use any radio frequency, but networks favor higher gigahertz ranges for better throughput (data rates).

- **Cost:** Radio transceivers are relatively inexpensive, but other equipment (antennas, repeaters, and so on) can make high-power, single-frequency radio moderately to very expensive.

- **Installation:** Installations are complex. Skilled technicians must install and maintain high-power equipment. The radio operators must be licensed by the FCC, and their equipment must be maintained in accordance with FCC regulations. Equipment that is improperly installed or tuned can cause low data transmission rates, signal loss, and even interference with local radio.

- **Capacity:** Bandwidth is typically between 1- and 10Mbps.

- **Node capacity:** This type of network is usually implemented as a single collision domain, so it has the same limitations as an Ethernet network using regular cables. This capacity is scaled down for reduced bandwidth and communications overhead. (A 1Mbps high-power, single-frequency network could not support the number of nodes a 10Mbps network could.)

- **Attenuation:** High-power rates improve the signal's resistance to attenuation, and repeaters can be used to extend signal range. Attenuation rates are fairly low.

- **EMI:** Much like low-power, single-frequency transmission, vulnerability to EMI is high. Vulnerability to eavesdropping is also high. Because the signal is broadcast over a large area, signals are more likely to be intercepted.

Spread-Spectrum

Spread-spectrum transmissions use the same frequencies as other radio frequency transmissions, but instead of using one frequency, they use several simultaneously. You can use two modulation schemes to accomplish this: direct-sequence modulation and frequency hopping.

Direct frequency modulation is the most common modulation scheme. It works by breaking the original data into parts (called chips), which are then transmitted on separate frequencies. To confuse eavesdroppers, spurious signals can also be transmitted. The transmission is coordinated with the intended receiver, who is aware of which frequencies are valid. The receiver can then isolate the chips and reassemble the data while ignoring the decoy information. Figure 2.22 illustrates how direct frequency modulation works.

The signal can be intercepted, but it is difficult to watch the right frequencies, gather the chips, know which chips are valid data, and find the right message. This makes eavesdropping difficult.

Current 900MHz direct-sequence systems support data rates of 2- to 6Mbps. Higher frequencies offer the possibility of higher data rates.

Frequency hopping rapidly switches among several predetermined frequencies. For this to work, the transmitter and receiver must be in nearly perfect synchronization. Bandwidth can be increased by simultaneously transmitting on several frequencies. Figure 2.23 shows how frequency hopping works.

FIGURE 2.22

Direct frequency
modulation

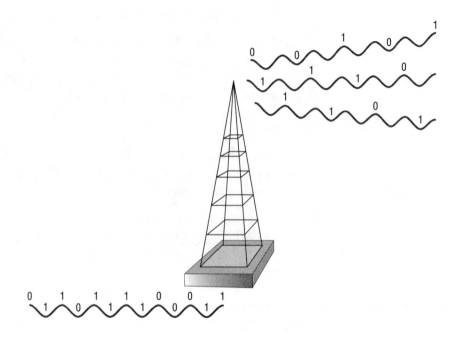

FIGURE 2.23

Frequency hopping

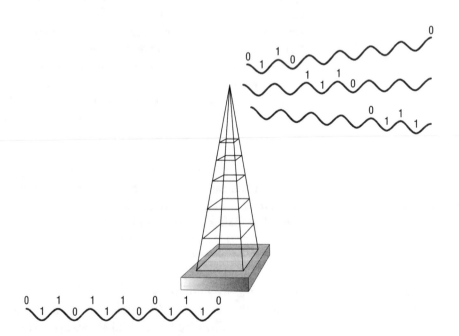

Spread-spectrum transceivers have the following characteristics:

- **Frequency range:** Spread-spectrum generally operates in the unlicensed frequency ranges. In the United States, devices using the 902- to 928MHz range are most common, but 2.4GHz devices are becoming available.

- **Cost:** Although costs depend on what kind of equipment you choose, they are typically fairly inexpensive when compared with other wireless media.

- **Installation:** Depending on the type of equipment you have in your system, installation problems can range from simple to fairly complex.

- **Bandwidth capacity:** The most common systems, the 900MHz systems, support data rates of 2- to 6Mbps, but newer systems operating in gigahertz produce higher data rates.

- **Node capacity:** This type of network is usually implemented as a single collision domain, so it has the same limitations as an Ethernet network using regular cables. This capacity is scaled down for reduced bandwidth and communications overhead. (A 2Mbps spread-spectrum network could not support the number of nodes a 10Mbps network could.)

- **Attenuation:** Attenuation depends on the frequency and power of the signal. Because spread-spectrum transmission systems operate at low power, which produces a weaker signal, they usually have high attenuation.

- **EMI:** Immunity to EMI is low, but because spread-spectrum uses different frequencies, interference would need to be across multiple frequencies to destroy the signal. Vulnerability to eavesdropping is low.

Microwave Transmission Systems

Microwave communication makes use of the lower gigahertz frequencies of the electromagnetic spectrum. These frequencies, which are higher than radio frequencies, produce better throughput and performance. There are two types of microwave data communication systems: terrestrial and satellite.

Table 2.3 shows a comparison of the terrestrial microwave and satellite microwave transmission systems, which are discussed in the following sections.

	FACTOR	TERRESTRIAL MICROWAVE	SATELLITE MICROWAVE
TABLE 2.3 Terrestrial Microwave and Satellite Microwave	Frequency range	Low gigahertz (typically between 4- to 6- or 21- to 23GHz)	Low gigahertz (typically 11 to 14)
	Cost	Moderate to high	High
	Installation	Moderately difficult	Difficult
	Bandwidth capacity	About 1- to 10Mbps	About 1- to 10Mbps
	Node capacity	2 (sender and receiver)	2 (sender and receiver)
	Attenuation	Depends on conditions (affected by atmospheric conditions)	Depends on conditions (affected by atmospheric conditions)
	EMI	Poor	Poor

Terrestrial Microwave

Terrestrial microwave systems typically use directional parabolic antennas to send and receive signals in the lower gigahertz range. The signals are highly focused, and the physical path must be line-of-sight. Relay towers are used to extend signals. Terrestrial microwave systems are typically used when using cabling is cost-prohibitive.

Because they do not use cable, microwave links often connect separate buildings where cabling would be too expensive, difficult to install, or prohibited. For example, if two buildings are separated by a public road, you may not be able to get permission to install cable over or under the road. Microwave links would be a good choice in this type of situation.

Because terrestrial microwave equipment often uses licensed frequencies, additional costs and time constraints may be imposed by licensing commissions or government agencies (the FCC, in the United States).

Figure 2.24 shows a microwave system connecting separate buildings. Smaller terrestrial microwave systems can be used within a building, as well. Microwave LANs operate at low power, using small transmitters that communicate with omnidirectional hubs. Hubs can then be connected to form an entire network.

Terrestrial microwave systems have the following characteristics:

- **Frequency range:** Most terrestrial microwave systems produce signals in the low gigahertz range, usually at 4- to 6GHz and 21- to 23GHz.

- **Cost:** Short-distance systems can be relatively inexpensive, and they are effective in the range of hundreds of meters. Long-distance systems can be very expensive. Terrestrial systems may be leased from providers to reduce startup costs, although the cost of the lease over a long term may prove more expensive than purchasing a system.

- **Installation:** Line-of-sight requirements for microwave systems can make installation difficult. Antennas must be carefully aligned. A licensed technician may be required. Also, because the transmission must be line-of-sight, suitable transceiver sites could be a problem. If your organization does not have a clear line-of-sight between two antennas, you must either purchase or lease a site.

- **Bandwidth capacity:** Capacity varies depending on the frequency used, but typically, data rates are from 1- to 10Mbps.

- **Attenuation:** Attenuation is affected by frequency, signal strength, antenna size, and atmospheric conditions. Normally, over short distances, attenuation is not significant. But rain and fog can negatively affect higher-frequency microwaves.

- **EMI:** Microwave signals are vulnerable to EMI, jamming, and eavesdropping (although microwave transmissions are often encrypted to reduce eavesdropping). Microwave systems are also affected by atmospheric conditions.

Satellite

Satellite microwave systems transmit signals between directional parabolic antennas. Like terrestrial microwave systems, they use low gigahertz frequencies and must be in line-of-sight. The main difference with satellite systems is that one antenna is on a satellite in geosynchronous orbit about 50,000 kilometers (22,300 miles) above the earth. Because of this, satellite microwave systems can reach the most remote places on earth and communicate with mobile devices.

Here's how it usually works: a LAN sends a signal through cable media to an antenna (commonly known as a satellite dish), which beams the signal to the satellite in orbit above the earth. The orbiting antenna then transmits the signal to another location on the earth or, if the destination is on the opposite side of the earth, to another satellite, which then transmits to a location on earth.

Figure 2.25 shows a transmission being beamed from a satellite dish on earth to an orbiting satellite and then back to earth.

Because the signal must be transmitted 50,000 kilometers to the satellite and 50,000 kilometers back to earth, satellite microwave transmissions take about as long to cover a few kilometers as they do to span continents. Because

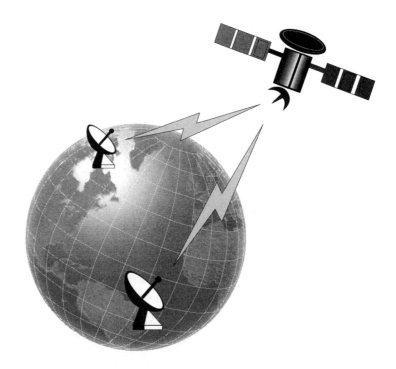

FIGURE 2.25

Satellite microwave
transmission

the transmission must travel long distances, satellite microwave systems experience delays between the transmission of a signal and its reception. These delays are called propagation delays. Propagation delays range from .5 to 5 seconds.

Satellite microwave systems have the following characteristics:

- **Frequency range:** Satellite links operate in the low gigahertz range, typically between 11- and 14GHz.

- **Cost:** The cost of building and launching a satellite is extremely expensive—as high as several hundred million dollars or more. Companies such as AT&T, Hughes Network Systems, and Scientific-Atlanta lease services, making them affordable for a slightly larger number of organizations. Although satellite communications are expensive, the cost of cable to cover the same distance may be even more expensive.

- **Installation:** Satellite microwave installation for orbiting satellites is extremely technical and difficult; it must be left to professionals in that field. The earth-based systems may require difficult, exact adjustments. Commercial providers can help with installation.

- **Bandwidth capacity:** Capacity depends on the frequency used. Typical data rates are 1- to 10Mbps.

- **Attenuation:** Attenuation depends on frequency, power, antenna size, and atmospheric conditions. Higher-frequency microwaves are more affected by rain and fog.

- **EMI:** Microwave systems are vulnerable to EMI, jamming, and eavesdropping. (Microwave transmissions are often encrypted to reduce eavesdropping.) Microwave systems are also affected by atmospheric conditions.

Infrared Transmission Systems

Infrared media use infrared light to transmit signals. LEDs or ILDs transmit the signals, and photodiodes receive the signals. Infrared media use the terahertz range of the electromagnetic spectrum. The remote controls we use for television, VCR, and CD players use infrared technology to send and receive signals.

Because infrared signals are in the terahertz (higher-frequency) range, they have good throughput. Infrared signals do have a downside: the signals cannot penetrate walls or other objects, and they are diluted by strong light sources.

Infrared media use pure light, normally containing only electromagnetic waves or photons from a small range of the electromagnetic spectrum. Infrared light is transmitted either line-of-sight (point-to-point) or broadcast omnidirectionally, allowing it to reflect off walls and ceilings. Point-to-point transmission allows for better data rates, but devices must remain in their locations. Broadcast, on the other hand, allows for more flexibility but with lower data rates. (Part of the signal strength is lost with each reflection.)

Point-to-Point

Infrared beams can be tightly focused and directed at a specific target. Laser transmitters can transmit line-of-sight across several thousand meters.

One advantage of infrared is that an FCC license is not required to use it. Also, using point-to-point infrared media reduces attenuation and makes eavesdropping difficult. Typical point-to-point infrared computer equipment is similar to that used for consumer products with remote controls. Careful alignment of transmitter and receiver is required. Figure 2.26 shows how a network might use point-to-point infrared transmission.

FIGURE 2.26

Point-to-point infrared media in a network

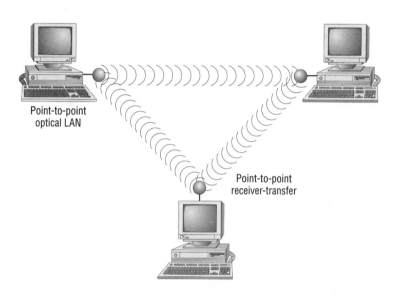

Point-to-point optical LAN

Point-to-point receiver-transfer

Point-to-point infrared systems have the following characteristics:

- **Frequency range:** Infrared light usually uses the lowest range of light frequencies, between 100GHz and 1000 terahertz (THz).

- **Cost:** The cost depends on the kind of equipment used. Long-distance systems, which typically use high-power lasers, can be very expensive. Equipment that is mass-produced for the consumer market and can be adapted for network use is generally inexpensive.

- **Installation:** Infrared point-to-point requires precise alignment. If high-powered lasers are used, take extra care because they can damage or burn eyes.

- **Bandwidth capacity:** Data rates vary between 100Kbps and 16Mbps (at 1 kilometer).

- **Attenuation:** The amount of attenuation depends on the quality of emitted light and its purity, as well as general atmospheric conditions and signal obstructions.

- **EMI:** Infrared transmission can be affected by intense light. Tightly focused beams are fairly immune to eavesdropping because tampering usually becomes evident by the disruption in the signal. Furthermore, the area in which the signal may be picked up is very limited.

Broadcast

Broadcast infrared systems spread the signal to cover a wider area and allow reception of the signal by several receivers. One of the major advantages is mobility; the workstations or other devices can be moved more easily than with point-to-point infrared media. Figure 2.27 shows how a broadcast infrared system might be used.

FIGURE 2.27

An implementation of broadcast infrared media

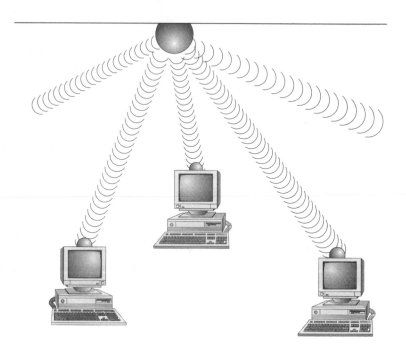

Because broadcast infrared signals are not as focused as point-to-point, this type of system cannot offer the same throughput. Broadcast infrared is typically limited to less than 1Mbps, making it too slow for most network needs. Broadcast infrared systems have the following characteristics:

- **Frequency range:** Infrared systems usually use the lowest range of light frequencies, between 100GHz and 1000THz.

- **Cost:** The cost of infrared equipment depends on the quality of light required. Typical equipment used for infrared systems is quite inexpensive. High-power laser equipment is much more expensive.

- **Installation:** Installation is fairly simple. When devices have clear paths and strong signals, they can be placed anywhere the signal can reach. This also makes reconfiguration easy. One concern should be the control of strong light sources that might affect infrared transmission.

- **Bandwidth capacity:** Although data rates are less than 1Mbps, it is theoretically possible to reach much higher throughput.

- **Node capacity:** Because of the low data rates of this type of network, you will not be able to network more than a handful of personal computers with this technology. However, for other applications where only small amounts of data need to be exchanged, you could connect any number of devices in this manner. Therefore, the node capacity of this type of network is highly application dependent.

- **Attenuation:** Broadcast infrared, like point-to-point, is affected by the quality of the emitted light and its purity and by atmospheric conditions. Because devices can be moved easily, however, obstructions are generally not of great concern.

- **EMI:** Intense light can dilute infrared transmissions. Because broadcast infrared transmissions cover a wide area, they are more easily intercepted for eavesdropping.

REAL WORLD PROBLEMS

You need to connect two buildings across a public road, and it is not feasible to use a direct cable connection.

■ Under what circumstances would you use a microwave link?

■ Under what circumstances would you use an infrared laser link?

■ Under what circumstances would you use a radio link?

You are the CIO of an interstate trucking company. You need to maintain constant contact with your fleet of trucks.

■ Which wireless technologies will enable you to do this?

You need to provide a network connection between an oil platform off the coast of Alaska and a shore-based installation. The platform is within line-of-sight of the shore installation. The harsh weather conditions often experienced in this location must not interfere with the network link.

■ Which types of wireless links are not appropriate in this situation? Why?

You wish to provide waiters in your restaurant with palm-top computers and wireless links so orders can be immediately transmitted to the kitchen and the waiters can be immediately notified when orders are ready.

■ What kind of wireless network will you implement in your restaurant? Why?

Network Adapters

NETWORK ADAPTERS, SOMETIMES called Network Interface Cards (NICs), are peripheral cards that plug into the motherboard of your computer and into a network cable. It is through the network adapter that your computer communicates on the network. Some computers, such as Apple Macintosh computers, have Ethernet network interfaces built in. Many newer IBM-compatible computers also have built-in networking adapters for Ethernet.

Microsoft ✓ **Exam** **Objective**

Given the manufacturer's documentation for the network adapter, install, configure, and resolve hardware conflicts for multiple network adapters in a token-ring or Ethernet network.

Network adapters perform all the functions required to communicate on a network. They convert data from the form stored in the computer to the form transmitted or received (or *transceived*) on the cable and provide a physical connection to the network.

Exactly what those functions are depends on the type of network you are using. For instance, on an Ethernet network, the adapter listens for silence before transmitting, filters out transmissions not addressed to it, and deals with collisions. Token Ring adapters wait to receive a token before transmitting and pass the token off after transmitting. Fiber-optic Ethernet adapters convert the data from 8-, 16-, or 32-bit words to serial pulses of light. Microwave network interfaces convert the computer data to serial radio waves. Figure 2.28 shows how an adapter plugs into a computer and attaches to a network cable.

FIGURE 2.28

Network interface adapter

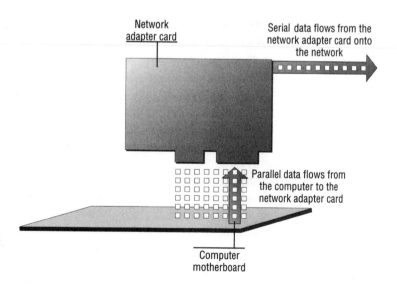

Network adapter card

Serial data flows from the network adapter card onto the network

Parallel data flows from the computer to the network adapter card

Computer motherboard

Adapters in Abstract

Your computer software does not have to be aware of how the network adapter performs its function because the network driver software handles all the specifics for your computer. The applications running on your computer need only address data and hand it to the adapter card.

This is much the way the post office or a parcel delivery service works. You don't care about the details of postal delivery; you simply address your parcel and hand it to the delivery driver. The postal service manages the process of delivering it for you.

This abstraction allows your computer to use a microwave radio transmitter just as easily as a fiber-optic network adapter or an adapter that works over coaxial cable. Everything in your computer remains the same except for the actual network adapter and the driver software for that adapter.

How Network Adapters Work

Network adapters receive the data to be transmitted from the motherboard of your computer into a small amount of RAM called a buffer. The data in the buffer is moved into a chip that calculates a checksum value for the chunk and adds address information, which includes the address of the destination card and its own address, which indicates where the data is from. Ethernet adapter addresses are permanently assigned when the adapter is made at the factory. This chunk is now referred to as a frame.

For example, in Ethernet, the adapter listens for silence on the network when no other adapters are transmitting. It then begins transmitting the frame one bit at a time, starting with the address information, then the chunk of data, and then the checksum.

The network adapter must still convert the serial bits of data to the appropriate media in use on the network. For instance, if the data is being transmitted over optical fiber, the bits are used to light up an infrared LED (light emitting diode) or laser diode, which transmits light pulses down the fiber to the receiving device's APD (avalanche photo diode) or photo-transistor. If the data is being sent over twisted-pair cable, the adapter must convert the bits of data from the 5-volt logic used in computers to the differential logic used for digital twisted-pair transmission.

The circuitry used to perform this media conversion is called a transceiver. Ethernet is the same no matter what type of media you use—only the transceiver changes. Transceivers can be external devices attached through the AUI port on an Ethernet adapter, or they can be internal on the card. Some cards (usually called combo cards) have more than one type of transceiver built in so you can use them with your choice of media. AUI interfaces on Ethernet adapters are not transceivers—they are where you attach a transceiver for the different media types.

Because a network signal travels through copper and optical fiber at about 66 percent as fast as the speed of light, there's a chance that one of two adapters far away from each other could still be hearing silence when the other has in fact started transmitting. In this case, they could transmit simultaneously and garble their data. This is referred to as a *collision*.

While adapters transmit, they listen to the wire to make sure the data on the line matches the data being transmitted. As long as it does, everything is fine. If another adapter has interrupted, the data being "heard" by the transmitting network adapter will not match the data being transmitted. If this happens, the adapter ceases transmitting and transmits a solid on state instead, which indicates to all computers that it has detected a collision and that they should discard the current frame because it has been corrupted. The network adapter waits a random amount of time and then again attempts to transmit the frame.

Configuring Network Adapters

Because network adapters have not been around since computers were invented, there is no assigned place for cards to be set to. Most adapter cards require their own interrupt, port address, and upper memory range. PCI motherboards automatically assign IRQ and port settings to your PCI card, so you don't need to worry about it.

Unfortunately, network adapters in computers with ISA buses can conflict with other devices, since no two devices should share the same interrupt or port. No software that comes with your computer will tell you every interrupt and port in use unless your computer is already running Windows NT, so you must be somewhat familiar with the hardware in your computer or use a program that can probe for free resources to find one. Many adapters have test programs that can tell you whether the adapter is working correctly with the settings you've assigned.

ISA (Industry Standard Architecture) is the original bus of the IBM PC and IBM AT computers. ISA is a 16-bit bus. PCI (Peripheral Component Interconnect) is the bus used in most personal computers (and Macintoshes) being manufactured today. PCI is a 32- or (in some cases) 64-bit bus, and is much faster than ISA. Some other busses you might encounter are: EISA (Extended Industry Standard Architecture) and VLB (VESA Local Bus). Most PC-compatible computers support ISA cards, but very few motherboards support mixing PCI, EISA, and VLB cards. You must know which kind of card(s) your motherboard supports.

In PCs, the interrupt assignments listed in Table 2.4 are standard.

	IRQ	COMMON USE
TABLE 2.4 Standard Interrupt Assignments	0	Timer
	1	Keyboard
	2	Secondary IRQ controller
	3	COM 2 and 4
	4	COM 1 and 3
	5	LPT2 or MIDI device
	6	Floppy disk drive
	7	LPT1
	8	Real-time clock
	9	Free or sound card
	10	Free or primary SCSI adapter
	11	Free or secondary SCSI adapter
	12	PS/2 Mouse
	13	Floating-point processor
	14	Primary hard disk controller
	15	Free or secondary hard disk controller

The most commonly used IRQ setting for LAN adapters is IRQ 5, since few computers on networks have sound cards or second printers. Other commonly used settings are IRQ 3 (which takes over the IRQ normally used for COM 2 and COM 4), IRQ 9 if it's not in use by another device, and IRQ 15 if there's not a second hard disk controller. Many motherboards come with two IDE hard disk controllers on the motherboard, however, so this interrupt isn't usually free unless the second controller is disabled.

Port settings are somewhat easier to select since most computers have free port memory. The following ports are generally free for use with LAN adapters:

- 280h

- 300h

- 320h

- 360h

Upper memory ranges are usually easy to assign because very few devices actually use them. The default memory range suggested by your NIC software will probably be free.

Selecting an Adapter

Before you get a network adapter for your computer, you need to determine three things:

- What type of network are you attaching to? This could be Ethernet, Fast Ethernet, Token Ring, ARCnet, ATM, or a proprietary network standard.

- What type of media are you using? This could be coaxial cable, unshielded twisted-pair, optical fiber, radio, or wireless IR.

- What type of bus does your computer have? This could be ISA, EISA, Micro Channel, VESA Local Bus, PCI, NuBUS, PC Card (PCMCIA), or a proprietary local bus.

Before selecting your network adapter card, you'll also want to consider the performance of the different types of adapters. For example, an ISA card offers only a 16-bit path, while EISA, Micro Channel, or PCI cards offer the possibility of a 32-bit path, which means higher performance potential. The type of memory transfer used by the card can also influence performance. Remember that the shared memory method provides faster memory transfer than Direct Memory Access (DMA) or basic I/O methods provide. Choose a card that provides the largest data transfer method and bit width. This can improve network transfers and reduce system bottlenecks.

Some computers have more than one bus. For instance, most modern computers have both an ISA and a PCI bus. For Ethernet and Token Ring, ISA is sufficiently fast, but for all higher-speed networks you should only use the PCI bus. In general, use the fastest bus in your computer for your network connection to ensure that the bus does not become a bottleneck.

Some computers, such as laptops and computers with proprietary buses, cannot easily be connected to networks because there isn't anywhere to attach a network adapter. Special adapters that run through the parallel printer port or SCSI ports are available to solve these sorts of problems.

REAL WORLD PROBLEMS

You have an Ethernet card and a sound card with a MIDI interface in your computer. You cannot attach to the network.

■ What is most likely the problem? How would you solve it?

You would like to attach your notebook computer to your LAN, but it does not have a PCMCIA slot or a place for a proprietary network card.

■ How can you attach it to the network?

Review

COMPUTERS MUST SEND signals to communicate. Digital encoding ensures that the signal will be communicated without losing information. Baseband and broadband are two ways of signaling information over a communications channel.

In most networks today, cables are what tie computers together into networks. The most commonly used cable types are coaxial, twisted-pair, and fiber-optic. Wireless (infrared and radio) is a way to tie computers together without cables, or with less cabling. IBM has specified a cabling system that uses a special connector.

Network adapter cards in the computer place the information on the network. A network adapter card must match both the bus of the computer it is placed in and the network to which it will be attached. The card must be configured to communicate with the computer.

Review Questions

1. One cable run in your UTP network is nearly 100 meters long. Which of the following should first be considered if this run experiences communication problems?

   A. EMI

   B. Crosstalk

   C. Attenuation

   D. Dispersion

2. The cabling in your new building must be run through walls and drop ceilings. To meet the fire codes, what type of cable must be used?

   A. Fire-retardant

   B. Gel-filled

   C. Plenum

   D. PVC

3. Which of the following cable types supports the highest bandwidth?

   A. Coaxial

   B. Fiber-optic

   C. STP

   D. UTP

4. Which of the following cable types would be used to transmit at speeds of 1.2 Gbps and higher?

   A. Coaxial

   B. Fiber-optic

   C. STP

   D. UTP

5. You have recently installed a new network adapter card in your computer and connected it to the twisted-pair network. However, when you try to communicate on the network, you get no response. The NIC is configured with IRQ 7 and port address 320h. Which of the following is most likely the problem?

   A. The network has another adapter with the same Ethernet MAC address.

   B. The network cable is improperly terminated.

   C. LPT 1 is conflicting with the adapter's interrupt setting.

   D. COM 2 is conflicting with the adapter's interrupt setting.

6. What is the standard cable type used with IBM's Token Ring network specification?

   A. Coaxial

   B. Fiber-optic

   C. STP

   D. UTP

7. By nature, fiber-optic cables are less susceptible to outside factors than are other types of cable. Which of the following do not significantly affect fiber-optic LAN cables? Choose all that apply:

   A. EMI

   B. Crosstalk

   C. Attenuation

   D. Dispersion

8. The four buildings on your campus form a rough square, approximately 250 meters on a side. You have been asked to provide your boss with cable specifications that will provide connectivity between the buildings. Which of the following cable types could you easily use without additional equipment? Choose all that apply:

   A. Coaxial

   B. Fiber-optic

C. STP

D. UTP

9. Which of the following cable types is the least expensive that can support 100 Mbps?

   A. Coaxial

   B. Fiber-optic

   C. STP

   D. UTP

10. Your production facility has a new inventory program that requires access to the network. However, as with most production environments, EMI is a concern. Because of the layout of the building, additional cables cannot be run. Which of the following radio technologies is least susceptible to EMI?

    A. AM

    B. Low power, single frequency

    C. High power, single frequency

    D. Spread spectrum

11. Which type of cabling is considered "Category 5" by the Electrical Industries Association (EIA)?

    A. STP

    B. unshielded twisted-pair

    C. token ring

    D. coaxial

12. Which type of network card offers the best performance?

    A. An EISA card with I/O memory transfer

    B. An EISA card with shared memory transfer

    C. An ISA card with I/O memory transfer

    D. An ISA card with shared memory transfer

13. The design for the network you are implementing calls for numerous cable runs in a production plant. The plant makes silicon molds and uses many machines that are powered by electricity. What should your primary concern be for these cables?

    A. EMI

    B. Crosstalk

    C. Attenuation

    D. Dispersion

CHAPTER

3

The Theoretical Network

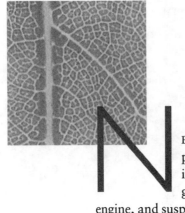

NETWORKS ARE COMPLICATED structures with many interrelated parts. To better understand how the various parts fit together, it is useful to have a network model. A network model is like a generic car: just as every car has wheels, a drive-train, an engine, and suspension, every network has a physical layer, a data link layer, a network layer, and so on.

One car may have an automatic transmission and another a manual one; one car may have disk brakes and another drums. Likewise, one network may implement the physical or data link layer differently than another, but they both are networks, and they both have the layers in one form or another.

The first part of this chapter introduces you to the OSI and IEEE networking models. These models will help you identify the various parts that make up networks and understand how the parts work together.

The OSI and IEEE theoretical definition of networking technology helps to explain networking concepts; but just as a theoretical car will not get you to the grocery store, a theoretical network will not get your data to the server.

The second half of this chapter examines the drivers and protocols used in Microsoft networks and how they relate to the OSI model.

OSI and 802

THIS SECTION INTRODUCES you to the OSI networking model and to the IEEE 802 enhancements to that model.

The OSI Model

The International Organization for Standardization (ISO) began developing the Open Systems Interconnection (OSI) reference model in 1977. It has since become the most widely accepted model for understanding network communication.

As you know, in order for computers to communicate, there must be accepted rules of communication. For communication to take place on a network composed of a variety of network devices, these rules must be clearly defined. The OSI model (and networking models developed by other organizations) attempts to define rules that apply to the following issues:

- How network devices contact each other and, if they have different languages, how they communicate with each other

- Methods by which a device on a network knows when to transmit data and when not to

- Methods to ensure that network transmissions are received correctly and by the right recipient

- How the physical transmission media are arranged and connected

- How to ensure that network devices maintain a proper rate of data flow

- How bits are represented on the network media

The OSI model is nothing tangible; it is simply a conceptual framework you can use to better understand the complex interactions taking place among the various devices on a network. The OSI model does not perform any functions in the communication process. The actual work is done by the appropriate software and hardware. The OSI model simply defines which tasks need to be done and which protocols will handle those tasks, at each of the seven layers of the model.

1. Physical

2. Data link

3. Network

4. Transport

5. Session

6. Presentation

7. Application

The OSI model divides communication tasks into smaller pieces called subtasks. Protocol implementations are computer processes that relate to these subtasks. Specific protocols fulfill subtasks at specific layers of the OSI model. When these protocols are grouped together to complete a whole task, you have what is called a protocol stack. The following sections examine how protocol stacks work and how they communicate with protocol stacks on other computers.

Protocol Stacks

A *protocol stack* is a group of protocols arranged on top of each other as part of a communication process. Each layer of the OSI model has different protocols associated with it. When more than one protocol is needed to complete a communication process, the protocols are grouped together in a stack. An example of a protocol stack is TCP/IP, which is widely used for Unix and the Internet.

Each layer in the protocol stack receives services from the layer below it and provides services to the layer above it. Novell explains the relationship like this: layer N uses the services of the layer below it (layer N–1) and provides services to the layer above it (layer N+1).

For two computers to communicate, the same protocol stacks must be running on each computer. Each layer of the protocol stack on one computer communicates with its equivalent, or peer, on the other computer. The computers can have different operating systems and still be able to communicate if they are running the same protocol stacks. For example, a DOS machine running TCP/IP can communicate with a Macintosh machine running TCP/IP. This is illustrated in Figure 3.1.

Peer-Layer Communication between Stacks

When a message is sent from one machine to another, it travels down the layers on one machine and then up the layers on the other machine. This route is illustrated in Figure 3.2.

Microsoft ✓ *Exam* *Objective*

Define the communication devices that communicate at each level of the OSI model.

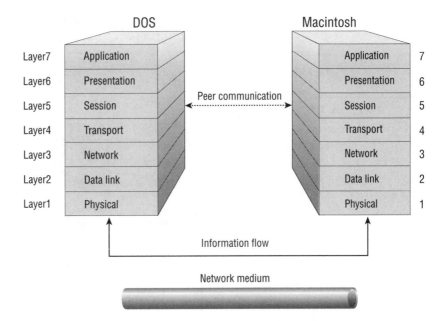

FIGURE 3.1

Peer communication
between two computers

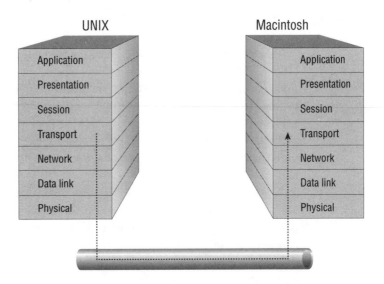

FIGURE 3.2

A message sent from one
peer layer to another

As the message travels down the first stack, each layer it passes through (except the physical layer) adds a header. These headers contain pieces of control information that are read and processed by the corresponding layer on the receiving stack. As the message travels up the stack of the other machine, each layer strips the header added by its peer layer. This process is illustrated in Figure 3.3.

FIGURE 3.3

The OSI model and headers

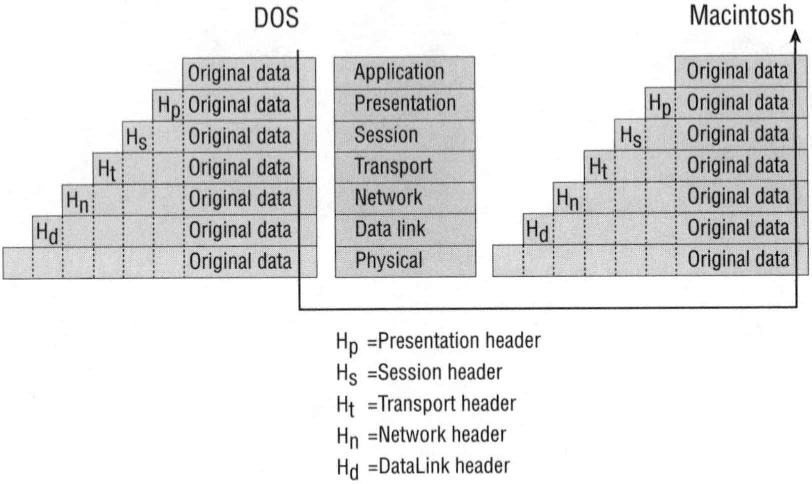

H_p = Presentation header
H_s = Session header
H_t = Transport header
H_n = Network header
H_d = DataLink header

As an example, suppose you are using two networked applications based on the DOS and Macintosh operating systems. At layer 7, the DOS application requests something from the Macintosh application. This request is sent to the DOS application's layer 6. This layer receives the request as a data packet, adds its own header, and passes the packet down to layer 5, where the process is repeated. As the request travels down the layers, headers are added until the request reaches the physical layer (which does not add a header), loaded down with headers.

Next, this request packet travels across the network transmission media and begins its journey up the layers on the Macintosh. The header that was put on at the data link layer of the DOS application is stripped at the data link layer of the Macintosh application. The Macintosh data link layer performs the tasks requested in the header and passes the requests to the next higher layer. This process is repeated until the Macintosh application's layer 7 receives the packet and interprets the request inside.

At each layer, the data packages, called service data units, are made up of data and headers from the layers above. For this reason they are commonly referred to by different names when they are at different layers, as shown in Figure 3.4. The term packet is applicable to a service data unit at any layer.

FIGURE 3.4

Common data package names

Application		Messages&Packets
Presentation	H₁	Packets
Session	H₂	Packets
Transport	H₃ Datagrams,Segments&Packets	
Network	H₄	Datagrams&Packets
DataLink	H₅	Frames&Packets
Physical		Bits&Packets

Physical Layer

The physical layer is simply responsible for sending bits (bits are the binary 1's and 0's of digital communication you learned about in Chapter 2) from one computer to another. The physical layer is not concerned with the meaning of the bits; instead it deals with the physical connection to the network and with transmission and reception of signals.

This level defines physical and electrical details, such as what will represent a 1 or a 0, how many pins a network connector will have, how data will be synchronized, and when the network adapter may or may not transmit the data (see Figure 3.5).

FIGURE 3.5

The physical layer makes a physical circuit with electrical, optical, or radio signals.

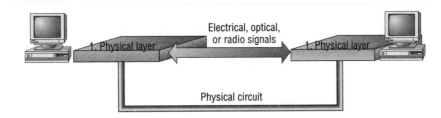

Passive hubs, simple active hubs, terminators, couplers, cables and cabling, connectors, repeaters, multiplexers, transmitters, receivers, and transceivers are devices associated with the physical layer.

The following items are addressed at the physical layer:

- Network connection types, including multipoint and point-to-point connections

- Physical topologies, which are physical layouts of networks, such as bus, star, or ring

- Analog and digital signaling, which include several methods for encoding data in analog and digital signals

- Bit synchronization, which deals with synchronization between sender and receiver

- Baseband and broadband transmissions, which are different methods for using media bandwidth

- Multiplexing, which involves combining several data channels into one

- Termination, which prevents signals from reflecting back through the cable and causing signal and packets errors. It also indicates the last node in a network segment.

Data Link Layer

The data link layer provides for the flow of data over a single link from one device to another. It accepts packets from the network layer and packages the information into data units called *frames* to be presented to the physical layer for transmission. The data link layer adds control information, such as frame type, routing, and segmentation information, to the data being sent.

This layer provides for the error-free transfer of frames from one computer to another. A Cyclic Redundancy Check (CRC) added to the data frame can detect damaged frames, and the data link layer in the receiving computer can request that the information be present. The data link layer can also detect when frames are lost and request that those frames be sent again.

Frames and packets are discussed in greater detail later in this chapter in the section "Network Protocols" and in Chapter 4 in the sections on physical network types, such as Ethernet and Token Ring.

In broadcast networks such as Ethernet (which Chapter 4 explains in more detail), all devices on the LAN receive the data that any device transmits. (Whether a network is broadcast or point-to-point [only the destination computer receives the information] is a matter of the network protocols, which were introduced in Chapter 1.) The data link layer recognizes frames for which the destination ID matches the computer and discards other packets. Figure 3.6 shows how the data link layer establishes an error-free connection between two devices.

FIGURE 3.6

The data link layer establishes an error-free link between two devices.

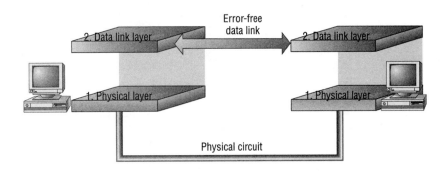

The IEEE committee felt that the data link layer needed to be defined in greater detail, so they split it into two sub-layers:

Bridges, intelligent hubs, and network interface cards are devices typically associated with the data link layer.

- Logical Link Control (LLC), which establishes and maintains links between the communicating devices

- Media Access Control (MAC), which controls the way multiple devices share the same media channel

Figure 3.7 illustrates the division of the data link layer into the MAC and LLC layers.

The logical link control sub-layer provides Service Access Points (SAPs) that other computers can refer to and use to transfer information from the logical link control sub-layer to the upper OSI layers. This is defined in the 802.2 standard.

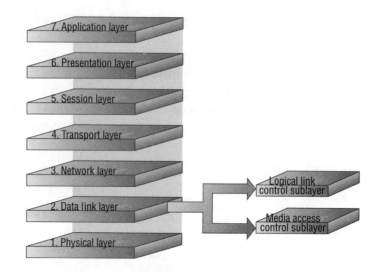

The media access control sub-layer, the lower of the two sub-layers, provides for shared access to the network adapter and communicates directly with network interface cards. Network interface cards have a unique 12-digit hexadecimal MAC Address assigned before they leave the factory where they are made (although there have been rare cases of adapters having the same addresses). These MAC addresses are used to establish the logical link between computers on the same LAN. Figure 3.8 shows the functions of the media access control sub-layer and logical link control sub-layer.

Network Layer

The network layer makes routing decisions and forwards packets for devices that are farther away than a single link. (A link connects two network devices and is implemented by the data link layer. Two devices connected by a link communicate directly with each other and not through a third device.) In larger networks there may be *intermediate systems* between any two *end systems,* and the network layer makes it possible for the transport layer and layers above it to send packets without being concerned about whether the end system is immediately adjacent or several hops away.

The network layer translates logical network addresses into physical machine addresses (the numbers used as destination IDs in the physical network cards). This layer also determines the quality of service (such as the priority of the message) and the route a message will take if there are several ways a message can get to its destination.

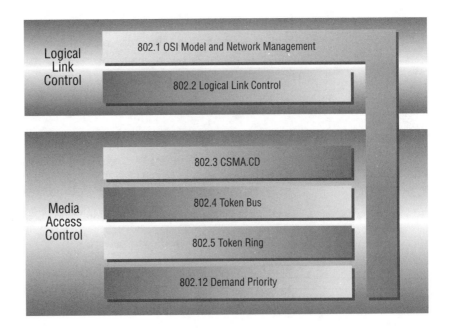

The network layer also may break large packets into smaller chunks if the packet is larger than the largest data frame the data link layer will accept. The network reassembles the chunks into packets at the receiving end.

Intermediate systems that perform only routing and relaying functions and do not provide an environment for executing user programs can implement just the first three OSI network layers. Figure 3.9 shows how the network layer moves packets across multiple links in a network.

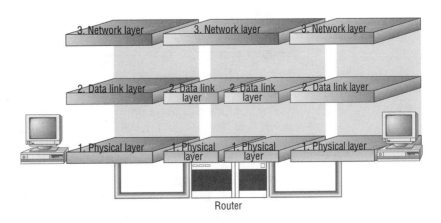

The network layer performs several important functions that enable data to arrive at its destination. The protocols at this layer may choose a specific route through an internetwork to avoid the excess traffic caused by sending data over networks and segments that don't need access to it.

Routers and gateways operate in the network layer.

The network layer serves to support communications between logically separate networks. This layer is concerned with the following:

- Addressing, including logical network addresses and services addresses

- Circuit, message, and packet switching

- Route discovery and route selection

- Connection services, including network layer flow control, network layer error control, and packet sequence control

- Gateway services

Transport Layer

The transport layer ensures that packets are delivered error free, in sequence, and with no losses or duplications. The transport layer breaks large messages from the session layer (which we'll look at next) into packets to be sent to the destination computer and reassembles packets into messages to be presented to the session layer.

The transport layer typically sends an acknowledgment to the originator for messages received. Figure 3.10 shows how the transport layer operates.

Session Layer

The session layer allows applications on separate computers to share a connection called a *session*. This layer provides services such as name lookup and security to allow two programs to find each other and establish the communications link. The session layer also provides for data synchronization and checkpointing so that in the event of a network failure, only the data sent after the point of failure need be re-sent.

This layer also controls the dialog between two processes, determining who can transmit and who can receive at what point during the communication. Figure 3.11 illustrates the operation of the session layer.

FIGURE 3.10

The transport layer provides end-to-end communication with integrity and performance guarantees.

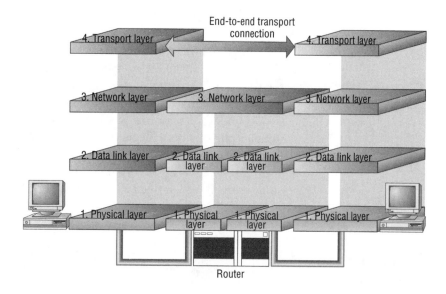

FIGURE 3.11

The session layer provides for dialog between application programs.

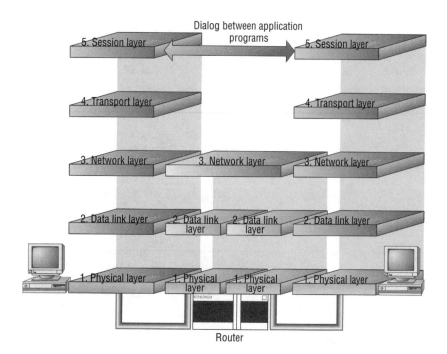

Presentation Layer

The presentation layer translates data between the formats the network requires and the formats the computer expects. The presentation layer does protocol conversion, data translation, compression and encryption, character set conversion, and the interpretation of graphics commands.

The network redirector operates at this level. The network redirector is what makes the files on a file server visible to the client computer. The network redirector also makes remote printers act as though they are attached to the local computer. The network redirector is an important part of networking and will be described in more detail in Chapter 6. Figure 3.12 illustrates the operation of the presentation layer.

FIGURE 3.12

The presentation layer adapts information to the local environment.

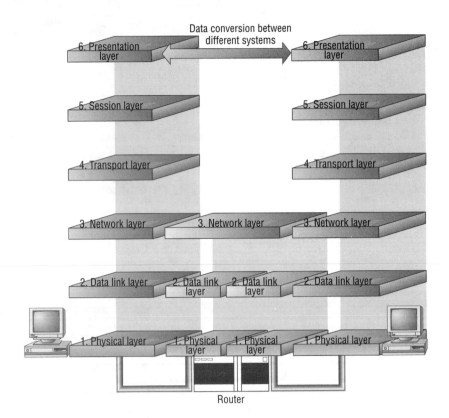

Application Layer

The application layer is the topmost layer of the OSI model, and it provides services that directly support user applications, such as database access, e-mail, and file transfers. It also allows applications to communicate with applications on other computers as though they were on the same computer. When a programmer writes an application program that uses network services, this is the layer the application program will access (see Figure 3.13).

FIGURE 3.13

The application layer provides for the connection of application programs on separate machines.

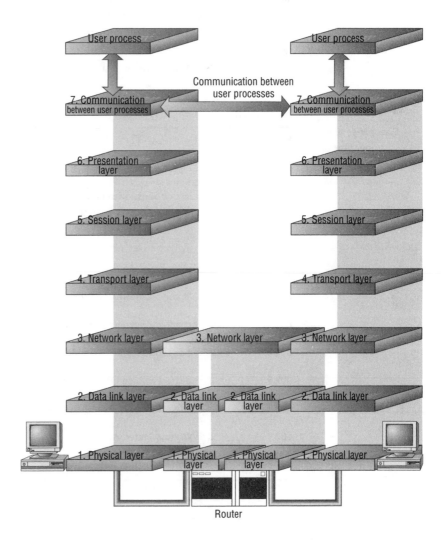

The IEEE 802 Categories

The Institute for Electrical and Electronic Engineers, Inc. (IEEE) in February 1980 formed a project called Project 802 (after the year and month the project started) to help define certain LAN standards.

The published IEEE 802 standards predate the OSI standards, but both were developed simultaneously and in cooperation, so the two standards share many features and interoperate well.

Project 802 defines aspects of the network relating to physical cabling and data transmission, corresponding to the physical and data link layers of the OSI model. The 802 specifications fall into 12 categories that are identified by the 802 numbers listed in Table 3.1.

TABLE 3.1 Categories of 802 Specifications	NUMBER	CATEGORY
	802.1	Internetworking
	802.2	Logical Link Control
	802.3	Carrier Sense with Multiple Access and Collision Detection (CSMA/CD, or Ethernet)
	802.4	Token Bus LAN
	802.5	Token Ring LAN
	802.6	Metropolitan Area Network (MAN)
	802.7	Broadband Technical Advisory Group
	802.8	Fiber-Optic Technical Advisory Group
	802.9	Integrated Voice/Data Networks
	802.10	Network Security
	802.11	Wireless Networks
	802.12	Demand Priority Access LAN, 100baseVG-AnyLAN

REAL WORLD PROBLEMS

Your company wants to use data link layer encryption devices to send private data over a public wide area network.

■ What effect will this have on devices in other layers?

When troubleshooting your network with a packet sniffer, you find a device generating spurious TCP/IP packets.

■ Which devices are suspect?

When troubleshooting your network, you determine that some device is creating an Ethernet broadcast storm.

■ Which devices are suspect?

You've heard that UDP/IP is a faster transport protocol than TCP/IP, and you want to use it on your network.

■ Will your routers be able to handle UDP/IP traffic?

You need to connect a building on the other side of your campus, but the distance involved is too far for twisted-pair or coaxial cable to work with Ethernet. You'd like to use optical fiber, but you don't want to have to use FDDI or another fiber-specific protocol because the routers are too expensive.

■ Can you use Ethernet over fiber-optic cable? If so, which layer would a device that converts Ethernet/twisted-pair to Ethernet/optical fiber operate in?

You are currently using IPX as your transport protocol in a Windows NT network. You want to switch to TCP/IP to allow Internet access.

■ What effect will this have on user applications and the way clients attach to servers?

Microsoft Networking Components within the OSI Framework

THIS SECTION DISCUSSES the networking components found in Microsoft Windows NT and Windows 95 networks in the context of what you learned in the preceding section about the OSI model. Specifically, this section is concerned with the drivers and protocols you will encounter in common networking environments today.

Drivers

Every device in a computer requires a driver to operate. Some drivers—for instance, the driver for an IDE hard disk or for the keyboard—are built into the operating system. Other devices require that drivers be installed separately when the device is attached or installed in the computer. Network adapter cards are of the second type; driver software must be provided by the manufacturer and installed in the computer so that the computer will be able to access the network adapter card.

Installable device drivers make a computer more flexible because the range of options and capabilities in devices is wide and it would be difficult or impossible for the writers of operating systems to foresee every possible feature a device might allow the computer to use. Rather than even attempt such a feat of programming, the operating systems writers provide a generic device driver interface and allow the manufacturers to write device drivers that will exploit the special capabilities of their devices.

Drivers and the Client Operating System

The network redirector in the client operating system uses the driver for the network adapter card to provide services such as file storage and printing to the users' applications. The driver must reside on the computer's hard disk or on a boot ROM (see the section "Network Adapter Cards" in Chapter 2) because the computer cannot access the card until it loads the driver for that card.

Driver Interfaces

In the early days of networking, drivers could be bound only to a unique instance of a protocol stack. For most computers this was okay because a single card needed only a single protocol stack. Servers, however, often needed to respond to more than one protocol and often used more than one card.

Microsoft ✓ *Exam Objective*

Explain the purpose of NDIS and Novell® ODI network standards.

The solution to this problem is driver interfaces, which allow multiple cards to be bound to multiple transport protocols. Two incompatible driver interfaces exist:

- Open Driver Interface (ODI), developed by Apple, Novell, and other major networking companies

- Network Driver Interface Specification (NDIS), developed by Microsoft

The driver interface you use is determined by the network operating system you select. Windows NT networking products use NDIS rather than ODI. For most other network products, such as Novell NetWare, you will be using ODI.

NDIS and ODI were created to allow multiple network drivers to be bound to multiple transports. This allows you to use both TCP/IP and IPX on a single network adapter or to use four network adapters all with the same TCP/IP stack.

The Place of Drivers in the OSI Model

Network adapter cards and drivers provide the services corresponding to the data link layer in OSI model. In the IEEE model, the data link is split into the Logical Link Control (LLC) sublayer, which corresponds to the software drivers and the Media Access Control (MAC) sublayer, which corresponds to the network adapter.

Installing and Configuring Drivers

Device drivers usually come on a disk with the device. Many common device drivers are included with the operating system software, and sometimes device drivers are made available for download from a service, such as the Microsoft Network or CompuServe, or from the Internet.

The driver must match both the network adapter and the computer's operating system. For instance, the same driver for a network interface card cannot be used in both Windows 95 and Windows NT Workstation. It is common for manufacturers to ship several drivers on a disk with the network interface card; it is up to you when you install the card to select the right driver for your operating system.

Make sure when you select a network interface card that there is a driver for the operating system you will use. You can check the Hardware Compatibility List (HCL) for your operating system (the HCL should come with the operating system documentation, but you can also get it by contacting the operating system vendor) or examine the vendor's product information to determine which operating systems a card will support.

Most drivers come with a setup program that helps the network administrator install the driver on the computer.

To install and configure or remove driver software, you must be familiar with the installation and configuration process in the operating system. This process is different for each operating system and is explained in the documentation for that operating system. Many network interface cards also explain how to install the card in the context of each of the operating systems that card supports. See Figure 3.14 for a view of the network configuration software for Windows NT.

FIGURE 3.14

Microsoft Windows 95 and Windows NT Server have graphical interfaces for installing and configuring network drivers.

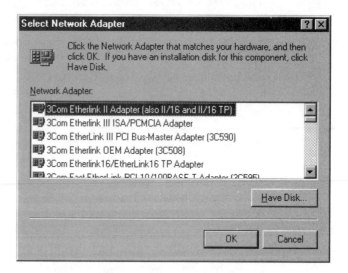

The network driver software must be configured to match the settings used to configure the network adapter card. If the adapter card is configured to use interrupt 5, for example, and the driver is expecting interrupt 3, the computer will not be able to communicate with the network card and will therefore be isolated from the rest of the network.

Network Protocols

As discussed in Chapter 1, protocols are the agreed-upon ways in which computers exchange information. Computers need to communicate at many levels and in many different ways, so there are many corresponding network protocols.

Microsoft ✓ ***Exam Objective***

Select the appropriate network and transport protocol or protocols for various token-ring and Ethernet networks. Protocol choices include:

- DLC
- AppleTalk®
- IPX
- TCP/IP
- NFS
- SMB

There are protocols at various levels in the OSI model. In fact, it is the protocols at a level in the OSI model that provide the functionality of that level. Protocols that work together to provide a layer or layers of the OSI model are known as a *protocol stack,* or *suite.*

How Protocols Work

A protocol is a set of basic steps that both parties (or computers) must perform in the right order. For instance, for one computer to send a message to another computer, the first computer must perform the following steps. (This is a general example; the actual steps are much more detailed.)

1. Break the data into small sections called *packets.*

2. Add addressing information to the packets identifying the destination computer.

3. Deliver the data to the network card for transmission over the network.

The receiving computer must perform the same steps, but in reverse order:

1. Accept the data from the network adapter card.

2. Remove the transmitting information that was added by the transmitting computer.

3. Reassemble the packets of data into the original message.

Each computer needs to perform the same steps the same way so that the data will arrive and reassemble properly. If one computer uses a protocol with different steps or even the same steps with different parameters (such as different sequencing, timing, or error correction), the two computers will not be able to communicate with each other.

Network Packets

Networks primarily send and receive the small chunks of data called packets. Network protocols (which we discuss in the sections "Protocol Stacks" and "Standard Protocol Stacks" later in this chapter) at various levels of the OSI model construct, modify, and disassemble packets as they move data down the sending stack, across the network, and back up the OSI stack of the receiving computer.

PACKET STRUCTURE Packets have the following components:

- A source address specifying the sending computer

- A destination address

- Instructions that tell the computer how to pass the data along

- Reassembly information for when the packet is part of a longer message

- The data to be transmitted to the remote computer

- Error-checking information to ensure that the data arrives intact

The components are combined into three sections:

- **Header:** A typical header includes an alert signal to indicate that the data is being transmitted, source and destination addresses, and clock information to synchronize the transmission.

- **Data:** The actual data being sent. This can vary (depending on the network type) from 48 bytes to 4K.

- **Trailer:** The contents of the trailer (or even the existence of a trailer) varies among network types, but it typically includes a Cyclic Redundancy Check (CRC). The CRC helps the network determine whether a packet has been damaged in transmission.

Figure 3.15 illustrates the composition of a packet.

ASSEMBLING PACKETS Each layer of the OSI model adds some information to the packet. The information at each level is meant to be read by the OSI layer at the same level in the destination computer. For example, information added at the network layer of one computer will be read by the network layer of the next computer. Figure 3.16 shows how information added at each layer is read by the corresponding layer on the next computer.

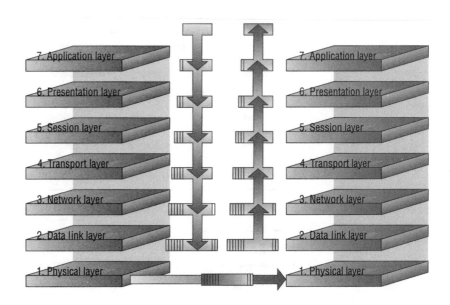

Routing

Early LANs were seldom connected to one another, but after the mid-1980s businesses began to realize the benefits of connecting LANs together into larger networks.

The process of moving information from one LAN to another over one or more paths between LANs is called *routing*. Protocols that support multipath LAN-to-LAN communication are called *routable protocols*. As more and more LANs are integrated into larger networks, it is becoming increasingly important that the protocols used to implement those LANs are routable.

Protocol Stacks

Protocols that work together to provide a layer or layers of the OSI model are known as a protocol stack, or suite. Each layer handles a different part of the communications process and has its own rules and requirements. Table 3.2 shows the layers of the OSI stack. The higher in the stack a protocol resides, the more sophisticated the protocol must be.

TABLE 3.2 Layers of the OSI Stack	**LAYER**	**DESCRIPTION**
	7. Application	Provides services that directly support user applications
	6. Presentation	Translates data formats and adds encryption
	5. Session	Sets up and tears down connections, or sessions. Administers sessions
	4. Transport	Adds identifiers to processes and deals with error-handling information
	3. Network	Handles internetwork sequencing, addressing, and routing
	2. Data link	Adds error-checking information and organizes bits into frames
	1. Physical	Transmits and receives bits over the physical media

Binding Protocols

Many different protocol stacks can perform network functions, and many different types of network interface cards can be installed in a computer. A computer may have more than one card, and a computer may use more than one protocol stack.

The *binding process* is what links the protocol stack to the network device driver for the network interface adapter. Several protocols can be bound to the same card; for instance, both TCP/IP and IPX/SPX can be bound to the same Ethernet adapter. In addition, one computer with several interface adapters—for instance, a server that must be able to communicate with both a local area network and a network backbone—can have the same protocol bound to two or more network cards.

The binding process can be used throughout the OSI layers to link one protocol stack to another. The device driver (implementing the data link layer) is bound to the network interface card (implementing the physical layer). TCP/IP can be bound to the device driver, and the NetBIOS session layer can be bound to TCP/IP.

Connectionless vs. Connection Oriented Protocols

There are two ways that communications between computers can be arranged: connectionless and connection oriented.

Microsoft ✓ *Exam* *Objective*	**Compare the implications of using connection-oriented communications with connectionless communications.**

Connectionless systems optimistically assume that all data will get through, so there's no protocol overhead for guaranteed delivery or sequential packet ordering. This makes them fast. User Datagram Protocol (UDP/IP) is an example of a connectionless Internet transport protocol.

Connection oriented systems pessimistically presume that some data will be lost or disordered in most transmissions. Connection oriented protocols guarantee that transmitted data will reach its destination in sequential order by retaining the data and negotiating for retransmission until sequential data can be handed to higher level protocols. This means that any application can rely upon a connection oriented transport to reliably deliver data as it was transmitted. Transmission Control Protocol (TCP/IP) is an example of a connection oriented Internet protocol.

Connectionless systems, on the other hand, simply transmit data and assume that it reaches its destination. While this normally works in a local area network environment, it breaks down quickly in a large area networks where packets can be dropped due to line noise or router congestion.

All is not lost for connectionless transports, however, since higher level protocols will know what data has not reached its destination after some time and request retransmission. Connectionless systems also do not return data in sequential order necessarily, so the higher level protocol must sort out the data packets.

For local area systems where data isn't likely to be dropped, it makes sense to push serialization and guaranteed delivery up to higher level protocols that are less efficient, since it won't be used often anyway. But in wide area networks like the Internet, it would simply take too much time for higher level protocols to sort out what data had been sent and what was missing, so the transport protocol simply takes measures that guarantee that all data gets through in order.

Standard Protocol Stacks

Several standard protocol stacks are commonly used in networks today:

- The ISO/OSI protocol suite
- IBM Systems Network Architecture (SNA)
- Digital DECnet
- Novell NetWare
- Apple AppleTalk
- The Internet protocol suite, TCP/IP

Protocols within the stacks exist at all levels of the seven-layer OSI model, but they may be divided roughly into three types:

- Application protocols provide for application-to-application interaction and data exchange.
- Transport protocols establish the communications sessions between computers.
- Network protocols handle issues such as routing and addressing information, error checking, and retransmission requests.

Figure 3.17 illustrates the three types.

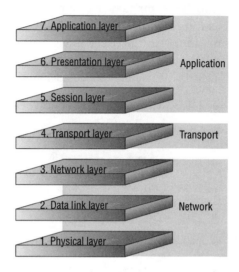

Microsoft-Supplied Network Protocols

Microsoft networking products come with three network transports, each intended for networks of different sizes with different requirements. They are

- NetBEUI

- NWLink

- TCP/IP

Each network transport has different strengths and weaknesses. In general, NetBEUI is intended for small, single-server networks. NWLink is intended for medium-sized networks (in a single facility, perhaps) or for networks that require access to Novell NetWare file servers. TCP/IP is a complex transport sufficient for globe-spanning networks such as the Internet. These protocols are covered in detail in the following sections.

NETBEUI NetBEUI stands for NetBIOS Extended User Interface. (NetBIOS stands for Network Basic Input/Output System.) NetBEUI implements the NetBIOS Frame (NBF) transport protocol, which was developed by IBM in the mid 1980s to support LAN workgroups under OS/2 and LAN Manager.

When IBM developed NetBEUI, they did not target networked PCs for enterprise-wide connectivity. Rather, NetBEUI was developed for workgroups of 2 to 200 computers. NetBEUI cannot be routed between networks, so it is constrained to small local area networks consisting of Microsoft and IBM clients and servers. NetBEUI 3.0 is the Microsoft update of IBM's NetBEUI protocol, included with Windows NT.

NetBEUI has a number of advantages, including:

- High speed on small networks

- Ability to handle more than 254 sessions (a limitation of earlier versions)

- Better performance over slow serial links than previous versions

- Ease of implementation

- Self-tuning features

- Good error protection

- Small memory overhead

NetBEUI can be thought of as the sports car of transport protocols. You can't rely on it for long trips (routing), but it's faster than any other TDI-compliant transport protocol for small networks that do not need to take advantage of routing to other networks.

NetBEUI has these disadvantages:

- It cannot be routed between networks.

- There are few tools for NetBEUI such as protocol analyzers.

- It offers very little cross-platform support.

The disadvantages of NetBEUI are similar to those of a sports car. It's not suitable for long trips because it can't be routed. Because it's not widely used, there is, outside the realm of Microsoft operating systems, very little software available to help you analyze NetBEUI problems.

NWLINK NWLink is Microsoft's implementation of Novell's IPX/SPX protocol stack, used in Novell NetWare. IPX is an outgrowth of the XNS protocol stack developed by Xerox in the late 1970s.

NWLink is IPX for Windows NT. IPX is the protocol; NWLink is the networking component that provides the protocol.

IPX is included with Microsoft Windows NT primarily to support interconnection to Novell NetWare servers. Microsoft clients and servers can then be added to existing network installations, over time, easing the migration between platforms and obviating the need for a complete cut-over from one networking standard to another.

NWLink does not by itself allow file and print sharing to and from NetWare clients or servers. Those functions are performed by the Client Services for NetWare (CSNW) redirector that also comes with Windows NT.

NWLink also includes enhancements to Novell's version of the NetBIOS programming interface. NWLink will allow Windows NT to act as either the client or server in Novell IPX/NetBIOS client-server applications.

The advantages of NWLink include the following:

- Ease of setup

- Support for routing between networks

- Speeds greater than the current Windows NT implementation of TCP/IP

- Ease of connection to installed NetWare servers and clients

Think of NWLink as the sedan of network protocols. NWLink provides a reasonable middle ground between the simple, nonroutable NetBEUI transport protocol and the complex, routable TCP/IP protocol. Like NetBEUI, IPX has many self-tuning characteristics, and it does not require much administrative burden to set up. The disadvantages of NWLink include the following:

- Lack of an effective centralized network numbering agency stymies interconnection between independent organizations

- Slower than NetBEUI over slow serial connections

- Doesn't support standard network management protocols

Truly large networks (networks that connect many organizations) may find it difficult to work over IPX because there is no effective central IPX addressing scheme to ensure that two networks don't use the same address numbers, as there is with TCP/IP. IPX does not support the wide range of network management tools available for TCP/IP.

TCP/IP TCP/IP is the Transmission Control Protocol and the Internet Protocol, as well as a suite of related protocols developed by the Department of Defense's Advanced Projects Research Agency (ARPA; later DARPA) under its project on network interconnection, started in 1969. TCP/IP is by far the most widely used protocol for interconnecting computers, and it is the protocol of the Internet. ARPA originally created TCP/IP to connect military networks together, but it provided the protocol standards to government agencies and universities free of charge.

Universities quickly adopted the protocol to interconnect their networks. Many academicians collaborated to create higher-level protocols for everything from news groups, mail transfer, file transfer, printing, remote booting, and even document browsing.

TCP/IP became the standard for interoperating Unix computers, especially in military and university environments. With the development of the Hypertext Transfer Protocol (HTTP) for sharing Hypertext Markup Language (HTML) documents freely on the large global network that interconnected universities and government agencies, the World Wide Web (WWW) was born, and Internet use exploded into the private sector. TCP/IP rode this wave of expansion to quickly eclipse IPX as the commercial protocol of choice among all network operating systems.

To support NetBIOS over TCP/IP, Microsoft has included NetBT (NetBIOS over TCP/IP) in accordance with Internet Protocol Request for Comments (RFC) 1001 and 1002.

TCP/IP protocol definitions are called Requests for Comments (RFC). They are freely available on the World Wide Web.

The advantages of TCP/IP include the following:

- Broad connectivity among all types of computers and servers
- Direct access to the global Internet
- Strong support for routing
- Simple Network Management Protocol support (SNMP)
- Support for Dynamic Host Configuration Protocol (DHCP) to dynamically assign client IP addresses
- Support for the Windows Internet Name Service (WINS) to allow name browsing among Microsoft clients and servers

- Support for most other Internet protocols, such as Post Office Protocol, Hypertext Transfer Protocol, and any other protocol acronym ending in *P*

- Centralized TCP/IP domain assignment, which allows internetworking between organizations

If you have a network that spans more than one metropolitan area, you will probably need to use TCP/IP. Think of TCP/IP as the truck of transport protocols. It's not fast or easy to use, but it is routable over wide, complex networks and provides more error correction than any other protocol. TCP/IP is supported on every modern computer and operating system.

Like a truck, TCP/IP has some disadvantages:

- Centralized TCP/IP domain assignment, which requires registration effort and cost

- Global expansion of the Internet, which has seriously limited availability of unique domain numbers. A new version of IP will be able to correct this problem when it is implemented.

- Difficulty of setup

- Relatively high overhead to support seamless connectivity and routing

- Slower speed than IPX and NetBEUI

TCP/IP is the slowest of all the protocols included with Windows NT. It is also relatively difficult to administer correctly, although new tools, such as DHCP, make it a little easier.

Other Protocols

Sometimes it seems that every computer company in the history of computers has created a protocol or two. Many of these protocols are no longer in widespread use, or they only apply to a certain brand of mini or mainframe computers. Some protocols, like those described in previous sections, have attained widespread use.

Other protocols you may encounter as you connect computers in your network to other computing systems are:

- DLC: IBM uses this protocol to link computers together in its SNA mainframe networks. You may need to use this protocol if you must connect your PCs to IBM equipment that does not support a more common network protocol such as TCP/IP.

- **SMB:** Server Message Block is a protocol that can be used to share resources such as files and devices. NetBIOS is based on the SMB format. Windows NT uses SMB, as do a number of other products. Samba, for example, is a product that uses SMB to enable UNIX and Windows machines to share directories and files.

- **X Windows:** This is the networked windowing protocol of most UNIX workstations. You may need to use this protocol if you will be connecting desktop computers running client programs to server programs running on UNIX workstations.

- **X.25:** This protocol is commonly used in wide area communications with multiple communicating devices. TCP/IP has grown much more popular as a wide area networking standard, but you may need to interface to equipment or networks that use this simpler protocol.

- **NFS:** Many UNIX computers use NFS (Network File System) to share file storage over a TCP/IP network. You may need to use the NFS protocol if you are using a UNIX workstation as a file server or if you need to give your UNIX workstations access to your PC-based file server.

- **SMTP:** This is the mail protocol of the Internet. If you are integrating your LAN e-mail system with the Internet, you will most likely interface with the Simple Mail Transport Protocol.

- **SNMP:** The Simple Network Management Protocol is widely used to control network communications devices using TCP/IP. Most network analyzer software can interface to SNMP, and an SNMP monitor is a very useful tool in a network of more than moderate complexity.

Physical Level Protocols

The IEEE protocols that map to the physical layer are

- 802.3 (Ethernet)

- 802.4 (Token Passing Bus)

- 802.5 (Token Ring)

802.3 (ETHERNET) The Ethernet protocol implements a logical bus network that can transmit at 10Mbps. Every computer receives the information, but only the intended destination acknowledges the transmission. Ethernet uses CSMA/CD to share the network media.

802.4 (TOKEN PASSING BUS) The Token Passing Bus protocol implements a bus network where each computer receives the information, but only the addressed computer responds. This protocol uses token passing to determine which computer may transmit at any one moment.

802.5 (TOKEN RING) Token Ring is a logical ring network that looks like a star network because the ring is actually formed inside a central hub. Token Ring devices can transmit at 4- or 16Mbps, and token passing is used to determine who may transmit at any one moment.

Review

THE OSI AND IEEE models provide frameworks that help describe the functions of a network. The layers in the OSI model encapsulate networking functions, and each layer builds on the next to provide a complete networking environment.

Groups of protocols that work together to provide portions of the OSI model are called protocol stacks. Computers must have the same protocol stacks in order to communicate with each other.

Network protocols place data in packets to be transported over the network. Each layer of the OSI model adds information to the packet.

Device drivers enable the operating system to communicate with the network interface adapters. A device driver must be configured to match the network interface adapter it supports.

Microsoft operating systems provide a graphical interface for the installation and configuration of device drivers and network protocol stacks.

REAL WORLD PROBLEMS

Your boss wants you to speed up the office LAN without spending any money. You are currently using 10-megabit Ethernet and TCP/IP. Users connect to the Internet using dial-up modems, and a single Ethernet domain is in use.

- What do you do?

Your company network has become very slow, so you decide to break it up into multiple domains and use a router to connect the domains. As soon as you disconnect the networks, even with the router running properly, you can't get data between networks. You are using four Windows NT servers (one in each subnetwork) running on Ethernet with NetBEUI. You've spent your budget money on the router and can't afford to purchase new hardware.

- What is wrong?

- How can you fix it without spending any more money?

You are evaluating a new connectionless protocol that works with Windows NT. The advertising brochure claims that the protocol is much faster than TCP/IP and that it can be used in almost every case where TCP/IP is used.

- Is the connectionless protocol likely to be faster than TCP/IP?

- Under which circumstances will the connectionless protocol fail?

You have just purchased a "packet sniffer" network troubleshooting device that can show you Ethernet frames and TCP/IP numbers. You notice that about 25 percent of all the Ethernet frames have the same "from" address. These frames contain TCP/IP packets that have the same IP "from" address.

- Which device is most likely to be transmitting these packets?

Using your trusty packet sniffer, you notice that about 25 percent of all the Ethernet frames in your network have the same "from" address but that the TCP/IP packets contained in these Ethernet frames have many different IP "from" addresses.

- Which device is the most likely to be transmitting these packets?

(continued)

REAL WORLD PROBLEMS (CONTINUED)

You are trying to attach an Ethernet network used by Marketing to a Token Ring network used in Engineering.

- Should you use a bridge or a router? Explain.

You need to connect two Ethernet networks in a small office.

- Should you use a bridge or a router? Explain.

You want to use both TCP/IP and IPX in your local area network because you have both Windows NT servers and Novell NetWare servers.

- Which device driver standard allows this on the Windows NT server?

- Which device driver standard allows this on the Novell NetWare server?

Review Questions

1. Historically, telegraph operators translated the Morse code they received into language their bosses understood. Which layer of the OSI model performs a similar function, translating binary data into language the application layer understands?

  A. 1 - Network

  B. 6 - Presentation layer

  C. 5 - Session layer

  D. 4 - Transport layer

2. Which layer of the OSI model is responsible for translating the data format?

  A. Application layer

  B. Network layer

  C. Presentation layer

  D. Data Link layer

3. Your MAN encompasses two offices on opposite sides of town that are connected via a leased 56K line. However, computers in each office are not able to communicate with computers in the other office. You believe there is a router configuration problem. At which layer of the OSI model does this problem reside?

   A. 4 - Transport

   B. 3 - Network

   C. 2 - Logical link

   D. 1 - Physical

4. Your network includes both NetWare 3.x and Windows NT servers. You prefer to use only one protocol. Which of the following protocols would best suit your situation?

   A. NWLink

   B. RFC

   C. AppleTalk

   D. NetBEUI

5. Which of the following connectivity devices typically work at the Physical layer of the OSI model?

   A. routers

   B. bridges

   C. repeaters

   D. gateways

6. Compression is often used to increase the speed on a network. Which of the following layers of the OSI model is responsible for compression and decompression of data?

   A. Application

   B. Presentation

   C. Session

   D. Transport

7. The IEEE 802 project divides the Data Link layer into two sublayers. Which sublayer of the Data Link layer communicates directly with the network interface card?

   A. Logical Link Control sublayer

   B. Logical Access Control sublayer

   C. Media Access Control sublayer

   D. Data Access Control sublayer

8. Which TCP/IP Transport layer protocol is the fastest?

   A. ICMP because it is connection-oriented

   B. TCP because it is connection-oriented

   C. IP because it is connectionless

   D. UDP because it is connectionless

9. At which layer of the OSI model would a communication problem due to an improperly terminated cable reside?

   A. 5 - Session

   B. 4 - Transport

   C. 2 - Data link

   D. 1 - Physical

10. Connection-oriented network communication is best described by which of the following statements?

   A. It is only used in Ethernet networks.

   B. It provides fast but unreliable delivery.

   C. It provides guaranteed delivery.

   D. All network communications are connection-oriented.

11. Which of the following network protocols do not contain Network layer information and thus cannot be routed? Choose all that apply:

    A. IPX/SPX (NWLink)

    B. NDS

    C. NetBEUI

    D. TCP/IP

12. Which layer of the OSI model packages raw data bits into data frames?

    A. Physical layer

    B. Network layer

    C. Presentation layer

    D. Data Link layer

13. If, through an error in manufacturing, two network cards were created with the same MAC address, which layer of the OSI model would discover the problem?

    A. 4 - Topological

    B. 3 - Application

    C. 2 - Data link

    D. 1 - Physical

14. Which layers of the OSI model are specified by IEEE 802?

    A. The Data Link and Network layers

    B. The Physical and Data Link layers

    C. The Transport and Session layers

    D. The Network and Transport layers

15. The speed of a protocol often depends on the amount of overhead information it carries. Which of the following protocols doesn't have routing overhead, and therefore is fairly fast?

A. DLC

B. NWLink

C. NetBEUI

D. TCP/IP

16. Part of IEEE Project 802 defined the sublayer (of the Data Link layer) at which bridges communicate. What is the name of this sublayer?

A. the Physical layer

B. the Transport layer

C. the Media Access Control layer

D. the Network layer

17. The IEEE 802 group has developed many networking standards. Which specification defines the rules for using Ethernet over fiber-optic cable?

A. 802.2

B. 802.3

C. 802.5

D. 802.8

18. Several companies in the computer network industry have developed driver interfaces that allow multiple cards to be bound to multiple transport protocols. There are two widely used driver interfaces; one developed by Microsoft, one developed by Apple, Novell and other networking companies. What are they? Choose two:

A. ATM

B. ODI

C. OSI

D. NDIS

CHAPTER

4

Real-World Networks

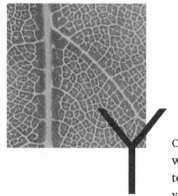

OU WILL ENCOUNTER several basic network architectures as you work with networks. These network architectures were designed to solve specific problems, and each has advantages and disadvantages. As networking technology improves and new uses for computers place different demands on networks, the number of architectures grows and networks become more sophisticated.

This chapter will introduce you to the most common network architectures today and will describe the advantages and disadvantages of each.

Ethernet

THERNET IS THE most popular physical network architecture in use today. First conceived in the 1960s at the University of Hawaii as the ALOHA network, it was a packet radio network that used the CSMA/CD (carrier sense multiple access with collision detect) protocol; we'll look at this in detail in a moment to arbitrate access to the network. Figure 4.1 shows a simple Ethernet network.

FIGURE 4.1

Ethernet is a simple method of connecting computers together.

In 1972 Robert Metcalfe and David Boffs at Xerox PARC implemented the network architecture with a cabling and signaling scheme, and in 1975 they introduced the first Ethernet product. This original Ethernet could connect over 100 computers at just under 3Mbps over a distance of up to a kilometer.

Xerox, Intel, and Digital took the original specification and extended it to 10 Mbps. This was the basis for the IEEE 802.3 specification. In 1990 the IEEE 802.3 committee released the specification for running Ethernet over twisted-pair wiring.

Ethernet is a bus- or star bus-based technology that uses baseband signaling and CSMA/CD to arbitrate network access. The Ethernet medium is passive, which means that the computers drive the signals over the network.

How Ethernet Works

Ethernet arbitrates access to the network with the *CSMA/CD (carrier sense multiple access with collision detection)* media access method. This means that only one workstation can use the network at a time. CSMA/CD functions are much like the old party-line telephone systems used in rural areas. If you wanted to use the telephone, you picked up the line and listened to see whether someone was already using it. If you heard someone on the line, you did not try to dial or speak; you simply hung up and waited a while before you picked up the phone to listen again.

If you picked up the phone and heard a dial tone, you knew the line was free. You and your phone system operated by *carrier sense.* You sensed the dial tone or carrier and, if it was present, you used it. *Multiple access* means that more than one party shared the line. *Collision detection* means that if two people picked up the phone at the same time and dialed, they would "collide," and both would need to hang up the phone and try again. The first one back on the free line would gain control and be able to make a call.

In the case of Ethernet, workstations send signals (packets) across the network. When a collision takes place, the workstations transmitting the packets stop transmitting and wait a random period of time before retransmitting.

Using the rules of this model, the workstations must *contend* for the opportunity to transmit across the network. For this reason, Ethernet is referred to as a contention-based system. Most Ethernet networks currently run at 10Mbps.

10Mbps Ethernet

Ethernet is available for many types of cable (or physical media). The different types of Ethernet use different signaling characteristics, but they share the Ethernet framing specification, the 10Mbps speed, and the use of CSMA/CD to arbitrate access.

Microsoft ✓ *Exam* *Objective*

Describe the characteristics and purpose of the media used in IEEE 802.3 and IEEE 802.5 standards.

The four commonly used 10Mbps Ethernet cabling systems are

- 10Base5, or *thicknet*, which uses thick coaxial cable

- 10base2, or *thinnet*, which uses thin coaxial cable

- 10baseT, which uses unshielded *twisted-pair* cable

- 10baseFL, which uses single- or multimode optical fiber

10Base5 (Thicknet) Ethernet

The original wiring used for Ethernet is called thicknet or 10Base5. The 5 stands for its maximum length: 500 meters (1650 feet). It is named for the size of the wire used, which is about as big around as your thumb. The coaxial (coax) cable is marked every 2.5 meters (8.25 feet) for connection points. This is done so you do not try to connect devices closer than 2.5 meters, since a shorter distance degrades the signal.

Most coax is made using PVC coating. If burned, one of the gases it creates is chlorine, which, when inhaled into the lungs, turns into hydrochloric acid. This can do great damage to lung tissue. Teflon-coated cable is much more expensive but is safer to use in ceilings where ventilation systems are located. Some fire codes require the use of plenum-rated cable if the wiring is run through ceilings.

10Base5 (thicknet) Ethernet has the following specifications:

Maximum segment length	500 meters (1650 feet)
Maximum taps	100
Maximum segments	5
Maximum segments with nodes	3
Minimum distance between taps	2.5 meters (8.25 feet)
Maximum repeaters	4
Maximum overall length with repeaters	2.5 kilometers (1.5 miles)
Maximum AUI drop cable length	50 meters (165 feet)

You normally use a device called a vampire tap to connect new connections to the thicknet. To do so, you use a tool that drills a small hole into the coaxial cable. Then you attach the tap and tighten it down, with its connector, into the hole. Although in some cases you can tap coaxial cable with users up and running, you should try to do it after working hours. A mistake can short the center conductor with the shielding and take down the entire segment.

The tap is also a *transceiver*, a device that handles transmission data signal generation and reception. Thicknet uses a BNC connector. At both ends of the cable, you must install a terminator to complete the electrical circuit and to cut down on signal reflections. Figure 4.2 shows some components of thicknet Ethernet, as well as thinnet Ethernet, which is discussed in the next section.

Thicknet cable has the following disadvantages:

- Large size

- High cost

- Connection method (drilling into the wire)

FIGURE 4.2

Some common thick and
thin Ethernet components

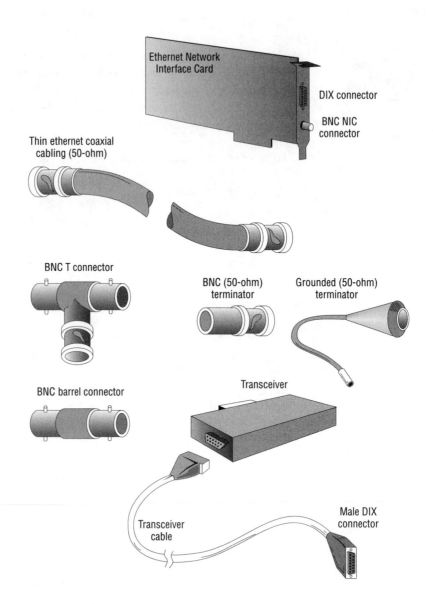

FIGURE 4.2

Some common thick and thin Ethernet components

The advantages of thicknet cabling are few for today's networks, but many
thicknet networks are still in use and are reliable.

The 10Base5 wiring specification allows you to increase the length of the
overall network by using repeaters, which are devices that pick up signals and
repeat them to another segment of the cable. You may use a maximum of four
repeaters on one network, with only three of the segments populated with

nodes. Thus, the overall length of a network that implements repeaters to extend the length is 2.5 kilometers (1.5 miles).

10Base2 (Thinnet Coax) Ethernet

When thinnet coax (10Base2) cable was introduced, it quickly became a popular choice of network cabling, since it costs, appears, and handles just like its affordable and useful cousin, the 75-ohm coaxial cable used for television cable. Because of its low cost, it is sometimes referred to as *cheapernet*.

10Base2 has the following specifications:

Maximum segment length	185 meters (610.5 feet)
Maximum segments	5
Maximum segments with nodes	3
Maximum repeaters	4
Maximum devices per segment	30
Maximum overall length with repeaters	925 meters (3052.5 feet)

The term 10Base2 is a little misleading since the maximum length is not actually 200 meters (660 feet) but only 185 meters (610.5 feet). Someone took the liberty of rounding up to make it fit in with the other specifications. Some vendors advertise that by using their hardware you can extend the 185 meters to 300 meters (990 feet). However, if you later mix LAN cards or repeaters from different vendors into your network, you may have problems, since most manufacturers adhere strictly to the IEEE specifications.

The specification for thinnet is 50-ohm RG-58A/U or RG-58C/U coaxial cable (commonly referred to as coax). RG-58A/U is the most widely used type. You should also avoid using RG-59 cable, which is intended for television signals. Another type of cable you may see is RG-58U cable. Installing this type of wiring is a mistake because it does not meet the IEEE specification for 10Base2.

You use BNC connectors for thinnet, along with the T connectors required to connect to the BNC female connectors on the LAN card. As with 10Base5 (thicknet), each end of the cable must have a terminator. Only one end of the cable must be grounded.

The 10Base2 wiring specification differs significantly from 10Base5 in that the transceiver is built into the LAN card itself and is not a device you must attach to the cable. A cable connecting the T connector to the workstation, called a pigtail, cannot be used with this standard. The T connector must connect directly to the back of the card in a daisy-chain fashion. If it doesn't connect this way, the network connections will fail.

As with 10Base5, you can use up to four repeaters on a network, with only three of the segments populated with nodes. You can mix 10Base2 and fiber-optic cabling by using a fiber/thinnet repeater. If you have repeaters on your thinnet network, be sure that all devices have SQE (Signal Quality Error) or Heart Beat turned off. If SQE is on, the SQE signal will appear as excessive collisions on the network and slow down the network.

To remember what you can put between any two nodes on a coaxial Ethernet network, keep in mind the "5-4-3 rule." As you may have noticed from the specifications, Ethernet topologies have a five-segment, four-repeater theme. The 3 part of the rule states that only three segments can be populated with nodes. The 5-4-3 rule does not apply to UTP or fiber-optic cable segments. With UTP, hubs act as repeaters. You cannot have two devices separated by more than four hubs.

The disadvantages of thinnet include the high cost compared to UTP cable and the fact that the bus configuration makes the network unreliable. If any node's cable is broken, the entire segment, and probably the entire network, will be affected. Nevertheless, because it was the most economical solution for a long time, thinnet is used in many existing installations.

Thicknet and thinnet are often used together, thicknet for covering large distances between thinnet segments and thinnet for connecting a number of computers to the thicknet backbone. This combines the advantages of both types of Ethernet in one network.

10BaseT (Twisted-Pair) Ethernet

The use of *unshielded twisted-pair* (*UTP*) cable is now a well-established trend in Ethernet network wiring schemes. UTP costs less and is more flexible than 10Base5 or 10Base2 cabling. The specification for UTP was created by the IEEE 802.3 subcommittee in the 1980s. Do not substitute *shielded twisted-pair* (*STP*) cable for UTP; the IEEE 10BaseT specification is for UTP only.

10BaseT (twisted-pair) Ethernet has the following specifications:

Maximum segments	1024
Maximum segments with nodes	1024
Maximum segment length	100 meters (330 feet)
Maximum nodes per segment	2
Maximum nodes per network	1024
Maximum hubs in a chain	4

10BaseT is wired as a star, which means that each device has its own set of wires connected directly to a hub. Although the physical topology of 10BaseT is a star, its logical topology is a bus. This gives you the advantages of a star wiring scheme and a bus in one specification. 10BaseT is easy to troubleshoot because problems on one segment of wiring usually do not affect the other segments. (Each node uses its own separate segment.)

You can also isolate a device that is causing problems by just disconnecting its cable from the hub. Some hubs have built-in management capabilities that will report errors or problems, as well as allow you to disconnect remotely the devices from the hub. These types of hubs are known as intelligent hubs. Figure 4.3 shows an Ethernet network with a 10BaseT hub.

The connection to the hub and the LAN cards is made with an RJ-45 connector. You can also connect 10BaseT to a DIX connector or an AUI connector by using a transceiver or twisted-pair access unit (TPAU). Thinnet connections on LAN cards can also be used with special transceiver devices.

UTP cable is classified in categories defined by the Electrical Industries Association. Categories 1 and 2 are voice-grade cable. Categories 3, 4, and 5 are data-grade. Be sure to ask the vendor for a performance specification sheet when you purchase Category 5 cable to be sure it meets the specifications for your network.

Some buildings that are wired for telephone service with twisted-pair wires have extra installed pairs available for your use on your network. If the wiring is Category 3 or better, you can use the existing wiring to add a 10BaseT network inexpensively. You can purchase wall jacks that have an RJ-45 connector for 10BaseT and an RJ-11 connector for traditional phone lines.

FIGURE 4.3

An Ethernet network with
a 10BaseT hub

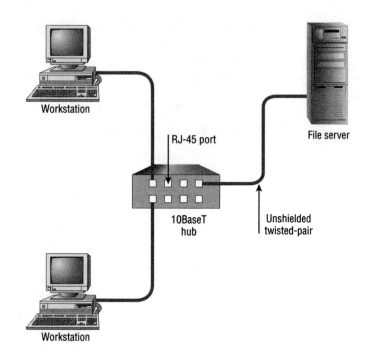

There are also Teflon-coated versions of UTP cable for areas that require plenum-rated wire. The cable is light and flexible, which makes it easy to pull through during construction. The cable is typically 22- or 24-gauge AWG (American Wire Gauge), with an impedance (resistance based on signal frequency) of 85 to 115 ohms at 10MHz.

10BaseFL

10baseFL (10Mbps data rate, baseband signaling over a fiber-optic cable) uses light rather than electricity to transmit Ethernet frames. 10baseFL is a star-wired network because it requires a network hub (also called a concentrator) to receive the light signal from each network station and send the same signal to all stations. The hub can be either active, with electronics to detect and retransmit the signal, or passive, with optics to split the light and reflect or guide it out to all the network stations.

You need to connect, with Ethernet, two buildings in the same college campus. The buildings are 980 meters apart as the crow flies.

- Which medium will you use?

You have four Ethernet stations to attach for a small accounting firm on a tight budget. All the stations are located in the same room.

- Which medium will you use?

Every once in a while, your 20-station 10Base2 network goes down. You've traced the problem to a secretary who occasionally rolls his chair over his thinnet cable, breaking the network connection momentarily, which causes your NetWare file server to drop connections to all the clients. You can't really move his computer, and since 10Base2 requires the network cabling to go in and out of the computer, you can't do anything about the location of the thinnet cable, either. All the network adapters in your LAN are 10Base2/10BaseT combo adapters.

- What can you do to make certain no single faulty cable can bring down your network?

You have a large (400-station) Ethernet network to design. Your client wants to use the most flexible architecture possible, because they intend to upgrade to either faster versions of Ethernet or possibly ATM in the next five years.

- Which medium will you use? Will you use any other types of media in portions of the network?

You need to connect two networks together across a busy street. The city will not grant a right-of-way to dig or tunnel under the street, and municipal ordinances prevent the use of an aerial cable.

- Which medium will you use?

10BaseFL Ethernet has the following specifications:

Maximum segments	1024
Maximum segments with nodes	1024
Maximum segment length	2000m
Maximum nodes per segment	2
Maximum nodes per network	1024
Maximum hubs in a chain	4

A passive fiber-optic hub requires no power to operate, but the intensity of the signal is divided among all the ports on the hub; therefore, the number of ports cannot be large and the signal from the network stations must be strong. Also, since there are no electronics in a passive fiber-optic hub, the passive hub cannot be managed or have error detection circuitry. This makes a network with a passive hub harder to troubleshoot.

A 10baseFL network segment can be up to 2000 meters long, four times that of a 10base5 segment. The great distances a 10baseFL segment can cover make it a common choice for network backbones. Figure 4.4 shows two networks linked by a fiber-optic segment.

FIGURE 4.4

A 10baseFL segment can link two LANs 2000 meters apart.

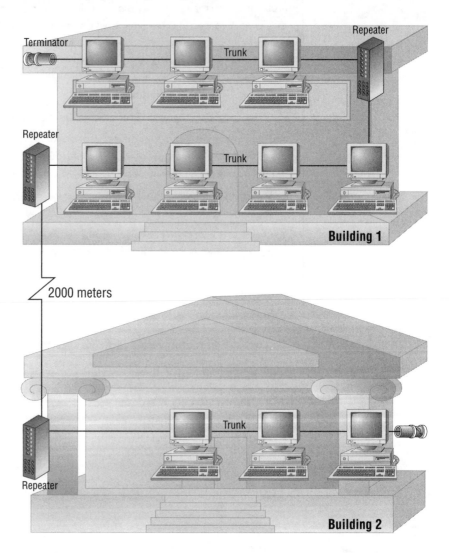

100Mbps Ethernet

For some networking applications, a 10Mbps data rate is not enough. Two competing standards extend traditional Ethernet to 100Mbps:

- 100VG-AnyLAN

- 100baseT Ethernet, also known as Fast Ethernet

100VG-AnyLAN

100VG-AnyLAN (100Mbps data rate, voice grade) combines elements of traditional Ethernet and Token Ring. It is referred to by any of the following designations:

- 100VG-AnyLAN

- 100baseVG

- VG

- AnyLAN

100VG-AnyLAN has the following advantages over regular Ethernet:

- It is faster.

- It supports both Ethernet and Token Ring packets.

- It uses a demand priority access method (as opposed to CSMA/CD) that allows for two priority levels.

- Hubs can filter individually addressed frames for enhanced privacy.

You can use 100VG-AnyLAN over categories 3, 4, and 5 twisted-pair and fiber-optic cable. It uses a star topology and defines how child hubs can be connected to a parent hub to extend the network. Several hubs are cascaded in Figure 4.5. The length of any two 100VG-AnyLAN cable segments combined must not exceed 250 meters.

FIGURE 4.5

You can cascade 100VG-AnyLAN hubs to form larger networks.

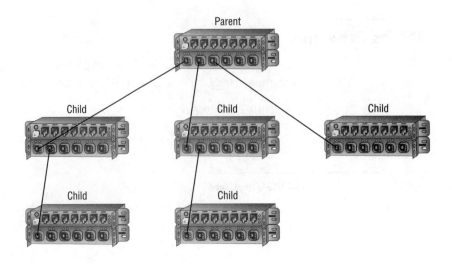

100BaseT Ethernet

100baseT, also called Fast Ethernet, is simply regular Ethernet run at a faster data rate over category 5 twisted-pair cable. 100baseT uses the same CSMA/CD protocol in a star wired bus as 10BaseT.

100baseT has been specified for three media types:

- 100baseT4 (four pairs categories 3, 4, or 5 UTP or STP)

- 100baseTX (two pairs category 5 UTP or STP)

- 100baseFX (two-strand fiber-optic cable)

In addition to the faster data rate and the higher quality cable required, 100baseX has the same advantages and drawbacks as 10BaseT.

Segmentation

As an Ethernet network grows and more stations are added to the LAN, performance can drop significantly. This is because Ethernet is a shared media network; when a lot of stations have data to transmit, the network gets congested, and many collisions occur. In a network with severe congestion, there may actually be more collisions occurring on a network than data being transmitted.

Segmentation is one solution to congestion on an Ethernet network. *Segmentation* is the process of splitting a larger Ethernet network into two or more segments linked by bridges or routers, as shown in Figure 4.6. The resulting segments have fewer stations to contend with for access to the network, and the bridge or router transfers data from one segment to the other only when the destination for the data is on the other segment. The rest of the network traffic stays in the segment where it belongs.

FIGURE 4.6

Segmentation reduces congestion on an Ethernet network.

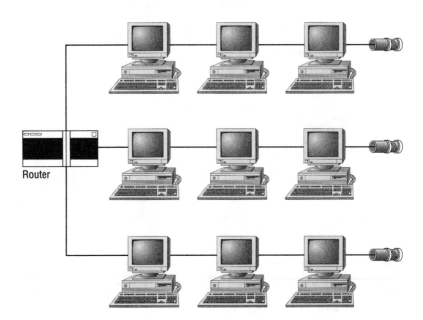

Router

REAL WORLD PROBLEMS

Your 10BaseT network is now very slow. You have six hubs connecting 120 Ethernet stations, all of which run Windows 95. Each 24-port UTP hub serves a single department and has a single 10BaseFL port connected to a central 8-port fiber-optic hub. Your budget won't support migrating to 100BaseT.

■ What can you do to relieve the traffic congestion on your network?

> **REAL WORLD PROBLEMS (CONTINUED)**
>
> You have a client who is installing a new UTP network with 50 new, Pentium class PCs. Her graphics design company will be using the computers to manipulate complex graphical advertising materials.
>
> ■ Which network architecture do you recommend?
>
> You have a client who wants to migrate to 100Mb Ethernet but doesn't have the budget to replace all the installed category 3 wiring in his building.
>
> ■ Which network architecture do you recommend?

Token Ring

TOKEN RING WAS developed by IBM as a robust, highly reliable network. It is more complex than Ethernet since it has self-healing properties. Token Ring is an IEEE 802.5 standard whose topology is physically a star but logically a ring.

Microsoft ✓ Exam Objective — **Select the appropriate topology for various token-ring and Ethernet networks.**

Workstations connect to the bus by means of individual cables that connect to an MSAU or controlled-access unit (CAU). This type of topology is illustrated in Figure 4.7.

FIGURE 4.7

A Token Ring network
in a physical star and a
logical ring.

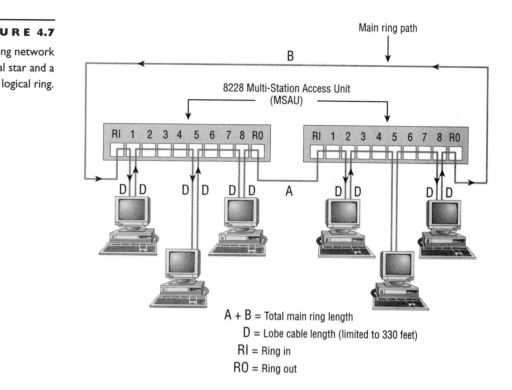

A + B = Total main ring length
D = Lobe cable length (limited to 330 feet)
RI = Ring in
RO = Ring out

Hubs (MAUs, MSAUs, and SMAUs)

Much of the functionality in a Token Ring network is in the hub. A Token
Ring hub may also be referred to in these ways:

- MAU (Multistation Access Unit)

- MSAU (Multistation Access Unit)

- SMAU (Smart Multistation Access Unit)

Microsoft
✓ *Exam*
Objective

**Describe the characteristics and purpose of the media used in IEEE 802.3
and IEEE 802.5 standards.**

IBM's Token Ring implementation has been the most popular implementation of the IEEE 802.5 standard. For this reason, when looking at Token Ring cabling and hardware, it is important to consider IBM's 8228 MSAU.

There are some differences between IBM's specifications for Token Ring and those of the IEEE 802.5. For example, each allows a different number of stations on an STP ring.

The IBM 8228 MSAU can connect up to eight workstations. It has a Ring In (RI) and a Ring Out (RO) connector for connecting to other MSAUs by means of a patch cable. The patch cable has an IBM Data Connector at both ends of the cable and is used to connect MSAUs, repeaters, and other IBM equipment.

Token Ring adapter cables are used to connect a workstation's Token Ring LAN adapter to a MSAU. The cable has a 9-pin male connector on one end and an IBM Data Connector on the other end. You will find the 9-pin connector only on Token Ring LAN cards. All other equipment uses the IBM Data Connector.

Token Ring Card Addressing and Settings

A Token Ring card has a unique address created and stored on each card during its manufacturing process. Some cards allow you to change this by using special configuration software provided by the card manufacturer.

A single workstation can have a maximum of two cards installed. One is designated as the primary card and the other as the alternate.

A Token Ring card normally uses DIP switch settings to configure the card, as shown in Figure 4.8. The connector to which the cable connects is a 9-pin female connector. A Token Ring network uses four wires to make the connection to each card, similar to UTP cable connections. Token Ring can also use STP cable.

When configuring a Token Ring network, you must remember that all Token Ring cards must be set to either 4Mbps or 16Mbps. You cannot mix speeds on the same segment.

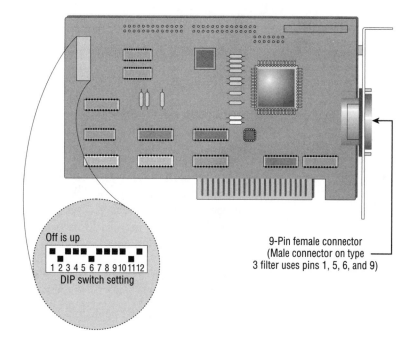

FIGURE 4.8

Token Ring NIC DIP switches

Cabling for Token Ring

The main purpose of Token Ring cabling is to connect the workstation's LAN card to the MSAU and connect other MSAUs with each other.

Here is a list of IBM standard cable types you can use with Token Ring:

- **Type 1:** STP cable used to connect terminals and distribution panels and to run through walls to wiring closets in the same building. It is made of two twisted pairs of solid-core, 22-gauge AWG copper wire surrounded by a braided shield. It can be run through conduit, inside walls, or in wire-ways for short distances.

- **Type 2:** Also STP cable, used for connecting terminals located in the same physical area or room and distribution panels in wiring closets. It is made just like Type 1 cable, with the exception that it incorporates four twisted pairs of telephone wires. This is so you can hook up both data and telephone equipment with one equipment run.

- **Type 3:** UTP cable with four pairs, each twisted two times for every 3.6 meters (12 feet) of length. It is cheaper than Type 1 or 2 cable. The disadvantage of Type 3 is that it is subject to crosstalk and noise, and you cannot use it for runs as long as those possible with Types 1 and 2 cable. It is made of either 22- or 24-gauge wire.

- **Type 5:** Optical cable used only on the main ring path. It consists of 62.5-micron diameter or 100-micron diameter fiber-optic cable.

- **Type 6:** STP cable that does not carry signals as far as Types 1 and 2. It is generally used only as patch cable or as extensions in wiring closets. It is made with two 26-gauge AWG stranded-core copper wires twisted together in a shielded jacket. Type 6 is much easier to work with than Type 1 because it is more flexible (since it consists of stranded copper wire rather than solid core).

- **Type 8:** Used for runs under carpets. Like Type 6 cable, it is made of two 26-gauge AWG stranded-core wires twisted together.

- **Type 9:** Basically the fire-retardant version of Type 6 cable. It is plenum-rated and used for runs in ceilings where ventilation systems exist. It is made with two 26-gauge AWG stranded-core copper wires twisted together in a shielded jacket.

The IEEE standards committee has developed a UTP/TR specification that replaces the old 4Mbps standard. Consequently, Token Ring networks that incorporate UTP are quickly becoming popular alternatives. You can now buy MSAUs that are designed for both Type 1 and Type 3 UTP cable. The UTP/TR standard uses Category 5 UTP cable, the same type used for Ethernet 10BaseT networks. Category 5 cable (not to be confused with Type 5 fiber-optic cable) has many more twists per foot than its cousin Category 3, so it is less susceptible to crosstalk and signal loss (attenuation) at 16Mbps speeds. You will also find it can handle larger distances that are close to the capabilities of Type 1 cable.

In noisy industrial situations, Type 1 cable is still preferred because STP cable is less susceptible to noise. Large network systems also still use Type 1 cable because it is very reliable.

Some typical Token Ring components are illustrated in Figure 4.9.

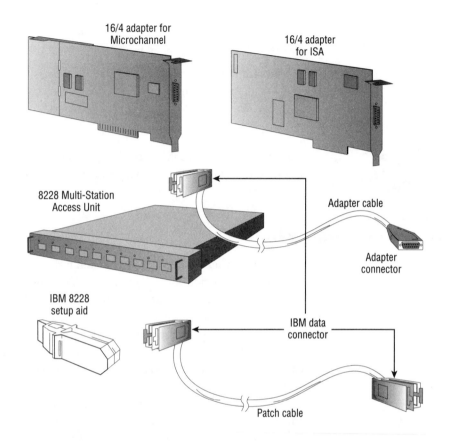

FIGURE 4.9

Token Ring components

Token Ring has the following specifications:

Cable type	UTP, STP, or fiber-optic
Maximum MSAUs	33
Maximum nodes	260
Maximum distance between node and MSAU	45.5 meters (150 feet) for UTP cable; up to 100 meters (330 feet) for STP or fiber-optic cable
Maximum patch cable distance connecting MSAUs	45.5 meters with UTP cable; 200 meters (660 feet) with STP; 1 kilometer (.6 mile) with fiber-optic cable

Minimum patch cable distance connecting MSAUs	2.5 meters (8 feet)
Maximum cumulative patch cable distance connecting all MSAUs	121.2 meters (400 feet) with UTP cable; fiber-optic cabling can span several kilometers

You can use fiber-optic cable in Token Ring networks to extend the above-listed distance limitations to up to ten times what copper cabling would allow.

How Token Ring Works

As we said earlier in this chapter, although the cards attach like a star to the MSAU, they function logically in a ring. The ring passes a free token (a small frame with a special format) around the ring in one consistent direction. A node receives the token from its nearest active upstream neighbor (NAUN) and passes it to its nearest active downstream neighbor (NADN). If a station receives a free token, it knows it can attach data and send it on down the ring. Each station is given an equal chance to have the token and take control in order to pass data. This is called media access.

Each station in the ring receives the data from the busy token with data attached and repeats the token and data, exactly as it received them, to the next active downstream neighbor on the ring. The addressed station (the station the data is intended for) keeps the data and passes it to its upper-layer protocols. It then switches two bits of the frame before it retransmits the information back to the ring to indicate that it received the data. The token and data are sent repeatedly until they reach the source workstation, and the process begins again.

Each station in the ring acts basically as a repeater. The data is received and retransmitted by each node on the network until it has gone full circle. This is something like the party game called Rumor or Telephone, in which one person whispers something into one player's ear, who in turn repeats it in someone else's ear, and so on, until it has gone full circle. The only difference is that, in the party game, when the person who initiated the message receives it back, it has usually undergone substantial permutations. When the originating node on the network receives the message, it is normally intact except that two bits have been flipped to show that the message made it to its intended destination.

Active Monitors and Standby Monitors

The station that has been up the longest normally becomes the active monitor. Token Ring allows only one active monitor on a ring at a time. All other stations on the ring become standby monitors. They wait in the wings in case the active monitor bites the dust, in which case a new active monitor is negotiated. Minor errors, such as the active monitor being turned off, are dealt with by the active monitor and standby monitors.

The active monitor does a sort of system check every seven seconds. In this check, the active monitor sends out a token to the next station on the ring. This token informs the station of the active monitor's address. This station also lists the active monitor as its upstream neighbor. The station then informs the station next in the ring of the active monitor's address. This process proceeds around the ring until the token returns to the active monitor. Through this process, each station learns three pieces of information: the address of the active monitor, who its upstream neighbor is, and who its downstream neighbor is.

Beaconing

If a station does not hear from its upstream neighbor in the seven seconds, it assumes something bad has happened and acts on its own. It sends a message down the ring announcing three basic pieces of information: who it is (its network address), its NAUN's address (the station it has not heard from in the allotted time), and the type of beacon (the condition being indicated, such as no response from the node). This action is called beaconing. It occurs when the Nearest Active Upstream Neighbor Notification fails, as illustrated in Figure 4.10.

The beaconing process serves to identify any area on the ring where there is a problem. (A problem area on the ring is called the fault domain.) Once the fault domain is located, the workstation that reported the problem—the downstream neighbor of the faulty workstation—has the job of removing the faulty station's packets from the network, ensuring that the network remains stable.

During the beaconing process, each Token Ring card takes itself out of the ring and does an internal diagnostic to determine whether it has a problem. If it

FIGURE 4.10

Beaconing points out
breaks on a Token Ring
network.

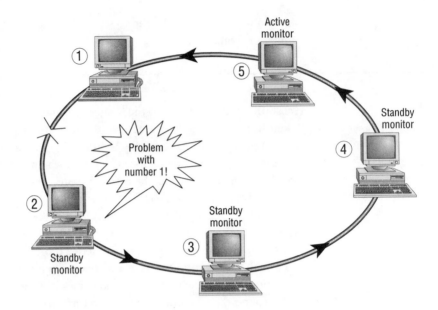

can, it repairs itself without administrator intervention. The automatic corrective action process of the card is called auto-reconfiguration. If the card finds an error during auto-reconfiguration, it does not attempt to reenter the ring.

If for some reason the card fails to correct itself and cannot safely get back on the ring, you must manually reconfigure the card or physically remove it and replace it with a functioning spare.

With the information obtained during auto-reconfiguration, the ring can repair itself without the network falling apart. This is sort of a built-in self-diagnostics and repair program.

Like other network standards, Token Ring has unique features and its own list of advantages. Here are some of the advantages:

- Unlike Ethernet, Token Ring continues to operate reliably under heavy loads.

- Built-in diagnostic and recovery mechanisms, such as beaconing and auto-reconfiguration, make the protocol more reliable.

- Token Ring makes connecting a LAN to an IBM mainframe easier since IBM created it and supports it.

- Fault-tolerance features are provided through ring reconfiguration, called ring-wrap. A single cable can create a ring when attached to two MSAUs.

Some of the disadvantages of Token Ring are as follows:

- Token Ring cards and equipment are more expensive than Ethernet or ARCnet systems.

- Token Ring can be very difficult to troubleshoot and requires considerable expertise.

FDDI

F DDI (FIBER DISTRIBUTED DATA INTERFACE) is another ring-based network. FDDI, unlike Token Ring, is implemented without hubs, although you can use devices called *concentrators* to perform a similar function. FDDI uses fiber-optic cables to implement very fast, reliable networks.

How FDDI Works

FDDI (like Token Ring) uses a token-passing scheme to control network access. Unlike Token Ring, several FDDI devices can transmit data simultaneously.

FDDI Token Passing

FDDI uses an even more sophisticated method of accessing the network than does Token Ring. Like Token Ring, a token is passed around the ring, and the possessor of the token is allowed to transmit FDDI frames. Unlike Token Ring, a FDDI network may have several frames simultaneously circulating on the network. This is possible because the possessor of the token may send multiple frames, without waiting for the first frame to circulate all the way around the ring before sending the next frame.

The possessor of the FDDI token is also allowed to release the token and send it to the next station in the ring as soon as it is through transmitting frames, rather than having to wait for the frames to make it all the way around the ring. This means that the next station may begin transmitting while the frames from the first station are still circulating, as you can see in Figure 4.11.

Dual counter-rotating rings allow FDDI to operate in spite of network faults.

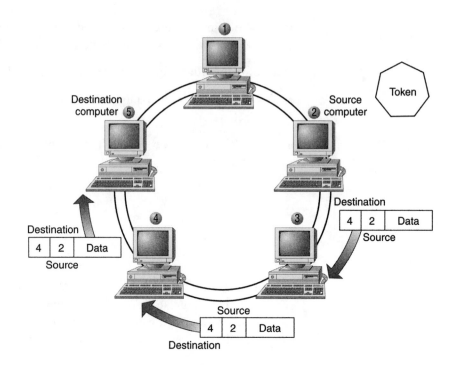

Some FDDI networks also have a method of reserving regular transmission times for certain stations; only those stations may transmit at those regular intervals, and those stations are not required to capture a token to transmit. Frames sent in such a manner are called *synchronous frames.* This is an optional feature in the FDDI standard.

Another optional feature is multiframe dialogs. *Multiframe dialogs* allow the station with the token to send a *limited token* (a token giving a station only the permission to reply to the originator) to another specific station, which is then allowed to transmit frames and limited tokens to the first station. In this manner two stations may communicate without interference from other stations.

Dual Counter-Rotating Rings

Another feature that sets FDDI apart from Token Ring is that it uses two counter-rotating rings (see Figure 4.12). Since there often is no central device to bypass network failures, another method must be used to ensure that a

FIGURE 4.12

Dual counter-rotating
rings allow FDDI to
operate in spite of
network faults.

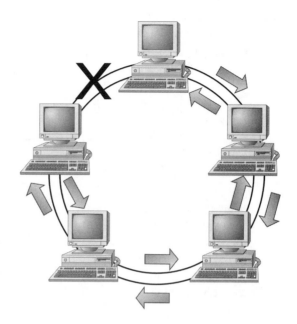

single failure does not take down the whole network. FDDI does this by
implementing two links in each device, one for the primary ring, the other for
the secondary ring.

In the event of a device or a cable failure, a single ring would be broken,
and the token (and the data frames) would not be able to proceed around the
ring. In FDDI, the data is then routed to the secondary ring, and the data
travels back around the ring, in the opposite direction from the way it originally traveled. When it reaches the other side of the break in the network and
is able to proceed no farther, it is routed back to the primary ring and proceeds normally.

Components

FDDI networks can be implemented just with stations (with FDDI network
interface cards) linked together in a ring by fiber-optic cable; however, concentrators make it possible to connect FDDI stations in a star or tree-like
structure.

Stations and Cards

The FDDI network interface cards in a station (computer) come in two types:

- Dual attachment station

- Single attachment station

In the dual attachment station there are two cable attachment points, type A and type B. These are called medium interface connectors, or MICs.

MIC type A is defined as the input path for the primary ring (and the output path for the secondary ring). MIC type B is defined as the output path of the primary ring (and the input path of the secondary ring).

The dual counter-rotating rings are implemented by connecting, via cable, the MIC type A of one station to the MIC type B of the next. The last is connected to the first, to complete the rings.

In the single attachment station there is one MIC, of type S. This is connected by a single cable to a concentrator.

Concentrators

There are three types of concentrators, as shown in Figure 4.13:

- Dual attachment concentrators

- Single attachment concentrators

- Null attachment concentrators

Each type of concentrator has several type M MICs for single attachment stations (and single attachment concentrators) to attach to. A dual attachment concentrator also has a type A and a type B MIC so it can be attached to a dual-counter rotating ring, just like a dual attachment station. A single attachment concentrator has a single type S MIC to allow it to be connected to another concentrator. You can use a null attachment concentrator if there will be no counter-rotating ring; it has only type M MICs and must be the topmost concentrator in a tree of concentrators.

With concentrators, an FDDI network can be constructed as a tree or ring of trees.

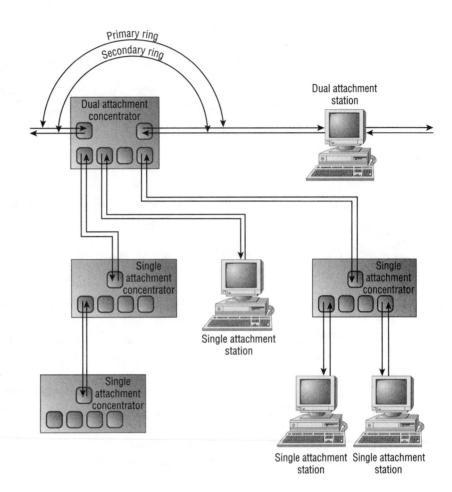

ATM (Asynchronous Transfer Mode)

ATM IS A NEW networking technology that is being used increasingly in network backbones and wide area networks. ATM is an attempt to meet the requirements of three different types of network traffic:

■ Audio (voice telephone over short and long distances)

- Video (cable television)

- Data (computer communications in LAN and WAN environments)

ATM is a high-speed network that uses fiber-optic cables or category 5 copper cables. It is a *point-to-point switched network,* meaning that central devices called *switches* are directly connected to end stations and to each other.

How ATM Works

Rather than transmitting frames, which can be variably sized, ATM communicates with *cells*. A cell is exactly 53 octets long.

An octet is exactly 8 bits of data. Octets are more precisely defined than bytes, which are usually but not always 8 bits.

Rather than specifying the source and destination addresses of the stations communicating, an ATM cell indicates the path the data will flow through. Small cells all of the same size are used to minimize latency and to make it easy for devices to process a cell, so intermediate devices (called switches) can maintain a very high data rate.

On an ATM network, every station is always transmitting. However, most of the cells transmitted are empty cells that can be discarded at the switch. When a cell that is not empty enters the switch, the VPI and VCI are read to determine where the cell will go next. The cell is then sent out in the next available slot, according to the type of cell it is.

ATM is a circuit-based network, in that a virtual circuit is set up between two devices to communicate over the network. There are two types of circuits in an ATM network:

- **Permanent virtual circuit (PVC):** A circuit that is set up once in the switches to allow communication between two devices

- **Switched Virtual Circuit (SVC):** A circuit that is temporarily set up just for the duration of a communication between two devices

The process of standardizing ATM is not complete. The classes of service may grow or change.

Several classes of service have been defined for ATM:

- Circuit emulation with constant bit rate

- Audio and/or video with a variable bit rate

- Connection-oriented service for data transmission

- Connectionless service for data transmission

A connectionless service provides for the sending of data units (messages or packets) from one endpoint (the computer) to another. Sequence control, flow control, and error control are not necessarily provided. A connection-oriented service maintains information about the flow of data from one endpoint to another and guarantees that the data units arrive in sequence and without error. Connection-oriented services also provide flow control. TCP/IP is another protocol that provides connectionless (UDP and IP) and connection-oriented (TCP) services.

Several data transmission speeds have been defined for ATM. They are listed in Table 4.1.

	NAME	DESCRIPTION
TABLE 4.1 ATM Data Transmission Speeds	T1 Carrier	1.544Mbps using conventional telephone transmission
	ATM-25	25Mbps over twisted-pair copper wire
	T3 Carrier	44.736Mbps using conventional telephone transmission
	OC-1 SONET	51Mbps transmission over optical fiber
	OC-3 SONET	155Mbps transmission over optical fiber
	OC-12 SONET	622Mbps transmission over optical fiber
	OC-48 SONET	2.4Gbps transmission over optical fiber

AppleTalk

APPLETALK IS A networking architecture that is built into every Macintosh computer. It was introduced in 1983 as a way of linking together Apple computers in small groups over a simple cabling scheme.

Select the appropriate network and transport protocol or protocols for various token-ring and Ethernet networks. Protocol choices include:

- DLC
- AppleTalk
- IPX
- TCP/IP
- NFS
- SMB

LocalTalk

AppleTalk is a complete networking architecture that can be operated over several different media, including Ethernet and Token Ring, but LocalTalk is the transmission medium developed for AppleTalk in Apple-specific networks. LocalTalk uses frames, like Ethernet and Token Ring, and uses CSMA/CA as a media access method.

LocalTalk Frame

The LocalTalk frame is similar in structure to the Ethernet and Token Ring frames.

CSMA/CA

LocalTalk uses carrier sense multiple access with collision avoidance (CSMA/CA) to arbitrate access to the network. CSMA/CA is similar to the scheme used in Ethernet (CSMA/CD). However, rather than transmitting as soon as it detects that the network is idle and detecting (the *D* in CSMA/CD) any collisions, CSMA/CA *avoids* collisions by waiting a random amount of time after transmissions by other stations.

Also, rather than detecting collisions and sending jamming signals, a transmitting station waits for a response from the destination station. If the transmitting station does not receive the response, it waits a little while and then, if the network appears to be idle, transmits the frame again.

Cables and connectors

LocalTalk networks are wired in a bus or tree topology and use shielded twisted-pair cable. Adapters are available to transmit LocalTalk frames over UTP or fiber-optic. A LocalTalk network can support up to 32 devices.

LocalTalk cables have an 8-pin plug at either end, and several cables can connect to a small connector module. See Figure 4.14 for an example of a LocalTalk network.

FIGURE 4.14

LocalTalk uses simple cables and connectors to link Apple devices together.

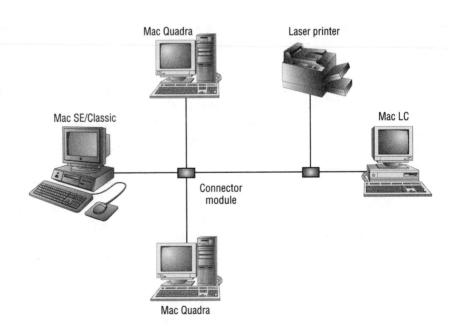

Because of the limitations of the built-in LocalTalk, other manufacturers have produced products that extend the capabilities of LocalTalk. Farallon PhoneNet, for example, can handle 254 devices using standard telephone cable and connectors.

LocalTalk is relatively slow when compared to other transmission mediums. For this reason, it is not often used in large business networks.

EtherTalk and TokenTalk

Apple computers with AppleTalk Phase 2 and a slot for expansion cards can use Ethernet (EtherTalk) or Token Ring (TokenTalk) as a transmission medium instead of LocalTalk. In addition to providing for higher data transmission rates and a wider choice of communications equipment, this allows Apple computers to fit more easily into non-Macintosh networks.

AppleShare

AppleShare is the Apple-specific file server on an AppleTalk network. Built into every Macintosh computer is the client-side software to talk to an AppleShare file server. There is also an AppleShare print server.

Zones

AppleTalk networks are divided into zones. A zone has a name, and the resources within a zone can be accessed by selecting that zone. Several zones can be connected, making a larger AppleTalk network. In addition, a single larger network can be divided into several zones to reduce congestion or to isolate certain resources.

ARCnet

O F THE DIFFERENT LAN options covered in this book, *ARCnet (Attached Resource Computer Network)* is the oldest. It was created by Datapoint Corporation in 1977. The ARCnet topology was developed before IBM's token-passing standards. Novell's version of this architecture is called RX-Net, and the Turbo version is called TRX-Net.

How ARCnet works

ARCnet combines a token-passing scheme with a star, bus, or tree topology, rather than a ring topology (such as IBM's Token Ring). A sample ARCnet network is illustrated in Figure 4.15.

FIGURE 4.15

An ARCnet network

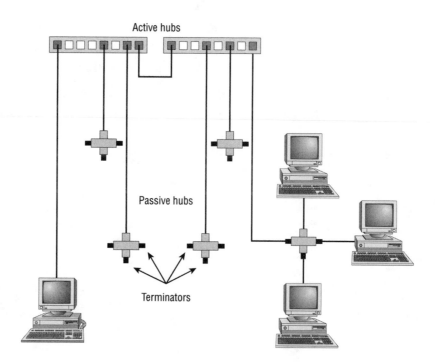

ARCnet broadcasts signals over a star topology, in the same way they are broadcast over an Ethernet bus, with one important difference: the ARCnet NIC cannot broadcast unless it has the token. The combination of token-passing with one of these topologies has made ARCnet a relatively flexible and reliable topology standard.

ARCnet is described by ANSI standard 878.1. ARCnet should not be confused with the IEEE Token Bus standard (IEEE 802.4).

Figure 4.16 shows several of the components used in an ARCnet topology with coaxial cable.

FIGURE 4.16

ARCnet components

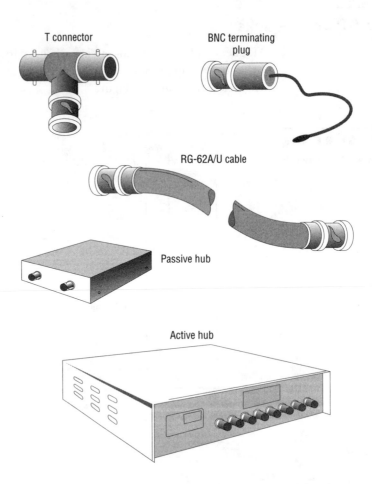

T connector

BNC terminating plug

RG-62A/U cable

Passive hub

Active hub

For many organizations, ARCnet remains a functional and cost-effective way to network. Theoretically, an ARCnet network can accommodate 255 nodes, but ARCnet systems of this size are impractical. New LAN installations rarely choose ARCnet because it is slower than the other technologies available and because of its proprietary nature.

ARCnet has the following specifications:

Maximum nodes	255
Maximum distance between nodes	6000 meters (20, 000 feet)
Maximum distance between passive hub and node	30 meters (100 feet)
Maximum distance between active hub and passive hub	30 meters

ARCnet has two main disadvantages. One is its slow speed. ARCnet has a data-transfer rate of 2.5Mbps. The ARCnet token-passing scheme uses a logical ring topology based on node address rather than on physical location. ARCnet doesn't pass the token to the next workstation on the cable; it passes the token to the network node with the next address (in ascending order). Using node addressing means that ARCnet passes the token to the next address whether that address is on a workstation in the same room or in a totally separate building. In addition, the ARCnet token travels at a fixed rate. This means that the LAN is slow. However, proper installation can help to alleviate the problem.

There is hope for improving the speed of ARCnet. A new design called ARCnet Plus increases the speed of ARCnet to 20Mbs. Thomas-Conrad Network Systems (TCNS) is something of a next-generation ARCnet. It has a top speed of 100Mbps, and it is inexpensive, especially when compared with FDDI.

The other reason for the waning popularity of ARCnet is its proprietary nature. It was not designed to facilitate interconnectivity. There has been some improvement in this area. ARCnet devices are standardized enough that any ARCnet device from any manufacturer will attach to any ARCnet LAN.

ARCnet also has some real advantages. Its star topology and cable filtering make it reliable. In a distributed star design, ARCnet uses passive and active hubs to control and route data tokens from one workstation to the next. Because token-passing is done at a fixed rate and there are no collisions, ARCnet is very stable.

ARCnet Card Addressing and Settings

Each network card on an ARCnet network must be given a unique node address for the network, in the form of an eight-digit binary number between 1 and 255 (0 is reserved for broadcast messages). Figure 4.17 shows an ARCnet card configured for working with UTP cable. (If it were to be used with coaxial cable, it would have a BNC twist-on connector.)

As stated earlier in this discussion, ARCnet uses token passing to manage access to the network. ARCnet passes the token, called an invitation to transmit, or ITT, from lowest node address to highest node address in ascending numerical order. Token passing starts with node 1 and passes to 2, to 3, and so on, up to 255, and then back to 1, forming a logical ring.

Because it is a logical ring, you should carefully plan the node addresses for each station. The addresses should proceed in a sequential, physical order. Proximity plays a major role in token passing. For example, if you choose numbers without planning carefully, node 41 could be in one building and node 42 could be in another building. Without careful planning and implementation, the signal

FIGURE 4.17

An ARCnet NIC

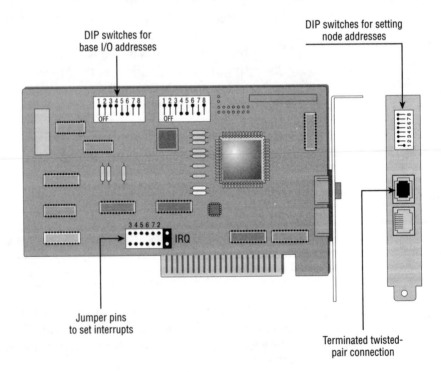

DIP switches for
base I/O addresses

DIP switches for setting
node addresses

Jumper pins
to set interrupts

IRQ

Terminated twisted-
pair connection

might travel in all sorts of directions before it reaches its destination. A better method is to sequentially number nodes in the same room to make token-passing easier.

Cabling for ARCnet

ARCnet can use three types of cable: coaxial, UTP, and fiber-optic. The most commonly used is RG-62/U coaxial cable. This choice allows for longer cable distances and provides greater stability in heavy-traffic environments.

You can use UTP cable with special boards and UTP hubs. UTP allows for cable lengths of 121 meters (400 feet), although with some specialized equipment (such as Thomas-Conrad), you may be able to extend it up to 242 meters (800 feet). A maximum of 32 stations can be on each cable. UTP uses 24- or 26-gauge wire or solid-core 22-, 24-, or 26- gauge wire. You must have at least two twists per foot and an impedance of 105 ohms. Many ARCnet designs, however, use UTP to easily and reliably connect to clients, while coaxial cable is used for longer cable runs.

Multiple nodes can share the same cable in a linear bus, attaching with BNC T connectors. This cable can be up to 303 meters (1000 feet) long. A maximum of eight nodes can share the bus.

Some newer ARCnet topology components support fiber-optic cabling. Fiber-optic cables have a maximum distance of 3485 meters (11,500 feet). One major advantage of this cable is that workstations long distances apart can be supported.

ARCnet Boards and Hubs

The following are three important components of ARCnet topology.

- Low-impedance boards
- Active hubs
- Passive hubs

Low-impedance boards create a signal strong enough to travel a maximum of 606 meters (2000 feet) to an active hub. They also perform filtering functions, as explained earlier in this discussion.

Active hubs boost incoming signals to allow for longer cable lengths. They then split the signals to multiple ports. If a network has more than four nodes, active hubs are required to configure the network. You can connect ports on active hubs to passive hubs, NICs, or other active hubs.

The server must be connected to an active hub. The active hub is the central anchoring device of ARCnet topology. Active hubs usually have eight ports, although this varies among manufacturers. Although you are not required to, it's a good idea to terminate unused ports on active hubs with 93-ohm resistors.

Passive hubs cannot connect to other passive hubs; they can connect only to active devices (such as active hubs or NICs). This is because passive hubs do not boost signals at all. Passive hubs usually have four ports. Any unused ports on a passive hub must be terminated with a 93-ohm terminator.

Figure 4.18 shows an example of ARCnet topology using active and passive hubs.

FIGURE 4.18

ARCnet topology with active and passive hubs

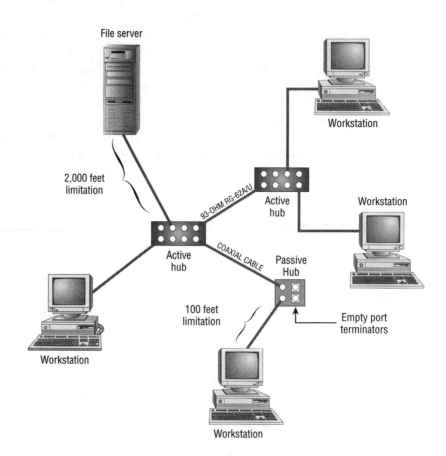

REAL WORLD PROBLEMS

You need to connect a campus consisting of 60 buildings in a five-square-mile area together with a backbone.

■ Which network topology is most appropriate?

You have a 300-station Ethernet network using eight UTP hubs connected via Ethernet to FDDI routers attached in a ring. All file servers are attached directly to the FDDI ring. Users are complaining that the client access times "feel sluggish" when they transmit large files, even though there are no congestion problems.

■ What can you do to improve client responsiveness?

Review

THERNET IS THE most widely used and most flexible network architecture. Its CSMA/CD media access protocol makes it a good choice for small or lightly loaded networks. Segmentation in Ethernet networks helps overcome Ethernet's limitations when you are creating larger networks. When an Ethernet network gets too large, the number of data retransmissions due to collisions can absorb all available bandwidth, making the network unusable.

Token Ring is a stable and fast architecture with an access protocol (Token Passing) that gives every network station fair access to the network. This allows Token Ring to scale to larger individual networks than can Ethernet; perceived performance in Token Ring just gradually diminishes as workstations are added.

FDDI is the fastest of the widely available networking architectures. It is often used in network backbones to link LANs together. Its dual-ring architecture makes it robust. You can implement the FDDI ring without a central hub or concentrator, or you can use concentrators to make the FDDI ring out of a physical tree topology.

ATM is a new network architecture that combines voice, video, and data. The ATM protocol encapsulates network data into 53-byte cells that ATM switches can efficiently route from the source to the destination over a virtual circuit. ATM provides several types of service, including constant bit rate and variable bit rate for audio and video streams and connection-oriented and connectionless service for data transmission.

AppleTalk is built into Macintosh computers and is simple to use. It natively uses LocalTalk, an Apple-specific networking protocol, as its transmission medium. AppleTalk can use other network architectures as the transmission medium, such as Ethernet and Token Ring.

Review Questions

1. When installing an Ethernet 10BaseT network, what type of cable is used?

    A. Fiber-optic cable

    B. None

    C. Thinnet coaxial

    D. Twisted-pair cable

2. You have been asked to implement a new high-speed network for your server connections. Because you are currently running Ethernet, you would like to remain within its standards. Which of the following will provide you with the highest possible speed?

    A. 10baseFL

    B. 10baseT

    C. 100VG-AnyLAN

    D. 10base5

3. In an Ethernet network, what method is used to access the media?

    A. Demand Priority

    B. CSMA/CD

    C. Polling

    D. CSMA/CA

4. To prevent signal attenuation, what is the maximum number of repeaters that can be placed on one 10Base5 or 10Base2 network?

   A. Three

   B. Four

   C. Five

   D. Any number

5. A Macintosh computer using LocalTalk for network communications ensures that data is successfully transmitted by using which of the following media access methods?

   A. Token Passing

   B. Polling

   C. CSMA/CD

   D. CSMA/CA

6. Which of the following are true of 10BaseT networks? Choose all that apply:

   A. They use fiber-optic cable.

   B. They use hubs as the central point of connection.

   C. They must be terminated at each end.

   D. They utilize Category 3 UTP.

7. Which of the following thicknet Ethernet components is used to make new connections?

   A. NCB T connector

   B. A Terminating Resistor

   C. A Vampire Tap

   D. A DIX connector

8. Fiber-optic cable is used in which of the following Ethernet networks?

   A. 10BaseFL

   B. 10Base5

   C. 10BaseT

   D. 10Base2

9. The building your company occupies has been pre-wired with Category 3 UTP. Which of the following fast Ethernet standards could you possibly implement without rewiring the building?

   A. 100baseT5

   B. 100baseFX

   C. 100baseT4

   D. 100baseTX

10. A BNC terminator is used in which of the following Ethernet networks? Choose all that apply:

    A. 10base5

    B. 10base2

    C. 10baseT

    D. 10baseFL

11. Through extensive testing you have learned that network utilization has steadily increased over the last year to over 66 percent. Your four file servers have increased utilization commensurate with the increase in network traffic. You are currently serving 153 clients on a 10BaseT Ethernet network.

    Required result: Reduce network utilization to below 50 percent.

    Optional desired results: The network is Ethernet. The new network must be easily expandable.

    Proposed solution: Upgrade network to 100BaseTX by replacing all hubs, NICs, and any wiring necessary.

Which result does the proposed solution produce?

A. The proposed solution produces the required result and produces both of the optional desired results.

B. The proposed solution produces the required result and produces only one of the optional desired results.

C. The proposed solution produces the required result but does not produce any of the optional desired results.

D. The proposed solution does not produce the required result.

12. In some types of networks, a special packet called the token is used to guarantee access to the network media. Which of the following networks use this method? Choose all that apply:

A. ARCnet

B. FDDI

C. ATM

D. Token Ring

13. The IEEE 10Base5 Ethernet standard specifies what type of cable?

A. Fiber-optic cable

B. Thicknet coaxial

C. Twisted-pair cable

D. None

14. A terminator prevents the electronic signal sent by a computer from bouncing across the network. Which of the following Ethernet implementations require terminators? Choose all that apply:

A. 100base5

B. 10base5

C. 10baseF

D. 10base2

15. In planning your Token Ring network, you have chosen to use STP cable. What is the maximum distance a client workstation can be from the MAU using STP?

   A. 50 feet

   B. 100 feet

   C. 50 meters

   D. 100 meters

16. A 10Base2 Ethernet network uses what type of cable?

   A. None

   B. Twisted-pair cable

   C. Thicknet coaxial

   D. Thinnet coaxial

17. In your new network design, there is a requirement to place a workstation at the far end of the building. You are going to be installing a 10BaseT Ethernet network, but are worried that this run might be too long. What is the maximum length of a 10BaseT cable?

   A. 25 meters

   B. 50 meters

   C. 75 meters

   D. 100 meters

18. Your company is expanding to include offices in the building next door. The buildings are approximately 400 meters apart. Which of the following Ethernet cable types could you use? Choose all that apply:

   A. 10base2

   B. 10base5

   C. 10baseT

   D. 10baseFL

19. The network design calls for one MAU to be placed on the south side of the first floor and another MAU to be placed on the north side of the second floor. The design also specifies that STP cable be used. What is the maximum distance allowable between the MAUs?

   A. 100 meters

   B. 200 meters

   C. 400 meters

   D. 800 meters

CHAPTER

5

Designing the Local Area Network

ESIGNING A NETWORK does not have to be difficult. If you are new to networking, the many options and trade-offs involved in installing a LAN can be intimidating. Experienced network integrators, who are familiar with the limitations and advantages of each networking component and cabling system, can tell after a few brief questions what would most likely meet your networking needs, both in terms of cost and performance.

This chapter will give you a view of today's networking technology and common practices and rules of thumb network integrators use when installing networks.

This chapter introduces several rules of thumb and makes generalizations that will change as networking technology changes. Computers get faster, storage grows cheaper, and networks carry more information as time goes by. Networks in the 21st century will be installed using different rules from the networks of the mid-1990s.

Network Scale

OW LARGE AND how complex a network do you need? Do you need no servers, one server, or many servers? Do you need special networking equipment, such as bridges, routers, and backbones? Do the users of your network require high bandwidth and therefore a fast (and expensive) network?

Determining your needs is the first and most important step in designing a network. This section will help you gather the information you need to design your network.

You will need to answer these questions:

- How many client computers do you have?

- How far apart are the computers?

- What software are you using?

- What software will you use?

- What special requirements do you have?

- How much can you spend?

How Many Client Computers?

The number of client computers you have is the most important factor in network design; your other design choices are all determined by the size of your network. There are basically five categories of design, separated by major differences. The supported client numbers within these categories are not firm. Some people will require a true client-server network with only four computers, while others may have no problem with a 30 station peer-to-peer network. For most circumstances, though, the guidelines given here serve as a good estimate for the type of network you should design.

Remember when designing your network to include computers you will add in the near future as part of your design size. For instance, if you already have nine computers but may add nine more in the next two years, you should design a single-server network rather than a peer network.

How many years should you take into account? That depends on how long you want your network design to last before you reengineer your network. You will eventually have to reengineer— technology will move quickly to make your current computers and software obsolete. Ten years is about the most you can expect from any network technology, although that number may stretch as time goes by. You should include at least three years' growth in your total client computer count.

Read through the following sections to determine which size network is right for your organization.

Peer Network (2–10 Users)

A peer network provides basic connectivity between computers but does not set apart any central computer as a server or provide many of the security features of a centralized client server network. Peer networks do not centralize data on servers; rather, they connect individual computers for purposes such as file sharing and e-mail.

If you have only a few users and security is not a major concern, consider using a peer network, as shown in Figure 5.1. Most operating systems, including Windows for Workgroups, Windows 95, Macintosh, OS/2 Warp, and Novell DOS have built-in peer networking, so you may not need to buy any software to set one up.

FIGURE 5.1

A peer-to-peer network has no specialized servers.

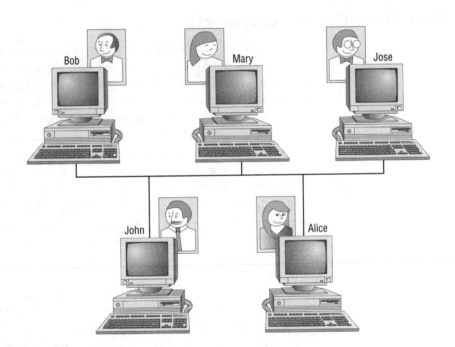

Peer networks are good for:

- File sharing
- Printer sharing
- E-mail
- Tight budgets
- Easy installation

They are not good for:

- Security

- Backup

- Organization of data

- Database applications

- Large networks

- Simple administration

- Internet/ WAN access

Single-Server Network (10–50 Users)

If you have fewer than about 50 people, you can run your entire organization with a single server. This allows you to centralize a number of services and maintain strong control over your network environment. Networking with a single server also has some benefits that can cost a lot in multiple-server networks, such as easy segmentation. Figure 5.2 illustrates a single-server network.

FIGURE 5.2

A server-based network has computers dedicated to serve files.

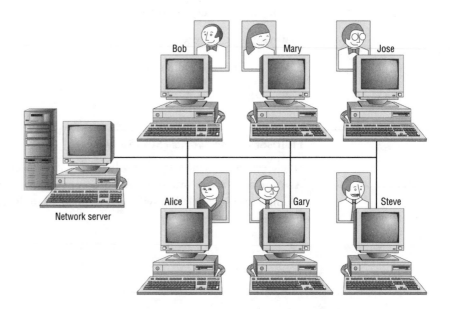

Running a single-server network requires the purchase of a network operating system, such as Windows NT, NetWare, or OS/2 Warp Server. (This program runs on the server and gives it its "server personality.") The operating system is what distinguishes a server from a client on the network.

Single-server networks are good for:

- Centralized file services

- Network printing

- E-mail

- Work flow and groupware

- Login security

- Archiving

- Organizing data

- Easy installation

- Simple administration

- Internet/WAN access

They are not very good for:

- Application serving

- Distributed organizations

- Large organizations

Multiserver Networks (50–250 Users)

Single-server networks are fine when you have fewer than around 50 nodes. As your network grows, however, a point will come when you need to begin adding more servers. You will need to create a multiserver network, as illustrated in Figure 5.3.

FIGURE 5.3

A multiserver network has multiple specialized servers.

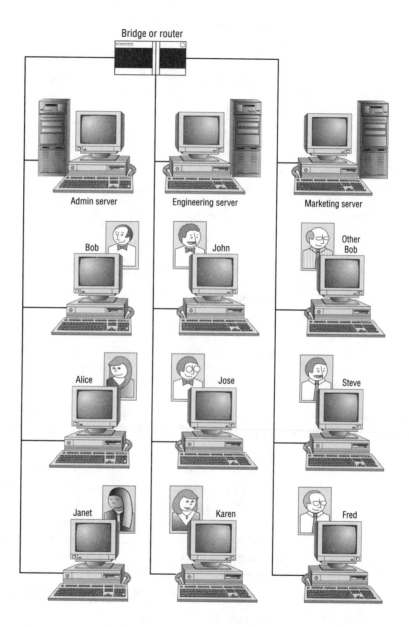

Using a multiserver network means you will have to consider your network architecture a little more carefully. Problems such as bottlenecks, the dreaded traffic jam of networking, need to be anticipated and prevented.

Multiserver networks are good for:

- Centralized file services

- Network printing

- E-mail

- Work flow and groupware

- Login security

- Application services

- Large databases

- Internet/WAN access

They are not very good for:

- Tight budgets

- Easy installation

- Organizing data

- Simple administration

Multiserver High-Speed Backbone Network (250–1000 Users)

With more than 250 clients, network planning becomes a lot more challenging. This number of clients tends to be spread out over larger areas than can be supported from a central computer room. This geographic aspect requires both a distributed network and a lot of servers (see Figure 5.4). Usually, a network of this size will be connected with a high-speed backbone that runs between servers. Because of the cost of high-speed protocol network equipment, high-speed backbone networks tend to be dramatically more expensive than the smaller networks presented above.

High-speed backbone networks are good for:

- Centralized file services

- Network printing

- E-mail

- Work flow and groupware

- Login security

- Application services

- Client-server database

- Internet/WAN access

They are not very good for:

- Tight budgets

- Easy installation

- Organizing data

- Speed

FIGURE 5.4

Networks with backbones serve large organizations.

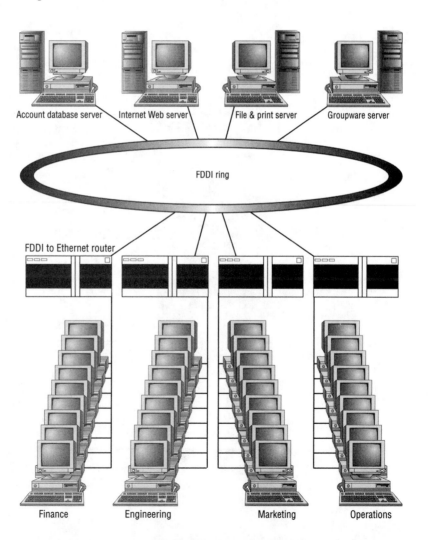

Enterprise Network (1000+ Users)

Enterprise networks are so large they are no longer really considered a single network. With more than 1000 users, it's best to break down the network into multiple connected networks that have different directory services and are split along some natural boundary, such as departments or buildings.

These smaller networks are then designed according to the criteria presented above for smaller networks and then connected with the network and internetwork connectivity devices described in Chapter 10. Sometimes, very large servers called mainframes or minicomputers are located on the internetwork and provide application services to users, in addition to the normal servers used for file and security services. See Figure 5.5 for an example of an enterprise network.

FIGURE 5.5

Enterprise networks tie large organizations together

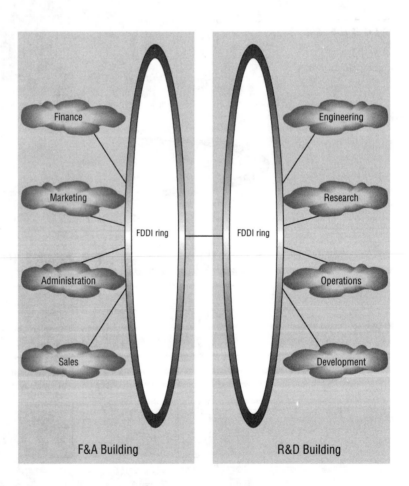

Enterprise networks are good for:

- Network printing
- E-mail
- Work flow and groupware
- Login security
- Application services
- Client-server database
- Internet access

They are not very good for:

- Tight budgets
- Easy installation
- Centralized file services
- Organizing data
- Speed

REAL WORLD PROBLEMS

You are in charge of putting together a network for a small company. There are only seven employees, and each employee needs a computer to share e-mail and files with other people in the company. Security is not a vital concern, but cost is, and all individuals can be depended upon to maintain their own computers.

- Will you install a peer-to-peer mnetwork or will you install a single-server network? Why?

Your company has grown, and the peer-to-peer network originally installed no longer meets your company's networking requirements. You need to convince your boss to move to a single-server network.

- Explain the advantages a single-server network has over a peer-to-peer network when there are 30 computers on the network.

(continued)

Your company has four departments—Marketing, Engineering, Production, and Administration—with 35, 55, 25, and 10 computers in each division, respectively. You have a server running Windows NT that provides file storage for everyone; it also hosts a SQL database back end for Administration and maintains the Internet connection for e-mail and Marketing's World Wide Web pages. The network is slow and getting slower. You have adequate funds for a modest improvement to your network.

- Explain the advantages of providing each department with its own departmental file server.

- Do you need a high-speed backbone between the servers? Explain your answer.

- You are a networking consultant to a large manufacturing corporation that is replacing its mainframe computing system with a network of specialized servers and personal computers. The headquarters occupies several large businesses on a campus, and there will be over 700 client computers connected to the network when installation is complete. Huge amounts of information will be transferred from department to department (and from building to building) as products move through the stages of research, development, production, and support.

- How will you tie the servers together?

How Far Apart Are the Computers?

The distance to the most distant client computer is important; it will help you determine which network protocol you should use and what type of cabling will work for your situation. To determine this number, select an area central to most of your client computers that can be used to install network equipment (such as the closet space in Figure 5.6). Then figure out how far the most distant client computer is by walking along the hallways from this point to that, using a consistent but comfortable pace. If you are less than 6 feet tall, multiply the number of paces by 2 feet. If you are over 6 feet, multiply the number of paces by 30 inches; then divide by 12 to get the number of feet. Add 20 feet for vertical rise to the ceiling and back down. The result will be a good estimate of the number of cable-feet between your most distant client and your network equipment area. You will use this number later in the design process to determine what type of cable you can use in your network.

FIGURE 5.6

You can get a rough estimate of the length of cable runs by walking from one location to the other.

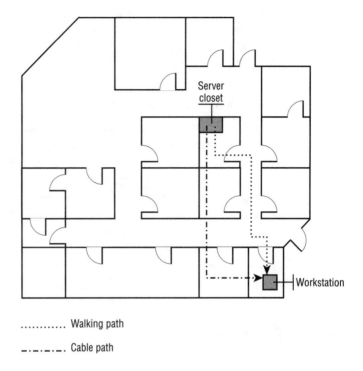

.... Walking path

_._._._. Cable path

What Software Are You Using?

Software and files are the data that flows over a network, so knowing what type of software is in use will give you a good estimate of how much data per client will traverse the network.

Word Processors and Spreadsheets

Word processor and spreadsheet programs generate very little in terms of network traffic because they are typically loaded once, their data is edited for some time, and then the programs and data are saved.

Graphics and CAD

Graphics and CAD (computer-aided design) applications tend to place a heavier load on the network than spreadsheets and word processor documents. This is because they are larger and take longer to load, which can slow performance of the network for other users. However, because they are loaded, their data is edited for some time, and then they are saved with their accompanying data, they can be considered *bursty* traffic. This means they slow the network while they are loading, but they don't cause a continuous load on the network.

Database Software

Shared databases tend to put a low level of constant traffic on the network. Since records have to be consistent among a number of users, each change made to a database is generally uploaded to the file server, and very little information is stored in the client computer. This results in frequent packet exchanges across the network. However, since most database transactions are relatively small, they typically don't impact the network until a large number of users is working on the network.

If you have a lot of database software and graphics software in use at the same time throughout your organization, you will want to consider high-speed networks.

What Software Will You Use?

An important software consideration in addition to the software currently in use is the software you will add once your network is up and running. Networks naturally improve the communications processes in networked organizations with tools such as e-mail, Internet connectivity, and groupware.

E-Mail

E-mail replaces the interoffice memo with a faster, more reliable, and less expensive form of written communication. E-mail is very easy to use, offers an immediacy not available with postal mail, and provides a written transcript of conversations for all parties involved.

Internet Service

The global Internet is simply a vast computer network. Many businesses, schools, and government agencies have banded together to connect their proprietary internal networks using a common set of protocols (network standard procedures), thus forming the Internet. Internet service extends many of the benefits of internal networking to include the entire networked world.

Such services as the World Wide Web, which provides advertising and subscription information services, e-mail, file storage, real-time e-mail (known as chatting), and even limited voice service, are provided to anyone connected to the global Internet.

In addition, the Internet can be used with a fair level of security between widely separated private networks. Ever-improving encryption technologies make this possible.

Groupware

Groupware is an extension of simple file and e-mail services that provides an extra layer of organization and process control to organizational data. With groupware, information is passed around to working teams automatically. Groupware is designed to get information where it is needed in a timely manner inside an organization, without relying on people to forward it.

Video Teleconferencing

Now that digital cameras are becoming more affordable and available, video teleconferencing is fast becoming a reality in local area networking. Users can transmit and receive real-time video between any two computers connected on a high-speed network. Some video-teleconferencing equipment even uses compression and slow frame rates to provide service over low-speed phone lines.

REAL WORLD PROBLEMS

You have been given the assignment to install a network for a small law firm. The computers will mostly be used for e-mail, scheduling, word processing, and searching for information on legal reference CD-ROMs. The senior partner in the firm has heard about fiber-optics and high-speed networking and asks you if an FDDI ring would be appropriate for the law firm network.

- What is your reply to the senior partner?

Your engineering firm is expanding. To accommodate the growth, the Research and Development department is moved to a new floor of the office building. Your supervisor discovers that an ARCnet network had been installed by the previous tenants. She asks if the existing ARCnet network will support the CAD and graphics traffic the R&D group will generate.

- What is your reply?

What Special Requirements Do You Have?

Do you have some special need for security on your network? Are any of your computers more than 100 meters from where you will locate your hub? Have there been any problems with electrical interference that you know about? These issues will play a part in determining what sort of cabling and network devices you will need to install. It will also impact the software you implement.

How Much Can You Spend?

The amount of money you can spend is a factor that will determine which solutions are available to you. Be sure to take the time to determine how much money you will be able to justify spending on your network. This is the dollar amount beyond the cost of the computers and software. The dollar amount includes such items as network interface adapters, hubs, cable cost, and the labor cost of installing the cable. Once you've determined the amount you can spend on *linking* your computers together, divide it by the number of clients you intend to network and compare it against the guidelines listed in Table 5.1.

	BUDGET	NETWORK
TABLE 5.1 Per-Client Network Connection Costs	Less than $100 per client	You will have a difficult time installing any sort of network for this amount of money. Consider a peer-to-peer solution if you have a small number of computers. If you are trying to network more than ten computers, you will need to determine how important a network is and budget more money.
	$100–$150 per client	You will be hard pressed to put together a client-server network with this budget constraint, unless your building is already network wired. It can be done, but you will have to find some very cost-effective contractors and commit to doing a lot of the work yourself.
	$150–$250 per client	This is the normal range for Ethernet client-server solutions. You should have enough with this budget to put together a network of up to 250 stations with no problem.

TABLE 5.1	BUDGET	NETWORK
Per-Client Network Connection Costs	$250–$500	With this budget, you have a lot of options. You can use high-speed solutions and should be able to connect any number of client stations together.
	$500+ per client	You will be able to use almost any networking protocol available, and you can have optical fiber installed at each location if you desire. High-speed servers and backbones will also fall within your budget.

REAL WORLD PROBLEMS

You have $7500 with which to network 100 computers.

■ What sort of network can you implement?

You have $75,000 with which to network 500 computers.

■ What sort of network can you implement?

Networking Technologies

THE PREVIOUS SECTION helped you determine how complex a network you need. This section will help you decide which network technology layer to use (Ethernet, Token Ring, and so on). It presents a comparison of the common network types you learned about in Chapter 4, in the context of current network integration and cabling practices.

Because the equipment you buy depends upon the logical link protocol you choose, make that decision before deciding on cable plant or other equipment.

Microsoft
Exam
Objective

Select the appropriate media for various situations. Media choices include:

- Twisted-pair cable
- Coaxial cable
- Fiber-optic cable
- Wireless

Situational elements include:

- Cost
- Distance limitations
- Number of nodes

Ethernet

In addition to what you learned in Chapter 4, it is important to understand the following about Ethernet in networks today:

- There is no guarantee that a computer will ever be able to transmit data in a heavily loaded network.

- A computer only has to wait for silence before transmitting.

The trick to designing Ethernet networks is to ensure plenty of silence on the network by keeping the number of clients below about 30 per network segment and bridging or switching between the segments as necessary.

Because there is no need to configure each device on the network, and because different variants support almost all architectures and cable types, there is very little reason to use any network access protocol other than Ethernet. Unless you have some special need for faster bandwidth or you already have a network cable plant installed that was designed for Token Ring, you should use Ethernet.

Fast Ethernet

Fast Ethernet is new and currently somewhat more expensive than Ethernet. This situation may change very quickly, depending on market forces. At the moment, however, unless you need the speed or have money to burn on your network, consider using Fast Ethernet as a transport between your servers and only the most demanding clients.

Fast Ethernet is quite simply Ethernet, but ten times faster. Older computers that have ISA buses (most computers built before 1993) are not fast enough to use the speed Fast Ethernet provides, so consider using Ethernet for those clients instead.

Token Ring

In addition to what you learned in Chapter 4, you should be aware that:

- All computers will eventually get to transmit data, no matter how loaded the network is.

- All computers will suffer some delay before being able to transmit while they wait for the token.

Token Ring is a contemporary of Ethernet, but because the electronics required to control the network process are inherently more costly, it never caught on as well as Ethernet. At one time Token Ring comprised 25 percent of all network stations, but that number is quickly dwindling.

FDDI (Fiber Distributed Data Interface)

FDDI is essentially a fast fiber version of Token Ring and has been the choice for high-speed backbones for some time, mostly because it was the first fast, commercially successful protocol available. FDDI, however, faces stiff competition from Fast Ethernet and ATM. Fast Ethernet runs at a comparable speed, uses less expensive devices, and can run over less expensive cable. ATM can be considerably faster (although it is typically more expensive).

FDDI rings can be quite large, up to about 13 kilometers between devices with single-mode fiber. And since the ring goes from device to device in a loop, it is possible for an FDDI ring to circle an entire city. For this reason FDDI is an ideal choice for campus areas or multi-building network backbones.

Fiber Channel

Fiber Channel is a new, fiber-specific, high-speed backbone network technology that is still in its infancy and is still relatively expensive. It currently operates at very high speeds and will eventually make a good choice for backbone connectivity in very large networks.

ATM

ATM is replacing frame relay as the digital network over which public telephone systems operate worldwide. It was, however, designed with service for computers in mind and is being used with much success as a high-speed backbone. ATM will eventually provide direct connection between private networks and public telephone networks for very high-speed access to the Internet.

REAL WORLD PROBLEMS

You have been asked to prepare a plan for the future growth of your organization's network. The Chief Information Officer wants you to consider new technologies that will support the bandwidth-intensive applications of the future.

■ Which technologies will be the focus of your report?

You have an installed network of several hundred stations and several servers on a 10baseT Ethernet network. You would like to increase the bandwidth between the servers and the most demanding clients but leave the rest of the network on 10baseT Ethernet.

■ How will you achieve this goal?

Physical Cables

THE PREVIOUS SECTION introduced some design considerations of the most popular networking technologies. This section discusses some of the design considerations of the *physical plant,* or the wires that connect the computers together.

Topology Again

The logical link layer you use will pretty much determine which physical plant topology you should install. However, keep in mind that of the three common topologies, only the star architecture can emulate all the other architectures. If you are at all uncertain as to which architecture to use, you will not go wrong by installing a star architecture. Buses and rings should be wired only in cases where compatibility with existing equipment is an issue.

Cable Types

This section describes three cable types: optical fiber, metallic cable (usually copper), and wireless. The metallic cable includes twisted-pair and coaxial. Fiber includes single-mode and multi-mode. Wireless includes microwave and infrared.

Microsoft ✓ *Exam Objective*

Describe the characteristics and purpose of the media used in IEEE 802.3 and IEEE 802.5 standards.

Twisted-Pair

Twisted-pair cables for networking are descended from the original cables used by AT&T to provide telephone service. Many types have evolved over the years, culminating in the creation of the most modern type, category 5, which is unshielded twisted-pair (UTP).

TWISTED-PAIR TYPES Shielded twisted-pair was developed for high-speed networking before categories 4 and 5 were available. It relies on a constant ground shield to reduce interference. Its high cost and installation difficulty have made it less common in the U.S., but it is very common in Europe, where in many places it is mandated by law.

If you are installing new twisted-pair wiring, you should not consider any cable type other than category 5. All other categories are obsolete and are not recommended by the International Telecommunications Union (ITU) for new installations.

COST PER LOCATION The cable cost per location for category 5 unshielded twisted-pair wiring is about $100 per location. You should not install any other type of UTP for new installations. If radio-frequency interference is an issue, consider using optical fiber rather than shielded twisted-pair.

DISTANCE LIMITATIONS Category 5 UTP is limited in total length to 100 meters. No more than 80 meters should be permanently installed between the wall outlet and the patch panel in the computer room.

OTHER LIMITATIONS Category 5 UTP is susceptible to interference from sources that generate electromagnetic interference, such as motors, HVAC units, fluorescent lights, and telephone ringing equipment. If interference is an issue, use optical fiber.

BANDWIDTH The maximum bandwidth of category 5 UTP is 100MHz. Because many transmission schemes can pack more than 1 bit per cycle, higher bit rates may be achieved.

MHz stands for megahertz *and refers to the number of positive-to-negative transitions (cycles) that occur in one second. This is a measure of analog bandwidth. It does not specify exactly how many bits per second can be transmitted (digital bandwidth) because encoding schemes such as non-return to zero can transmit more than 1 bit per cycle. For instance, ATM STS-3 at 155 megabits per second can be transmitted over category 5 UTP because the analog bandwidth is much lower.*

Because of its sensitivity to electromagnetic interference and crosstalk, you may have difficulty operating 100Mbps standards such as Fast Ethernet and ATM-155 near the distance limitation of category 5 wiring. If you intend to run 100Mbps protocols or faster at distances greater than 75 meters, consider multi-mode optical fiber instead.

Coax

Coax comes in many styles. The most commonly used types in computer networking are thicknet and thinnet.

Do not try to use 75-ohm video cabling in a computer network. It is more common, but it will not work for computer network devices.

COST PER LOCATION Thinnet coaxial cable has the lowest cost per station of any type of cable, at around $25 dollars. These cables can be purchased with connectors already attached and can be installed by just about anyone; they are simply daisy chained from one computer to another.

Installing thicknet coaxial cable typically costs about $50 per station, and transceivers must be included for each station, at a cost of about $100.

DISTANCE LIMITATIONS Thinnet is limited to a total bus distance of 185 meters. Thicknet is limited to 500 meters total.

OTHER LIMITATIONS Because they are bus networks, the path of the installed cable must match the locations of existing computers. For this reason, adding computers that are not near the bus cabling is difficult and expensive.

BANDWIDTH The useful bandwidth of coaxial cabling is 10Mbps, the speed of Ethernet. No other popular network standard allows the use of coaxial cabling. The theoretical limit, however, may be as much as 550MHz in point-to-point wiring.

Fiber

Although many types of optical fiber are available, most network devices specify the use of only two types: multi-mode, with a core diameter of 62.5 microns (one micron equals 1/1,000,000 of a meter) and a *cladding* (a layer of glass surrounding the core) diameter of 125 microns, and single-mode, with a core diameter of 8.3 microns and a cladding diameter of 125 microns. The other types of multi-mode cable are all obsolete and not recommended for use in networks.

SINGLE-MODE Single-mode fiber is much more difficult to make than multi-mode fiber, so it costs quite a bit more. Current theoretical guesses put the bandwidth limit at about 4 terabits per second (that's 4000 billion), but the upper limit for distance has not been established. Testing has confirmed 8 gigabits per second over 15 million meters without the use of amplification or signal repeaters.

MULTI-MODE Multi-mode fiber is far less expensive than single-mode fiber and has many features in common with it. It does not, however, have nearly infinite bandwidth and distance characteristics.

Multi-mode fiber is generally rated at 100Mbps at 1 kilometer, but modern cables easily exceed that. Modern cables should operate at 622Mbps at 1 kilometer and have no problem with 2200Mbps at 100 meters. Obviously, if you need speed, fiber is the way to go.

COST PER LOCATION Fiber should always be installed in a star architecture so that future switched networks will be able to take advantage of it. You can figure costs of $250 per multi-mode station location.

DISTANCE LIMITATIONS Multi-mode fiber is limited to 2000 meters when using Ethernet 10BaseFL and to 400 meters when using Fast Ethernet 100BaseF. Both of these limitations are due to timing constraints for Ethernet, however, and not because of some limitation of the fiber. The bandwidth limit of modern cables is about 622Mbps at 1000 meters. That bandwidth can be doubled each time the cable distance is halved.

OTHER LIMITATIONS Since fiber is immune to electromagnetic interference, and because it is nearly impossible to tap, there are very few limitations about where it can be run. Also, since optical fiber does not transmit electricity, it is not subject to electrical building codes. Optical fiber is not delicate, but it should be handled with care during the installation. You must be careful not to exceed the bend radius of the fiber or to go around right angles without some slack; otherwise, light will escape the fiber and reduce its ability to transmit data. Fiber can require considerable skill to install.

BANDWIDTH The useful bandwidth of optical fiber depends on the network standard you use. Single-mode optical fiber can carry any network signal at any speed, and multi-mode fiber can carry all current network signals within buildings.

CONNECTORS AND JACKS Although a number of optical fiber connectors are available, you should consider only two types for network installations: ST and SC. ST is the current industry standard. Most networking equipment uses the ST connector. However, ST connectors can be difficult to plug and unplug, and they are rather bulky for large count cables. For these reasons the SC connector is becoming more popular, but only time will tell whether it manages to replace ST as the industry standard.

Wireless Radio

Wireless radio is very expensive, but it can be extremely useful in situations where running cable is prohibitively expensive or not possible. The different types of wireless radio solutions in existence all serve different needs at different ranges. If you intend to use wireless radio in your network, you should contact the manufacturers of different devices to determine exactly which radio will fit your requirement. Table 5.2 describes several wireless solutions.

TABLE 5.2 Wireless Networking Solutions	FREQUENCY	DESCRIPTION
	900MHz spread spectrum	900MHz solutions generally provide about 2Mbps of network bandwidth at ranges up to 5000 meters. These radios operate much like cellular telephones in that they do not have to be line of sight. They typically cost about $5000 per station.
	2.4GHz spread spectrum	The 2.4GHz spectrum has been released by the FCC for unlicensed use, and many network devices are being planned that will operate in this range. None however, are currently available.
	6GHz spread spectrum	The 5.8GHz solutions generally provide about 6Mbps of throughput at ranges up to 800 feet. These devices consume less power and provide more speed than their 900MHz counterparts but are not suitable for long-distance links. They cost about $1000 per station.
	23GHz microwave	23GHz microwave is the distance and bandwidth winner for wireless solutions. These radios are point-to-point and must have a clear line of sight between the transmitter and receiver, but they are capable of transmitting up to 6Mbps at ranges up to 50 kilometers under ideal circumstances. They are very susceptible to weather, however, and they are very expensive; cost per station is typically $15,000.

Wireless IR

Wireless infrared is broken down into local area and point-to-point solutions. All operate at full network speed, generally 10Mbps for Ethernet. Infrared LED solutions are typically less expensive and easier to set up. Some point-to-point solutions use infrared laser diodes for greater distance. All infrared solutions require a clear line of sight and are greatly impacted by weather, such as rain or fog, unless they are indoor-only solutions. Table 5.3 describes short-, medium-, and long-distance LED and laser diode (LD) solutions.

TABLE 5.3	TYPE	DESCRIPTION
Infrared LED and Laser Diode Network Solutions	Short-distance intra-building LED	Short-distance intra-building infrared LED solutions operate at full Ethernet speed and cost about $400 per station. These devices are generally aimed at a central infrared hub that can be mounted on a ceiling for total room coverage
	Medium-distance inter-building LED	Medium-distance inter-building LED solutions operate at full Ethernet or Token Ring speed and cost about $5000 per station. These devices must be aimed in each other's general direction because they are generally highly focused and are limited to fewer than 500 meters
	Long-distance point-to-point LD	Long-distance point-to-point infrared laser diode solutions can operate at full network speed for a variety of protocols up to 155Mbps. At those speeds they are limited to 500 meters, but at 20Mbps or less they can operate at distances up to 1200 meters. These solutions typically cost about $8000 per station

Review

DESIGNING A NETWORK does not have to be difficult. The most important points to consider are the number of users, where they are located, the types of software, special requirements such as security and electromagnetic interference, and the amount of money that can be spent on a network. All impact how a network is designed.

The most common network types include Ethernet, Fast Ethernet, Token Ring, FDDI, Fiber Channel, and ATM. These network types use a variety of physical transmission media, including twisted-pair copper cables, coaxial copper cables, fiber-optic cables, wireless radio, and wireless infrared.

Review Questions

1. Suppose the following situation exists: Your company occupies three building on a campus. Each of these buildings has a 10BaseT network running to all floors. The buildings form a rough triangle, 1,500 meters on each side. Each are within sight of the others. You must choose a network type to connect the buildings.

   Required result: The network must support 100Mbps transfer speeds.

   Optional desired result: The network must be easy to install and maintain. The network should be immune to EMI.

   Proposed solution: Implement a fiber-optic network between buildings.

   Which results does the proposed solution produce? Choose one:

   A. The proposed solution produces the required result and produces both of the optional desired results.

   B. The proposed solution produces the required result and produces only one of the optional desired results.

   C. The proposed solution produces the required result but does not produce any of the optional desired results.

   D. The proposed solution does not produce the required result.

2. You have just been hired to manage the network for a law firm. Currently, no network is installed, but each of the 42 employees has a computer. Because of the type of data being processed, security is very important, and centralized backups are required. However, speed is not of the utmost importance. Which of the following network types is best suited to your environment?

   A. Multi-Server with a high-speed backbone

   B. Enterprise

   C. Hybrid

   D. Single Server

3. Suppose the following situation exists: Your company is installing five new computer kiosks for general employee information. The wiring closet is centrally located in the building. However, the cable runs range anywhere from 200 to 600 feet.

   Required result: Select a single type of cable that will enable all computers on the network to communicate with each other.

   Optional desired results: Keep costs to a minimum. The cable must be resistant to EMI.

   Proposed solution: Select fiber-optic cable as the standard.

   Which results does the proposed solution produce? Choose one:

   A. The proposed solution produces the required result and produces both of the optional desired results.

   B. The proposed solution produces the required result and produces only one of the optional desired results.

   C. The proposed solution produces the required result but does not produce any of the optional desired results.

   D. The proposed solution does not produce the required result.

4. As a consultant, you have been hired by an advertising firm to optimize their network performance. They currently have 180 computers and printers connected to the network. They use centralized file storage and backups, and have groupware applications, Internet access, and a database of client information. Which of the following network types is best suited to their company?

   A. Multi-Server

   B. Enterprise

   C. Peer

   D. Mesh

5. Suppose the following situation exists: Your company occupies three building on a campus. Each of these buildings has a 10BaseT network running to all floors. The buildings form a rough triangle, 1,500 meters on each side. Each are within sight of the others. You must choose a network type to connect the buildings.

Required result: The network must support 100Mbps transfer speeds.

Optional desired result: The network must be Ethernet. The network should be immune to EMI.

Proposed solution: Implement a fiber-optic network between buildings.

Which results does the proposed solution produce? Choose one:

A. The proposed solution produces the required result and produces both of the optional desired results.

B. The proposed solution produces the required result and produces only one of the optional desired results.

C. The proposed solution produces the required result but does not produce any of the optional desired results.

D. The proposed solution does not produce the required result.

CHAPTER

6

Configuring the Network Server

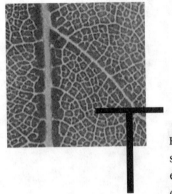

THIS CHAPTER FOCUSES on the brain of the network, which is the server. The server stores files, prints documents, coordinates e-mail and groupware, and hosts the server applications in client-server computing.

This chapter describes the server and illustrates the interaction of client and server computers. You will see how to install Windows NT Server and how to share printers and volumes. You will also learn about several applications that must have a network to operate: e-mail, group scheduling, groupware, and client-server computing. In addition, you will learn about two ways of integrating computers from different vendors, such as Apple and IBM, into the same network.

Server Hardware and Operating System

THE SERVER IS a computer like any other. It has a hard disk on which to store data, a CPU to compute with, and a network interface adapter to connect it to the rest of the network. It also has an operating system to control the hardware and to provide the network services that make a server the heart of network activity.

Your choice of server hardware and network operating system will greatly influence the speed, usability, and ease of administration of your network.

Server Hardware

The server is the focal point of your network. Most network operations are communications with the server. For this reason the server must be fast, in order to quickly respond to client requests, and it must have enough capacity (hard disk space and memory) to store files and perform tasks for many users. For these reasons the server computer should be more powerful than the average personal computer, as Table 6.1 describes.

TABLE 6.1	COMPONENT	CLIENT	SERVER
Client and Server Hardware Requirements	Processor	486 or greater	Pentium or RISC-based preferred, 486 for very small networks
	Display	VGA or better	VGA or better
	Hard disk space	About 50MB plus the storage space for a single user and applications	About 90MB (110 for RISC) plus storage space for a single user (times the number of users) and applications
	Memory	At least 8MB	At least 16MB

You will also want to put the fastest network cards in the server, as well as use the fastest hard drives you can reasonably afford. All the server files must come off the hard drive and go out through the network adapter, so any improvement in these two items will enhance all aspects of the server's performance.

If you have a demanding network environment (many client stations, or heavy data storage requirements, such as for graphics, video, or large, complex documents), you should consider how a RISC-based server would enhance your network's performance. RISC-based servers generally require more RAM and more hard disk space than do x86- (Intel and Intel clone) based computers, but this is because RISC-based computers are optimized for speed. You must be careful when selecting peripherals to place in or connect to a RISC-based computer because drivers must be specially written for a RISC-based computer, and many adapter cards will not work in a RISC-based computer.

The Hardware Compatibility List (HCL) for the network operating system you choose will describe the devices that will work with your operating system. A RISC-based computer will also have an HCL for the hardware, listing the adapter cards and hardware devices that will work with that system.

You can protect your investment in hardware by selecting devices (adapter cards and peripheral components) that are widely supported. The more HCLs the device is on, the more likely you will be able to use that device when you upgrade your computer or switch to another network operating system.

REAL WORLD PROBLEMS

You are planning a network for a medical practice that doesn't have many client computers to support but that stores very large graphical files, such as MRI and X-ray images, on their server.

■ Which hardware component will require more than average capacity?

You are planning a network for a computer-assisted drafting company. They use very powerful client computers running windows NT Workstation and they transfer very large files. You have the option of using Ethernet or Fast Ethernet, at your discretion.

■ Which will you recommend, and why?

You have a client who makes sandwiches for delicatessens around the city. He uses ten computers for accounting and order entry that he would like to network with a server. He doesn't think he will add more than three computers in the next five years. You have the option of using Ethernet or Fast Ethernet, at your discretion.

■ Which will you recommend, and why?

You would like to use a multiport serial board from an old BBS computer for your new Windows NT remote access server, but you are worried that it might not be compatible with Windows NT.

■ How can you check?

The Network Operating System

A network operating system (NOS) is very similar to a regular client operating system such as Windows or OS/2 in than it controls the basic functions of the computer. Unlike regular operating systems, network operating systems provide network services such as file and print sharing and user account management.

Because many computers rely on the services of a server, good network operating systems are implemented with features such as protected preemptive multitasking, which prevents poorly written server component software from crashing the server, and strong security, which allows you to manage who has access to the different resources stored or provided by the server.

Technically, the only difference between a server and a client computer is the software each one runs. Servers run network operating systems, and clients run client network access software. A complete network requires two types of network software:

- The network operating system, which runs on the server and allows you to share server resources such as hard disk space, printers, and CD-ROMs.

- Client network access software, which runs on the client and provides access to the resources shared by the server.

Client Software

The purpose of client network software is to make the services that are available on the network appear to be local to the client computer. This way, application software can be written without regard to where printers, hard drives, and so on, are located.

When a program needs to open a file, it sends a request to the operating system (such as DOS) that includes the drive, path, and file name. It relies on the operating system to return the contents of the file requested. When a program prints, it merely sends data to a software port. It relies on the operating system to transfer the contents of the software port to the printer port.

Client software works by intercepting calls to DOS for print and file services. The network client software determines whether the drive letter (or *drive designator*, as it is sometimes called) refers to a local drive or to a network drive. If the drive letter refers to a local drive, the network client software simply passes the request to the local operating system (such as DOS). If the request refers to a network resource, the client software intervenes, communicates with the server to get the contents of the file or to transfer print data, and returns information to the application program the same way the local operating system would.

For instance, when you access a file on your computer, you use syntax like this:

```
edit c:\files\readme.txt
```

The network client software intercepts the request before DOS gets it and checks the syntax of the line to determine whether the drive letter designator refers to shared resource. If the request refers to a local drive, it is passed to the operating system. If the request refers to a network resource, the network client software negotiates with the server to service the request.

This way, application programs don't have to know anything about networks in order to use network resources. They can simply treat networks as very large hard disk drives and as local printers. The network client software intervenes whenever necessary to communicate with the network.

Network client software is referred to differently in different operating systems. In Novell NetWare, the network client software is called a *requester*, (because it requests services from the server), whereas in Microsoft and IBM networks, client software is called a *redirector* (because it redirects requests to the network) (see Figure 6.1).

FIGURE 6.1

A redirector intercepts network requests and forwards them to the server.

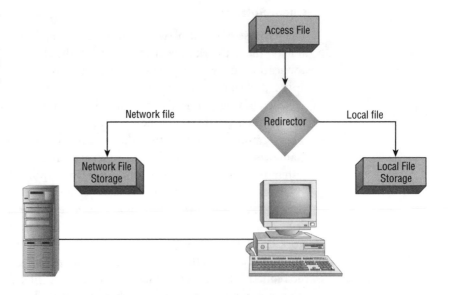

PERIPHERALS Requesters and redirectors must know how to handle input/output requests other than files, such as print requests, in order to support printing to a print server. These are handled in much the same way as file requests; the only difference is that rather than intercepting file requests, the redirector intercepts peripheral ports.

Peripheral ports are operating system services that receive data destined for a physical input/output port. The operating system receives the data through the peripheral port service and transfers the data to the physical input/output port, where it is received by the destination device, such as a printer.

Requesters and redirectors intercept the peripheral port data and check to see whether it is destined for a network resource. If it is, they send the data to the server that handles that resource. The server then sends the data to its physical input/output port, where the data is received by its destination device.

Server Software

Servers are the waiters of the network world—they exist simply to listen for and satisfy the requirements of clients. Because servers actually store most of the data on a network, they provide a convenient location to perform a number of other services, such as:

- Managing user accounts

- Security

- Central licensing

- Data protection

- Multitasking and multiprocessing

Each of these functions is more applicable to server operating systems than client operating systems. Most client operating systems do not normally provide these functions.

MANAGING USER ACCOUNTS Network operating systems require that users pass a security test by providing a username and a secret password. The process of passing this security test is called logging in or logging on, depending on the network operating system in use. Once logged on, users have access to network resources until they close their session by logging out or logging off.

To keep track of users and passwords, networks implement user accounts in a user accounts database. This database is managed by the network administrator, who can add, change, and delete user accounts. Individual users of a network usually have their own user account. The server keeps track of who has logged in and is usually capable of recording which resources the logged-in user requested. In Chapter 8 you find out how to create and work with user accounts in Windows NT.

SECURITY Since a server knows who you are when you log in, it can keep track of the resources you have permission to use. The network administrator can assign permission to use each different network resource to each user. This allows users to have private storage and keep sensitive information such as finances away from prying eyes. Chapter 8 shows you how you can use the log in security mechanisms and other security features of a network operating system to create a secure network environment.

CENTRALIZED LICENSING Software licensing laws allow companies to buy only as many copies of a program as are in use at one time, no matter how many people may eventually use it. This is called *like-a-book licensing* because the software is treated as though it were a copy of a book. For example, just as a book can be located on a central bookshelf and a user can check it out and later return it to make it available to another user, more than one user can use software. The company has to pay only for the number of copies that are actually in use simultaneously.

The only catch is that the company must take measures to monitor exactly how many copies are in use. This is nearly impossible if individual computers are used. However, if the software is loaded on a server, the server can simply keep track of the number of users using the software. By centralizing the licensing on the file server, companies can fully comply with copyright law while paying only for the software they actually use.

DATA PROTECTION Again because most important data is stored on servers, they make a convenient point to implement data protection. Data protection refers to any measures taken to protect the integrity of the information stored on the server. There are many ways to do this:

- Archiving

- Fault-tolerant file system

- Uninterruptible power supplies

- Replication

These data protection features are implemented by most network operating systems.

Archiving, or backing up your data, is the most common way to protect data. Archiving works by making a copy of all the information stored on a computer. This copy is then kept for safekeeping. The copy does not usually need to be accessed, so slow offline storage methods such as magnetic tape are used because they are very inexpensive. Many backup tapes can be made of server information and stored in various places.

If a server becomes damaged or destroyed, a backup tape can be restored into a new server, which will then contain all the data files of the old server.

Fault-tolerant file systems are components of a network operating system that stores files in a special way to ensure that the operating system will not corrupt them. For instance, most computer operating systems, such as MS-DOS, will leave a file in an inconsistent state if the computer loses power or a program crashes while the file is open. Server operating systems, such as Windows NT, complete the operation that writes a file to a disk only after the operating system knows that the complete file has been written. This way, a partial file (which can confuse the operating system and cause further data loss) is never stored on a hard drive.

Fault tolerance for file systems also works by storing some redundant information on an extra hard disk drive. Network file servers let you add an additional hard disk that contains redundant information. That way, if any one hard disk fails, you can restore the information contained on the failed drive from the redundant drive.

An *uninterruptible power supply* (UPS) is a smart battery that powers a network file server. UPSs are powered by normal power, and the server plugs into them. If power fails, the UPS keeps the server running and sends a signal telling it to shut down properly. This allows the server to close all open files and complete any operations it may have pending. Then the server closes down the operating system and the UPS shuts it off.

Replication is the process of making a copy of the data stored on one server on another server. This allows the server with the copied data to take over immediately if the first server goes down unexpectedly.

MULTITASKING AND MULTIPROCESSING Servers must usually respond to a large number of clients. For this reason they must be fast, and they should be able to do more than one thing at a time. These requirements are made easier by multitasking and multiprocessing.

Multitasking refers to executing multiple tasks at the same time. Actually, CPUs cannot run more than one process at a time, but they can switch between processes so quickly that they appear to be running simultaneously.

The ability of a CPU to switch tasks quickly also allows processes to operate at the same time, which gives the illusion of having a number of slower CPUs, each dedicated to a specific process. A side effect of this process is that time spent waiting for something to happen isn't wasted. This makes it easy to handle multiple client requests, perform a backup, and create the redundant information for a fault-tolerant file system all at the same time.

Multiprocessing is useful if you have too many processes multitasking at once and the server becomes sluggish. If you can't pare down the number of running processes or upgrade to a faster CPU, good network operating systems will allow you to add more CPUs. The network operating system then parcels out processes to different CPUs, managing which CPU is executing which task. This allows multiple CPUs to work in the same computer and on the same file storage.

Peers as Servers

Some server software is more sophisticated than others. For instance, every Windows 95 client can operate as a server, sharing hard drives and peripheral devices; however, Windows NT Server is optimized for speed and efficiency in satisfying network requests and provides additional features such as security and data integrity.

When a computer shares some resources but is not dedicated to sharing resources (perhaps someone uses it as a client computer also), the computer is a peer. Peers both share and request network resources.

Most network and client operating systems are capable of being used in a peer network environment.

REAL WORLD PROBLEMS

Your boss tells you he doesn't want to get a server because a company he used to work for had one that crashed all the time.

- Which features of modern network operating systems can you point out that reduce this risk?

You are installing a network for a small company that is on a tight budget. They ask if they can have a very powerful workstation they already own converted into a server.

- Is this possible? If so, what hardware and software will be required?

Your boss asks if you can think of any way to save on software costs in the company. Your company uses a number of different packages, such as word processors, spreadsheets, database software, and accounting packages. Everyone uses them periodically, but only occasionally does more than one user actually have the same program running at the same time.

- What is your response?

(continued)

REAL WORLD PROBLEMS (CONTINUED)

Your boss gets fired. The company vice president comes to you and asks if you can make sure your ex-boss can't access network files or data.

- What can you tell the vice president?

You are consulting to a traditional accounting firm. The senior partner resists automating their record storage and operations because he doesn't trust computers not to lose the data.

- Which features of server-based networks can you point out that will prevent data loss?

You notice that your departmental server has become bogged down with its normal tasks. Some users are beginning to report slow responses when accessing files and printing. You check the performance monitor and determine that the bottleneck must be the CPU in the server. There is plenty of storage space left. Your company doesn't have quite enough money to buy a new server, but you could upgrade the computer. You already have the fastest microprocessor available.

- What can you do to improve CPU performance?

Windows NT Server Installation

YOU WILL NEED to know how to install the server operating system on the server computer. This is because the server software is usually installed when a network is put together, unlike the software for a client personal computer, which often comes preinstalled by the manufacturer. You will also want to know how the installation process works; you may have to reinstall the server software because of hardware failure or to upgrade to a newer version of the operating system.

The remainder of this chapter assumes you will be installing Windows NT Server as your network operating system; however, the issues presented are the same issues you would face when installing any other network operating system.

You should prepare or determine several things in advance to make the installation process go smoothly:

- Hardware Compatibility List
- Server naming information
- Server responsibilities
- Hard drive partitioning
- Network adapter card settings
- TCP/IP installation information

The operating system installation process is not the same every time you install the operating system. It varies, depending on the following:

- The CPU(s) and memory in the server computer
- The number and partitioning of the hard drives in the computer
- The jobs the server will perform on the network
- Whether the software is being installed for the first time or being upgraded
- The hardware devices and adapter cards installed in the computer
- The size and type of network on which the server will be installed
- The type of file system(s) the server will use

The Hardware Compatibility List

You must first determine that the hardware (processor, adapter cards, peripheral devices, and so on) will operate with the server software. As discussed in Chapter 3, the Hardware Compatibility List (HCL) for the operating system will describe the hardware components the operating system vendor (in this case, Microsoft) has tested to work properly with the operating system.

If you have a device that is not on the Hardware Compatibility List, it may still work properly, but you will probably have to determine that yourself, either by contacting the manufacturer of the device or by testing it in your system. Microsoft, and most operating system vendors, will provide technical support only for devices in their Hardware Compatibility List.

Server Naming Information

Whichever server operating system you install, you will need to give it a name. Providing a name allows client stations to identify the server on the network and find the services the server shares on the network.

<table>
<tr>
<td>

Microsoft
✓ **Exam**
Objective

</td>
<td>

Implement a NetBIOS naming scheme for all computers on a given network.

</td>
</tr>
</table>

Microsoft networks use a scheme of unique identifiers, called NetBIOS names, for printers, workstations, servers, domains, and workgroups. These names can be up to 15 characters long, plus a sixteenth character, not visible to the user, that is assigned by the system based on services and functions.

In addition, you need to give a name to your network. This allows clients and servers to distinguish between network environments, so you can set up different networks for different parts of your company. Even in a small network you may need two network names—one for your server-based network (the domain name) and one for the Windows 95 peer-to-peer network (the workgroup name). As you install the server software, you will be asked for the name of the server.

Before you begin installing servers and naming computers, you should come up with a coherent plan to keep track of networked resources. Often, networks are brought online chaotically, and servers are named as if they were pets. While this is fun for the network administrator, it's not fun for new users who are trying to figure out where certain files might reside.

The primary responsibility of a network administrator is to make network resources as easily available as possible. Part of this responsibility is coming up with a coherent naming scheme for all network resources.

To make a naming scheme, think about what is important in your organization. Are resources divided up by department? By use? Is there an obvious name you should use?

For instance, if you have a server dedicated to the accounting department, "ACCOUNTING" might be a good name for it. Or, if the server only stores X-ray files, "XRAYS" might be a good name for it. A printer loaded with invoices should probably be called "INVOICE PRINTER."

The rule for naming conventions is consistency and uniqueness. If you name one server by department or location, name them all by department or location. If you find you can't, that's a good indication that department or location naming isn't the right scheme for your situation.

It's okay to change schemes based on major resource types. For instance, it's acceptable to name servers by department but printers by function, such as "Invoices" or "Checks," because most printers are used exclusively within departments anyway, whereas servers are accessed throughout the organization. For this reason, names must be unique within domains, and should be unique throughout your organization. A "CHECKS" printer in the accounting domain and a "CHECKS" printer in the finance domain will most certainly be accidentally accessed incorrectly by someone.

Create a set of rules for naming shared resources. Give each department or location or purpose or function a unique mnemonic, and combine them to create unique names. For instance, "ACCSRV" would be the accounting server, whereas "MKTLPR" would be the marketing laser printer, and "ACCIPR" would be the accounting invoices printer. When users are familiar with your naming scheme, they will know exactly what your named resources refer to when they see them in lists.

Small organizations should create naming schemes with an eye towards the future. Naming your server "SERVER" because it's the only one you have leaves you out in the cold when you add a second one. "PRIMARY" might be a bit better, but your organization location or even "HEADQUARTERS" could easily support the addition of more servers down the line without changing your naming scheme.

Server Roles

Many servers can participate in the same network. In the past, this meant that user accounts were scattered around the various servers and that a separate account had to be maintained on each server a user attached to. Obviously, this was inconvenient.

Microsoft avoids this problem in Windows NT by allowing servers grouped together in a domain to share login information without intervention from the user. If a user attempts to use a resource and the resource server has not logged in the user, that resource server will ask the server the user logged in to whether the user has permission to use the resource. If this server responds favorably, the resource server allows the user access. This procedure is invisible to the user.

REAL WORLD PROBLEMS

You must install two hundred computers in a new network for your new company headquarters. There will be three physical LANs in you headquarters, reflecting your company's division into Acquisitions, Financing, and Operations. Each LAN will be linked to the other LANs. Each will have its own server, and approximately one-third of the client computers. Each will have its own set of printers. You expect that each department will grow in the number of server computers and the number of client computers. You also expect to add another LAN for Financing sometime in the future.

■ Implement a NetBIOS naming scheme for this network.

You have just installed a network in your home office, linking you and your husband's Windows 95 computers and your son's Windows NT Workstation computer. Your son has a scanner and a printer hooked up to his computer, and you have a printer and a fax-modem hooked up to your computer.

■ Implement a NetBIOS naming scheme for this network.

In Windows NT, users all log into a central computer called a domain controller. Domain controllers contain a complete copy of the user accounts for each user on the network. There are two types of domain controllers: the primary domain controller (PDC), which contains the master list of users and performs the login function for each user, and backup domain controllers (BDC), which keep copies of the user list and substitute for the primary domain controller if it is not available.

Primary and backup domain controllers are simply regular servers with special roles. Servers do not have to be primary or backup domain controllers—they can simply share resources on the network.

You will have to determine the role of your server—PDC, BDC, or simple server—when you install the network operating system.

Partitioning the Hard Drive

Before you install the network operating system, you will need to partition the computer's hard disks. Partitioning is the process of dividing the space on the hard disks for the operating system, user files, shared files, programs, and other purposes, as illustrated in Figure 6.2.

FIGURE 6.2

The server's hard disk can be partitioned into system and user areas.

Tower box

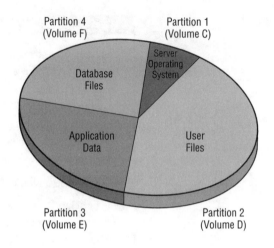

Server Hard Drive
Partitions

At a minimum, you will have as many partitions as you have hard disk drives in the computer. You may wish to divide a large hard drive into smaller partitions. One reason to do this is to keep the storage requirements of one service, such as user files or e-mail, from overflowing all the available storage space and crashing the system. Another reason is to separate data according to purpose—for instance, to keep operating system files in one partition and application files in another. This way, when the operating system is reinstalled, the application files will not be affected.

Configuring the Network Adapter Card

Servers communicate on the network through their network adapter cards. When you install Windows NT, you tell it which type of network adapter card you have, and you may need to provide a driver for the card.

Depending on the type of card you use, you may have to provide the IRQ and port settings for the card. Your adapter card manual will tell you whether or not you will need this information and how to set or determine what the settings are.

You will also have to determine which network protocols you want to use. Windows NT gives you three choices:

- **TCP/IP:** Good for large networks that use routers, networks directly connected to the Internet, and experienced network administrators. TPC/IP is the most versatile, but slowest, transport protocol provided with Windows NT. Installing TCP/IP requires you to know the TCP/IP number for your server.

- **IPX:** Good for large routed networks and networks connected to Novell NetWare file servers, IPX is fast and easy to set up.

- **NetBEUI:** Good for small non-routed networks or workgroups, Net-BEUI is the fastest and easiest to setup of all the transport protocols.

TCP/IP Installation

TCP/IP requires a little more information than the other network transports when you install the server software, especially if you intend to attach your Windows NT server to the Internet.

If you check the TCP/IP option while installing Windows NT, you are asked to provide the following information in the Microsoft TCP/IP Properties window (see Figure 6.3):

- **IP address:** Every computer in a TCP/IP network requires an IP address. An IP address is four numbers (between 0 and 255, inclusive) separated by periods. 128.110.121.45 is a valid IP address.

- **Subnet mask:** The subnet mask distinguishes the portion of the IP address that is the network ID from the portion that is the station ID. The subnet mask 255.255.0.0, when applied to the IP address given above, would identify the network ID as 128.110 and the station ID as 121.45. All stations in the same LAN should have the same network ID but different station IDs.

- **Default gateway:** A TCP/IP network must have a *gateway* to communicate beyond the LAN identified by the network ID. A gateway is a computer or electronic device that is connected to two different networks and can move TCP/IP data from one to the other. If your TCP/IP network has more than one LAN or if you are connecting to the Internet, you will need to know the IP address of the gateway that will transfer TCP/IP data in

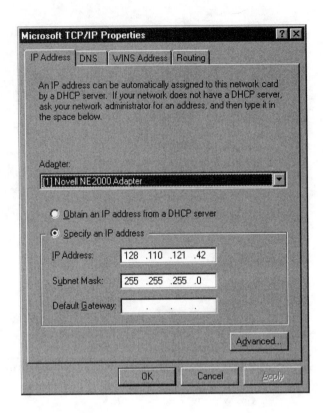

and out of your LAN. A single LAN that is not connected to other LANs
does not require a default gateway setting.

- **Automatic versus manual configuration:** If your LAN is part of a larger
  network that uses TCP/IP and also provides a network service called the
  dynamic host configuration protocol (DHCP), you can set the server's
  TCP/IP settings to be configured automatically. You do this by checking
  the Enable DHCP box in the TCP/IP settings panel. This setting indicates
  to the server that it should query a central server for its TCP/IP settings.
  Otherwise, you will have to provide the above settings yourself for each
  network interface card in the server computer that will be using the
  TCP/IP protocol.

You can install TCP/IP later by double-clicking the Network icon in the
Control Panel, clicking the Protocols tab, and then selecting Add. Selecting the
TCP/IP option from the list of protocols you see at this point will allow you to

install the TCP/IP services. You can reconfigure the TCP/IP settings by double-clicking the network icon in the Control Panel, clicking the Protocols tab, and selecting the TCP/IP service from the list of protocols you see.

REAL WORLD PROBLEMS

You are installing the first server for your company.

- Which server role is most appropriate for this server?

You are installing a server for a small recycling business. After interviewing the customer, you determine that the network will most likely never grow beyond a single server, that Internet access is not required, and that the company does not want to pay for network administration costs once the network is installed.

- Which transport protocol is most appropriate?

You are designing a network for a computer software design group with many offices around the country. They tell you they would like to connect the servers in their various offices using the Internet.

- Which transport protocol is most appropriate?

Network Printing

THE PREVIOUS SECTION showed you how to install the Windows NT operating system. This section introduces network printing and shows you how to install, configure, and share a network printer.

About Network Printing

A network printer accepts requests to print documents from redirectors on client computers. A network printer can be a printer attached to a server, a printer attached to a client computer, or a printer attached directly to the network with a network print interface. The printer prints the documents, but the network software on the server makes the printer visible to the network and accepts print jobs for the printer to print.

The network software also *spools* the print jobs (see Figure 6.4). Because many computers may print to the network printer at the same time, the *spooler* on the server computer holds print jobs in its memory or on its hard drive while they are waiting to be printed. The print jobs are usually printed in the order in which they were received.

FIGURE 6.4

The print server can spool print jobs from several client computers at the same time while printing them one at a time.

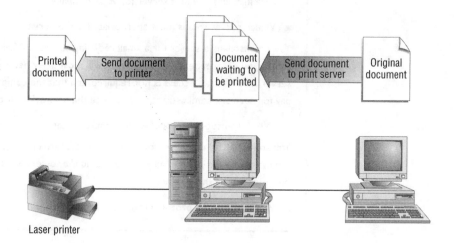

Because many computers may print to the network printer at the same time, the *spooler* on the server computer holds print jobs in its memory or on its hard drive while they are waiting to be printed.

Print Drivers

There are many different types of printers, each with its own printing language (sometimes called a page description language, or PDL). Hewlett-Packard LaserJet printers have different command codes from Epson or Olivetti printers (although many printers can be configured to understand Hewlett-Packard Graphics Language, or HPGL). PostScript printers speak a very different and very powerful page description language.

Because of this, computers must have print drivers to allow application software to communicate with the printer. The print driver translates printing operations from the application into the language the printer understands.

A print server is not concerned with which language a printer speaks. Its only job is to connect client print requests to the printer. For this reason each client that will print to a specific printer on the network should have a print driver for that type of printer. If you have three identical HP printers and one PostScript printer on your network, you should have two print drivers on each of your client computers—one for the HP printers and one for PostScript printers. These drivers may reside on the server, in which case the server will need to be configured to download the drivers to the client automatically, or you will need to install the drivers manually on the client.

The server must also have a print driver for the printer in order to spool print requests to the printer. The print driver allows the server to determine fault conditions in the printer, such as out-of-paper or toner-low conditions.

Sharing a Printer

Sharing a printer in Windows NT is much the same as sharing a file resource. You must provide a unique network name for the printer, identify its printer driver to Windows NT, and select the port to which the printer is connected. Additionally, you may want to provide a description of the printer and a description of its location (such as Third Floor or Marketing). Figure 6.5 shows the Add Printer Wizard for Windows NT Server.

FIGURE 6.5

The Add Printer Wizard allows you to configure a printer to be shared on the network.

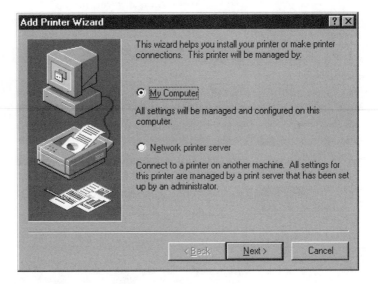

Connecting to a Shared Printer

Once a printer has been made available to the network, it is a simple matter to connect a client computer to it. In Windows 95, the Printers option under the Start button's Settings option has an icon called Add Printer. Add Printer is a Wizard that walks you through the steps of adding a printer either locally or on a network.

When you are given the choice of Local Printer or Network Printer, you can choose Network Printer and specify the printer you prepared according to the preceding section, "Sharing a Printer." You specify the printer by giving the name of the server it is attached to (preceded by two backslashes), followed by the name of the printer (preceded by one backslash). For instance, \\server\hplj4 is a valid printer name.

You can also browse the network for the printer (see Figure 6.6). The Network Printer option in the Add Printer Wizard opens the Connect to Printer window, which shows you the computers on the network and the printers attached to them that have been shared. If you select one of the printers displayed, the information is entered for you.

FIGURE 6.6

The Network Printer option opens a Connect to Printer window that shows you the shared printers on the network and allows you to select one.

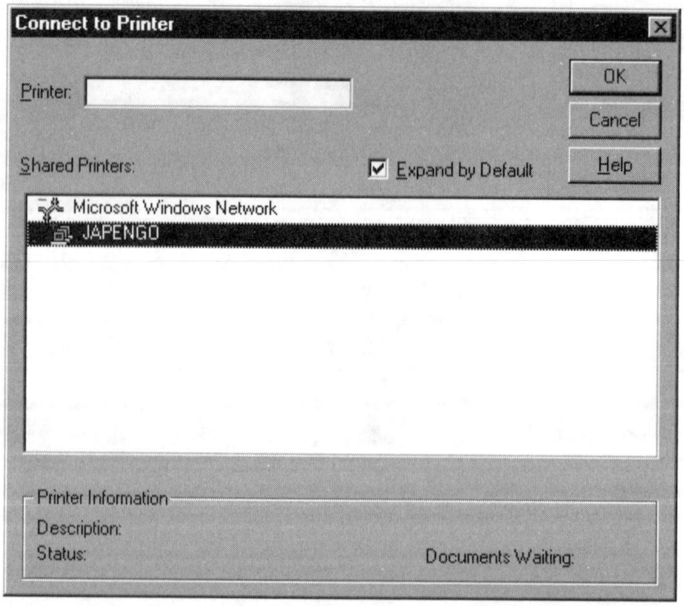

Sharing Fax Modems

A fax server provides shared faxing, just as a print server provides shared printing. In fact, a fax server can be treated just like a shared printer; a document can be printed directly to it, and the document image can be sent out electronically over the facsimile machine without ever having been printed on paper. This is less wasteful of paper supplies and much more convenient than printing the document and then taking it to a shared conventional fax machine.

A fax server can also receive faxes and store them electronically for review. Useful faxes can then be printed or forwarded to the appropriate recipient, and the rest can be discarded without ever being set on paper.

REAL WORLD PROBLEMS

When one of the users on your network prints to the central laser printer, nothing but strange characters appear. The printer works fine for everyone else.

- What is wrong? How can you fix it?

You have six printers attached to your network. Four are HP LaserJet 4 laser printers, and two are HP 855C color ink jet printers.

- How many printer drivers do you need?

All the employees in your company have fax modems installed in their computers, and a single phone line running to all of them. Occasionally, users interrupt each other's faxes by accidentally trying to fax out while someone else is on the line.

- What is the best solution to this problem?

Network Applications

NOT ONLY CAN a network help you do things more efficiently than you can with a stand-alone computer, such as print documents and send faxes, it makes possible new types of applications that require a network to operate. Network applications such as e-mail, scheduling, and groupware can make your business more productive by automating tasks that would otherwise take valuable time, and also by providing new ways for the people in your business to communicate.

E-Mail

Electronic mail (e-mail) is an application or suite of applications that allow users connected to the same network to exchange memoranda and files without having to be logged in at the same time. Users can compose e-mail messages and send them to the mailbox (sometimes called the message box) of anyone with an e-mail account on the network by including that user's e-mail address in the address line of the e-mail message. E-mail mimics the way regular postal mail works, but because it is transferred electronically between e-mail servers (post offices), it is nearly instantaneous, free of per-use charges, and does not waste paper.

As with regular postal mail, users must periodically check their mailboxes. Some e-mail programs have the ability to pop up a notice when new e-mail arrives. Figure 6.7 shows Microsoft Exchange, the e-mail program included with Windows 95.

FIGURE 6.7

Network users can send messages to each other with e-mail.

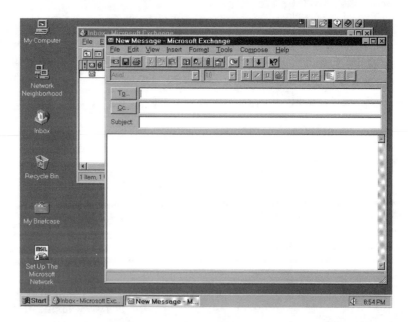

Components of an E-Mail system

A single application on your computer can provide the functionality of e-mail if it checks a central database stored on a server or on your client computer for new mail. This functionality can also be supplied by a client application that queries an e-mail server for mail functions. Small LAN and peer-to-peer networks typically rely on the first type, and larger networks and the Internet rely on the second type. Some e-mail applications, such as Microsoft Exchange, can work in either capacity.

E-Mail Clients

E-mail clients provide a view of each user's mailbox. They allow users to:

- Compose e-mail

- Read e-mail

- Forward e-mail messages to other users

- Save or delete e-mail messages

- Attach files to messages

- Request a return receipt

- Check for new mail (e-mail server systems only)

- Provide an "address book" or directory of e-mail users

E-Mail Servers

E-mail servers store and transfer messages on the network. Think of e-mail servers as the post offices of e-mail. In fact, the primary Internet e-mail server protocol is called the Post Office Protocol (POP). E-mail servers also typically act as e-mail gateways to convert the message contents and attachments between different proprietary e-mail systems.

You may need to convert mail from one system to another. For instance, your network may use MHS and you want to receive mail from the Internet, which uses SMTP, or you are using an X.400 mail system and you need to connect to the MHS mail on a Novell network.

A gateway (see Figure 6.8) is a device that converts mail from one standard to another. It is usually a dedicated computer, although it can be a program that is run on the network server.

FIGURE 6.8

A gateway converts mail from one standard to another.

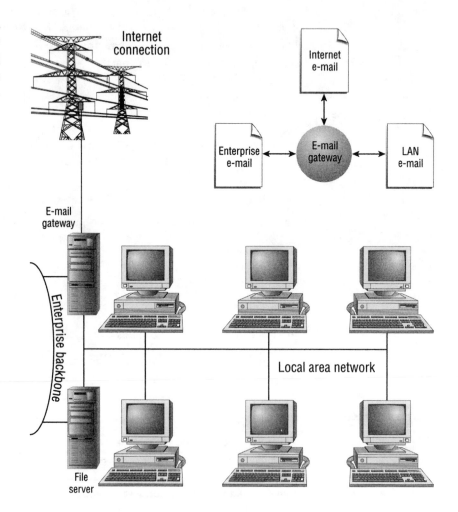

E-mail Protocols

As with any client-server application, e-mail software has communication standards in regard to transmitting messages and attachments. Unfortunately, many proprietary standards exist, although the Internet mail protocols are becoming dominant.

POP and SMTP

Internet mail uses the Post Office Protocol (POP), which describes how e-mail clients interact with e-mail servers, and the Simple Mail Transport Protocol (SMTP), which describes how e-mail servers transfer e-mail messages to their intended recipients.

X.400 and X.500

Some cross-platform e-mail systems use the ITU (International Telephony Union, formerly the CCITT) X.400 messaging protocol and the X.500 directory services protocol to implement mail standards. These protocols are international standards, but they are not the predominant e-mail protocols.

MHS

Message Handling Service (MHS) is the Novell NetWare e-mail standard. It is similar to X.400, but it does not follow X.400 standards. Many older local area networks use the MHS e-mail standard.

MAPI

Message Application Programming Interface (MAPI) is the Microsoft standard for messaging in Microsoft networks and is the internal mail standard used by Exchange. Microsoft Exchange now supports both MAPI and the Internet protocols, but it uses MAPI for it's internal storage and messages generated by applications.

Group Scheduling

Another of the amazingly productive tools networks support is group scheduling. Essentially an outgrowth of e-mail, group scheduling allows groups of users to share their diaries and calendars on a network so that everyone in the organization can easily tell what commitments others have on their time. This allows meetings to be scheduled for times when everyone involved is available and provides a systematic way of unobtrusively alerting users to upcoming events. Group scheduling also allows users to view users' published schedules.

Most scheduling programs, such as Microsoft Schedule+, simulate the look and interface of a paper-based day timer. These programs typically have a daily calendar of events and meetings; alarms; and a to-do list. The alarms can usually be set to provide a visual and audible signal that alerts users to upcoming events.

Network-enabled or group schedulers can automatically find times when everyone in a group is free to schedule meetings and other group activities.

Groupware

Groupware is a term that encompasses any mechanism for group interaction that is more complex than e-mail. Examples of groupware include

- Bulletin board systems
- Internet News
- Interactive conferences
- Microsoft Exchange
- Lotus Notes

Groupware also encompasses systems that make it possible for members of a group to cooperatively create documents, to track revisions of documents and changes from one revision to another, to track who has and has not seen a document, and to keep track of other types of group project information.

Group Messaging

Group messaging systems go beyond simple e-mail by allowing several people to join a conversation. Messages on a particular topic are presented together, and you can join the conversation on that topic or establish a new topic to discuss.

All the messages posted on a particular topic are usually kept by the group messaging software. This way, another person can join the conversation and know what has already been discussed. Bulletin board systems and Internet News are examples of group messaging.

Cooperative Document Construction

Traditional applications, such as word processors and spreadsheets, can take on aspects of groupware when they make it possible for several people to work simultaneously on a document. For instance, using Microsoft Word and Windows 95 Object Linking and Embedding, one person can prepare the graphics parts of a document while another produces a spreadsheet view of data to be included and a third individual writes the document text and links the work of the others into the main document (see Figure 6.9).

Document Exchange and Tracking Revisions

Some groupware products can use e-mail and other methods of document exchange and will keep track of document revisions and document routing (who has or has not seen the document). This way, distributed groups can work cooperatively on a document even when a direct network connection is not available.

Shared Network Applications

In a network environment the applications a user uses can reside on either the client computer's hard disk or the server's shared hard disk. You should know the many advantages of storing the applications on the server, as well as some of the disadvantages.

Applications can be divided into two types: stand-alone and network aware. (All groupware programs are network-aware applications.)

FIGURE 6.9

Several people using groupware can work on a document at the same time.

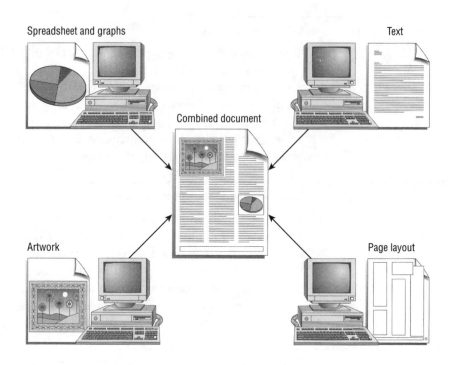

Spreadsheet and graphs

Text

Combined document

Artwork

Page layout

Stand-Alone Applications

Your network can benefit from storing stand-alone applications on the server even when the applications make no direct use of the network. A stand-alone application is one that operates on a stand-alone computer (a computer not connected to a network) the same way it operates on a computer connected to a network.

These are the benefits of storing the application on the server:

- **Lower licensing costs:** It is often less expensive to purchase a site license for software for a certain number of stations than it is to purchase that many copies of the software. It is also possible, when the software is on the server, to buy just as many licenses as users will simultaneously use instead of the (larger) total number that would have to be installed on all the clients, even when that software was not being used, if the software was stored on the client computer's hard drive.

- **Version control:** When one copy of the application resides on the server, you can be sure everyone is using the same version of the software.

- **Administration:** It is easier to install the software once on the server than once each for every client on the network. If you install the software on the server, when you replace, upgrade, or otherwise alter the software, you will have to do so in only one place.

One drawback of storing applications on the server is that when the network goes down, the applications are not available to the client computers, as they would be if they were stored on the client computer's local hard drive.

Network-Aware Applications

The same advantages and disadvantages of installing stand-alone applications on the server apply to network-aware applications. Network-aware applications are programs that adapt to the presence of a network. Some of the ways an application may do this are by:

- Locking files so only one user at a time may modify them

- Providing for security at the application level so you can give users different levels of access

- Connecting to e-mail services to exchange application data among users

Installing Network Applications

Most network applications have special requirements for installation on a network server, but most modern applications automatically take care of these requirements when they are installed. Be aware that you will probably need to find the application directory and set user permissions on that directory manually, however, because the installation software may not have access to your group accounts. Check the documentation for each network application for any special installation requirements.

REAL WORLD PROBLEMS

You work for a bank that has an interoffice memo system run by couriers who make mail runs past each employee twice a day and transfer memos between branches once a day. You've just installed a new network.

■ Which network application can you use to make this process more efficient?

You are setting up an e-mail system to exchange mail with the Internet.

■ Which e-mail protocols should you use?

Your boss tells you that employees are responding to her attempts to plan weekly meetings just by using e-mail. She asks you if there's a better way to coordinate the activities of many busy people.

■ Which network application do you recommend?

Your company has branches in London, Paris, New York, Sydney, Tokyo, and Los Angeles. The company president would like to cut the expense of the weekly executive staff meeting currently being conducted by conference call to these locations by using the Internet, but wants to retain the immediacy of conversation that e-mail does not provide.

■ Which class of network applications do you recommend?

You have a client who is debating whether to store applications locally on users' computers or on the network. She asks you for advice.

■ What do you tell her the advantages of server-based applications are? What are the disadvantages?

Client-Server

THE TERM *CLIENT-SERVER* can describe hardware, in which case it is referring to network servers and client computers, or it can refer to a way of organizing software applications and services on a network. Client-server computing is a powerful way of constructing programs on a network. In order to describe its advantages and how it works, we will first describe two alternatives to client-server computing:

- Centralized computing
- Client computing with central file storage

Centralized Computing

Centralized computing originated with mainframe computers and time-sharing. The principle behind centralized computing is that a central computer executes a program, such as a database or a transaction-processing program (for instance, an airline reservations system or a bank records program), and remote terminals merely display data on a screen and convey keyboard data back to the central computer.

In modern networks, personal computers can perform the role of dumb terminals. With Windows software, the PC can appear to the central computer as many terminals, each virtual terminal accessing different data or performing a separate transaction on the mainframe.

In centralized computing it is the central computer that does all the work. The data resides on the central computer, and the program executes on the central computer. The personal computer or dumb terminal only displays screen data and accepts keystrokes for the central computer to process. Centralized computing does not fully use the capabilities of today's powerful network clients. Figure 6.10 illustrates centralized computing.

Client Computing with Central File Storage

At the opposite end of the spectrum from centralized computing is client computing with central file storage (see Figure 6.11). In this way of organizing an application, the client computer does all the work. A central file server stores, but that is all.

Client computers cooperate to ensure that central files are not corrupted by attempts by several computers to access them at the same time. When a client computer needs to perform an operation, the file is transferred to the client computer to perform the operation. Two examples of this type of application are networked database programs that do not use a SQL (Structured Query Language) server and any network-aware application that does not communicate with a special program executing on the server, such as network scheduling programs and groupware.

F I G U R E 6.10

Centralized computing
uses dumb terminals to
display information to the
user. All programs are run
on a central computer.

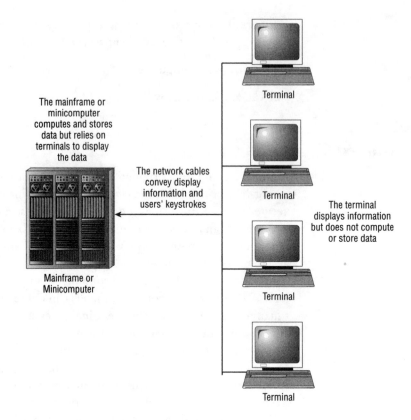

The mainframe or
minicomputer
computes and stores
data but relies on
terminals to display
the data

The network cables
convey display
information and
users' keystrokes

Mainframe or
Minicomputer

Terminal

Terminal

The terminal
displays information
but does not compute
or store data

Terminal

Terminal

F I G U R E 6.11

Client computing with
central file storage stores
the files on the server, but
all programs are run on
the client computers.

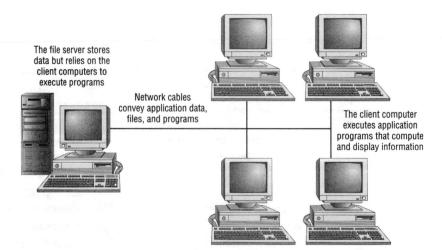

The file server stores
data but relies on the
client computers to
execute programs

Network cables
convey application data,
files, and programs

The client computer
executes application
programs that compute
and display information

While it more fully exploits the capabilities of client computers and provides a richer and more customizable environment for the user, this type of program can place heavy demands on the network if the data files the program works with are large. It also takes time to transmit data from the server to the client, process the data, and transfer it back to the server so other network programs can access the data.

The Client-Server Model

The client-server model combines the advantages of both the centralized computing model and the client model of computing. It does this by performing the operations that are best executed by a central computer on the file server and performing those operations that are best done close to the user on the client computer (see Figure 6.12). The client-server model works best when many people need access to large amounts of data. Simply stated, a client-server system is any system in which the client computer makes a request over a network to a server computer that then satisfies the request.

FIGURE 6.12

Client-server splits a program between the client and the server. Each performs the tasks it does best.

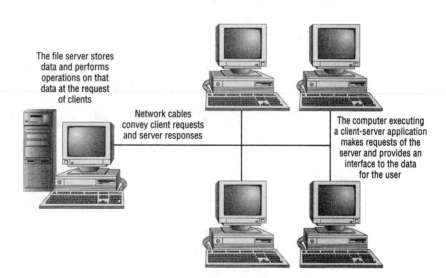

The file server stores data and performs operations on that data at the request of clients

Network cables convey client requests and server responses

The computer executing a client-server application makes requests of the server and provides an interface to the data for the user

The Client

When you use a client-server system, what you see is the client, or front end. It presents the interface you use to manipulate or search for data. The request you make by manipulating windows, menus, check boxes, and so on, is translated into a compact form that the client transmits over the network for the server to perform.

One example of a front end is Microsoft Access when it is used with a SQL back end. (You can also use Access without a SQL back end but it doesn't scale well to provide high performance when large numbers of applications query the database.) Access displays tables in windows or in forms you can browse. It allows you to modify and search the tables in an easy-to-use graphical environment. All the actual data manipulation, however, occurs on the SQL server. Access translates all the database operations into SQL for the server to perform. The results of the operations are transmitted back to Access to display in an intuitive, graphical form.

SQL is not limited to database programs such as Microsoft Access. User programs such as Microsoft Excel can use SQL to query the back-end database server for values to use in spreadsheet calculations. Program tools allow custom programs to store and retrieve data in server-based databases. Query tools provide direct access to the SQL data.

The Server

The server is where data operations in a client-server system occur. The central computer can service many client requests quickly and efficiently, which is the traditional advantage of centralized computing. The central computer can also provide enhanced security by performing only authorized operations on the data.

Back-end database software is optimized to perform searches and sorts, and the back-end computer is often more powerful than the front-end computer.

REAL WORLD PROBLEMS

Your company uses a job-tracking database developed under Microsoft Access. The database has become quite large, and when a lot of users are accessing the database it takes quite a while to search for information in the system.

■ What can be done to speed up the database system?

You are consulting to an industrial engine parts distributor who uses an old mainframe system for inventory, order entry, and invoicing. Although this company's software works just fine, it usually takes new users about six months to become familiar with the system, and many mistakes are made because the character-based system is hard to use. They like the central storage and speed of their central computer, but they have heard that local area networks with personal computers are the wave of the future.

■ Which architecture do you recommend they migrate to?

Review

A SERVER REQUIRES A more powerful computer than a client. Features such as preemptive multitasking, support for multiprocessing, a log-based file system, and support for RISC-based CPUs make an operating system more effective as a network server. Hardware driver software must be specifically written to work with a server operating system, so you should check the Hardware Compatibility List to be sure it will work with your operating system.

Client-server computing is a way of organizing programs on a network so the best aspects of both centralized and personal computing are emphasized. The server and client cooperate to provide the illusion that remote services are local to the computer. A redirector intercepts file and print requests and sends network requests out to the server. The server responds with the requested file or prints the document.

A network supports programs such as e-mail, groupware, and group scheduling that were not nearly as effective on stand-alone computers. By taking advantage of network connectivity, network applications can provide new ways for the people in your business to communicate.

Review Questions

1. Historically, computing installations used a single, very powerful computer for processing. What type of computing model does this situation represent?

   A. Client/Server computing

   B. Standalone computing

   C. Distributed computing

   D. Centralized computing

2. You are expanding your Windows NT network to include a second server. To ensure that the new server will act as a Domain Controller if the Primary Domain Controller fails, how should you install Windows NT?

   A. As a Standby Domain Controller

   B. As a Standalone Server

   C. As a Backup Domain Controller

   D. As a Primary Domain Controller

3. Suppose the following situation exists: You administer the network for a large, multinational corporation. You must design a naming system that will scale easily across the wide-area network as it is implemented. The total network covers 56 offices in 14 countries, with a total of 15,000 clients and 75 servers.

   Required result: Design a naming system which uniquely identifies each of the clients and servers.

   Optional desired results: The naming system for clients should include the primary user's logon name. The naming system for servers should describe their function as well as their location.

   Proposed solution: Assign each client and server a 12-character random, unique, alphanumeric name. Track the list of computers and names via a Microsoft Access database.

   What result does the proposed solution provide?

   A. The proposed solution produces the required result and produces all of the optional desired results.

   B. The proposed solution produces the required result but produces only one of the optional desired results.

   C. The proposed solution produces the required result but does not produce any of the optional desired results.

   D. The proposed solution does not produce the required result.

4. Your database, which was originally created in Microsoft Access, is stored on the Windows NT file server so that multiple people have access. However, as the database has grown and more people have required access, you've noticed that performance has suffered. Which of the following steps can you take to increase the performance of your database?

   A. Import the database into SQL and run MS-SQL Server on the file server.

   B. Install a faster network card in the server.

   C. Increase the memory in the client computers.

   D. Buy copies of Access for workstations. Import the database into each workstation and keep the master database on the server.

5. For computers to communicate on a network using TCP/IP, which of the following settings must be unique for each computer?

   A. IP Address

   B. Subnet Mask

   C. Default Gateway

   D. WINS Server Address

6. It is possible to automatically configure TCP/IP settings on computers running Microsoft operating systems. Which of the following protocols perform this function?

   A. ICMP

   B. SMTP

   C. RARP

   D. DHCP

7. Suppose the following situation exists: Your company has recently merged with another company of approximately the same size. Both companies have been running peer-to-peer networks, but are looking for new ideas. The companies are located in different cities and must have access to each other's files. In addition, a database has been created merging the client information for both companies that must be accessed by all employees.

Required result: Recommend a centralized network model for the new company.

Optional desired results: The network needs to accommodate extensive security. The network must have room for growth.

Proposed solution: Implement a Windows NT domain multi-server network using user- and group-level security.

Which result does the proposed solution produce? Choose one:

A. The proposed solution produces the required result and produces both of the optional desired results.

B. The proposed solution produces the required result and produces only one of the optional desired results.

C. The proposed solution produces the required result but does not produce any of the optional desired results.

D. The proposed solution does not produce the required result.

8. Which of the following network printing components hold a print job until it can be processed by the printer?

A. Spooler

B. Print Server

C. Redirector

D. Printer Share

9. One of the benefits to networking is the ability to share devices. Which of the two following devices can be shared as a print job destination?

A. A Cannon Color Laser printer

B. A Hayes 56K fax modem

C. A Hewlett-Packard CD-R drive

D. A Hewlett-Packard Scanjet attached to LPT1

10. You have just purchased an Ethernet card for your Windows NT Server. Which of the following can you reference to verify your new card will work in your server? Choose all that apply:

A. TechNet

B. MSDL

C. WinMSD

D. HCL

11. Your network includes the following printers: three HP Laserjet 860s, one Okidata dot-matrix, and two Tektronix color laser. In addition, you have an HP Laserjet 860 connected directly to the back of your computer. How many printer drivers need to be installed on your computer for you to utilize all printers available to you?

A. Seven

B. Four

C. Three

D. Two

12. You are planning a new Windows NT Server implementation and would like to ensure that the system files have enough room to operate and are not overrun by user and application files. Which of the following partition configurations best suits your situation?

A. Create a single partition and install all files there.

B. Create multiple partitions; one containing the system files, one the applications, and one the user data.

C. Create a mirrored partition utilizing one disk set for system files, and one for other files.

D. Use a RAID5 array to ensure no files are lost.

13. Your PC utilizes the file storage and backup facilities on the file server, but runs all applications locally. Which of the following computing models does this represent?

    A. Client computing with Central File Storage

    B. Centralized computing

    C. Standalone computing

    D. Peer-to-peer computing

14. In an effort to centralize management of applications, your boss has recommended that all programs be installed on the server, rather than on each individual client. Which of the arguments can be made for storing applications on the server? Choose all that apply:

    A. Software upgrades are easier because the files are centrally located.

    B. The server handles fewer requests.

    C. Software licensing is often easier to manage because you pay for the number of concurrent users.

    D. Access to the software can be controlled through user and group permissions.

15. Suppose the following situation exists: You have been hired to design and manage a mid-size network for a law firm. The firm occupies three offices in the metropolitan area. Because the computers contain confidential client information, file access control is of the utmost importance. The firm is planning to implement a database and an internal e-mail system once the network is up and running.

    Required result: Implement a centralized network design that will suit the firm's needs.

    Optional desired results: The network design must handle the plans for expansion. The network design must prevent unauthorized access to files.

    Proposed solution: Implement a Windows NT server-based network with user-level security. As more servers become necessary, add dedicated e-mail and/or database servers.

What results does the proposed solution produce?

A. The proposed solution produces the required result and both of the optional desired results.

B. The proposed solution produces the required result and only one of the optional desired results.

C. The proposed solution produces the required result but does not produce any of the optional desired results.

D. The proposed solution does not produce the required result.

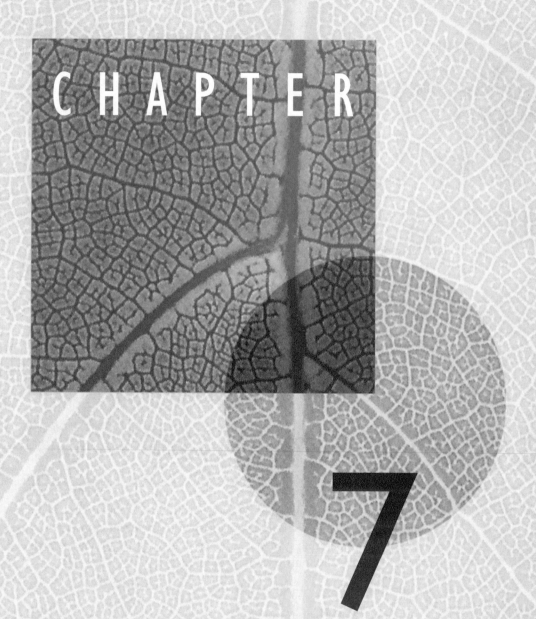

CHAPTER

7

Configuring Network Clients

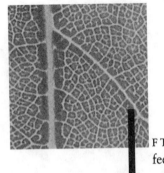

F THE SERVER is the brain of a network, the clients are the hands and feet. You use network clients to run application software, such as word processors and spreadsheets. You also use them to access network services. Your network clients can also share local printers and directories on their local hard drives.

This chapter will introduce you to the major client operating systems and show you their strengths and weaknesses. The discussion will then focus on Windows 95 to show you how to configure the operating system to recognize a network card and connect to network services. Finally, you will find out how clients can share files and printers and how to connect to files and printers that others have shared.

Client Operating Systems

HE SERVER SERVES files, shares printers, redirects communications, and otherwise supports the network, but the client computer is where you get work done on a network. The client computer is governed by a client operating system. In this section you learn about six client operating systems commonly used in networks:

- Windows 95

- Windows NT Workstation

- OS/2

- MS-DOS

- Macintosh

- Unix

You will also learn how each operating system interacts with the network.

The client operating system performs several important tasks on a network:

- Executes user applications

- Provides the user interface to the network

- Provides the network connection

Windows 95

Windows 95 (its opening screen is shown in Figure 7.1) is Microsoft's latest operating system designed specifically for personal use on a personal computer.

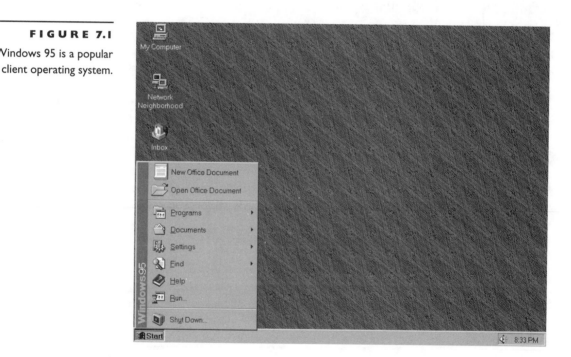

Applications

Windows 95, which provides a new user interface, was engineered to be fully compatible with previous versions of the Windows operating system. Both application software and hardware device drivers that were developed for previous versions of Windows will run on Windows 95.

Windows 95 is both a 16-bit and 32-bit operating system. It can execute older 16-bit Windows and DOS applications, as well as newer 32-bit applications written for Windows 95 and Windows NT.

Multitasking

Windows 95 supports both cooperative and preemptive multitasking. Older Windows programs expect a cooperative environment, but newer software that is written for the more powerful 32-bit environment of Windows 95 and Windows NT uses the preemptive capabilities of the two operating systems.

Windows 95 is widely supported by software developers. Many business and personal software applications have been written for the Windows 95 operating system.

Hardware

The Windows 95 operating system is widely supported by personal computer hardware manufacturers. Windows 95 runs only on Intel-based computers. This means the computer must have a 386, 486, Pentium, or Pentium Pro microprocessor, or a microprocessor compatible with one of these. Windows 95 will not run on RISC chips such as the PowerPC, Digital Alpha, MIPS, and ARM.

Windows 95 is also a single-processor operating system. It cannot take advantage of two (or more) processors in a computer system. Windows 95 uses the first microprocessor to do all its processing and leaves the others idle.

Drivers

Windows 95 can use many drivers written for DOS and earlier versions of Windows (but not any version of Windows NT). However, Windows 95 works best when you use drivers written for Windows 95. Some drivers for DOS or earlier versions of Windows can cause Windows to run more slowly or operate erratically. Fortunately, almost every hardware device now has a Windows 95 driver.

Windows NT Workstation

Windows NT Workstation is a powerful client operating system that uses Windows NT technology to support users' applications instead of (or in addition to) serving network files. Figure 7.2 shows the Windows NT desktop.

FIGURE 7.2
Windows NT
Workstation is a powerful
client operating system.

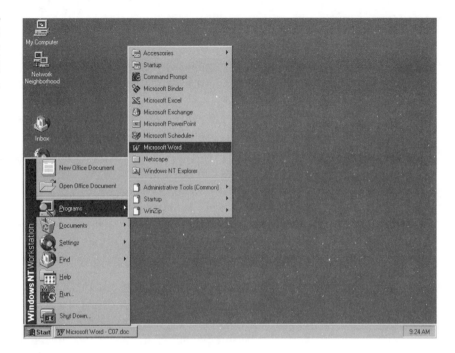

Applications

Windows NT Workstation can run most of the applications Windows 95 can run, but some applications that use special hardware functions of Windows 95 or older versions of Windows will not run correctly on Windows NT Workstation. New programs that use the 32-bit features of Windows 95 or Windows NT can run on either system.

Multitasking

Windows NT Workstation uses preemptive multitasking so that no one program can take over control of the computer. The operating system guarantees that each program will get a fair share of microprocessor time.

Applications on Windows NT Workstation are isolated from each other so no one application can crash another. If one application crashes, you can tell the operating system to clean up that application, and you can continue to use your other applications. It is not necessary to reboot the computer, and the system does not become unstable when applications misbehave.

Hardware

The additional features of Windows NT Workstation require a more powerful computer than Windows 95. Whereas Windows 95 runs well on 486-class computers and 8MB of RAM, Windows NT Workstation needs at least a 486/66 microprocessor (preferably a Pentium microprocessor) and 16MB of RAM.

Windows NT Workstation supports RISC microprocessors in addition to the Intel family of microprocessor chips. Specifically, it currently supports Intel, MIPS, Digital Alpha, and PowerPC microprocessors. As more powerful microprocessors become available, Windows NT Workstation will be easily portable to other microprocessors.

The Windows NT Workstation operating system also supports multiprocessing. This means the operating system will use more than one microprocessor if any are available. The operating system shares the microprocessors fairly among all the programs in the computer that need microprocessor time.

Drivers

Windows NT Workstation does not use the same device drivers as Windows 95. You must be sure the hardware devices you attach to a Windows NT Workstation computer support that operating system. Windows NT Workstation does use the same device drivers as Windows NT Server.

OS/2

OS/2 is a 32-bit operating system developed by IBM and Microsoft but now supported primarily by IBM. OS/2 was designed to be the successor to MS-DOS.

Applications

OS/2 supports MS-DOS applications and applications specifically written for OS/2. Some versions of the OS/2 operating system also support Windows software.

Multitasking

OS/2 uses preemptive multitasking. Like Windows NT Workstation, OS/2 protects running applications from each other to prevent one application from crashing into another or crashing the operating system.

OS/2 is more sophisticated than other operating systems in the way it schedules programs; in addition to providing preemptive multitasking, OS/2 supports multithreading. This ability allows application programs to be made of many small communicating parts, each of which gets its own slice of micro-processor time. Programmers can use multithreading to make sophisticated programs that need to do many things at one time, such as communications or multimedia programs that have to coordinate audio, video, text, and voice.

Hardware

OS/2 was first written to be used on Intel and Intel-compatible computers but has since been ported to the PowerPC RISC chip. OS/2 has the same hardware requirements as Windows 95 (a 386 microprocessor and 8MB of RAM), but if you also wish to run Windows programs, you may need more RAM. Like Windows 95, OS/2 supports only one processor in the computer.

Drivers

Drivers for most hardware devices must be written for OS/2, but some MS-DOS drivers will work. You will get the best performance out of your hardware with drivers written specifically for OS/2.

MS-DOS

MS-DOS (Microsoft Disk Operating System) was produced by Microsoft for the original IBM PC. Unlike Windows 95, NT Workstation, OS/2, and the Macintosh, MS-DOS does not provide a graphical interface. With MS-DOS you use a *command line* to run applications and to instruct the operating system to perform tasks such as creating directories and connecting to a net-work server.

MS-DOS is a 16-bit operating system. It does not use the advanced features of more powerful processors, such as the 486 and Pentium. It cannot use more than one processor.

MS-DOS can only run applications written for MS/DOS.

Multitasking

MS-DOS does not multitask. Only one program is run at a time, and that program uses all of the microprocessor. That program does not share memory or hardware with any other programs. It has complete control of the computer.

Hardware

MS-DOS can run on computers that Windows 95 can run on, but it can also run on much less powerful computers. MS-DOS needs an Intel or Intel-compatible microprocessor to execute, but in addition to the more powerful Pentium and 486 processors, MS-DOS can run on 386, 286, and even 8086 and 8088 processors. These are the processors often found in older personal computers that cannot run Windows well, or at all.

MS-DOS is also often found in specialized devices and portable and hand-held computers. The meager requirements of MS-DOS allow it to work in many situations that would be too constrained for a larger operating system.

Drivers

Drivers must be specifically written for MS-DOS to use hardware other than the screen, hard drives, communications, and printer ports that have support built in to MS-DOS.

You can sometimes use MS-DOS drivers with other operating systems, such as Windows 95 and OS/2. Because MS-DOS has been around for a long time, most older devices and many newer devices support it.

Macintosh

The Macintosh operating system is one of the easiest-to-use operating systems available for personal computers. It was the first widely available system to provide a graphical user interface, and it gave many people their first introduction to the windows/icons/mouse pointer (WIMP) environment.

Applications

The Macintosh operating system as sold by Apple supports only Macintosh applications. However, some MS-DOS and Windows emulator programs allow you to run DOS and Windows applications on a Macintosh computer.

There are even hardware cards with an Intel microprocessor that you can install in your Macintosh to run DOS and Windows applications at full speed. These are not part of the basic operating system, however.

Multitasking

The latest version of the Macintosh operating system supports both cooperative and preemptive multitasking. Older Macintosh programs use the cooperative environment, while newer programs use the more sophisticated preemptive services provided by the new operating system.

Older programs are all run in the same environment so they can interact in the same manner older operating systems allowed them to. Programs written for the newer operating systems are separated and protected from each other to prevent one program from crashing another program or the operating system.

Hardware

The Macintosh operating system does not run on IBM-compatible PCs. Apple Computer Company manufactures Apple Macintosh computers and has licensed the design to several clone manufacturers. Apple is working with Motorola, IBM, and several other companies to make a common hardware platform that any manufacturer can produce to run the Macintosh operating system, but the operating system for the platform is not yet available.

The Motorola 68000 family of processors and the PowerPC RISC family of processors are the two microprocessor types the Macintosh operating system has been ported to. The operating system can use more than one microprocessor but does not yet share multiple processes fairly among all the available microprocessors, so multiprocessing is not yet an integral part of the operating system.

Drivers

Hardware drivers must be written specifically for the Macintosh operating system. However, network software comes built in to the operating system, so most networks that support Macintosh clients load Macintosh services on the server and use the built-in software on the Macintosh clients.

Unix

Unix is an operating system with very fast RISC microprocessors and lots of memory and hard disk space. There are, however, versions of Unix for personal computers, and Unix can run on Intel 386, 486, and Pentium computers, as well as on RISC microprocessor computers.

Unix is often used in powerful engineering and scientific environments in peer networks. It is a powerful operating system that can be a server as well as a client. In many cases a few powerful Unix workstations are part of a LAN made of client personal computers and servers. In such an environment the Unix computers can use the network server for file storage and printing services.

Applications

Unix operating systems generally run only Unix software, but as with the Macintosh operating system, some Unix manufacturers also make hardware or software packages that allow a Unix computer to emulate a DOS or Windows computer. There are also packages for some Unix computers to emulate the Macintosh operating system, and Apple itself has sold a version of Unix (called A/UX) with the Macintosh environment built in.

Multitasking

All Unix operating systems multitask preemptively, and most support multithreading.

Hardware

Unix, like Windows NT, can run on a variety of hardware platforms. There are versions of Unix for each type of processor that NT supports, and many workstation manufacturers make RISC computers that are designed specifically to run their version of Unix. SUN workstations and Hewlett-Packard workstations are examples of Unix hardware platforms that do not have wide operating system support beyond the operating system provided by the workstation vendor.

Drivers

Unix drivers can be used only with Unix, and Unix does not use drivers written for other operating systems. Also, one version of Unix cannot use drivers from other versions; if you have a driver for Solaris, for example, you cannot use that driver under HP/UX.

REAL WORLD PROBLEMS

You are the administrator of a network with several Windows NT servers and 50 Windows 3.11 client computers. You wish to upgrade the operating systems on your client computers to take advantage of modern 32-bit programs, but you also need to continue to run certain Windows programs that were developed specifically for your company.

- Under what circumstances would you choose Windows NT Workstation as your client computer operating system?

- Under what circumstances would you choose Windows 95 as your client computer operating system?

- Under what circumstances would you choose OS/2 as your client computer operating system?

You need a client operating system for a number of powerful computers in your software development department. It is vital that when programs under development crash, they not crash the whole computer. Your company develops database software for the Windows 32-bit environment.

- Which operating system best fits your needs, and why?

You are selecting client computers for a graphics design studio. The graphic artists prefer to concentrate on product design and illustration rather than on figuring out how their computers work.

- Which operating systems are appropriate for this situation?

Your biotech company's tissue-sample testing process uses a simple DOS-based program to automatically control a tissue-sampling device and report sample data back to a central program running on another computer. Your company would like to fill a laboratory with computers running this program, each computer controlling a separate device.

- Which client operating system will allow you to implement the network with a minimum of cost?

Network Adapters

NETWORK INTERFACE CARDS were introduced in Chapter 2. In that chapter you learned what they are and how they work. In this section you will learn how to install a network card in a client computer and configure a client operating system (Windows 95) to use that card to talk to the network.

Microsoft ✓ **Exam Objective**	**Given the manufacturer's documentation for the network adapter, install, configure, and resolve hardware conflicts for multiple network adapters in a token-ring or Ethernet network.**

Card Installation

The first step in putting a client computer on the network is to put the network interface card in the computer. This usually involves opening the computer and inserting the card in an empty expansion slot on the computer's motherboard (see Figure 7.3).

Computer circuitry is sensitive, and electricity can be deadly, so use caution. Turn off the power and remove the power source (unplug the computer) before opening the case.

Some network interface cards use jumpers or switches on the card to configure such settings as the IRQ and DMA. Figure 7.4 shows an adapter card with jumpers and DIP switches. See Chapter 2 of this book and the documentation for the network interface card for information about card settings. You need to know the settings for the card when you put it in the computer so you can tell the client operating system how to talk to the card. Some cards use software to configure their settings, so you may have to run a DOS configuration program to configure the card before you configure the client operating system to talk to the card.

FIGURE 7.3

Network interface cards
are placed in expansion
slots on the personal
computer's motherboard.

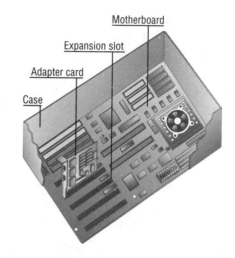

FIGURE 7.4

Dip switches and jumpers
can configure card
settings.

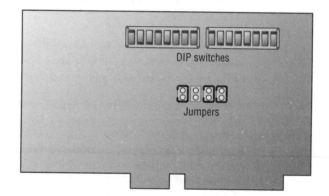

In Windows 95 you have the option of using device drivers from DOS as well as Windows 95 device drivers (as mentioned in the section "Windows 95" earlier in this chapter). One common network type of network driver for DOS and earlier versions of Windows is ODI. ODI drivers were introduced by Novell for connecting to Novell NetWare. ODI is an interface for device drivers. It makes device drivers interchangeable—one device driver for one card that implements the ODI interface can be exchanged for another device driver and card. ODI also allows several network protocols (see the section "Protocol Stacks" later in this chapter) to all talk to the same card.

Included with Windows 95 is another type of interface for device drivers, called NDIS. NDIS performs the same function as ODI, but NDIS is written for Windows 95 and is integrated into the operating system.

You should use ODI device drivers if you are using software that requires the ODI interface to function or if no NDIS driver is available; otherwise, choose NDIS device drivers for use with Windows 95.

OS Configuration

Once you have installed the network adapter card, you need to configure the client operating system to recognize the card. Windows 95 provides you with several ways of doing this:

- The Add New Hardware Wizard attempts to find new hardware you have installed and then guides you through the process of configuring the hardware.

- The Windows 95 Plug and Play software may auto-detect and auto-configure the operating system to match your card if you have a Plug and Play motherboard and a Plug and Play network interface card.

- You can install the network card driver and set the card's parameters in the Network Control Panel yourself.

To add network adapter software to Windows 95, follow these steps:

1. Double-click the Network icon in the Control Panel (see Figure 7.5). The Configure Network dialog box appears.

2. Select the Add button to add a networking component.

3. Select Adapter to add an adapter.

4. Find the network interface card installed in the computer (see Figure 7.6). If your adapter is not included in the list, select Have Disk and select the adapter from the floppy disk provided by the manufacturer.

FIGURE 7.5

Select the Network icon in the Control Panel to add a network adapter to Windows 95.

FIGURE 7.6

Windows 95 comes with drivers for many network adapters. You can select Have Disk if your adapter is not included with Windows 95.

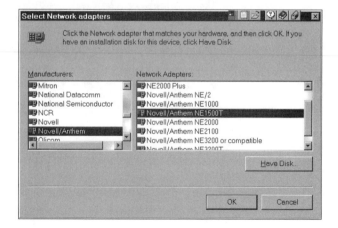

5. Back at the Configure Network dialog box, double-click the adapter card that is now listed in the window.

6. Set the software to match the settings (DMA, IRQ, Base Address, and so on) you used when you installed the card. Figure 7.7 shows the Configure Network Card Control Panel.

FIGURE 7.7

You can configure the network adapter card from the Configure Network Control Panel.

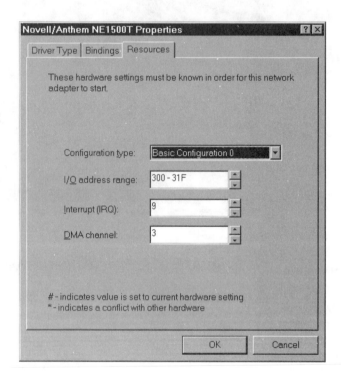

Protocol Stacks

After you load the device driver for the network interface card, you need to select the protocol your client operating system will use to connect to the network. The three protocols included with Windows 95 are IPX/SPX, NetBEUI, and TCP/IP. You need to select at least one of the three protocols. If you select more than one, Windows 95 will use the first one listed to connect to the network server. You must select a protocol the server uses.

Microsoft
Exam
Objective

Select the appropriate network and transport protocol or protocols for various token-ring and Ethernet networks. Protocol choices include:

- DLC
- AppleTalk
- IPX
- TCP/IP
- NFS
- SMB

You can select more than one protocol to connect to several services. For instance, you can choose IPX/SPX to connect to your Windows NT Server and TCP/IP to connect to the Internet.

IPX/SPX

IPX/SPX is the network protocol used by Novell NetWare clients to connect to NetWare servers. If your network contains NetWare servers, you may wish to use this protocol.

Under Windows 95 and Windows NT, IPX/SPX is very easy to install and configure. IPX/SPX can be used for both large and small networks, and the interoperability it provides between both NetWare and Microsoft network operating systems makes IPX/SPX an attractive choice for multivendor networks.

NetBEUI

Also known as the Server Message Block protocol, or SMB, NetBEUI is the protocol first implemented by Microsoft for use in LAN Manager networks. It is the native protocol for Microsoft Windows NT networks.

NetBEUI is an efficient network protocol. It is a good choice for connecting to other Microsoft operating systems over low-speed links, such as modem connections.

A disadvantage of NetBEUI is that it is not a routable protocol. This means you cannot use NetBEUI alone to make large internetworks of many LANS; NetBEUI is more useful for small networks than large ones.

TCP/IP

TCP/IP is the transport protocol for Unix networks and the Internet. If you plan to connect to the Internet, you will need to install this protocol.

TCP/IP is also a good protocol to use if your LAN is part of a larger organizational network. TCP/IP supports network sizes ranging from a small workgroup (ten or fewer users) up to any size of large network. One drawback of this flexibility is that TCP/IP is more difficult to set up and administer than NetBEUI and IPX/SPX.

REAL WORLD PROBLEMS

You are installing Windows 95 clients in a mixed Windows NT and NetWare server network. Your CIO wants your company to use only one transport protocol.

■ Which transport protocol best fits this situation?

You have a number of telecommuting employees in your company who connect to your network from home. They use Windows 95 as a client operating system.

■ Which protocol do you configure the Windows 95 clients to use? Why?

You are configuring your Windows NT server and Windows 95 clients from scratch. You have the choice of configuring any supported protocol.

■ Under what circumstances would you select TCP/IP as the protocol for use by your client computers?

Network Clients and Network Services Software

THE FINAL LINKS to connecting your client computer to the network are the network clients and the network services software. These are software packages that log you in to the network and redirect file accesses and print requests to file and print servers. Some packages that come with Windows 95 are

- Client for Microsoft Networks
- Client for NetWare Networks
- File and Printer Sharing for Microsoft Networks
- File and Printer Sharing for NetWare Networks

Connecting to Workgroups and Domains

To use network services you first need to log in to the network, and to do that you need the network client package for that network. In Windows 95 you can install a client package from the Network dialog box in the Control Panel.

You need to configure the client to attach it to the network. For Microsoft Workgroup (peer) networks, you select the Identification tab in the Network dialog box. There you enter your computer's name and the name of the workgroup the client will be a part of (as shown in Figure 7.8).

Every computer in the domain and workgroup must have a different name. You should decide on a computer-naming scheme so you can identify the computers on the network. The Windows 95 default (the first part of an individual's first name) may not be appropriate for computers that several people will use; you may wish to identify the computer by room number, for example, instead.

To connect a Windows 95 computer to a Windows NT server *domain* (server-based network), you specify the domain name in the properties section of the Client for Microsoft Networks software package (see Figure 7.9).

FIGURE 7.8

You specify the
workgroup name in the
Identification section of
the Network dialog box.

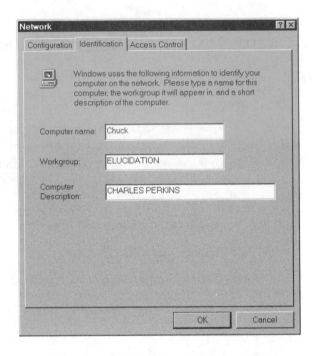

FIGURE 7.8

You specify the
workgroup name in the
Identification section of
the Network dialog box.

FIGURE 7.9

You specify the domain
name in the Properties
section of Client for
Microsoft Networks.

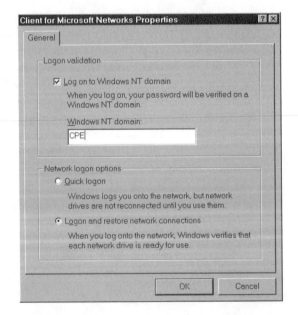

Computer names, workgroup names, and domain names have certain restrictions. They must be unique. They are also limited to 15 characters. (The operating system may add a 16th hidden character.)

Sharing Drives and Printers

To share files and printers, you must enable the options in File and Print Sharing in the Network dialog box. To do this, click the File and Print Sharing button in the Configuration tab of the Network window. Then check the following options in the panel that appears:

- I want to be able to give others access to my files.

- I want to be able to allow others to print to my printers.

After you have done that, click OK and close the Network window.

Connecting to Drives and Printers

Once you have connected to a workgroup or domain, you can access files and disk volumes on the server and on other computers in your workgroup.

You can select Network Neighborhood on your Windows 95 desktop and select from the other computers in your workgroup. If, instead, you select Whole Network, you can also access files on the Windows NT servers in your domain.

Windows allows you to make a permanent connection to a network resource in two ways:

- By making a shadow of the resource

- By mapping a drive to the file or directory

You can make a shadow of a network resource by right-clicking and dragging on the resource you find in Network Neighborhood or Whole Network. When you release the icon on your desktop, a menu appears asking whether you wish to copy the object or make a shadow. If you make a shadow, you have a connection to the actual object on the other computer.

You can map a drive letter to a shared directory on the network by selecting Tools ➤ Map Network Drive in Windows Explorer. This drive letter will then appear like any other drive letter.

You connect to a network printer by selecting the Add Printer icon in the Printers panel. (Click the Start button and select Settings ➤ Printers.) The Select Printer Wizard walks you through the process of selecting either a local printer or a network printer. It also allows you to browse the network to find the printer you wish to attach to.

E-Mail Mailboxes

At the time you connect the network to the network file and print services, you may also wish to connect the client e-mail to the server's storage location for e-mail boxes. This is done in most LAN file server–based e-mail systems by configuring the e-mail software to look in a certain directory on the file server for e-mail information. Check the documentation for the e-mail package you will use to learn how to configure the e-mail software.

Troubleshooting Client Connections

ONCE YOU HAVE installed the network adapter in the client computer and configured the operating system to talk to the card and to the network, you still may have problems connecting to the network. This section will help you solve some of the common problems administrators face when connecting client computers to a network.

Microsoft ✓ **Exam Objective**

Identify common errors associated with components required for communications.

Diagnose and resolve common connectivity problems with cards, cables, and related hardware.

Troubleshooting Ethernet

Ethernet troubleshooting involves checking cards (including IRQ and port settings) and cables (10base2 being the cable type most likely to require troubleshooting).

Ethernet Card Problems

Each Ethernet adapter on a network must have a unique MAC address. This is normally not a problem because Ethernet adapters are made with unique addresses burned in at the factory. Unfortunately, an Ethernet adapter manufacturer once shipped a batch of Ethernet cards with duplicate MAC addresses by mistake, which caused address conflicts on a few networks.

To prevent this problem from occurring again, some Ethernet adapters allow you to override the default MAC address burned into the card at the factory with your own setting. This ability is provided for the extremely rare possibility that you have two network adapters with the same MAC address setting. You should not use this feature unless you know for certain that you have a MAC address duplication problem. If you are having MAC address problems, reset all the Ethernet adapters on your network to the default factory MAC addresses.

Some Ethernet adapters have more than one transceiver on board. These cards are usually referred to as combo cards because they have a combination of transceivers available. The cards may have any combination of twisted-pair, AUI, BNC, and optical-fiber transceivers. Generally they have two, but in rare cases they have three.

These cards either have a jumper setting or a software-configurable setting to select which transceiver is in use. You must select the transceiver for the type of cable you are using in your network. If you have the wrong transceiver selected, the card will not work.

Some cards have an "auto-sense" feature that allows the adapter to select the transceiver to use if one of the ports has electrical current or light present. This feature does not always work properly on every card in every situation, so if you have a combo network adapter set to auto-sense that appears to be malfunctioning, try setting the port you are actually using.

When a workstation's NIC goes out and begins to talk continuously and incoherently on the network, it will create packets that are larger than 1518 bytes and have CRC errors. This type of packet is called a *jabber packet*. To find the faulty card, disconnect workstations or hubs one at a time until you pinpoint the rogue card.

In some cases, resource conflicts can cause network communications problems. You may need to take all the boards out of your system except the network adapter. Once you have it working, add one board at a time until you find the board that has the conflicts. Reconfigure and continue adding cards until the system is up and running.

Remember that COM1 uses IRQ 4 and COM2 uses IRQ 3. Try to avoid these when configuring IRQs because they are commonly used by a serial mouse and modem. Sometimes, just the presence of the serial port will interfere with these IRQs.

Check for the frequent error of not having common frame types bound to the workstation and the file server. If they are not bound, your workstation will respond with the message "File server not found."

Be sure to use the diagnostics program that ships with the LAN card. You will be able to test and configure the card in the machine rather than having to remove it. If you use a card that has two or more ports, be sure you have set the jumpers or configuration to use the correct port on the card.

Some network adapter cards do not make a very good connection in the card socket. Cleaning the card connector and resetting the card can usually solve this problem. (Don't be tempted to use an eraser to clean the connector—it will leave grit on the card.) If you have checked the settings and cleaned the card and it still doesn't work, replace it with a spare that you know is functional.

10Base2 Problems

If your 10Base2 network goes down, it is likely that the bus continuity has been damaged or disconnected. (Perhaps someone moved a PC.) Check terminators at both ends of the cable with a volt-ohm meter to be sure they still read 50 ohms resistance. Check the resistance of the entire segment of cable by using the center conductor of a T and the T's outside shield. It should measure 25 ohms or slightly above. If it measures close to 50 ohms, you may have a faulty terminator, a missing terminator, a break in the wire, or a missing T-connector. Also, check that one end of the cable is still grounded.

If you are working with 10Base2, make sure the cable has not grown too long as a result of the consistent addition of users without consideration of wiring lengths. This is a very common problem with bus topology networks.

Because some people see no difference between RG-59, RG-58A/C, and RG-62, make sure someone did not just add a black piece of coax to extend or repair the cable. Also check for the wrong connector types on your cable.

If only one workstation is having a problem on a 10Base2 or 10Base5 network, you can be sure it is not the cabling but rather the LAN card, the transceiver, or the AUI cable. You will probably need to swap out the card to nail this one down, so make sure you have a spare. Remember to configure the card before you attempt this solution.

Ethernet, IPX, and Frame Types

One frequently encountered problem with the IPX protocol stack is frame type incompatibility. IPX comes with four frame types:

- Ethernet_802.2

- Ethernet_802.3

- Ethernet_SNAP

- Ethernet_II

The differences between these frame types are minor, involving such issues as checksum and addressing. They are incompatible with each other, however. For any two computers to communicate on your network, they must both support the same frame type.

The simplest way to deal with this problem is to set each device in your network to the same single frame type. Microsoft and Novell both recommend using Ethernet_802.2. This is, unfortunately, difficult for some users because many early Ethernet adapters support only one frame type, usually

Ethernet_802.3. To avoid this problem, your server should be configured to support all necessary frame types. Doing so may cause a slight performance penalty, but it will allow all computers on the network to communicate with the server.

This problem with frame type incompatibility is also a common problem with NWLink.

Note that although many operating systems support frame type auto-detection, some Ethernet cards do not. For this reason you should set the frame type manually if you know what it should be.

If you have a computer using IPX that does not appear to be communicating on the network, set the IPX frame type to the frame type supported on the network file server.

Cable Problems and Cable-Testing Tools

Check to make sure the cabling does not run near high-voltage cables or is wrapped in cable trays. Fluorescent lights can also cause electromagnetic interference (EMI). Check that the wires are not run against or across these lights. Electrical motors also cause EMI if wires are run across them.

Microsoft ✓ *Exam Objective*   **Identify and resolve network performance problems.**

Network cable testing equipment can locate wiring faults quickly. If you suspect you will be troubleshooting on a regular basis, a network cable tester is a good investment.

A time-domain reflectometer is a cable-testing device that can tell you whether the cable is shorted, broken, or crimped, and how far down the cable problem resides. The device sends a signal down the wire and measures the characteristics of the reflected signal. From the reflection it can determine the type of problem with the cable. (This is like throwing a rock down a well and determining how long it takes before you hear it hit the bottom, as well as sensing whether it hit water, dirt, or other rocks.)

Troubleshooting Token Ring

Most Token Ring problems come from obvious mistakes. You can begin by asking questions such as these:

- Are the patch cables and adapter cables to the workstations of the correct specifications?

- Are the correct types of cables in the right places?

- Are the connectors tight and properly secured?

Token Ring Card Problems

Start your troubleshooting of card problems by confirming that there are no resource conflicts with the Token Ring NIC and other devices installed in the workstation. This is especially important if you are adding a card or have recently added other devices to the workstation.

Check the Token Ring card's custom statistics to see whether any internal errors are listed. Internal errors are usually a sign that the card has malfunctioned and should be replaced.

Token Ring card addresses are hardcoded into the ROMs, but some cards allow you to override these addresses with custom addresses. Make sure you do not have two cards with exactly the same node address. This has been known to happen with Ethernet, Token Ring, and ARCnet networks.

Be sure all Token Ring cards are configured for the same speed. In other words, if a network is set for 16Mbps, make sure the card you are troubleshooting is configured for 16Mbps as well. If the system is an IBM/PS2 and the user used the IBM reference disk to set up a new or existing piece of hardware in the machine, the Token Ring card is automatically reset to the 4Mbps speed. If you do happen to place a card in the network that is configured with an inappropriate Token Ring speed, it will cause network traffic to halt temporarily while the ring reconfigures.

You can specify three settings for a Token Ring card merely by using the device drivers supplied with the card:

- The adapter address, which you can change to override the internal address built in by the manufacturer

- Shared RAM locations the card uses

- Activation of the early token release feature (but only with 16Mbps Token Ring cards set to 16Mbps)

Cabling and MSAU Problems

Be sure your network cabling and associated hardware are well documented. This will help you quickly identify the cable and MSAU of a malfunctioning station. This type of information is critical when isolating a hardware-related problem.

Do not mix MSAUs from different vendors. Internal electrical characteristics, such as impedance, can cause problems with Token Ring networks.

If your network does not have bridges or routers, you can try a trouble-shooting fix that is often used to reset the Token Ring network:

1. Disconnect all of the patch cables from the MSAUs.

2. With the setup tool, reset each port.

3. Reconnect each port one at a time with the patch cables.

It's also a good idea to have on hand special cable testers and equipment that are built specifically for troubleshooting Token Ring.

Troubleshooting Multiple Adapters

When you have multiple adapters in your server, you are introducing the possibility of conflict and the necessity of routing data between the cards. These problems, which can prevent client connections, appear to originate on the client side—some clients will work and other clients will not.

Each adapter in a server must have its own unique IRQ and port setting and may require its own upper memory address space. If two cards try to occupy the same hardware resource, neither will work reliably.

You must make sure each adapter is bound to a transport protocol and has a unique network number (IPX) or IP number (TCP/IP). Adapters with conflicting network or IP numbers will not operate correctly. Conflicting network or IP numbers may allow some clients to attach and others to be denied service.

You will need to enable routing between multiple adapters unless your server is the only destination for traffic on your network. Peer computers attached to networks on different adapters in the server will not be able to see one another unless the server is routing traffic between the network adapters. In Windows NT, routing is enabled between all transport protocols and adapters by default. In most other network operating systems, you must specifically enable routing between network adapter cards.

Troubleshooting ARCnet

As with other types of networks, ARCnet troubleshooting involves checking NIC settings and cable connections.

ARCnet Card Problems

Duplicate node addresses can cause problems on an ARCnet network. NICs come from the factory set to a default address of 0. You must manually set the NIC address on each card, and each node on the network must have a unique address on that network. If more than one node has the same address, one of the nodes will be unable to either find or connect to the network.

Different impedance levels may also be the source of your troubles. If the ARCnet bus uses NICs that have different impedance levels, signals will be either reflected or attenuated, causing interference with other network signals.

ARCnet Cable and Connection Problems

A number of problems can exist with cabling. First, cable length may be longer than the specifications dictate, which could cause signal degradation, resulting in loss of data or communication failure.

If you are using UTP in a bus topology rather than a star, you usually cannot have more than ten nodes (NICs) per segment. (Check with the manufacturer; this number can vary.) In an ARCnet bus topology, disconnected cables can bring down the network.

Connectors for coax that are not crimped or built correctly are a problem. Also, because of their design, twist-on connectors can cause intermittent errors on a network.

You should also check for terminator problems. Unused ports on passive hubs that are not terminated can create signal reflections. Sometimes, the self-terminating capability of active hubs can fail. Make sure you use terminators with the right ohm rating: 93 ohm for coax or 100 ohm for twisted-pair. You can use a volt-ohm meter to test terminators.

Troubleshooting FDDI

The common problems that occur on FDDI networks involve connectors, cabling, and communication delays.

Connector Problems

Dirty connectors can cause problems in FDDI networks. To allow clear communication, the connector must be free of dirt and dust. Remember that the signals are being transmitted using light. If the connectors are dirty, you can clear them using a lint-free cloth and alcohol. (You should use only alcohol as a solvent to clean connectors.)

Another problem may be a bad connector or an open segment of cable. A loss of optical power over 11 decibels may indicate a problem of this nature. Faulty connectors, bad connections, or open segments (segments that are incorrectly terminated) may be responsible for this loss.

Cable Problems

If you use the wrong type of cable between nodes, you will experience problems. Multi-mode fiber is good for distances up to 2 kilometers (1.2 miles). Use single-mode fiber for longer distances.

The type of fiber-optic cable you use can affect network speed. You should probably replace any plastic fiber-optic cable if you want throughput of more than 10Mbps. Glass fiber-optic cable is the best alternative. Plastic should not be used on runs longer than 50 meters (165 feet).

There are several ways to find cable problems. If a complete break occurs in a cable segment, you can find the break using a flashlight. For small breaks, you can use an optical power meter and a source of light energy to test the cable. You can also use an optical time-domain reflectometer (OTDR), although this is the most expensive option.

REAL WORLD PROBLEMS

Your Windows 95 client computers connect to Windows NT and NetWare file servers using the IPX protocol. One client cannot access any servers. The network adapter card passes all diagnostic tests.

- What may be the problem?

- How can you solve this problem?

You have two clients with Ethernet network adapter cards that are configured the same in every detail, and either one can operate on the network without any problem when the other one is powered off. When both clients are powered on, however, both client computers experience network problems.

- What may be wrong in this situation?

- How can you solve this problem?

Your network adapter is set to use interrupt 4 and you cannot connect to the network.

- What may be the problem, and how can you resolve it?

You have a thinnet network that is performing erratically. You suspect that it may not be terminated correctly.

- How can you check the termination of the network?

You plan to link several networks together by installing several network cards in your server and attaching a network link to each card.

- What must you do to ensure that all network cards operate properly?

Review

WINDOWS 95 IS the modern operating system with the most software. Windows NT Workstation is a more robust operating system. OS/2 is a flexible operating system from IBM. The Apple Macintosh operating system is one of the easiest-to-use operating systems, and it is sophisticated and powerful. MS-DOS is an old operating system that will run on simple computers. Unix is a powerful operating system that can also be run on personal computers.

The client operating system must be given the same settings the network adapter card was configured with to allow the operating system to recognize the card.

All computers in the same workgroup must use the same workgroup name to share information as a workgroup. Each client computer must have the domain name of the Windows NT domain to access the server.

You can create a link to a shared directory by creating a shadow of it on your desktop or by assigning a drive letter to the directory.

To troubleshoot Ethernet networks, check for faulty NICs and be sure NICs are connected properly. To look for cable problems, use cable-testing tools, such as a time-domain reflectometer. Check for incorrect cable types. Also check for the wrong connector types on your cable.

When troubleshooting a Token Ring system, start by confirming that there are no resource conflicts with the Token Ring NIC and other devices installed in the workstation. Then check the Token Ring card (such as its custom statistics for internal errors, which indicate a faulty NIC, and for duplicate node addresses) and your network cabling. Be sure all Token Ring cards are configured for the same speed (4- or 16Mbps).

Some common problems in an ARCnet network are duplicate node addresses, different impedance levels, cable problems, connector problems, terminator problems, failed NICs, and active hubs.

Some common problems in an FDDI network are dirty connectors, bad connectors or open segments of cable, inappropriate cable usage, and breaks in the cable.

Review Questions

1. Which of the following operating systems will allow you to run Windows programs, but still use device drivers developed for MS-DOS?

   A. MS-DOS

   B. MacOS 8

   C. Windows NT Server

   D. Windows 95

2. In a networked computing environment, which of the following software components provides the means for computers to establish communications sessions over the network?

   A. The network interface card

   B. The network device driver

   C. The client software

   D. The protocol stack

3. What is the maximum size a computer's name may be in a Microsoft network?

   A. 12

   B. 8+3

   C. 8

   D. 15

4. You have begun to notice communications problems on your thinnet network. You use a volt-ohm meter to test the resistance between the conductor and the shield. It registers a resistance of 50-ohms. Which of the following is most likely the problem on your network?

   A. Your network is using the incorrect cable type.

   B. The resistance setting is incorrect on a network adapter card on your network.

   C. There is a defective network card interrupting communication.

   D. There is a faulty terminator on your network.

5. When configuring a new computer for a Token Ring network, which of the following must be considered?

   A. The IP address of the new computer should match the IP addresses of the other computers.

   B. The MAC address of the new computer should match the MAC address of the other computers.

   C. The NIC should be configured to operate at the same speed as the NICs on other computers.

   D. The node address of the new computer should be the next highest available address to preserve the continuity of the ring.

6. You must implement a new operating system for the client computers on your network. Which of the following operating systems will support both DOS and Windows applications? Choose all that apply:

   A. Windows 95

   B. LINUX

   C. MS-DOS

   D. Windows NT Workstation

7. The NDIS and ODI specifications define the rules for communication between the protocol stack and the network interface adapter. Which of the following components should be NDIS or ODI compliant to operate in a Windows 95 computer?

   A. The client software

   B. The operating system

   C. The network device driver

   D. The network interface adapter

8. Which of the following is used by Microsoft to describe a server-based network?

   A. Domain

   B. Session

   C. Workgroup

   D. LAN

9. If two computers running NWLink are unable to communicate, which of these situations is the most likely problem?

    A. The computers share the same MAC address.

    B. The IPX default gateway is set incorrectly on one of the computers.

    C. The IPX frame type is not the same on both computers.

    D. The network does not support NWLink.

10. The development staff for your company needs a desktop operating system that can gracefully handle a program crash without taking down the entire computer. In addition, certain developers need the power of multiple processors. Choose one operating system from the following list to install on all of your developer's computers.

    A. Windows NT Workstation

    B. DR-DOS

    C. Windows for Workgroups

    D. Windows 95

11. In a network that is using Windows 95 clients and Windows NT servers, which of the following protocols can be used for communication? Choose all that apply:

    A. AppleTalk

    B. DLC

    C. IPX/SPX

    D. NetBEUI

12. You have noticed recently that network performance is suffering. By using a protocol analyzer to capture network traffic, you find that one workstation on your network is consistently sending packets with CRC errors. You suspect this may be the problem with network performance. Which of the following can you do to correct the problem?

    A. Increase network speed to 100Mbps.

    B. Replace the network card because it has failed.

    C. Configure the network card to use a different MAC address.

    D. Change the protocols being used on the network.

13. You have decided to install a second Ethernet adapter in your server. To ensure that it works properly, you configured it with the same IRQ and port settings as the adapter already in the machine. Each card works independently, but when both are installed, neither works. Which of the following is the cause of the problem?

    A. The adapters must have unique settings, including IRQ and port.

    B. The server's BIOS must be configured to support multiple network adapters.

    C. The server does not support more than one Ethernet adapter.

    D. The adapters must be configured to recognize each other.

14. Which of the following operating systems includes support for both Intel and Digital Alpha architectures? Choose all that apply:

    A. Windows for Workgroups

    B. Windows NT Workstation

    C. OS/2

    D. Windows 95

15. What is the term Microsoft uses to describe a peer-to-peer Windows network?

    A. Domain

    B. Session

    C. Workgroup

    D. LAN

16. Your network consists of two LANs, one 10BaseT and one 10Base2. Your server is connected to both networks to allow easy communication. Each of your client workstations has a combo network adapter card with both RJ-45 and BNC connectors. You are in the process of moving a workstation from the Thinnet LAN to the UTP LAN. Which of the following must you do before the workstation will be able to communicate?

A. The computer name must be changed to reflect the new network.

B. The network adapter card must be assigned a new node address.

C. The network adapter must be configured to use the transceiver for the RJ-45 port.

D. The network adapter must be configured to use a new IRQ and port address.

17. One of the keys to troubleshooting a 10Base2 network is the ability to identify how far down the network segment the cable is broken. Which of the following troubleshooting devices will help you determine a cable break's location?

A. Time-domain reflectometer

B. SNMP manager

C. Volt-ohm meter

D. Sniffer

18. Which of the following Ethernet components is unique for each card created?

A. Frame type

B. CRC address

C. IRQ

D. MAC address

8

Administering Your Network

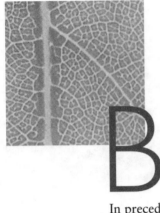

BEING AN ADMINISTRATOR requires more than just installing a network and forgetting about it. In fact, the greatest portion of a network administrator's time is spent managing the running network.

In preceding chapters you learned the basic principles of networking and how to install a network. This chapter takes you through the essential areas of network administration.

The Network Administrator

AS A NETWORK administrator, your task is to support network users as they use their computers and the network to do their jobs. A good network administrator tries to be unobtrusive. The ideal network is invisible; users should not even be aware that a structure of cables, adapters, servers, and administration staff supports them as they concentrate on getting their job done.

The best network administrator is the one you never see because you never have a network problem.

The network administrator is the individual primarily responsible for the uninterrupted proper operation of the network, including:

- Creating a useful network environment
- Managing the network environment
- Protecting the network environment

Each of these major areas of responsibility has many duties. For instance, creating a useful network environment covers the planning of the overall nature of the network, the creation of users and groups, the implementation of network policies, and the documentation of the network once it is installed. Protecting the network environment covers such activities as implementing fault-tolerant systems, scanning for viruses, and installing uninterruptible power supplies. Managing a network environment covers the periodic tasks of managing user accounts, upgrading servers, monitoring network performance, and backing up the network. Each of these duties and responsibilities is covered in detail in the remainder of this chapter.

Creating a Network Environment

YOUR NETWORK ENVIRONMENT will reflect the nature of your organization. A decentralized company with individuals pursuing their own projects and goals will certainly have a different network setup than a focused company in which each employee has a defined task in support of the company's production process.

Microsoft Exam Objective

> **Choose an administrative plan to meet specified needs, including performance management, account management, and security.**

Three facets of your network are most strongly affected by how your company works, and these three characteristics define how your network appears to your users:

- What network software is loaded on the server

- How user accounts are set up

- How group accounts are set up and how user accounts are assigned to them

Network Software

Organizations differ in many regards. Some organizations create a product based on the collaboration of many individuals. Other organizations have little interaction between individuals at all.

Why is your organization installing a network? Do users need access to the same data files? Will there be a central database? Are groupware tools, such as e-mail and scheduling programs, important? Is Internet connectivity important?

The network software you load on your server defines all the things, beyond saving files on the network, your client computers can use your network for. These are the applications that make your client computers more useful than stand-alone computers.

Database

Will your company use a database to store organizational or business-related information? If so, how that database is implemented will have an effect on how you configure your network. Most often, either a database is stored as a number of files on the server while the database program runs on the client computers, or a database server runs on the server computer and only the user interface runs on the client computers.

DATABASE FILES STORED ON THE SERVER A database that is not often accessed or is accessed by a only small number of people on the network is often implemented by storing only the database files on the file server and by running the database program on the client computer. Microsoft Access can work this way. The database program manipulates the database files directly and cooperates with other database programs on other computers to keep the data in a consistent state.

Because each database program must cooperate with other database programs to manipulate the files, when there are many clients accessing the database's data, database performance can degrade significantly, and the network can become swamped by database traffic. However, this type of database is simpler to configure and less expensive to implement than a client-server database, described in the next section.

The primary consideration for your network when you intend to install this type of database is that your file server have adequate disk space to contain the database files.

DATABASE BACK END RUN ON SERVER A database for which a database server runs on the server computer and only the user interface runs on the client computers is called a client-server database or a SQL database. (SQL stands for Structured Query Language, and a SQL server is a specific kind of client-server database.)

When your database is frequently accessed and a large number of network users need to interact with your database, a database back end provides better database performance and reduces network traffic. The database back end does this by running a program on the server computer that takes over the task of manipulating the database files stored on the file server. Then the client database programs, rather than manipulating the files, send requests to the back-end program to perform the manipulations for them. The back-end program can satisfy many requests at once and can arbitrate among requests to maximize database performance.

With a back-end server you still have to ensure that your file server has adequate file storage for the database files. However, in addition to file storage, you must ensure that your file server has sufficient processing power to satisfy database requests from client computers, as well as file storage and retrieval requests from regular programs. If database access will be heavy and you expect a lot of file storage activity on your network, you should consider installing the database back end on a server that is separate from your regular file storage server.

Shared Data Files

One important aspect of the network environment and how people use applications on your network is where data is stored on your network. This is even the case for applications that are not network specific, such as word processors and spreadsheets.

The primary incentive for installing a network with a file server is that you can store files on the server. But where on the server will you store the files? If you were to store all files in one big directory, you would soon discover that you could not find the files you need. Important documents would be lost or overwritten. You would not be able to restrict access to sensitive files, and you would not know who had placed which files in the directory, or for what purpose. Clearly, you must have a better organizational plan than this.

In most instances you will want to create a directory for each user account. Files pertinent only to that user should be stored in that user's account. Groups of users (see the section "Groups" later in this chapter) in many cases should have a directory for their use. For example, you may have several people in your accounting department, each with his or her own user account. A directory shared by all individuals in the Accounting group would hold data files pertinent to accounting. A similar group and shared directory could be created for marketing, and so on.

You can also create directories that have access restricted to certain users and groups. You can store sensitive information in these directories. You can also create directories that contain information the company as a whole will use. You can give everyone read access to these directories and limit write access to those individuals or groups responsible for the documents stored in the directories. For example, you might have a standard letterhead or memo style for your corporation and you want everyone to be able to create a document using that style, but you want only your advertising department to be able to change the style.

Groupware, E-Mail, and Scheduling

Database programs and file storage predate networks but are enhanced by them. However, it is networks that make groupware and e-mail possible by the network. E-mail in particular is one of the most useful applications a network can provide.

E-MAIL *E-mail* allows users of your network to send messages without requiring the recipient to be there at the time the message is sent. Transmission is instantaneous, and reams of paper are not required to send the same message to hundreds of people. Unlike voice mail and paper, you can attach programs and digital files to your electronic message. Some e-mail packages even indicate whether a message has been read.

You will want to ensure that all of your clients' e-mail packages work together. The easiest way to do that is to use only one e-mail package on all your client computers. If you cannot do that (for instance, if you have a mixed network of Windows, Macintosh, and Unix computers), you will want to select e-mail packages that interoperate.

Most e-mail packages store the clients' e-mail on the server computer. You must ensure that the file server has adequate disk space. You may wish to store your users' e-mail in a partition separate from other files on your server to prevent a deluge of mail from swamping all the available space and crashing your server.

If your network is connected to other networks or to the Internet, you may wish to run a mail server program such as Microsoft Exchange. This type of program runs on the server and routes mail between your network and other networks. If your network is particularly large or you have a lot of mail traffic to and from your network, you may wish to dedicate a server computer to run a mail server program.

GROUPWARE *Groupware* is software that allows a number of users on a network to work cooperatively over a network. E-mail is a simple form of groupware because it allows users to share information and exchange files. There are, however, many software packages that aid collaboration in ways far beyond the simple exchange of messages and files.

Bulletin boards, for example, provide an electronic setting for group communication. Teleconferencing and electronic white boards allow separated groups to exchange visual as well as audio information in real time. There are also products that allow a document to be constructed collaboratively, with the final document assembled electronically on the network from parts each collaborator can work on individually at his or her own computer.

Each groupware product has its own requirements, and you will have to ensure that your computer network supports the groupware products you intend to use in your organization.

SCHEDULING Scheduling can be made much easier in the presence of a network. Scheduling packages have long been available on individual computers, but a network makes it possible for those individual scheduling packages to communicate. If you have a networked scheduling package and each person in your organization keeps a schedule on the network, the software can interrogate other individuals' schedules to find good meeting times, and a support staff can work together to maintain an executive's busy schedule.

Like groupware, each scheduling package has its own requirements for how the network environment must be established. Check the software documentation to ensure that your network server and clients will support your scheduling application.

Internet Connectivity

Many networks today are being connected to the Internet. An Internet connection can make your network more useful in several ways.

EXTERNAL E-MAIL If your network is connected to the Internet, you can send e-mail from computers on your network to individuals connected to the Internet around the world. You can attach electronic documents to e-mail messages, and if the recipient's software is compatible, you can save time and money sending those documents electronically instead of via the regular mail. You can also participate in mailing lists, which bring together individuals who are interested in a certain topic, such as network administration. In this way you can share your problems and successes and learn from the experiences from others. This can enable you to perform your job more effectively.

To connect your desktop mail to the Internet you will need to either select an e-mail package that uses the Internet mail protocols directly or install an e-mail server that can transfer mail between your LAN's e-mail system and the Internet.

WEB HOSTING When you have an Internet connection, you can make information about your organization or your organization's products available to others on the Internet via the World Wide Web. This can be a valuable tool for spreading information about your organization or for providing support for your product. It also makes a good sales tool.

To host Web pages, you need a connection to the Internet with enough bandwidth to support the network activity your Web page will generate. The more popular your Web page is, the greater the bandwidth you must provide. A regular modem, for example, will support only the most limited amount of occasional access. A dedicated 56K frame relay link will allow several people to access your Web site at once, but it will quickly become saturated when more than a handful of people attempt to access your site. A T1 line is the minimum you will need if you intend to establish a serious Web presence.

ALLOWING WEB ACCESS With Internet access, you can also use World Wide Web browsers on your desktop computers to gather information from other companies and individuals. Search engines and other Internet tools can automate the process of searching for information and help you find exactly what you need to know about virtually any subject.

Configuring your network so your client computers can connect to the Internet through your network requires you to configure each network client to use the TCP/IP protocol stack and to ensure that each computer has a TCP/IP address and other TCP/IP configuration information. As with Web hosting, you need to provide enough bandwidth for the number of users you intend to support. You also need to register your network on the Internet so that your network and the Internet will interoperate properly.

REAL WORLD PROBLEMS

You will install a network for a company that needs a SQL database and wishes to host World Wide Web pages for its sales department.

■ How will the database and Internet requirements affect the network environment you will install?

A company with several hundred employees in offices in several cities needs e-mail for the whole company. They would like to use the Internet to transport the mail between office LANs.

■ What must you do to enable this company to send their e-mail over the Internet, and how might it affect their LAN requirements?

A busy senatorial staff currently keeps the senator's schedule on paper. Several staff members must have access to the schedule. Keeping the schedule consistent becomes difficult, especially around reelection time.

■ What type of software would help the senator's staff?

You must create a directory structure for the file server for the administrative department of your corporation.

■ How would you organize the directory structure on your file server so that all the secretaries in the department can access a shared set of files, only some of them can change them, each secretary can have his or her own set of files, and Eastern Division can have a separate set of shared files from Western Division's?

Your parts and inventory database, which was created in Access, has become less and less responsive as large amounts of data have been added to the database and as more individuals access the data.

■ What can you do to speed up database access?

User Accounts

User accounts are what identify the people in your organization to the computer network. Each person is given a username and a password. The person uses that username and secret password to access network resources and to establish a personal computing environment, including such things as the background pattern on the screen and the location of personal files.

Groups help you organize user accounts by needs, functions, and attributes. You can assign permissions to groups so that individuals within a group can share resources, such as a common directory or printer.

The Default Accounts

Most network operating systems come with two accounts already created for you: the Administrator account and the Guest account.

The Administrator account is always present and should be protected with a strong password. This account manages the overall configuration of the computer and can be used for managing security policies, creating or changing users and groups, setting shared directories for networking, and for other hardware and software maintenance tasks. Under Windows NT, this account has network access rights to do anything on the network. This account can be renamed in some operating systems, but it cannot be deleted.

The Guest account enables one-time users or users with low or no security access to use the computer in a limited fashion. The Guest account is often installed with a blank password. If the password is left blank, remote users can connect to the computer using the Guest account. Under Windows NT Server version 4.0, the Guest account can be renamed, but it cannot be deleted, and it is disabled by default; you must enable it in order to use it.

Creating User Accounts in Windows NT

Most network operating systems maintain similar information about users of those operating systems. They must record usernames and passwords and usually assign a home directory on the network server to the user. Often, a network operating system will maintain additional information about the user, such as the default connections to apply to the user, the user's security permissions, the groups the user belongs to, the background pattern for the user's desktop, and so on. In a Windows NT network, this additional information is called the user's profile.

You can add additional user accounts to your Windows NT network in two ways: You can create new user accounts, or you can make copies of existing user accounts. In either case you may make changes in three areas:

- User account information

- Group membership information

- User account profile information

To add a new user account, you will be working with the New User dialog box, as shown in Figure 8.1.

FIGURE 8.1

New User dialog box

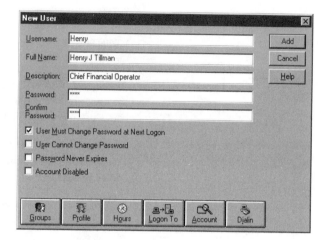

When you create an account, it must have a unique username. It cannot be the same as another username or group name on the server or network domain.

The passwords on your network should be hard to guess. Easy-to-guess passwords such as your birth date, your name, or your children's names are not good choices. If you wish to create an account that does not require a password (such as the guest account in many networks), you can leave the password field blank. This, however, is a serious security hole in your network, and you should create such an account only if it is really needed and you have taken adequate security precautions to ensure that the guest account cannot be used to damage your network or access sensitive information.

Remember your passwords. They are your keys to the network. Windows NT will not tell you what a password is after it has been entered, even if you are the system administrator. If you or another user forgets the password, you can create another password for that user account, but you cannot determine what the original password was.

Table 8.1 describes the properties of the User account that are accessible from the New User dialog box in Windows NT Server version 4.0. User accounts are administered with the User Manager administrative tool.

TABLE 8.1	FIELD	VALUE
User Account Properties	Username	A required text field of up to 20 characters. Uses both uppercase and lowercase letters except " / \ [ ] : ; | = , + * ? < > but is not case sensitive. This name must be unique among workstation users or among network domain members if attached to a network.
	Full Name	An optional text field typically used for the complete name of the user. For instance, a user whose full name is Mae West may have a username of mwest.
	Description	An optional text field for more fully describing the user, that user's position in the firm, home office, and so on. This field is limited to any 48 characters.
	Password	A required text field up to 14 characters, case sensitive. This field displays asterisks, rather than the characters typed, to keep your password secure.
	Confirm Password	A required text field for confirming the password field. This method avoids typing errors, which result in unknown passwords. As with the Password field, the Confirm Password field displays asterisks.
	User Must Change Password at Next Logon	A check box field that forces a password change at the next logon. Note that Windows NT will not allow you to apply changes to a User account if this field and the User Cannot Change Password field are both checked.
	User Cannot Change Password	A check box field that makes it impossible for users to change their own password. This feature is used for shared accounts (such as the Guest account), where a user changing the account password would make it impossible for other users of the account to log on. You would normally not check this field for typical users.
	Password Never Expires	A check box field that prevents a password from expiring according to the password policy. This setting is normally used for automated software services that must be logged in as a user. Note that setting Password Never Expires overrides the User Must Change Password at Next Logon field.
	Account Disabled	A check box field that, when set, prevents users from logging onto the network with this account. This field provides an easy way to place an account temporarily out of service.

	FIELD	VALUE
TABLE 8.1 User Account Properties (continued)	Account Locked Out	This option is checked if the account is currently locked out due to failed logon attempts. You can clear it to restore access to the account, but it cannot be set.
	Groups button	Assigns Group membership
	Profile button	A button used to set the user environment profile information
	Dial-In button	Allows users to dial into the computer using Remote Access Service (See Chapter 12 for more information.)

You should record the Administrator account password, seal it in an envelope, and place it in a secure location. Make sure at least one other trusted individual knows where the password is stored in case you get hit by a meteor.

REAL WORLD PROBLEMS

You have 35 people in your company, all of whom need user accounts. You consider assigning accounts using first names as account names.

- What are the drawbacks of this method of naming accounts?

You are the administrator of a 75-station network. You are about to go on a much-needed vacation. Until now, you have always been available to handle any emergency.

- What should you do in case there is trouble while you are gone?

Copying User Accounts

If you have to create accounts for a large number of users—for instance, in an academic environment where hundreds of students come and go every year—you can create a few basic User account templates and copy them as needed. A User account template is a User account that provides all the features new users will need and has its Account Disabled field (in Windows NT; most network operating systems have a similar option) enabled. When you need to add a User account, you can copy the template. When you copy a User account, Windows NT automatically copies some of the User account field values from the template; you provide the remaining necessary information.

Windows NT copies these values from the template to the new User account:

- Description
- Group Account Memberships
- Profile Settings
- User Cannot Change Password
- Password Never Expires

Windows NT leaves the following fields blank in the new User account dialog:

- Username
- Full Name
- User Must Change Password at Next Logon
- Account Disabled

The Username and Full Name fields are left blank for you to enter the new user information. The User Must Change Password at Next Logon check box is set by default. As a security precaution, leave this setting if you want to force new users to change from your assigned password when they first log on.

Disabling and Deleting User Accounts

When access to the account is no longer appropriate for a user, that account should be disabled. Leaving unused active accounts in the user accounts database makes it easy for potential intruders to continue logon attempts after accounts they've already tried lock them out. Disabling an account prevents it from being used but retains the account information for future use.

This technique is useful for employees who are absent or for temporarily denying access to an account that may have been compromised. Deleting an account removes all the user account information from the system. If a user account has been deleted and that user requires access again, a new account will have to be set up with all new permissions. Creating a new user account with the same name in Windows NT will not restore previous account information since each user account is internally identified by a unique security identifier, not by username.

If a user will no longer be using the system, you should disable the user's account. After removing anything important stored by that account, you can then delete the account. Deleting an account destroys all user preferences and permissions, so be certain the user will never again require access before taking this step.

Renaming User Accounts

You can rename any user account in Windows NT, including the Administrator and Guest default accounts, with User Manager. You may need to change an account user name if an account associated with a specific job is passed to another individual or if your organization changes its network naming policy.

Changing the name does not change any other properties of the account. You may want to change the names of the Administrator and Guest accounts so an intruder familiar with Windows NT default user account names cannot gain access to your system simply by guessing a password.

Home Directories

Home directories give users a place to store their own files. By changing the home directory location through the user profile, you can allow each user to have a private location in which to store files. In general, you should set permissions on home directories so that only that user has access to the data in the directory.

Windows NT makes the home directory the default save location for programs that do not specify one in their Save dialog box. The home directory is also the default directory when launching an MS-DOS prompt.

Windows NT cannot automatically create more than one level of directory structure in the User Profile dialog box. If you had entered the path to the directory location above without having created the user directory first, Windows NT would have set the profile but warned you to create the directory manually. Creating the path for user directories prior to changing the profile information ensures you will not forget to do this or misspell the user name when you create the directory.

REAL WORLD PROBLEMS

The head of the eastern sales division has been hired away by a competitor.

- What should you do with his account?

You must create 300 new accounts for the freshman class of the college where you manage a network.

- What is the best way to do this quickly and efficiently?

- In what circumstances will you rename accounts instead of creating new ones?

Groups

Setting specific permissions for many users of a workstation can be an error-prone and time-consuming exercise. Most organizations do not have security requirements that change for every user. Setting permissions is more manageable with the security groups concept: permissions are assigned to groups rather than to individual users. Users who are members of a group have all the permissions assigned to that group. Group memberships are especially important in large networks.

Groups are useful in many situations. For instance, the finance department in your organization can have permissions set to access all the financial data stored on a computer. You would then create a group called Finance in User Manager and make each individual in the finance department a member of this group. Every member of the Finance group will have access to all the financial data.

Groups also make changing permissions easier. Permissions assigned to a group affect every member of the group, so changes can be made across the entire group by changing permissions for the group. For instance, adding a new directory for the finance group requires merely assigning the group permission to the directory to give each member access. This is much easier than assigning permission to a number of individual accounts.

The two basic types of groups in Windows NT networks are local groups and global groups. Local groups affect only a single Windows NT workstation or server. Global groups affect the entire network and are stored on the primary domain controller. Windows 95 and earlier versions of Windows do not maintain group information because these operating systems do not secure resources in relation to individual users.

One individual account can belong to many groups. This arrangement facilitates setting up groups for many purposes. For instance, you might define groups corresponding to the functional areas in your organization—administration, marketing, finance, manufacturing, and so on. You might create another group for supervisors, another for network support staff, and another for new employees. This procedure enables you to set default permissions for all finance members; the permissions can be modified if the Finance group member is also a new employee by making that account a member of both groups.

For example, a member of the finance group may have permission to access accounting information and financial statements, but new users may be denied permission to access accounting information. By assigning membership in both groups, you would be allowing access to financial statements without permitting access to accounting information until the user is a trusted employee and removed from the New Users group.

Windows NT has a default group called Users that can be used to assign rights and permissions for every user on the network. When accounts are created, they are automatically assigned membership in the default Users group. Changing permissions assigned to the default Users group will change permissions for everyone who has access to the computer.

Microsoft Exchange uses the Windows NT group information to define its groups. Therefore, all members of a security group defined now will also become message groups when you install Microsoft Exchange.

Planning Groups

Planning your groups correctly will make administering the users on your workstation easier. Experienced administrators seldom assign access rights to individual accounts. Instead, they create a group and then make individual accounts a part of that group. For instance, rather than giving individual users the access rights to back up the system, the administrator creates a Backup group with those rights and then adds users to that group. That way, when the backup process changes, only the group account must be changed to match the new process. Also, the administrator now has a convenient way to send messages to all individuals who can back up the network.

Windows NT Server uses Global groups to maintain groups across all computers on a network. This is different from the local groups you can create using Windows NT Workstation.

Assigning users to groups allows you to keep track of who needs which resource. For example, word processing users might need access to the word processing package itself, its data files, and also a shared directory that contains your organization's common documents and templates. You can give all three rights to a group called Word Processing and then in one action give the rights to an individual account by adding the account to the group.

In Windows NT, you can give rights to everyone by assigning those access rights to the group Users.

When you are creating the network groups for your network, you should determine which network resources the users on your network will need to access. Observe what different users have in common, and create groups to give users that access. Ideally, you will assign rights to groups and grant rights to users by making them a part of the appropriate groups. You can base groups on criteria such as the following:

- Organization functional units, such as marketing

- Network programs, such as word processing, graphics, and so on

- Events, such as a company party

- Network resources, such as a laser printer

- Location, such as Hanger 18

- Individual function, such as backup operator

When a user is a member of many groups, some of those groups may specifically allow access to a resource while other group memberships deny it. A specific denial in Windows NT always overrides access to a resource.

Suppose a new employee is a member of the Finance and New Employees groups. In the Finance group, she is allowed access to the financial directory, but all members of the New Employees group are specifically denied access to this directory. The new user will not have access to this directory.

When resolving conflicting permissions, Windows NT always chooses the most restrictive permission specifically encountered.

Built-in Groups

Most network operating systems have several predefined groups for specific network administration purposes. Windows NT creates several groups at installation that are meant to provide convenient group features for administration. They may be all you need, but if you have many users you will probably modify these default groups and add your own. These built-in groups are

- Account Operators

- Administrators

- Backup Operators

- Domain Admins

- Domain Guests

- Domain Users

- Guests

- Print Operators

- Replicator

- Server Operators

- Users

You can use an additional special group, named Everyone, to assign global permissions or rights to all users.

ACCOUNT OPERATORS Account Operators can administer users and groups. They have the ability to create and delete accounts and to modify account settings for certain groups of accounts. Many organizations find it useful to assign one individual the task of adding new accounts to the network and assigning non-sensitive privileges to user accounts. The ability of Account Operators to assign rights to other accounts is limited by the security policy of the domain for Account Operators.

ADMINISTRATORS Administrators can fully administer the workstation. They have full rights and privileges over all files and other resources on the workstation or server. The default Administrator account and the Initial User account, if created automatically, have membership in the Administrators group. If the workstation is part of a network domain, all domain administrators are automatically members of the Administrators group.

BACKUP OPERATORS Backup Operators can bypass security to back up and restore all files on the workstation using the Backup and Restore commands provided with NT. Any user may use the backup and restore utilities to back up and restore files they have full access to. Members of the Backup Operators group are granted full rights for all files on the workstation, but only while using the Backup and Restore commands.

DOMAIN ADMINS Members of the Domain Admins group can administer the domain. Accounts in this group are automatically added to the Administrators groups of each server or workstation within the domain, and Domain Admins have all the privileges of Administrators.

DOMAIN GUESTS Members of the Domain Guests group can log in to the domain with relaxed security. This group provides limited access to basic network resources.

DOMAIN USERS Domain Users are users of the domain with generic privileges. Accounts in the Domain Users group are automatically added to the Users groups of each server or workstation within the domain. Domain Users have all of the privileges of Users.

REPLICATOR The Replicator group is used for the setup of the Replicator service. The Replicator service automatically updates files from one workstation to another.

SERVER OPERATORS Members of the Server Operators group can administer servers in the domain. The Server Operators group allows its members to perform some administrative functions on severs within a domain, such as configuring devices and modifying system settings.

USERS Members of the Users group have normal user rights and permissions. This group is designed for the vast majority of people who need to use the workstation or server but are not system or network administrators. Members of the Users group can run applications, manage files on the workstation, and use local and network printers. They can create and manage their own local groups and may manage their own profiles. All new User accounts you create will automatically have membership in the Users group.

Creating Groups

In Windows NT, you create groups much the way you create users. Select New Local Group from the User menu in the User Manager window. Then you can enter the group name, description, and members in the New Local Group dialog box (see Figure 8.2).

FIGURE 8.2

The New Local Group dialog box allows you to create a group and add users to that group.

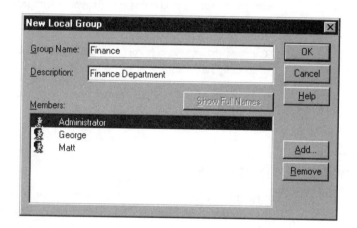

The Group Name field identifies the local group. The group name has the same restrictions as a username. It must be unique and can contain any upper- or lowercase letters, numbers, or symbols other than the following:

" / \ : ; | = + * ? < >

The Description field is where you type a description of the group.

REAL WORLD PROBLEMS

Your company has several departments: Marketing, Sales, Production, and Administration. It has several levels of staff status: Temporary, Wage, Salary, and Officer. There are three floors in your office building, and the users in your company have varying levels of computer competence. You have two assistants to help you administer the network. Your company has an informal party-planning committee and a softball team.

■ What groups will you create in your network?

(continued)

REAL WORLD PROBLEMS (CONTINUED)

You wish to allow certain users limited access to the network, but you don't want those users to have the level of access that regular users have.

■ What group will you assign these users to?

It would be a lot easier administratively to assign everyone to the Domain Administrators group instead of creating specific groups for specific purposes.

■ Why don't you do this?

You must ensure that only certain users can use a specific software package because of licensing restrictions.

■ How can groups help you restrict access to the software package?

Documenting the Network

Your network should be well documented. Network documentation not only helps you keep track of your network, it becomes indispensable if someone else needs to perform your network administration duties. Be sure to keep all network information in one log and make all changes in that log. You can, of course, make copies of the log, but there should be just one place to record new network information. Documenting your network has three primary purposes:

■ Clearly defines the network in your own mind

■ Records information so others can maintain the network

■ Tracks material for warranty and costing purposes

You need network documentation because your network will almost certainly not stay the same as when you installed it. Eventually your network will grow, and you will add equipment. You will also do maintenance tasks and reinstall or upgrade the server and client systems. By documenting what you did the first time, you can perform these tasks more easily the next time you need them.

Your network documentation should be broken down into major sections to help you or others find information quickly. You should keep track of the following information:

■ Physical plant diagram, station locations, and cable test results

- Network hardware and software, which should include the following:

  - Item description and serial number

  - Location

  - Purchase date, vendor, and warranty information

  - Network name, number, or other logical value that could identify it on the network.

  - Documentation (or location of the documentation)

- Current network diagram/architecture/layout

- Number of software licenses for each application and location of the license certificates

- A history of network problems and their solutions

If you keep your documentation as a network file, it is a good idea to print it out and to store the file away from the network—you may need to use the information when the network is not functioning.

Protecting Your Network Environment

YOU MUST PROTECT your network from intentional and accidental damage. A security plan will help keep your network safe from intruders and you can protect your network from viruses by using virus scanning software. You can use an uninterruptible power supply to protect your computer equipment from power surges, failures, and brownouts.

You should implement a backup plan so you can recover data from hardware failure and from inadvertent deletion, and you can use replication, striping, and mirroring to make your system less susceptible to failure and to allow you to quickly recover from hardware problems.

Security

Providing security means more than controlling a system to prevent theft. It means controlling the system to prevent loss of any nature. Accidental loss, especially in information systems, is quite common. Users sometimes delete files to make space without really knowing what they've deleted. Computers can crash, sometimes losing data in the process. A file can be overwritten with a different document of the same name.

The security measures implemented in networks are designed to prevent both accidental and intentional loss. All network operating systems requires a logon so that no access to information is given without accountability.

Unlike many network operating systems, Windows NT implements resource-level security whereby individual information resources are secured by type, and access to the resource is controlled by lists of trusted users called Access Control Lists. These measures are quite effective in preventing loss, and they form an important part of the total networking process.

When a user or group has an access control entry in an access control list for a specific resource that allows access, that user has permission to use that object. The set of access control lists is called Permissions.

As the network administrator, it is your job to define and implement a security policy that will protect critical resources without preventing people from performing their work. The balance between protection and usability changes for every organization, and it is up to the network administrator to strike the appropriate balance for each individual organization.

How Much Security Is Enough?

Before you begin securing shared resources, you need to determine exactly what your security requirement is. If your organization has a security policy, you should read that document before implementing security on your network.

Remember that the purpose of security is to prevent loss (including unauthorized disclosure) of any type. Before implementing security, ask yourself how likely it is the different sorts of loss will occur. Remember that a good backup policy will prevent most data loss, so you should really only be concerned with unauthorized disclosure in your security policy. The following sections present a series of questions you should answer before creating a security policy.

WHAT ARE YOU TRYING TO PREVENT? You should understand what losses you are trying to prevent before implementing security. The following problems can occur on computer networks, so consider them when you create a security policy.

- **Accessory to copyright violation:** The owners of computers that are used for public data receptacles are liable for the content on them. For instance, if you are running a BBS with your computer and one of your clients stores pirated software on it, you may be liable for copyright violation. This specific circumstance does not apply to most users, but similar problems may.

- **Accidental loss:** Users may accidentally delete or change important data files or programs that they should have read access to. Preventing this is easy, but it does require specific action on your part because the default share permission is full control for everyone.

- **Unauthorized disclosure:** Trade secrets, Privacy Act information, and financial data are important information resources to protect, but these resources must be shared among users on a network. For most shares containing this sort of data, you should deny access for everyone and then allow access only for the specific groups that require it to perform their jobs.

- **Malicious destruction of data:** This can occur when a computer isn't properly secured on the Internet or when someone gains physical access to your computer or network with the intent to destroy information. Assess the likelihood of this sort of access to your computer when formulating a security plan.

HOW IMPORTANT IS YOUR DATA? This may seem obvious, but if your data doesn't have much value or is naturally secure, there isn't much reason to secure it.

For instance, directories that contain non–work related software such as games or programs that can easily be reinstalled if something goes wrong are not big security risks. On the other hand, trade secrets or private employee information must be secured to prevent its accidental disclosure.

WHAT IS THE RISK OF INTRUSION? If your computer is part of a physically secure network and you trust everyone who logs in, you don't have much risk of intrusion. If, however, your computer is not secure from untrusted individuals or there is sensitive information on it, you should take steps to prevent that information from being shared or restrict access to certain groups.

WHAT IS THE PROBABILITY OF ACCIDENTAL LOSS? Sometimes people with access to your files accidentally delete files or change them without understanding the consequences. If your shared resources are accessible to inexperienced computer users, you may accidentally lose data.

Creating a Security Plan

If you have a rigorous security requirement, create a plan listing all the shared resources on your computer and the groups that will require access to them. When complete, use the exercises shown in the remainder of this chapter to implement security according to your plan.

EXTERNAL REQUIREMENTS Many organizations have external security regulations that require certain protections. Companies involved with classified government work, for instance, have a number of security policies mandated by government with which they must comply. The network administrator must adapt any mandated external security policies to the network security policy.

INHERENT POLICY There are two ways to implement network security: optimistically and pessimistically. An optimistic policy optimizes the usability of the network by securing only those resources that are known to require unusual security. A pessimistic policy optimizes security by restricting all resources and granting access only to those individuals who are known to need access in order to perform their work. These are also referred to as *need to know* policies.

Whether you use an optimistic or pessimistic approach to network security depends on your needs, the value of your data, and any external requirements that may apply.

If your data is extremely valuable, you should consider taking a pessimistic approach to network security. For instance, banks have legal requirements to keep their data secure. Intrusions could cost many times more than the lag in productivity required by their security measures, so a pessimistic security policy is warranted.

A building contractor, however, probably does not have much to worry about in terms of network security. The competition is not likely to attempt to gain access to network files, and even if they did, there isn't much chance they'd find anything useful other than perhaps financial records. A good backup policy is all that is really required to keep data secure, so an optimistic security policy is warranted.

Pessimistic security can cost a tremendous amount of money in lost productivity. Every minute users must wait for specific access to a network resource costs money. The time an administrator takes to implement a detailed security policy costs money. The additional time required to secure new resources when they are installed costs money. Encryption devices cost money.

No individual instance of these costs would amount to much, but over the life of a network they represent quite a bit of time and money. You should be certain your data and situation warrant a pessimistic security policy before implementing it.

REAL WORLD PROBLEMS

You are creating a security policy for the research and design department of a high-tech company. The information stored on the servers in this LAN is vital to the company, but the engineers and researchers will not accept intrusive security measures.

■ What sort of security can you implement?

You are the LAN administrator for a defense contractor. Your LAN contains very sensitive information.

■ What type of security is warranted in this case?

You are the network administrator for a university LAN. You maintain student accounts and faculty accounts on your LAN.

■ What security issues do you face on your LAN?

Virus Protection

Unfortunately, not only do you have to protect your network from deliberate or unintentional tampering, you must protect your network data from the indiscriminate destruction and system unreliability caused by computer viruses.

A virus is a computer program that modifies your computer system to allow it to reproduce itself. Bootable floppy disks and executable programs can transmit viruses. When a virus first runs on your system, it searches for other bootable floppies, bootable hard drive partitions, or executable programs and modifies them to include the virus. Once your computer has become infected, you run the risk of infecting other computers by exchanging floppy disks or executable programs.

You may have heard that Windows NT is immune to viruses. This is not true. No viruses are known that can get past Windows NT security on the server, but that protection does not apply to the server before the operating system is started or to clients attached to the server. The server can be affected by a boot sector virus, especially if it is sometimes booted with another operating system such as DOS or Windows, and any computer that can write a file to the server can propagate a virus over the network to other clients, even though the virus won't infect the server.

You may wish to install virus-scanning software on your file server and client computers. This type of software watches network traffic and files on floppy disks and intercepts suspicious files. Most virus-scanning software asks if you wish to disinfect the offending file by removing the virus. It is important to always have a current version of your virus-scanning software. The current version will detect viruses that older versions will miss. Microsoft produces the virus-scanning program VIRSCAN; there are many other commercial virus-scanning products available on the market, and you can download virus scanners from the Internet.

Uninterruptible Power Supply

Your file server is an electrical device; when the power fails, so does your server. This can be a disaster. If your file server is in the middle of an important operation when the power fails, you could lose important data. One way to protect your computer from power failure is with an uninterruptible power supply (UPS), as shown in Figure 8.3.

FIGURE 8.3

A uninterruptible power supply can protect your computer from power outages and power spikes.

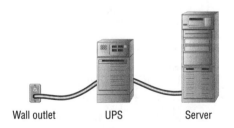

Wall outlet   UPS   Server

A UPS stores electricity while your computer and the power supplying it are acting normally. When a power failure occurs, the UPS continues to provide power to your computer for a period of time. How long it provides power depends on the UPS you purchase; it can range from several minutes to several hours. Five or ten minutes is a common UPS capacity.

The UPS will signal your file server that power has failed and that it may be necessary for the file server to save its data. This allows the file server operating system to gracefully shut down when power fails instead of being halted in the middle of an important operation, which might cause data to be lost.

You can provide a UPS for your servers, or you can provide it for your entire network. There are many available options, and the cost depends on the degree of protection you need for your network.

The best UPS systems are always active. In other words, the network equipment draws power from the UPS and the UPS draws power from the power source. Some UPS systems are inactive while there is normal power but activate and provide power when normal power fails. This type of UPS system is less expensive but also less reliable.

Your UPS should protect your equipment from power spikes as well as power failures and brownouts. The UPS should come with software to communicate with the server and notify it of a power problem. The UPS should be powerful enough to drive all the devices that will depend on it if a power failure occurs, and it should give the network systems enough time to gracefully shut down.

For critical network operations, you may wish to consider an independent source of power, such as a gasoline-powered generator. The UPS can provide electrical power until the generator comes online. This way your network can continue to function even when the power is out for an extended period of time.

You should remember to include network devices such as hubs, bridges, and routers in your UPS planning. Some server functions will not be able to continue or be able to shut down gracefully if communications with other equipment is cut off by power failure.

Disaster Recovery

In spite of all of your preparation, your network can still fail. You can reduce the cost of failure of a device on your network, such as a hard disk drive or other server component, by implementing a backup policy. You can make your system fault tolerant by replicating, striping, or mirroring your server's data.

Microsoft
Exam
Objective

Choose a disaster recovery plan for various situations.

Backup Policy

Every network should have some form of backup. The most common form is backup on magnetic tape, because it is reliable, inexpensive, and has enough capacity to back up the entire network on a single tape. If you have a tape backup of your important data files and something does happen to your file server, you can restore the data to that server or to another server. Without a tape backup, the data could be lost permanently.

A tape backup of your data can also be useful when data files are inadvertently or intentionally deleted. You can restore those deleted files from the backup tape. You will lose any changes that were made since the files were last backed up, but the files themselves will be restored.

THE TAPE DRIVE The tape drive should match the data backup needs of your network. Here are some things to consider when choosing a tape drive:

- Amount of data you will need to back up

- Speed of the drive

- Capacity of the drive

- Reliability of the drive

- Cost of the drive

- Cost of the media

- Media interchangeability with other tape drives

- Drivers and backup software for the operating system

You should select a tape drive that can back up all the data on your largest server on a single tape.

THE BACKUP POLICY The simplest backup policy is to leave a tape in the drive and back up your system whenever you remember to. That is not a good backup policy.

A better backup policy is to have a set time every day (or every night) when the file server backs up its data to the tape drive. After the backup, remove the tape and insert another. You can rotate the tapes on a weekly or monthly schedule to make economical use of your backup medium while keeping backups of your data for a period of time.

You should also consider taking some of the backup tapes (every other tape, for instance, or make two backups and take one) *offsite*, or away from the location of the network. This protects your data in case of a disaster such as a fire, which might destroy the file server and any data stored on backup tapes in the same location.

You should perform a full backup of your server data fairly often—at least once a week. The full backup will store all your data. You can use incremental backups, which store only what has changed since your last backup, for daily backups between full backups. If your network holds critical data that changes often, you may wish to perform a full backup every night and several incremental backups during the day to minimize the amount of data that can be lost. If even that is not sufficient, you should consider fault-tolerant systems, as described a little later in this chapter.

You should also test your backups to ensure that the backup system is performing properly. You can do this by creating some data, backing it up, deleting it, and then attempting to restore it from the backup tape. Experienced administrators do this every so often to make sure the backup system is still working as they expect it to.

LOCATION OF THE BACKUP SYSTEM Backups can be performed locally on each server in your network, or they can be performed over the network to a client or central tape backup computer. Each method has advantages and disadvantages.

Tape backups that are local to the server do not load down the network with backup traffic. Consider that during a backup, you will be moving the entire contents of all your server's hard disk drives. This amount of traffic over your network is probably not feasible during the day, but at night most organizations have little or no network traffic. Local backups are less convenient for multiple server environments, however, because you have to change tapes at a number of locations each day.

Networks with several servers often have an isolated segment for backup; all data for backup is transferred over that segment. This arrangement frees other network segments from the load of backing up the data, and it isolates the data backup from the effects of network use.

In general, when you have only one or two servers, you should probably keep your backups local. When you have more than two, you should probably opt for centralized backup as long as it doesn't interfere with your normal network traffic.

Replication

If the data on your file servers must be available even if an individual file server goes down, you should consider replicating the data on your servers. Replication is the process by which servers maintain a copy of other servers' data. For example, suppose you have three file servers in your organization: one for Manufacturing (named MANSRV), one for Customer Support (named CUSTSRV), and one for Research and Design (named RDSRV). You might then configure MANSRV to replicate CUSTSRV's important customer list and order data, CUSTSRV to replicate RDSRV's specifications and preliminary test data for your next product, and RDSRV to replicate MANSRV's inventory and control database. This way, if any one server fails, the data is still available on a different server.

Fault Tolerance

Sometimes being able to recover your data from a hardware failure is not enough. Some LANs must not experience any down time, or data or money will be lost. You can use replication to allow the network to continue to operate in the absence of a server, and you can implement fault tolerance in your servers to make it less likely for a hardware failure to cause a server to go down.

You can make your file server less susceptible to hard disk failure by using the fault tolerance characteristics of your server operating system or hardware. Windows NT Server, for example, allows you to perform disk striping and mirroring.

Windows NT Server supports RAID (Redundant Arrays of Inexpensive Disks) levels 0 (Striping), 1 (Mirroring), and 5 (Striping with Parity). Level 0 increases disk performance but does not make your server more fault tolerant—in fact, if any one disk fails in a Level 0 RAID stripe set, the data on all the disks in the set is lost. Therefore, a Level 0 RAID set makes your file server less fault tolerant.

While many operating systems directly support the various levels of RAID, you can also buy hard drive controller cards that perform the RAID functions. This way you can use RAID in an operating system that does not support RAID, or you can reduce the workload on an operating system that does support it by having the controller card perform the function instead of having the microprocessor do it.

STRIPING WITH PARITY Disk Striping with Parity, also called RAID level 5, protects you from failure of any one disk in your computer by spreading the information to be stored on disk across several disks and by including some error-correction information on the disks. If any one of the striped disks fails, the operating system can recover the information that was on that disk from the other disks in the stripe set.

Disk Striping with Parity requires at least three partitions of the same size, and each partition should be on a different physical drive. Striping with Parity wastes less disk space than does mirroring, and it also often results in faster disk performance because the operating system can request data from all the striped drives at the same time.

MIRRORING Disk Mirroring, or RAID level 1, makes an exact copy of your hard drive partition on another hard drive partition in your system. Ideally, each partition would be on a separate hard drive. Any information written to one drive will also be written to the other drive, so the exact copy is maintained by the operating system. If at any time one hard drive fails, the other hard drive partition can take over the data storage functions.

Mirroring requires at least two partitions of the same size, and each partition should be on a different physical drive. Some operating systems, such as Windows NT, cannot boot if their operating system files are on a stripe set. However, Windows NT can operate when the partition that contains its operating system files are mirrored. Many organizations that require fault tolerance in their file servers mirror the system partition and stripe all other partitions.

REAL WORLD PROBLEMS

You must protect your LAN from viruses.

- How will you do it?

Power outages are a problem in your area.

- What is your solution to this problem?

You are creating a disaster recovery plan for your network.

- In what circumstances is a nightly backup sufficient?

- What circumstances would make it necessary for you to implement fault tolerance in your servers?

You must ensure that the failure of any one server on your network will not make vital data inaccessible.

- How will you do this?

Your operating system does not support RAID but you need to be able to stripe data across several drives for fault tolerance and for increased performance.

- How can you implement RAID in this situation?

Managing Your Network Environment

A NETWORK IS A dynamic construct. It will grow and change as your organization grows and changes. Once you have configured the network, you must manage it to ensure that it continues to serve your organization's needs. A primary concern of every network administrator is that the network perform well. Growing networks commonly develop *bottlenecks* that slow down the system, and it is your job to find and remove those bottlenecks.

Monitoring Network Performance

To detect when your network performance decreases, you must be able to recognize a network that is performing well. You should use the monitoring tools available to you to get a performance *baseline* for your network. A baseline is a record of the response characteristics of your network when it is not heavily loaded or otherwise performing badly. You can later refer to this baseline to recognize anomalous situations.

Microsoft Exam Objective

Select the appropriate hardware and software tools to monitor trends in the network.

Each operating system has its own tools to monitor network performance. Windows NT has two tools you will find very useful for managing your network: Performance Monitor and Network Monitor.

Performance Monitor

The Windows NT Performance Monitor shows you how your Windows NT server is performing. Almost any aspect of your Windows NT server can be graphed or logged using the Performance Monitor. It can present information about your system in charts, logs, and reports so you can view the information in several ways.

Network Monitor

A similar utility for monitoring network traffic is the Windows NT Network Monitor. The Network Monitor can show you information such as the current network utilization, frames per second, communicating stations on the network and their station addresses, and sources of broadcasts.

Automated Network Management

Software packages are available for most network operating systems that will help you automate the management of your network. These packages can track key parameters of your network server and client operating systems, such as the amount of free disk space and the peak amount of traffic on your network.

Many of these packages also help you manage other things such as the configuration of client computers and the software distributed to each client computer. Several such packages can actually upgrade the software on your client computers for you.

Hardware Upgrade Policy

As computer technology progresses, as your network grows, and as you upgrade applications on your network and install new software packages, you will find that the hardware on your network (the computers, NICs, hubs, and so on) become increasingly obsolete. This is a natural occurrence in the world of networks, and you should prepare for it.

Some components of your network will last longer than others. If you install new copper network cables today to the Category 5 specification, your physical cables could last you a decade or longer. If you install fiber-optic cables, you may never need to replace them. Commodity Ethernet NICs (capable of 10Mbps) will probably be useful for five years or so, before network applications require greater bandwidth. (For some applications today, 10Mbps is already inadequate.) The cutting-edge computer today will be merely adequate a year and a half from now, and in three years it will be underpowered.

You should have a plan for upgrading your computers and network equipment as they become obsolete. Expect to replace the computers in your network every three years. The life cycle of other components in your network will depend on the performance you require from your network. A data entry firm that exchanges little more than text files over the network will be able to use installed network cables much longer than an engineering firm that is always exchanging huge archives of structural data.

Review

A GOOD NETWORK ADMINISTRATOR is seldom seen by network users because a good network administrator keeps problems from happening that would otherwise interfere with users' work. The administrator creates, manages, and protects the network environment so the users can use the network to do their jobs.

The network environment you create will reflect the nature of your organization. Your software needs, including network software and the support of regular software, will affect how you set up your server. You may have more than one server if you have a large organization or if the nature of your organization would place too great a load on a single server.

You will create user accounts for the people in your organization, and you can use groups to simplify your administration of the network. You can assign privileges to groups and then put users in groups, thereby giving those users those privileges.

By documenting your network, you make your own job easier and you make it easier for others to work with your network. You should store the network documentation in a safe place not on the network, or you may not have a network when you need to access the data.

You should evaluate your organization's security needs and provide appropriate security mechanisms in your network. Network operating systems provide many ways of ensuring that only authorized individuals have access to private data. You also need to protect your network data from other forms of damage and loss, such as viruses, power failure, and hardware failure.

Once you have planned and configured your network environment, you need to manage your network environment. Most operating systems come with tools to help you do this, and you can purchase additional software packages that can automate many management tasks for you.

Finally, you should recognize that the hardware and software you install today will be obsolete tomorrow. You should plan to replace your computers, network components, and applications as time goes by.

Review Questions

1. The manager of the accounting department has decided not to return from maternity leave. Her replacement has been hired from outside the company. Which of the following is the best way to ensure that her replacement has the same access to the network she had?

   A. Change the password on the old manager's account and let the new manager use the same account.

   B. Disable the old manager's account. Create a new account with the same settings as the old account.

   C. Delete the old account. Create a new account for the new manager.

   D. Rename the account to the new manager's username and assign a new password.

2. When designing a disaster recovery and prevention plan, it is always a good idea to include a UPS. When connected to your server, what will a UPS do?

   A. Ensure that the server is protected from virus attacks.

   B. Ensure that the server is protected from unauthorized access.

   C. Ensure that the server is protected from power failure.

   D. Ensure that the server is protected from fire.

3. You are planning the installation of a new Windows NT server. You would like to provide some hard disk fault-tolerance. Which of the following could you use in your new server to provide fault tolerance? Choose all that apply:

   A. UPS

   B. Disk striping with parity

   C. Disk duplexing

   D. Disk striping

4. What is the maximum length a username can be when using Microsoft products such as Windows NT?

A. 15 characters

B. 12 characters

C. 16 characters

D. 20 characters

5. A number of user groups are automatically created when Windows NT Server is installed on a computer. Which of the following groups provides no special privileges to its members?

A. Users

B. Server Operators

C. Replicator

D. Administrators

6. You manage a rather large 100BaseTX network. It encompasses 20 servers and 900 client computers. You have been tasked with implementing a security plan that will withstand audits by clients.

Required result: Provide a security plan that will ensure solid security and provide centralized control of resources.

Optional desired results: Your plan should include a mechanism to track failed logon attempts as well as other network events. Include plans to protect your network from password discovery programs.

Proposed solution: Implement Windows NT user-level security on NTFS partitions including access-control security to shared resources. Set password restrictions to require users to change their passwords every 30 days and limit the number of failed attempts before an account is locked.

What results does the proposed solution provide?

A. The proposed solution produces the required result and produces all of the optional desired results.

B. The proposed solution produces the required result but produces only one of the optional desired results.

C. The proposed solution produces the required result but does not produce any of the optional desired results.

D. The proposed solution does not produce the required result.

7. When the Windows NT operating system, either Workstation or Server, is installed on a computer, two accounts are created. Which of the accounts in the following list are created when the operating system is installed? Choose two:

A. Manager

B. Guest

C. Administrator

D. Supervisor

8. The manager of the accounting department is going on maternity leave. When she returns she will need to maintain the access level she has now. However, you are concerned about someone else using her logon while she is gone. Which of the following can you do to ensure this doesn't happen?

A. Delete her account and re-create it when she returns.

B. Change the password on her account so that no one knows it.

C. Disable her account and re-enable it when she returns.

D. Enable password protection on her computer so that no one can access it.

9. When implementing a virus-protection system for your network, which of the following will provide reliable protection? Choose all that apply:

   A. Remove floppy drives from client computers.

   B. Install virus scanning software on all client and server computers.

   C. Update virus protection software regularly.

   D. Restrict physical access to the servers.

10. You have been asked to develop a naming system for the users on your Windows NT network. Which of the following statements apply to usernames on Microsoft networks? Choose all that apply:

    A. Must be unique among domain members.

    B. Must coincide with the computer name.

    C. Can include /, \, and ?

    D. Can use mixed case, but are not case sensitive.

11. When Windows NT Server is installed on a computer, a number of global and local groups are created. Which of the following groups provides its members with the ability to administer any computer in the domain?

    A. Domain Guests

    B. Domain Users

    C. Domain Operators

    D. Domain Admins

12. Which of the following RAID levels provides the fastest reads and best fault tolerance?

    A. RAID Level X

    B. RAID Level 5

    C. RAID Level 1

    D. RAID Level 0

13. Suppose the following situation exists: In an audit of your network security you learn that more than 100 of your 500 users have been granted Administrator privileges. This is too large a security risk to accept on your network.

   Required result: Implement a new security structure that restricts user access.

   Optional desired results: The new structure must ensure that only specific personnel are granted Administrator privileges. The new security structure should include auditing of logon events.

   Proposed solution: Create departmental groups encompassing the entire company structure. Include an Administrators group for yourself and other network administrators. Remove all Administrator and equivalent privileges from all users.

   Which result does the proposed solution produce?

   A. The proposed solution produces the required result and produces both of the optional desired results.

   B. The proposed solution produces the required result and produces only one of the optional desired results.

   C. The proposed solution produces the required result but does not produce any of the optional desired results.

   D. The proposed solution does not produce the required result.

CHAPTER

9

Remote Access

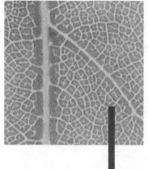

L OCAL AREA NETWORKS (LANS) allow you to connect computers together, but they have limitations. By definition, a LAN is local, which means that if you need to connect to the network from a distance, you must use a different method. Remote access is a method of connecting computers to networks over telephone lines. If you connect your home computer to your business Windows NT network over the phone lines, you will most likely use Microsoft's Remote Access Service for Windows NT.

This chapter will show you some of the technologies used to access a computer network remotely, as well as how to set up Remote Access Service on a Windows NT server. You will also learn how to connect a Windows 95 client computer to the server using a dial-up connection and Remote Access Service.

Modem Technology

T HE EASIEST WAY to connect computers over long distances is over telephone lines; you can reach almost anywhere by telephone. However, it would be prohibitively expensive to run a network cable to every location that has a telephone outlet. If it were not for modems, that would be the only way to make computer communication as pervasive as telephones are today.

How a Modem Works

Today's public telephone systems transfer analog signals from your phone to the destination of your call. (See Chapter 2 to refresh your memory on the difference between analog and digital signals.) Usually, the analog signal that is transferred is your voice. Computers, however, communicate using digital signals. This would seem to make the public phone system an inappropriate way to connect computers. Figure 9.1 illustrates how the telephone system works.

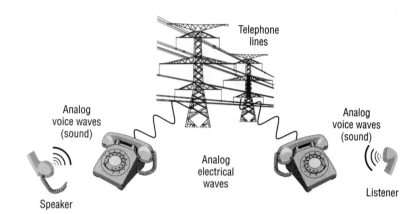

Modems, however, convert communications signals from a form the computer can understand to a form the phone system can convey, and vice versa. Modulation is the process of converting a digital signal from a computer into an analog signal the telephone system will accept. When you pick up the phone while your computer modem is communicating, or while you are sending a fax from your fax machine, you hear the sound of digital information that has been converted to analog signals.

At the other end of the connection, whether it be across town or across the world, another modem interprets those analog signals the telephone system has conveyed and converts them back into digital form so the receiving computer can understand them. See Figure 9.2 for an example of computers communicating via modems.

Connecting to the Computer

A modem can be installed internally, in the computer, in which case it is called an internal modem, or it can be an external device that is connected to the computer with a *serial cable*. Figure 9.3 shows an example of each type of modem.

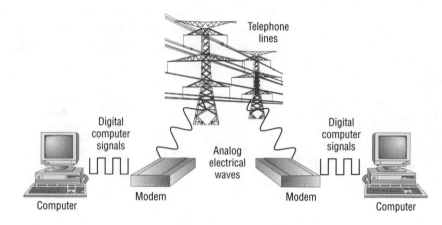

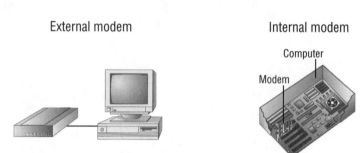

The serial (RS-232) cable must have connectors that match the modem at one end and the computer at the other end. On the modem end, most external modems have a female DB 25 (the *25* stands for *25-pin*) connector and need a cable that has a DB 25 male connector. (The male connector is the one with two rows of pins sticking out; the female connector has matching holes to accept the pins.) The other end of the cable, which connects to the computer, can have one of three types of connectors, depending on the computer:

- A DB 25 female connector to match the computer's 25-pin male connector

- A DB 9 male DIN connector to match the computer's 9-pin female DIN connector

- A small, round, male connector to match the PS/2-style female connector on the computer

Figure 9.4 illustrates the various types of serial connections.

PS/2-style serial connectors were introduced by IBM with the IBM PS/2 line of computers. Their small size makes them more convenient for manufacturers to use when they put serial connectors on the computer's motherboard, where space is at a premium.

FIGURE 9.4

Common serial cables have one of four connector types (including the connector on the modem-end of the cable).

DB 9 male PS/2 male

DB 25 male DB 25 female

Connecting to the Phone System

You connect a modem to the phone system just as you would a regular telephone or fax machine. The modem should accept a regular telephone cord—the kind that connects a telephone to a wall outlet.

Some special modems described later in this chapter require different connectors and special phone lines from the telephone company, but regular (asynchronous, used to connect to public dial network lines, as explained later in this chapter) modems can be connected to any telephone wall outlet.

Many businesses do not use regular analog telephones. Modems will work only with telephone lines that regular analog telephones can use. If you have a digital telephone system, sometimes called a key system, you must not plug your modem into the digital phone system lines, even if the telephone cord connector will fit. You could damage your modem or your digital telephone system if you do. Make sure a telephone line is a "plain old telephone system" (POTS) before you plug your modem into it.

Transfer Speed

Just as some computers are faster than others, some modems are faster than others. As with computers and just about everything else, the faster you go, the more it costs.

Modem speed is often discussed in baud rates or BPS, which are similar terms, but they do not mean exactly the same thing. *Baud rate* refers to the oscillation of a sound wave on which a single bit of data is carried. *BPS,* or bits per second, is the amount of data transferred in a second.

In early modems, there was a direct correlation between the oscillation of a sound wave and the number of bits per second transmitted, so the baud rate and the BPS were in fact the same thing. Now, however, engineers have found ways of transmitting more than 1 bit per oscillation of a sound wave. By employing special techniques that manipulate analog signals so that more than 1 bit of data can be transferred in a single cycle of the signal, a modem can encode data and achieve higher throughput. A modem that is modulating its sound waves at 9600 baud may actually be transmitting 28,800 BPS.

Compression

Another feature of most modern modems is data compression. Compression can greatly speed up the transfer of some types of information, such as text and graphics. It is less effective at speeding up other forms of data, such as program files and already compressed data.

Many modems can, when establishing a connection with another modem, compress the data flowing between the two modems. This compression happens without the intervention of the two computers involved. The two computers merely recognize a connection that is faster than would ordinarily occur without compression.

The two modems must compress and decompress data in the same way for the compression to happen. If the modems do not use the same compression scheme, they send the data back and forth uncompressed, which results in a slower link between the two computers. The most common compression standards today use the terms v.42bis and MNP class 5. (See the section "Asynchronous Modem Standards" later in this chapter for more information.)

Compression makes modem communication faster, but compression works in addition to, rather than being dependent on, the bits per second of the modem. BPS is an indicator of how fast the modems can communicate with each other; compression makes that communication appear faster than it is to the communicating computers. A modem can use compression at any number of bits per second, and a faster modem without compression can transfer data more quickly than a slower modem with compression when the data does not compress well. On the other hand, the slower modem with compression may transfer data more quickly than the faster modem if the data does compress well. The best of both worlds is, of course, a fast modem with compression.

Error Detection and Correction

Another feature modems provide is error correction. A bad telephone connection can cause bits of data to be scrambled or lost. If the erroneous bits are not detected and the damaged data is not corrected, the data being transmitted could be lost or permanently corrupted.

The simplest form of error detection, which all asynchronous modems can perform, is *parity checking*. In parity checking, there must be an odd number of 1 bits in a data word transmitted, in which case the modem is using odd parity, or there must be an even number, in which case the modem is using even parity. Parity can also be disabled, and it often is, because it uses some of the available bits per second to transmit the parity information.

Parity checking does not correct data errors. It simply signals that an error has occurred. It is up to the receiving computer to request that the transmitting computer resend the data.

Another commonly used method to make sure data is sent intact is counting the number of data words sent and received, making sure they are the same, and calculating a checksum, or final tally, on both the sent and received data to make sure the checksums match. These are operations the computers, not the modems, perform. If there is an error in the data transmission, all the data may have to be re-sent.

Modems, however, can assist in error control by detecting and correcting data errors themselves, without the assistance of the transmitting and receiving computers. Modems use several standards to perform error control and correction.

A company called Microcom developed a popular standard for early modems, called the Microcom Network Protocol, or MNP. Many modem vendors adopted the original MNP standard and its successors, MNP classes 2, 3, and 4.

An international standard for error control developed by the CCITT is V.42, which incorporates a protocol called Link Access Procedure for Modems, or LAPM. V.42, however, also incorporates the MNP class 4 protocol, so V.42 modems can perform error-control functions with MNP class 4 modems as well as with other V.42 modems.

REAL WORLD PROBLEMS

The telephone service at one of the outlying branches of your company is unreliable and noisy. You need to connect to the outlying branch via modem every night to download information.

■ Which modem feature will you most be interested in?

You must attach a modem to a computer that has no internal slots left.

■ Which type of modem will you be interested in?

A new digital key–system telephone and associated cabling were recently installed in your office. Your coworker wonders why his modem won't work when connected to the phone jack.

■ What is most likely the problem?

You are evaluating modems for use in your bank of dial-up modems in your network.

■ How does compression affect your choice of which modems you will buy?

Types of Modems

THERE ARE MANY types of modems because there are many different environments over which computers need to send data. As mentioned earlier in this chapter, modems are used whenever a computer's digital signals need to be converted to analog signals to be transmitted. The types of modems can be divided into two broad categories, depending on how they coordinate their data transmission:

■ Asynchronous

■ Synchronous

Asynchronous Communications

Asynchronous modems were developed specifically for use with telephone lines, and they are the most common type of modem. Almost any modem you purchase in a computer store will be an asynchronous modem.

Asynchronous Data Transfer

When your computer sends data to another computer using an asynchronous modem connection, the data is first divided into bytes. The bytes are sent 1 bit at a time (serially), and the byte is preceded by a start bit and followed by a stop bit. (See Chapter 2 for more details on serial and parallel communications.)

The computers do not coordinate in terms of when data will be sent. The receiving computer uses the start and stop bits to recognize when it has an entire byte of data. The start and stop bits and other coordination mechanisms in asynchronous communications can take up as much as 25 percent of data traffic. See Figure 9.5 for an example of data being sent asynchronously.

FIGURE 9.5

Data bytes sent asynchronously are framed by start and stop bits.

Asynchronous Modem Standards

Standards are especially important in computer communications equipment because it is the standards that make it possible for devices (such as modems) from different manufacturers to talk to each other. You have already been introduced to the MNP and V.42 error-correction standards and the V.35bis compression standard. There are several more standards you should know about to make an informed decision on which type of modem to use in your network.

Hayes Microcomputer products in the early 1980s introduced a modem that could dial the phone as well as send data; the person using the modem did not have to use a telephone to dial the number. A Hayes modem had many special commands to configure the modem and manage the phone line. Many other modem manufacturers adopted the Hayes set of commands, and the Hayes-compatible command set has become an industry standard. Any communications software you have is likely to use the Hayes-compatible setting as its default configuration.

The International Telecommunications Union (ITU) has developed a number of standards for modems. These standards usually start with a *V,* and may contain the word *bis,* which means *second* in French. If the standard includes the word *terbo,* it means third, not fast. Table 9.1 contains several of the ITU standards for modems.

TABLE 9.1 ITU Standards For Modems	STANDARD	BPS
	V.22bis	2400
	V.32	9600
	V.32bis	14,400
	V.32terbo	19,200
	V.FastClass (V.FC)	28,800
	V.34	28,800
	V.42	57,600

Microcom, in addition to specifying error-control protocols, created a data compression specification called MNP class 5. The ITU also specified the V.42bis compression protocol. As mentioned earlier in this chapter, fast modems can be combined with compression to provide even faster data transfer rates. For instance, a very good modem might have V.32bis signaling, V.42 error control, and V.42bis compression.

Synchronous Communications

As you learned in the previous section, an asynchronous modem can spend up to 25 percent of its time negotiating the transmission and reception of data. This process is called *handshaking*. Synchronous communications can more effectively use the available bits per second and give you a faster connection than asynchronous communications can.

Synchronous Data Transfer

Synchronous modems can transmit more data than asynchronous modems (at the same number of bits per second) because they use careful timing and coordination between modems to send large blocks of data, without start and stop bits. These large blocks, called frames, have multiple bytes within them. Special characters are used to facilitate synchronization.

Synchronous communication requires that some kind of clocking mechanism be put into place to keep the clocks of the sender and receiver synchronized. The following three methods are used for synchronous timing coordination:

- *Guaranteed state change* describes a method in which the clocking information is embedded in the data signal. This way, the receiver is guaranteed that transitions will occur in the signal at predefined intervals. These transitions allow the receiver to continually adjust its internal clock. Guaranteed state change is the most common method of synchronous timing coordination, and it is frequently used with digital signals.

- *Separate clock signal* is a method in which a separate channel is used between the transmitter and receiver to provide the clocking information. Because this method requires twice the channel capacity, it is inefficient. This method is most effective for shorter transmissions, such as those between a computer and a printer.

- *Oversampling* is a method in which the receiver samples the signal at a much faster rate than the data rate. This permits the use of an encoding method that does not add clocking transitions. If the receiver samples the signal ten times more quickly than the data rate, out of any ten measurements, one would provide the data information and the other nine would determine whether the receiver's clock is synchronized.

See Figure 9.6 for an example of synchronous communication.

Synchronous modems also do some things that asynchronous modems do not always do, including:

- Arrange data into blocks

- Add control information

- Check information to provide error control

FIGURE 9.6

Synchronous modems
transmit frames that have
special characters to begin
and end each frame but
no start or stop bits
around the bytes being
transmitted.

Synchronous Modem Standards

The three primary protocols in synchronous communications are

- Synchronous Data Link Control (SDLC)

- High-level Data Link Control (HDLC)

- Binary synchronous communications protocol (bisync)

Uses for Synchronous Modems

Synchronous modems are used most often to make dedicated connections to remote computers using telephone lines leased from the telephone company. Synchronous modems provide a better data transfer rate and better error control than do asynchronous modems. However, synchronous modems cost more than asynchronous modems, and most user software is written for an asynchronous modem, so you will probably not use a synchronous modem to provide Remote Access Service to your network. You may, however, use a synchronous modem to connect your network permanently to another network over a telephone connection.

Digital Modems

Digital modems are inappropriately named; they do not modulate or demodulate a signal. However, *modem* has come to mean a device that connects computers over a phone line, so the name has stuck.

An ISDN (Integrated Services Digital Network) modem is an example of a digital modem. Like a regular asynchronous or synchronous modem, an

ISDN modem can be installed in the computer on an expansion card or connected to the computer externally via a serial cable.

ISDN requires a special phone line from the telephone company. This phone line is not an analog phone line like the POTS line you may be used to. It is a digital connection to the telephone company's communications equipment. This line can carry more information than a regular phone line, anywhere from 56- or 64Kbps (for single-channel, basic rate ISDN) to over 1Mbps (for primary rate ISDN).

WARNING

Again, be careful what you plug your telephone or your modem into. The electrical characteristics of various types of communications lines are different and can damage equipment that is not meant for that type of line.

ISDN modems can communicate only with other ISDN modems.

Carriers

A CRITICAL PART OF remote access that we have not yet discussed is the carriers of the network information. The carrier in remote network access or in wide area networking is the phone company or other entity that carries the telephone connection from one network point to the other. For instance, the carrier of your modem data when you call your office from home is most likely your local telephone company. If you need to connect to a computer in another state, you will probably be connecting through two local telephone companies (one serving you and one serving the destination computer) and one or more long-distance carriers in between.

Microsoft ✓ *Exam Objective*

List the characteristics, requirements, and appropriate situations for WAN connection services. WAN connection services include:

- X.25
- ISDN
- Frame relay
- ATM

The carrier does not necessarily have to be a phone company. With the recent deregulation of the communications industry, other organizations can get into the communications business. You may in the future connect to your network at work through your cable TV service, through a digital cellular radio network, or perhaps even through a service provided by the power company. Any service that brings wires into your home may eventually provide data carrier service under the new telecommunications regulations.

However, today, the phone company is most likely the carrier you will use. You can connect computers together using phone company telephone lines in two ways:

- Public dial network lines

- Leased lines

Public Dial Network Lines

Public dial network lines are the very same lines that you use for regular telephone service. This is the type of phone line you use with regular asynchronous modems, as discussed earlier in this chapter. Public dial network lines are not very fast, but they are adequate for exchanging e-mail and transferring small files, such as word processing files. Large graphics files and entire databases take too long to regularly transfer over these lines.

ISDN is a new type of public dial network line that is faster than POTS. ISDN is capable of handling large graphics files and complete databases. ISDN requires a special phone line from the telephone company. ISDN is more expensive than regular asynchronous modems, so it is used less often.

With public dial network lines, you make a connection by dialing a number. Your connection is set up for the duration of your conversation (or data transfer), and when you hang up, the connection is dissolved. You can later call the same number and reestablish the connection, or you can call another number and connect to a different service (or person).

Leased Lines

A *leased line* is different from a public dial network line in that the line is dedicated to a connection between two predetermined numbers. The connection is set up for you by the phone company, and the connection stays in place whether or not you are using it. You cannot redirect the connection to another number, because you do not dial a number. For example, you could have a leased line between your office and your Internet service provider. This line would be dedicated in that you could not redirect it anywhere else, and it would be there for you all the time.

Leased lines are commonly used to give widely separated computers permanent connections. An organization with offices in several cities, for example, might purchase leased lines between each of the offices to provide a permanent connection between the servers on the networks at each office.

A leased line can also carry more data than a public dial network line. Telephone carriers offer lines from the basic capability level of a regular telephone line (which can carry up to 56Kbps with special synchronous modems and data compression) to T1 (a telephone standard line capacity that conveys about 1.5Mbps) or T3 (a telephone standard line capacity that conveys about 45Mbps, which is faster than most local area networks).

Leased lines can be very expensive, so unless your computers must always be connected and exchanging information, you may wish to use public dial network lines instead.

In the preceding sections of this chapter, you were shown the modem and telephone technology that makes it possible to access your network remotely. Now you will see how to install and configure the remote access software on Microsoft Windows NT and how to connect to a RAS server from a Windows 95 client.

REAL WORLD PROBLEMS

You must connect your central office with several branch offices around the state. They will be constantly connected with your home office, and you wish to maximize the bandwidth available to network applications.

- Which types of modems are best for this situation?

You will be outfitting each of your salespeople with a laptop and modem. When they are on the road they will be dialing in to your LAN to exchange e-mail and files with your headquarters. They must be able to dial in from hotel rooms and from customer sites.

- Which type of modem will you give your salespeople?

Several people in your company telecommute. Leased lines are too expensive, but they need a faster connection than regular modems allow.

- Which sort of modem is best for this situation?

Remote Access Software

AS MENTIONED EARLIER in this chapter, the remote access software in Windows NT is called the Remote Access Service (RAS). Microsoft RAS allows users to connect to a Windows NT computer over phone lines. If you have more than one modem attached to your RAS server, you can have more than one computer connect to it at a time. RAS on a Windows NT Server can accept up to 256 simultaneous connections from remote clients. See Figure 9.7 for an example of remote clients connected to a network via a RAS server.

FIGURE 9.7

Remote computers can connect to a network via a RAS server.

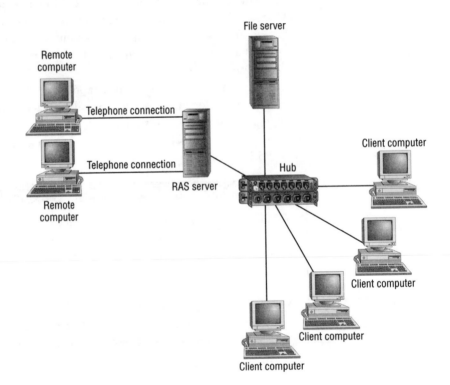

The client computers that are connected through RAS, instead of being directly connected to the network, can do anything they could do if they were actually on the network; however, the network will appear to be operating much more slowly. This is because the telephone lines they must use to connect to the RAS server do not have as much bandwidth (capacity to transfer information) as do your LAN cables.

If you connect to your RAS using a digital modem such as ISDN, the speed difference is not as noticeable as when you connect using a regular asynchronous modem. You could then use your computer as though it were directly connected to the network, even though you may be miles away.

When using a regular modem, because it is so much slower than your local area network, you will want to load all the executable programs you will use, and any data that does not change frequently, directly on the client computer. Remote Access Service is best used to access files and e-mail and to connect to remote interactive programs, such as bulletin boards and client-server databases.

Installing Remote Access Service

The following steps will lead you through the process of installing Remote Access Service on your Windows NT server.

1. From the Start button, select Settings ➤ Control Panel.

2. Double-click the Network icon. (The Network window will appear.)

3. Click the Services tab.

4. Check to see whether Remote Access Service has already been installed. If the Network Services list under the Services tab (see Figure 9.8) includes the item Remote Access Service, you do not need to install the software. Double-click the Remote Access Service item in the list and skip ahead to step 7.

5. Press the Add button. You are presented with a list of software you can add to your Windows NT Server. Select Remote Access Software from the list and click the Continue button.

At this point you may need to tell the installation software where to find the Windows NT files. The files will be on the installation CD or floppies and in the directory corresponding to the type of computer you have. For instance, if you have an Intel-based computer and the CD-ROM is drive F, you should enter **F:\i386**.

FIGURE 9.8

The Network Services tab
shows currently installed
network services.

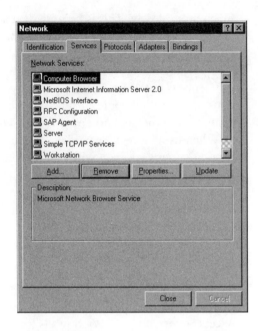

FIGURE 9.8

The Network Services tab
shows currently installed
network services.

6. After the installation program copies the RAS program files to your computer, you are prompted to specify which COM port RAS should use and whether the port should be dial out only, receive calls only, or dial out and receive calls (see Figure 9.9). For client computers to connect to this RAS service, you need to select Receive Calls Only or Dial Out and Receive calls. RAS interrogates the modem and asks you to confirm the type of modem it has found.

7. You should now see the Remote Access Setup window (see Figure 9.10). Press the Network button to access the Network Configuration window shown in Figure 9.11. For the simplest network configuration, make sure only the NetBEUI option in the Server Settings section is checked. If a Server Settings area appears within the Network Configuration window, also check the Allow Authentication Including Clear Text option.

The Server Settings area appears within the Network Configuration window when the communications port (shown in the Remote Access Setup window) is configured to dial out.

8. Click OK to see the Remote Access Setup window, click the Continue button to return to the Services tab of the Network window, and click the Close button.

When you are done, you see a message telling you to restart your computer. Choose Yes to restart now.

FIGURE 9.9

You select the ports for RAS and how they will be used (dial out, receive call, or both) in the Configure Port Usage window.

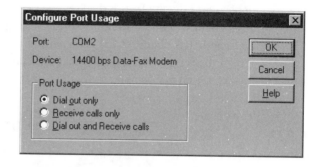

FIGURE 9.10

The Remote Access Setup window allows you to configure a port to be used with Remote Access Service.

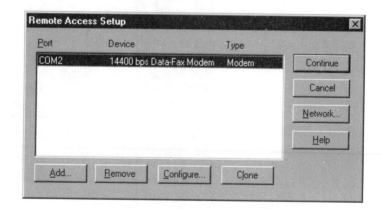

FIGURE 9.11

Select only the NetBEUI option in the Network Configuration window for the simplest Remote Access Service network setting.

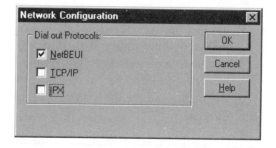

Administering Remote Access Service

If you wish Remote Access Service to start up when you start up your computer, you can enable it in the Services section of the Control Panel. In the Services window, choose Remote Access Service, select Startup, and select Automatic (see Figure 9.12). You can then either choose Remote Access Service in the Services dialog box and click Start or restart your computer to have it start automatically.

FIGURE 9.12

Make Remote Access Service start automatically by selecting Automatic.

Once you have installed the Remote Access Service software (as described in the previous section), you can use the Dial-Up Networking icon in the My Computer window (see Figure 9.13) to make dial-up connections to other computers. If you attempt to use the Dial-Up Networking icon before you have set up RAS, Windows NT walks you through the process of setting up RAS as outlined above. Also, once you have installed RAS, you will be able to use the Remote Access Admin program (located in the Administrative Tools section of the Start menu) to manage RAS connections.

To allow all the users on your server to use Remote Access Service, follow these steps:

1. Select Users ➤ Permissions on the Users menu in the Remote Access Admin program.

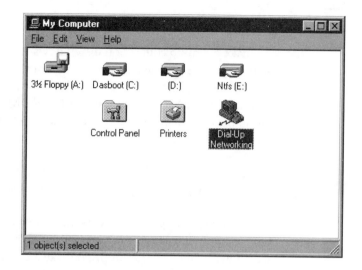

FIGURE 9.13

By clicking the Dial-Up Networking icon, you can establish connections to other computers using the Remote Access Service.

2. Select the Grant Dialin Permission to User option and click the Grant All button (see Figure 9.14).

3. Choose Yes to give the ability to access your server remotely to all your server's users.

FIGURE 9.14

Grant All will give all users on your network the ability to connect to your network remotely.

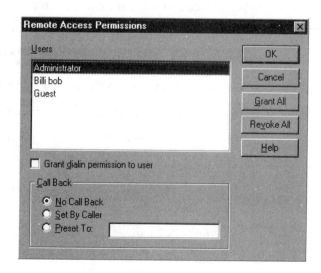

Making a Dial-Up Connection

To make a dial-up connection in Windows 95, you must have the dial-up adapter installed in the Network section of the Windows 95 Control Panel. If it is not installed, you can use the Add Software option on the Control Panel to add it. You need the Windows 95 CD-ROM or installation floppies to install the dial-up adapter software. The Add Software Wizard walks you through the steps.

A Wizard in Microsoft software is a software program that helps you perform a task. The Add Software Wizard helps you install software on your Windows 95 computer.

When the dial-up adapter is installed, a Dial-Up Networking selection appears within the My Computer window when you double-click the My Computer icon on the desktop. To make a dial-up connection, you double-click the Dial-Up Networking icon and then double-click the Make New Connection icon.

Another Wizard (the Make New Connection Wizard) walks you through the steps of making a new connection using the dial-up adapter. You are prompted to name the connection, confirm the modem selection, and enter the telephone number to dial.

A new icon then appears in the Dial-Up Networking window. Double-click the icon to make the connection to the Remote Access Service you set up in the previous section.

REAL WORLD PROBLEMS

You have installed several modems in your Windows NT Server computer.

■ What else must you do before people can call in and connect to your network?

You can dial out of your network, but no one can dial in and connect to your network.

■ What might be wrong? How can you fix it?

Users can dial in to your network and access Windows NT servers, but they cannot access Novell NetWare servers.

■ What might be wrong? How can you fix it?

Review

F YOU HAVE users who are not always in the office or you need to access network data from home, you may need to install Remote Access Service on your network. Remote Access Service uses modem technology to provide a network connection to your home or traveling computer.

Modems convert the digital communications of a computer into analog signals that can be carried over a regular telephone line. There are several standards for modem speed, error-correction capability, and data compression capability. A V.32bis signaling, V.42 error-control, and V.42bis data compression modem is a common type of modem. An alternative is a V.32bis, MNP class 4 error-control and MNP class 5 data compression modem.

Asynchronous modems such as these spend up to 25 percent of their bandwidth in handshaking. Synchronous modems are more efficient because they use careful timing and larger blocks to transfer data. Synchronous modems are less common, however, and more expensive.

Digital modems do not modulate and demodulate; instead, they connect a computer to a digital line. ISDN is a common type of digital modem. Digital modems are much faster then regular (analog) modems.

Regular asynchronous modems are used with public dial network lines, including plain old telephone service (POTS). This is the same telephone service you plug your regular telephone into. ISDN is a new type of public dial network line, and it is not POTS; you cannot plug your regular telephone into an ISDN line.

Leased lines are dedicated telephone lines you cannot dial. They provide a direct line connection with a predetermined number, at data rates ranging from that of regular telephone lines to T3 (45Mbps) and beyond.

Your Windows NT installation disks contain the Microsoft Remote Access Service, and your Windows 95 installation disks include dial-up networking software. Using these built-in services, you can connect your Windows 95 client computer to your Windows NT network.

Review Questions

1. Which of the following statements describe dedicated leased lines? Choose all that apply:

    A. Utilize CSU/DSUs

    B. Can provide data transfer rates between 56Kbps and 45Mbps

    C. Provide only a temporary connection between two sites

    D. Use packet switching technology

2. Most modems employ a number of functions that improve performance and reliability. Which of the following increases the reliability of a modem?

    A. Error detection

    B. Demodulation

    C. Encryption

    D. Compression

3. It is essential that communication between two devices be synchronized. Which of the following methods maintains synchronization without a clocking signal?

    A. Time division multiplexing

    B. Asynchronous data transmission

    C. Synchronous data transmission

    D. Asynchronous transfer mode

4. Which of the following cable types can be used to connect an analog modem to your computer?

    A. Parallel

    B. SCSI

    C. 10BaseT

    D. RS-232

5. When RAS is installed on a Windows NT server, what is the maximum number of concurrent dial-in connections?

   A. 144

   B. 256

   C. 64

   D. 128

6. To improve performance over a dial-up line, a modem can employ any number of functions. Which of the following increases the data rate of a modem?

   A. Error correction

   B. Asynchronous transfer

   C. Compression

   D. Encryption

7. When configuring an ISDN device, a single B channel can be set to what speed on a BRI (basic rate interface)?

   A. 28.8 Kbps

   B. 1.44 Mbps

   C. 64 Kbps or 56Kbps

   D. 128Kbps

8. For all intents and purposes, a RAS connection is an extension of the network. Which of the following is not possible over a RAS connection?

   A. Read and manipulate files

   B. Administer users and groups

   C. Execute programs

   D. None of the above. RAS will allow all network functions.

9. Which of the following Windows NT services could you install to allow remote Windows computers access to your network via modem?

A. CDS

B. SLIP

C. PPP

D. RAS

CHAPTER

10

Expanding Networks

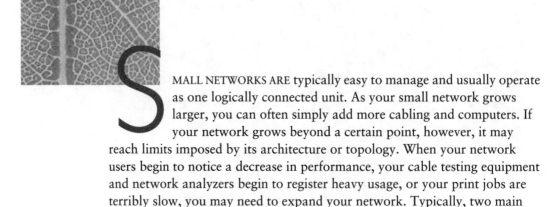

SMALL NETWORKS ARE typically easy to manage and usually operate as one logically connected unit. As your small network grows larger, you can often simply add more cabling and computers. If your network grows beyond a certain point, however, it may reach limits imposed by its architecture or topology. When your network users begin to notice a decrease in performance, your cable testing equipment and network analyzers begin to register heavy usage, or your print jobs are terribly slow, you may need to expand your network. Typically, two main types of expansion are possible:

- Expansion within a single network, called *network connectivity*

- Expansion that involves and joins two separate networks, called *inter-network connectivity*

This chapter introduces you to some basic strategies and tools for expanding your network.

Microsoft
Exam
Objective

Define the communication devices that communicate at each level of the OSI model.

Network Connectivity

O EXPAND A SINGLE network without breaking it into new parts or connecting it to other networks, you can usually use one of the following devices:

- Passive hubs
- Active hubs
- Intelligent hubs
- Repeaters
- Bridges
- Multiplexers

Let's look at each of these individually.

Hubs

All networks (except those using coaxial cable) require a central location to bring media segments together. These central locations are called *hubs* (or multiport repeaters or concentrators). The easiest way to understand this concept is to think of the necessity of connecting multiple cables. If you just connected the media segments together by soldering them, the signals would interfere with each other and create problems. A hub organizes the cables and relays signals to the other media segments. Figure 10.1 shows a hub.

FIGURE 10.1

Example of a hub

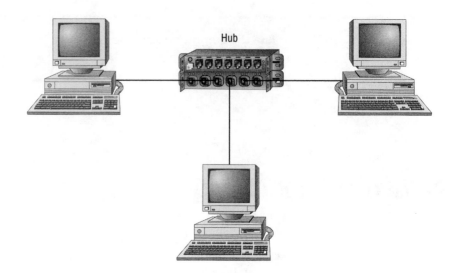

Hub

Keep the following items in mind when working with hubs:

- There is a limit to the number of hubs that can be connected to each other to extend a network. The limit is typically four, but the maximum number of hubs depends on the type of network topology used.

- When possible, connect each hub directly to a server network card rather than to another hub.

- Label the connections on the hub. This can save you hours of troubleshooting.

- The more hubs data passes through, the slower the connection.

There are three main types of hubs: passive, active, and intelligent.

Passive Hubs

A *passive hub* simply combines the signals of network segments. There is no signal processing or regeneration. Because it does not boost the signal and, in fact, absorbs some of the signal, a passive hub reduces by half the maximum cabling distances permitted. For example, if a segment normally allows a reliable transmission distance of 200 meters (656 feet), the distance between a passive hub and a device can be only 100 meters (328 feet). Also, with a passive hub, each computer receives the signals sent from all the other computers connected to the hub.

Active Hubs

Active hubs are like passive hubs except that they have electronic components that regenerate or amplify signals. Because of this, the distances between devices can be increased. The main drawback to some active hubs is that they amplify noise as well as the signal, depending on whether they function as simple amplifiers or as signal regenerators. They are also much more expensive than passive hubs. Because some active hubs function as repeaters (as described in the next section), they are sometimes called *multiport repeaters*.

Intelligent Hubs

In addition to signal regeneration, *intelligent hubs* perform some network management and intelligent path selection. A switching hub chooses only the port of the device where the signal needs to go, rather than sending the signal along all paths. Many switching hubs can choose which alternative path will be the quickest and send the signal that way. One advantage to this is that you can permanently connect all transmission media segments because each segment will be used only when a signal is sent to a device using that segment.

Repeaters

All transmission media attenuate (weaken) the electromagnetic waves that travel through them. Attenuation therefore limits the distance any medium can carry data. Adding a device that amplifies the signal can allow it to travel farther, increasing the size of the network. For example, if you are connecting computers that are more than 100 meters (328 feet) apart using a 10BaseT Ethernet cable, you will need a device that amplifies signals to ensure data transmission. Devices that amplify signals in this way are called *repeaters*.

Repeaters fall into two categories: amplifiers and signal-regenerating repeaters. *Amplifiers* simply amplify the entire incoming signal. Unfortunately, they amplify both the signal and the noise. *Signal-regenerating repeaters* create an exact duplicate of incoming data by identifying it amidst the noise, reconstructing it, and retransmitting only the desired information. This reduces the noise. The original signal is duplicated, boosted to its original strength, and sent. Figure 10.2 shows where a repeater might be used.

FIGURE 10.2

Example of repeater use
in a network

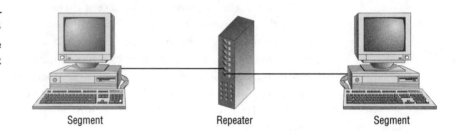

Segment   Repeater   Segment

Because repeaters simply deal with the actual, physical signals on a network, they operate at the Physical Layer of the OSI model.

Theoretically, repeaters can be used to combine an unlimited number of transmission media segments. In reality, though, network designs limit the number of repeaters.

Bridges

Bridges connect network segments. The use of a bridge increases the maximum possible size of your network. Unlike a repeater, which simply passes on all the signals it receives, a bridge selectively determines the appropriate segment to which it should pass a signal. It does this by reading the address of all the signals it receives. The bridge reads the physical location of the source and destination computers from this address. The process works like this:

1. A bridge receives all the signals from both segment A and segment B.

2. The bridge reads the addresses and discards (filters) all signals from segment A that are addressed to segment A, because they do not need to cross the bridge.

3. Signals from segment A addressed to a computer on segment B are retransmitted to segment B.

4. The signals from segment B are treated in the same way.

Like repeaters, bridges can regenerate signals in order to extend network lengths. However, because bridges actually read the packet address, they are considered to operate at the Data Link layer of the OSI model.

Figure 10.3 illustrates how signals pass through a bridge.

FIGURE 10.3

A bridge connects different types of networks.

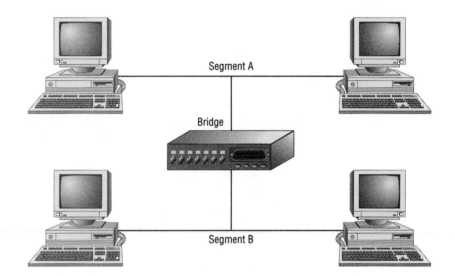

Through address filtering, bridges can divide busy networks into segments and reduce network traffic. Network traffic will be reduced if most signals are addressed to the same segment and do not cross the bridge. To use a bridge effectively, networks are often divided into groups by physical location and shared resources (such as printers, network servers, and applications). If most signals do not frequently cross the bridge, using bridges can help reduce traffic on your network.

For the exam, you will need to consider bridges as incapable of connecting LANs of different types. For example, an Ethernet segment and a Token Ring segment normally cannot be connected with a bridge. This is because each network type uses different physical addressing. There is, however, a type of bridge, called a "translation bridge", that allows you to connect different network types with different physical addressing. Translation bridges are not common, and are not the type of bridge referred to by the Networking Essentials exam questions.

There are two basic types of bridges:

- *Transparent bridges* keep a table of addresses in memory to determine where to send data.

- *Source-routing bridges* require the entire route to be included in the transmission and do not route packets intelligently. IBM Token Ring networks use this type of bridge.

If a segment on the network is being used at 60 percent or higher capacity, consider using a bridge to divert some of the data. A router, described in the section "Routers and Brouters" later in this chapter, may be a better option.

Multiplexers

In some cases, a transmission medium can handle a greater capacity than a single signal can occupy. *Multiplexing* allows you to use more bandwidth of the medium by combining two or more separate signals and transmitting them together. The original signals can then be extracted at the other end of the medium. This is called *demultiplexing*.

Multiplexing is a technique that allows both baseband and broadband media to support multiple data channels. In other words, multiplexing provides a way of sharing a single medium segment by combining several channels for transmission over that segment. There are different ways to combine the channels. The ideal method depends on whether the media in question is baseband or broadband.

A familiar example of multiplexing is cable TV. Most cable TV sends numerous signals (30 or more) through a single coaxial cable. The cable box or VCR demultiplexes the signals into what we think of as channels.

The three major methods of multiplexing are

- Frequency-division multiplexing

- Time-division multiplexing

- Statistical time-division multiplexing

Frequency-Division Multiplexing

Frequency-division multiplexing (FDM) uses separate frequencies to combine multiple data channels onto a broadband medium. You can use FDM to separate traffic traveling in different directions in a broadband LAN. Figure 10.4 illustrates frequency-division multiplexing.

FIGURE 10.4

Frequency-division
multiplexing (FDM)

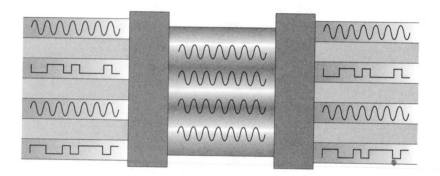

Time-Division Multiplexing

Time-division multiplexing (TDM) divides channels into time slots. Each of the devices communicating over this multiplexed line is allocated a time slot in a round-robin fashion, as shown in Figure 10.5. You can use TDM with baseband media or even with an individual channel of a broadband FDM system.

Conventional TDM multiplexers are sometimes called synchronous TDM *because the time slots do not vary. If a device does not use its time slot, that slot is wasted.*

FIGURE 10.5

Time-division
multiplexing (TDM)

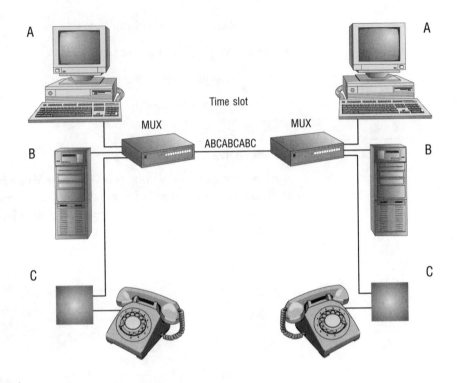

Statistical Time-Division multiplexing

Statistical time-division multiplexing, or StatTDM, addresses the issue mentioned above—that conventional TDM systems can be inefficient if many slot times are wasted. StatTDM provides an intelligent solution to this problem by dynamically allocating time slots to devices on a first-come, first-served basis. The number of time slots allocated to a particular device depends on how busy it is. You can use priorities to allow one device greater access to time slots than another. For the multiplexer on the receiving end to determine which signal a particular time slot is carrying, there must be a control field that identifies the owner attached to the data. Figure 10.6 shows statistical time-division multiplexing.

Because terms like statistical time-division multiplexer are a bit cumbersome, network technicians often use jargon terms to refer to them: a multiplexer is a mux or TDM, and a statistical multiplexer is commonly called a StatMux.

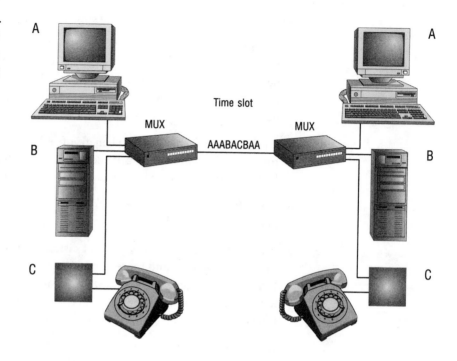

FIGURE 10.6

Statistical time-division
multiplexing

Internetwork Connectivity

AN *INTERNETWORK* CONSISTS of two or more independent networks that are connected and yet maintain independent identities. At some point in the growth of your network, you might want to consider breaking it into two relatively separate networks in order to limit network traffic.

An internetwork may include different types of networks (an Ethernet and a Token Ring network, for example). To connect independent networks, you use *internetwork connectivity devices.*

The internetwork connectivity devices discussed here are routers and brouters, gateways, and CSUs/DSUs. These are the most commonly used devices.

Some of the benefits of internetworking are

- **Reduces network traffic:** Without internetwork connectivity devices, packet traffic could affect the entire network. With internetwork connectivity devices, most traffic stays on the local network, and only packets destined for other networks cross internetwork connectivity devices.

- **Optimizes performance:** The benefit of reduced traffic is optimized performance. However, the optimized network performance can be offset by the increased server load when a server acts as a router.

- **Simplifies management:** Network problems can be more easily identified and isolated in smaller networks, as opposed to one large network.

- **Efficiently spans long geographical distances:** Because WAN links are many times slower and more expensive than LAN links, having a single large network spanning long distances can complicate network management and slow network performance. You can more efficiently span long distances by connecting multiple smaller networks.

Another good reason to internetwork is to connect your network to those of other organizations. This concept is at the core of the Internet. As you probably know, the Internet is not a single network, but a multitude of interconnected networks.

Routers and Brouters

One basic mechanism in internetworking is routers. *Routers* are devices that connect two or more networks. They consist of a combination of hardware and software. The hardware can be a network server, a separate computer, or a special black box device. The hardware includes the physical interfaces to the various networks in the internetwork. These interfaces can be Token Ring, Ethernet, T1, Frame Relay, Asynchronous Transfer Mode (ATM), or any number of other technologies. The two main pieces of software in a router are the operating system and the routing protocol. Management software can be another software component of a router.

Routers use logical and physical addressing to connect two or more logically separate networks. They accomplish this connection by organizing the large network into logical network segments (sometimes called *subnetworks* or *subnets*). Each of these subnetworks is given a logical address. This allows the networks to be separate but still access each other and exchange data when necessary. Data is grouped into packets, or blocks of data. Each packet, in addition to having a physical device address, has a logical network address. Figure 10.7 shows networks connected by routers.

FIGURE 10.7

Networks connected by routers

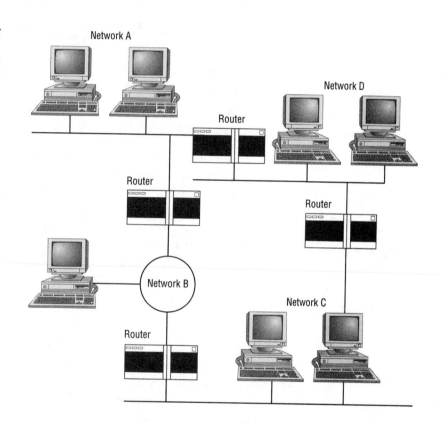

The network address allows routers to more accurately and efficiently calculate the optimal path to a workstation or computer. Routers perform a function very similar to that of a bridge, but routers keep the networks separate. Because they must check both the device address and the network address, router processing is generally slower than bridge processing. However, routers are more "intelligent" than bridges because they use algorithms to determine the best path to send a packet to a network. By passing packets only according to network addresses, routers can help prevent a broadcast storm.

Even if a router is not directly connected to a network, it will know the best way to get a packet there. Routers list network addresses in routing tables. These tables contain all known network addresses and possible paths. In addition to storing information about possible paths, routing tables (also known as route tables) store estimates of the *cost* to send a message through a given route. The cost of a particular route can be defined in several terms: a time estimate, a distance estimate, or an estimate that includes monetary terms, as in a situation in which one link is more expensive than another.

The following terms are used to quantify the routing cost:

- *Hop count* describes the number of routers a message must pass through to reach its destination.

- *Tick count* describes the amount of time required for a message to reach its destination. A *tick* is 1 /18 second.

- *Relative expense* is a number you can assign based on the actual monetary cost (if you are charged for the network link) or some other relevant criteria required to use a given link, such as bandwidth on busy links.

The network administrator can preprogram some routers with preset routing information. Unfortunately, preprogrammed routers cannot adjust to changing network conditions and are susceptible to delays when there are network problems. In most cases it makes more sense to use routers that can identify possible routes through the internetwork and store that information in routing tables they can quickly access (and indeed, most routers are built this way).

Route discovery is the process of finding the possible routes through the internetwork and then building routing tables to store that information. Because network conditions change over time, routers need to perform route discovery regularly (typically about once per minute) to ensure that their routing tables are up to date and accurate. The two methods of route discovery are distance-vector and link-state.

Distance-Vector Routing

In *distance-vector routing,* each router advertises its presence to other routers on the network. Periodically (for example, every 60 seconds), each router on the network broadcasts the information contained in its routing table. The other routers then update their routing tables with the broadcast information they receive.

As you can imagine, these periodic broadcasts of routing table information by the routers performing distance-vector route discovery add up to a noticeable amount of traffic. This traffic is not a problem in LANs, because plenty of bandwidth is available and the number of routers is usually low. However, it can seriously affect performance in a WAN. In a large internetwork, distance-vector routing tends to be quite inefficient. Because route changes must be broadcast through the network from router to router, and because changes are contained within complete routing tables, it can take a long time (as long as several minutes) before all the routers on the network know of a change.

Link-State Routing

Because distance-vector routing generates enough network traffic to cause a problem on internetworks that have a lot of routers, *link-state routing* was developed as an improvement. Link-state routers broadcast their complete routing tables only at startup and at certain intervals—much less frequently than distance-vector broadcasts. Thus, this type of routing generates less network traffic than the distance-vector method.

Open shortest path first (OSPF) is a link-state algorithm supported by TCP/IP. It facilitates the process of route selection based upon number of hops, traffic, and other factors.

The major difference between the link-state and distance-vector methods is that once the initial routing-table exchange has occurred, a link-state router will generally broadcast routing updates only when it detects a change in its routing table. And when it does broadcast, it sends only information about the change; it doesn't send its complete routing table.

Other routers that receive broadcast messages regarding changes in the state of network links use this information to update their own routing tables. Because only the changes are sent, these updates can be done in less time.

Once a router has created its routing table, it can use the cost information contained within that table to calculate the best path through the internetwork. Routing protocol can select the best path based on the minimum number of hops, number of ticks, or relative expense. Selection of the optimum route can be dynamic or static. *Dynamic route selection* permits routers to constantly adjust to changing network conditions. With static route selection, on the other hand, packets must always follow a predetermined path.

Dynamic route selection uses the cost information that is continually being generated by routing algorithms and placed in routing tables to select the best route for each packet. As network conditions change, the router can select different paths to maintain the lowest possible costs. The router can even select new paths "on the fly" as it is transmitting packets. If changes occur during a transmission that make one route suddenly less attractive than another, the router can send the remaining packets of the transmission along a different path (or several different paths) from the packets in the first part of the transmission.

Remember that each router along the path makes routing selections for the next hop. A router uses a protocol, such as a routing information protocol (RIP), in the process of determining which path to the destination involves the fewest hops.

With *static route selection,* the data path is not selected on the fly by the routers involved. Instead, the data path is designated in advance. Either the network administrator or a computer on the network (the initial router or a controlling device) selects a route for the data from a predefined table. All packets are then forced along that route, and intermediate routers are not allowed to make route-selection decisions. Static route selection tends to be less efficient than dynamic route selection because it cannot adapt to changing network conditions.

Many routers may be more appropriately called brouters. A *brouter* is a router that can also bridge. A brouter first tries to deliver the packet based on network protocol information. If the brouter does not support the protocol the packet is using or cannot deliver the packet based on protocol information, it bridges the packet using the physical address. True routers simply discard a packet if it doesn't have a correct logical address. A brouter can be a more affordable option to having both a router and a bridge. It can also make network management simpler.

Routers work at the Network Layer of the OSI model.

Keep the following items in mind when working with routers:

- Some routers, especially older ones, may not follow standards. This can cause problems when you use different vendors' routers on the same network.

- Be sure the router is rated to handle the speed of your network connections.

- Routers slow down network communications to a small extent, so don't use them unnecessarily.

The following protocols are routable:

- DECnet

- DDP (AppleTalk)

- TCP/IP

- NW Link IPX

- OSI

- XNS

The following protocols are NOT routable:

- LAT (from Digital Equipment Corporation)

- NetBEUI

Dealing with Broadcast Storms

A *broadcast storm* occurs when a network is so overwhelmed by messages being broadcast that its bandwidth limits are reached. This could be caused, for example, by a malfunctioning network interface card. A broadcast storm can bring a network to its knees. Repeaters serve only to repeat broadcast storms across the network.

Microsoft Exam Objective   **Resolve broadcast storms.**

When dealing with broadcast storms and other similar problems, bridges, too, typically present some problems. All broadcasts on bridged internetworks spread network wide, which make these internetworks susceptible to broadcast storms. Also, protocol addressing errors are not limited to an offending network segment, but instead disrupt the entire network, much like a broadcast storm.

Because routed internetworks are based on protocol addresses and logical groupings of workstations and network resources, they offer greater security than their bridged counterparts. Routers can provide "firewalls" that limit network-wide damage of broadcast storms or protocol address problems by confining incidents to a localized segment. As a result, routed internetworks are usually significantly more stable than bridged internetworks.

Broadcasting certain packets across an entire internetwork, however, is a useful and important capability, particularly when broadcast-oriented protocols such as the NetBIOS name service are supported. Many routers support "all nets broadcasting" with an algorithm that provides for effective broadcasts without creating loops. This prevents broadcast storms and improves network performance, yet it allows broadcast-oriented protocols to be used.

If you are dealing with a nonroutable protocol, such as NetBEUI, you may wish to isolate a broadcast storm by switching to a routable protocol, such as TCP/IP. This will allow you to use routing to separate the network into segments.

Bridges can, however, offer a type of defense against broadcast storms. Some types of bridges allow you to set, for a specific Ethernet address (host), the maximum number of broadcast packets that can occur during each one-second period. When that threshold is surpassed, it is determined that a storm is occurring. Any additional broadcast packets from that host address will be dropped until the storm is determined to be over. The storm is determined to be over after 30 seconds during which every one-second period has less than one half the stated threshold in broadcast packets. In addition to setting limits for an Ethernet address, you can set the maximum number of broadcasts or packets that can occur on a specific bridge interface.

It is, however, normally preferable to use a router to fight broadcast storms proactively. That is, they can be used in the network architecture to create subnets that will limit the number of clients that are affected by the storm. For the exam, remember that a router is the prescribed method.

Gateways

A router is often referred to, especially in the older literature on TCP/IP and the Internet, as a gateway. Here, however, a gateway has a slightly different meaning.

Routers can successfully connect networks with protocols that function in similar ways. When the networks that must be connected are using completely different protocols from each other, however, a more powerful and intelligent device is required. A *gateway* is a device that can interpret and translate the different protocols that are used on two distinct networks. Gateways can be comprised of software, dedicated hardware, or a combination of both. Although gateways can function at the Network layer, for the exam think of gateways as operating at the upper layers of the OSI model, above the Network layer. In other words, they function at the Transport, Session, Presentation, and Application layers. When you need to have different environments communicating, you may wish to consider a gateway.

A gateway can actually convert data so that it works with an application on a computer on the other side of the gateway. For example, a gateway can receive e-mail messages in one format and convert them into another format. You can connect systems with different communication protocols, languages, and architecture using a gateway.

You'll find many gateways used to connect mainframes and LANs. For example, IBM networks using SNA (Systems Network Architecture) have a totally different protocol architecture from LANs, so gateways are used to connect the two.

When considering use of a gateway, keep in mind that they can be slow, because they need to perform such intensive conversion, and that they can be expensive.

CSUs/DSUs

Sometimes, when expanding your network, it is less costly and easier to use existing public networks, such as the public telephone network in your area. Connecting to some of these networks requires the use of *CSUs/DSUs* (*channel service units/digital service units*).

Network service providers may require you to use a CSU/DSU to translate the signals of your LAN into a different signal format and strength for use on their transmission media. CSUs/DSUs are also useful for shielding your network from both noise and dangerous voltage currents that can come through the public network.

REAL WORLD PROBLEMS

You need to run cabling from your network to some new offices that were recently built on the other side of the building. Since you plan to use 10BaseT on this Ethernet network segment, your maximum cabling length is only 330 feet. This is 50 feet short of the new office.

■ Which network connectivity device would you consider adding to the network to make sure the signal strength is great enough to make it to the new office?

(continued)

You have a very busy network that is becoming bogged down with traffic. You decide that the layout of the network is conveniently organized in a way such that you could simply divide the network into two segments and most traffic would stay on the side of the segment on which it originated.

■ Which network connectivity device might you use to connect the two segments?

You are reorganizing a 10Base2 (thinnet coax) Ethernet network and need to install a device to bring everything together. Because of the size of the network, you are concerned about signal strength diminishing.

■ Which kind of device would you want to choose, making sure that signal strength is not compromised?

Your network frequently experiences network storms.

■ Which type of internetwork device would you use to prevent a storm from spreading? Why?

■ Why would you not use a repeater? Why would you not use a typical bridge?

A new employee in your company doesn't understand routing and you need to explain it.

■ What could you say about it? What are the different types of routing and how do they work?

You are going to hook up your LAN to a mainframe. You will need an internetwork connectivity device.

■ What would this device be? Why would you need it?

You are connecting your network to the PSTN in your area. A representative from the local telephone company tells you that you'll need to use a specific internetwork device that will change your network signal to another strength and format.

■ Which device is the representative referring to?

Review

W HEN NETWORKS GROW to a certain point, they need to have network or internetwork connectivity devices implemented in order to deal with the change. Network connectivity devices serve to expand a network. They include:

- Passive hubs

- Active hubs

- Intelligent hubs

- Repeaters

- Bridges

- Multiplexers

Sometimes you may need to divide a network into separate segments, or connect one network to another. For this, internetwork connectivity devices are best. They include:

- Routers and brouters

- Gateways

- CSU/DSUs

Review Questions

1. Which of the following would most effectively segment traffic on a network using NWLink? Choose the most correct answer:

   A. Repeater

   B. Router

   C. Modem

   D. Bridge

2. Of the devices listed below, which is capable of operating at all of the upper layers of the OSI model?

   A. Gateway

   B. Brouter

   C. Router

   D. Bridge

3. Some networking devices regenerate the signals they receive, effectively increasing the distance the signal can travel before succumbing to attenuation. Which of the following devices does not have this ability?

   A. Multiplexer

   B. Active hub

   C. Bridge

   D. Passive hub

4. Which of the following networking devices will allow you to transmit Ethernet, Token Ring, and voice over a single cable?

   A. Router

   B. Multiplexer

   C. Repeater

   D. Bridge

5. Which of the following steps can you take to control broadcast storms on a network?

   A. Segment the network with a router.

   B. Use a network analyzer to track which computers are sending the most broadcasts.

   C. Convert the network to 10BaseT.

   D. Segment the network with a bridge.

6. Your network consists solely of Windows 95 clients and Windows NT servers. You have recently acquired a smaller company that is using NetWare servers. You would like to provide access to the NetWare servers for your Windows 95 clients, but you do not want to install a new redirector on each client computer. Which of the following could you install to provide Windows 95 clients access to NetWare servers?

   A. Gateway

   B. Bridge

   C. Router

   D. Brouter

7. An excessive number of broadcasts on a network will cause the network media to be flooded, effectively halting network communication. What is this phenomenon called?

   A. A broadcast flood

   B. A broadcast storm

   C. A collision storm

   D. EMI

8. Which of the following networking devices operate below the network layer of the OSI model? Choose all that apply:

   A. Bridges

   B. Gateways

   C. Repeaters

   D. Routers

9. Suppose the following situation exists: Your Windows NT Workstation workgroup consists of 15 computers spread over 175 meters on a 10Base2 network. A repeater has been installed near the middle of the network, effectively creating two network segments. You notice, however, that because of high network traffic, performance is not as high as you would like.

   Required result: Increase network performance.

   Optional desired result: Continue to use NetBEUI as the transport protocol. Keep upgrade costs to a minimum.

   Proposed solution: Replace the repeater with a bridge between the two network segments.

   What result does the proposed solution produce?

   A. The proposed solution produces the required result and produces both of the optional desired results.

   B. The proposed solution produces the required result and produces only one of the optional desired results.

   C. The proposed solution produces the required result but does not produce any of the optional desired results.

   D. The proposed solution does not produce the required result.

10. Which of the following devices is able to increase the network segment length by increasing signal strength?

    A. BNC barrel connector

    B. Repeater

    C. Transceiver

    D. Passive hub

11. If your network requires a multiplexer to support the assignment of priorities to particular devices, which of the following forms of multiplexing would be used?

   A. Statistical Time Division Multiplexing

   B. Statistical Frequency Division Multiplexing

   C. Frequency Division Multiplexing

   D. Time Division Multiplexing

12. Broadcast storms are often a problem on networks. With which of the following protocols can broadcast storms not be controlled by installing a router?

   A. IPX/SPX

   B. NetBEUI

   C. DLC

   D. TCP/IP

13. Which of the following route-discovery techniques uses frequent broadcasts that can increase network traffic?

   A. Broadcast routing

   B. Distance-vector routing

   C. Comprehensive routing

   D. Link-state routing

14. Suppose the following situation exists: Your 10Base2 network is expanding rapidly as more and more computers are added. You are very concerned about attenuation and are beginning to notice inconsistent network behavior. Your network consists of 2 NT servers and 35 workstations, all using NetBEUI for transport.

   Required result: Install a networking device that will eliminate the effects of attenuation.

   Optional desired results: Ensure that broadcast storms do not incapacitate the network. Filter traffic based on MAC addresses.

   Proposed solution: Install a repeater at a central point of the network.

Which result does the proposed solution produce?

A. The proposed solution produces the required result and produces both of the optional desired results.

B. The proposed solution produces the required result and produces only one of the optional desired results.

C. The proposed solution produces the required result but does not produce any of the optional desired results.

D. The proposed solution does not produce the required result.

15. Generally, the more advanced a product is, the more expensive it is. Which of the following devices operates highest on the OSI model and is more expensive?

A. Repeater

B. Transceiver

C. Router

D. Bridge

16. A brouter generally provides greater functionality than a router. Which of the following statements accurately describes the differences?

A. A brouter works at all layers of the OSI model.

B. A brouter chooses the best path to a destination.

C. A brouter filters traffic according to network address.

D. A brouter is able to bridge those protocols that are not routable.

17. Which of the following terms describes the process employed by routers to determine possible routes through a network?

A. Segment discovery

B. Network discovery

C. Route discovery

D. Path discovery

18. There are two types of gateways in networking, one of which provides the next hop for TCP/IP packets whose destination is outside the local network. Which of the following describes the other type of gateway?

    A. It provides connectivity for computers to the Internet.

    B. It provides connectivity between physically dissimilar networks.

    C. It provides protocol translation.

    D. It provides a mechanism for sending data and voice over the same phone line.

19. Suppose the following situation exists: Your 10Base2 network is expanding rapidly as more and more computers are added. You are very concerned about attenuation and are beginning to notice inconsistent network behavior. Your network consists of 2 NT servers and 35 work-stations, all using NetBEUI for transport.

    Required result: Install a networking device that will eliminate the effects of attenuation.

    Optional desired results: Ensure that broadcast storms do not incapacitate the network. Filter traffic based on MAC addresses.

    Proposed solution: Install a typical bridge at a central point of the network.

    Which result does the proposed solution produce?

    A. The proposed solution produces the required result and produces both of the optional desired results.

    B. The proposed solution produces the required result and produces only one of the optional desired results.

    C. The proposed solution produces the required result but does not produce any of the optional desired results.

    D. The proposed solution does not produce the required result.

20. What type of multiplexing would a device use if it transmits each signal at a different frequency?

A. Time Division Multiplexing

B. Statistical Time Division Multiplexing

C. Statistical Frequency Division Multiplexing

D. Frequency Division Multiplexing

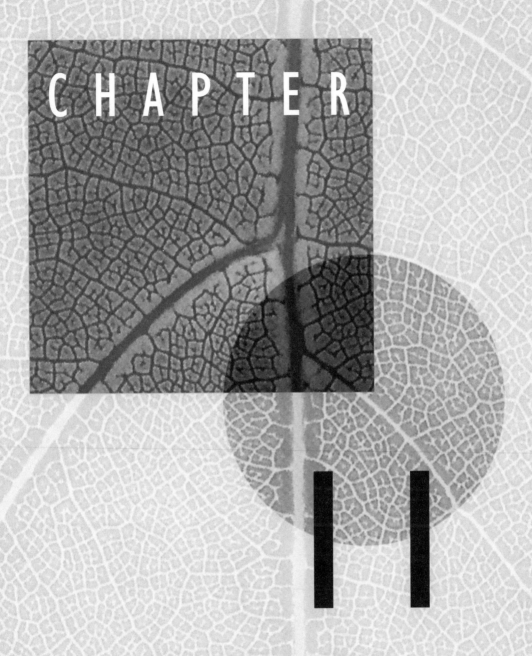

CHAPTER

11

Wide Area Networks

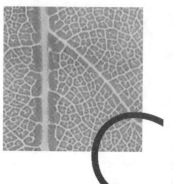

C HAPTER 10 DISCUSSED how expansion components such as repeaters, bridges, routers, brouters, and gateways enable LAN growth. As you know, you can add workstations in remote parts of a building or in separate buildings to a LAN, and you can connect separate LANs to the local physical media to create a larger integrated local network. However, sometimes LANs grow beyond the practical limits of their physical cable media. This chapter focuses on much larger networks called *wide area networks* (*WANs*) and the transmission media, data conventions, and hardware devices that support WAN communications. You will gain an overview of WAN transmission technology, including key concepts and terminology.

Microsoft ✓ ***Exam Objective***

List the characteristics, requirements, and appropriate situations for WAN connection services. WAN connection services include:

- X.25
- ISDN
- Frame relay
- ATM

WAN Overview

W IDE AREA NETWORKS originated to solve the problem of connecting a LAN to a distant workstation or another remote LAN when the distances exceed cable media specifications or when physical cable connections are not possible. WANs are usually required for high volume, long-distance data traffic. To implement WANs, you can use the following transmission media:

- The public switched telephone network (PSTN)

- High-speed, high-bandwidth dedicated leased circuits

- High-speed fiber-optic cable

- Microwave transmission links

- Satellite links

- Wireless radiated media (radio frequencies)

- The Internet

When a LAN uses modems, direct digital devices, and any of the media types listed above to outgrow its building or campus and connect to a distant LAN, it may become large enough to cover a metropolitan area. This type of LAN is sometimes called a *metropolitan area network (MAN)*, as illustrated in Figure 11.1.

FIGURE 11.1

A metropolitan area network (MAN) is similar to a LAN but spans a wider area—up to a good-sized metropolis.

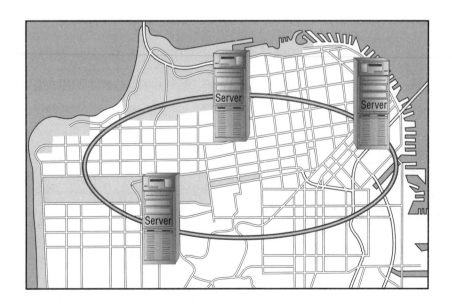

When a network grows even larger than a MAN, it becomes a WAN. There are two types of WANs:

- **Enterprise networks:** When a network connects a company's branch offices and divisions, it becomes an enterprise-wide network. For example, a corporation may have sites on every continent, all of which are interconnected to form one wide area network.

- **Global networks:** When a network spans several countries and continents and includes many types of organizations and individuals, it can be labeled global. These networks serve multinational corporations and scientific, academic, and military establishments. The Internet, often called the "network of networks," fits that definition.

Most often, WANs use high-speed leased telephone circuits (such as T1) to provide the links between different network sites. T1 bandwidth is 1.544Mbps, divisible into 24 channels of 64Kbps each. As the number of telephone lines an organization has approaches 24, it might begin to compare the cost of 24 separate phone lines, modem speed, and connect time to the cost, speed, and channel features of a T1 circuit.

Whichever carrier media you use, communication between LANs often involves one of the following data transmission methods:

- Analog lines

- Digital lines

- Packet-switched messaging on both analog and digital lines

These transmission methods are usually implemented across a public or private network service.

Public Network Services

HEN FACED WITH the costs of installing a WAN, rather than choosing to start your system from scratch, you may want to consider using the services (transmission media) of networks that already exist. Public networks can help you extend your own transmission media, and using provider services is often much less expensive (you pay to use their media) than installing your own transmission media.

A number of different services exist. Two of the most popular are the Public Switched Telephone Network and the Internet.

Public Switched Telephone Network

Virtually every country in the world has a Public Switched Telephone Network (PSTN). All of these networks together represent the world's largest network. PSTNs were originally designed exclusively for telephones but have become highly sophisticated, able to handle different kinds of data transmission, including digital data transmission.

The United States PSTN consists of a complex assortment of components, including the following:

- Subscriber wiring and equipment
- Demarcation point
- Local loops
- Central offices
- Switching offices
- Long-distance carriers
- Points of presence
- Data transmission services

Subscriber wiring and equipment is your wiring and equipment, such as telephones, modems, and other devices. Typically, subscriber wiring consists of UTP cabling with RJ-11 or RJ-45 connectors. Often, the wiring extends back to a telephone closet, which then connects to a *demarcation point,* or *demarc.* The demarc is the grounded, protected, physical connection point where the telephone company's wiring connects with your wiring. You are responsible for maintaining wiring and equipment on your side of the demarc.

Local loops begin at the demarc and extend back to the provider's central office (CO). The local loop normally consists of high-grade UTP cable, fiber-optic cable, or a combination of the two. The CO provides various services, the most important of which is switching incoming signals to outgoing trunk lines. It also provides reliable DC power to establish an electronic circuit on the local loop. A number of COs are connected by trunk lines to other switching offices.

Groups of central offices and switching offices then use long-distance carriers to provide transmission capability to COs almost anywhere in the world. Long-distance carriers often make use of a variety of transmission media, including high-bandwidth coaxial cable, fiber-optic cable, and microwave transmitters and receivers.

The lines from the long-distance carriers enter the central office at what is called a point of presence. Figure 11.2 shows how the components of a PSTN work together.

FIGURE 11.2

PSTN components

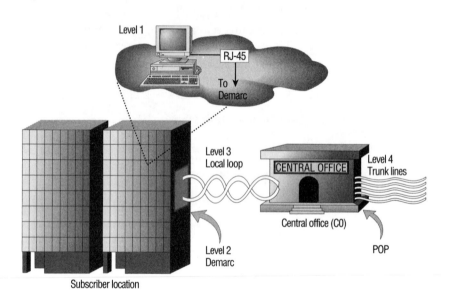

The PSTN provides a number of options for data transmissions, including services that route packets between different sites. Available services and some possible transmission rates include the following:

SERVICE	TRANSMISSION RATE
Switched 56	56Kbps
X.25	56Kbps
T1 circuits	1.544Mbps

SERVICE	TRANSMISSION RATE
T3 circuits	44.736Mbps
Frame relay	1.544Mbps
SMDS	1.544Mbps
ISDN	1.544Mbps
ATM	44.736Mbps

Compare these data transmission rates with common LAN services such as Ethernet (10Mbps), Token Ring/4 (4Mbps), and Token Ring/16 (16Mbps). Figure 11.3 shows an example of a PSTN.

FIGURE 11.3

Example of a PSTN

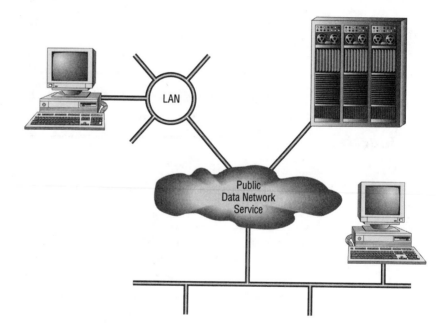

The Internet

You're probably familiar with the Internet. It is a shared network of government agencies, educational institutions, private organizations, and individuals from over a hundred nations. No one owns the Internet; anyone can have access to the transmission media. In fact, estimates of the number of people who have access to the Internet reach as high as 50 million worldwide.

The United States has begun to put its weight behind the development of the National Information Infrastructure (better known as the "information superhighway"). The stated goals are to connect networks through "superhighways" with data rates higher than 3Gbps. Research includes strategies for using fiber-optics and other high-bandwidth transmission media. As the National Information Infrastructure materializes, it will offer a whole new level of Internet service.

SLIP and PPP

Serial Line Internet Protocol (SLIP) and Point-to-Point Protocol (PPP) are two very common protocols used to transmit IP packets (IP is part of the TCP/IP protocol suite) over serial line and telephone connections, most often as part of a dial-up Internet connection.

Microsoft ✓ *Exam* *Objective*

Distinguish whether SLIP or PPP is used as the communications protocol for various situations.

The TCP/IP protocol suite runs over a variety of network media: IEEE 802.3 (Ethernet) and 802.5 (Token Ring) LAN's, X.25 lines, satellite links, and serial lines. There are defined standards for transporting IP packets across many of these networks. SLIP (Serial Line IP) and PPP are popular standards commonly used for point-to-point serial connections using TCP/IP.

SLIP and PPP are similar protocols. There are, however, some key differences that make PPP a more sophisticated option:

- PPP is a multiprotocol transport mechanism. While SLIP is designed to handle one type of traffic (TCP/IP traffic) at a time, PPP can transport TCP/IP traffic as well as IPX, AppleTalk, and other types of traffic simultaneously on the same connection. However, since SLIP and PPP are typically used to make single TCP/IP connections (to the Internet), the multiprotocol feature of PPP is not usually of benefit.

- With SLIP, you must know both the IP address assigned to you by an Internet service provider (ISP) and the IP address of the remote system your computer will be dialing into. If the IP addresses are assigned dynamically, you will need to set them up manually; SLIP software normally does not automatically register IP assignments. You may also need to make other manual configurations. PPP deals with these problems by negotiating configuration parameters at the beginning of your connection.

- PPP can negotiate header compression. Streams of packets in a single TCP connection have few changed fields in the IP and TCP headers, so simple compression algorithms can just send the changed parts of the headers instead of the complete headers. This can significantly improve packet throughput. SLIP does not offer this compression.

- PPP offers IP enhanced security.

Some people believe SLIP is faster than PPP because the protocol format calls for a packet size that is 3 bytes smaller than the packets PPP uses. Actually, this difference is so small that it is practically insignificant.

Many types of SLIP/PPP software offer automatic dial-up login to an Internet service provider. With these features, your SLIP/PPP software may need to know only your login userid/password and the telephone number of your service provider. The software can then dial-up into your service provider and figure out everything else on its own.

If, however, the ISP's system sends out prompts (for example, "login:" for the login name and "password:" for the password) in a nonstandard format, you will need to either create a script to automate the login process yourself or log in manually in the terminal emulation mode of your SLIP/PPP software.

PPP offers two methods for automating logins: PAP (Password Authentication Protocol) and CHAP (Challenge-Handshake Authentication Protocol).

For over a decade SLIP has been a very popular protocol that offers a simple, reliable way to connect to a TCP/IP host. SLIP is, however, a very simple protocol with some definite shortcomings. In recent years, PPP has slowly replaced SLIP. PPP was developed as an improvement over SLIP. Most people now seem to agree that new installations should start fresh with PPP.

Systems designers should use SLIP only for interim backward compatibility with existing installations that have not yet been upgraded to PPP. In other words, use PPP unless you are using SLIP already and aren't ready to upgrade.

REAL WORLD PROBLEMS

You are responsible for setting up some remote workstations and a server that will be connected to the Internet. The workstations will be connecting to the server using standard telephone lines. You know that SLIP and PPP are useful protocols for your situation. Your boss comes in and says, "I think SLIP is the protocol we should start using here. What do you think?"

- What protocol would you recommend?

- List three advantages of the protocol you recommended.

Your boss comes back a few hours later and says he's discovered that you won't be able to use the protocol you recommended because the company is currently committed to the other protocol.

- Do you expect any major problems with using the other protocol? Why or why not?

Switching

SWITCHING IS AN important technique that can determine how connections are made and how data movement is handled on a WAN. Data sent across the PSTN or other internetworks (the media connecting WANs) can travel along different paths from sender to receiver. *Switching* sends data along different routes, much the way trains are switched over multiple tracks. Three major switching techniques are available to route messages through internetworks: circuit switching, message switching, and packet switching.

Circuit switching connects the sender and receiver by a single physical path for the duration of the conversation. In contrast, *message switching* does not establish a dedicated path between two stations; instead, messages are stored and forwarded from one intermediate device to the next. *Packet switching* combines the advantages of both circuit and message switching by breaking longer messages into small parts called packets. Packet switching is the most efficient switching technique for data communications. The following sections discuss each of these switching techniques in detail.

Circuit Switching

In circuit switching, a dedicated physical connection is established between the sender and the receiver and maintained for the entire conversation. For example, the PSTN uses a circuit-switching system. When you make a call, a physical link between the two phones is dedicated during the entire conversation When one phone hangs up, the connection is terminated and the circuit is released. A computer network performs circuit switching in a similar way.

Before any two computers can transfer data, a dedicated circuit must be established between the two. The sending machine requests a connection to the destination, after which the destination machine signals that it is ready to accept data. The data is then sent from the source to the destination, and the destination sends acknowledgments back to the source. When the conversation is finished, the source sends a signal to the destination, indicating that the connection is no longer needed, and disconnects itself.

The major advantage of circuit switching is that the dedicated transmission channel the machines establish provides a guaranteed data rate. This is important for time-critical applications such as audio and video. Also, once the circuit is established, there is virtually no channel access delay; since the channel is always available, it does not need to be requested again.

Circuit switching does have its disadvantages. One is that it is often an inefficient use of the transmission media. Because the connection is dedicated even when it is idle, no other devices can use the channel. Dedicated channels require more bandwidth than nondedicated channels, so transmission media can be expensive. Also, this method can be subject to long connection delays; it may take several seconds to establish the connection.

Message Switching

Message switching is unlike circuit switching in that it does not establish a dedicated path between two communicating devices. Instead, each message is treated as an independent unit and includes its own destination and source addresses. Each complete message is then transmitted from device to device through the internetwork. Each intermediate device receives the message, stores it until the next device is ready to receive it, and then forwards it to the next device. For this reason, a message-switching network is sometimes referred to as a store-and-forward network.

Message switches can be programmed with information about the most efficient routes, as well as information regarding neighboring switches that can be used to forward messages to their ultimate destination. Because of this information, and because network conditions vary, message-switching systems typically route messages through the network along varying paths.

The devices that perform message switching are often PCs using custom software for this purpose. The PC must be prepared to store potentially long messages until those messages can be forwarded. These messages are stored on a hard disk or in RAM. The amount of storage space needed depends on the network traffic through the switch.

One example of a store-and-forward system is e-mail. An e-mail message is forwarded as a complete unit from server to server until it reaches the correct destination. It may take several seconds to several minutes (or in the case of slow connections to the Internet, several hours), but it usually beats the postal service. Clearly, e-mail would be an inefficient use of a dedicated connection. Scheduling and calendaring applications, as well as group databases such as Lotus Notes, can also send updates as messages in this system.

Advantages of message switching include the following:

- It provides efficient traffic management. By assigning priorities to the messages to be switched, you can ensure that higher-priority messages get through in a timely fashion, rather than being delayed by general traffic. Resources are set aside to handle these messages, similar to the extra resources a post office or parcel-delivery service maintains for priority mail.

- It reduces network traffic congestion. The intermediate devices (the message switches) are able to store messages until a communications channel becomes available, rather than choking the network by trying to transmit everything in real time.

- Its use of data channels is more efficient than circuit switching. With message switching, the network devices share the data channels. This increases efficiency because more of the available bandwidth can be used.

- It provides asynchronous communication across time zones. Messages can be sent even though the receiver may not be present, which can make communication across time zones easier. For example, if you have corporate offices in Sydney, Frankfurt, and Chicago, the last thing you'll want to do is communicate regularly in real time.

On the other hand, the delay introduced by storing and forwarding complete messages makes message switching unsuitable for real-time applications such as voice or video. For these applications (and especially video-conferencing), you need circuit switching. Another disadvantage of message switching is that it can be costly to equip intermediate devices with enough storage capacity to store potentially long messages.

Packet Switching

Packet switching provides the advantages of circuit switching and message switching and avoids the main disadvantages of both. In packet switching, messages are broken up into packets, each of which includes a header with source, destination, and intermediate node address information. Individual packets don't always follow the same route; this is called independent routing. Independent routing offers two advantages:

- Bandwidth can be managed by splitting data onto different routes in a busy circuit.

- If a certain link in the network goes down during the transmission, the remaining packets can be sent through another route.

How, then, is packet switching different from message switching? The main difference is that packet switching restricts packets to a maximum length. This length is short enough to allow the switching devices to store the packet data in memory without writing any of it to disk. By cutting the disk out of the process, packet switching works far more quickly and efficiently than message switching.

In the following sections we discuss two methods of packet switching: datagram packet switching, which has many similarities to message switching, and virtual-circuit packet switching, which is quite similar to circuit switching.

Datagram Packet Switching

In a datagram packet-switched network, a message is divided into a stream of packets. Each packet is separately addressed and treated as an independent unit with its own control instructions, rather than being a piece of something larger. The switching devices route each packet independently through the network, with each intermediate node determining the packet's next route segment. Before transmission starts, the sequence of packets and their destinations are established by the exchange of control information between the sending terminal, the network, and the receiving terminal. Packet sizes are kept small to prevent extended switch clogging and to make retransmission (to compensate for errors) a lot easier.

The switching devices can direct packets around busy network links (rather than blindly sending them into the thickest of the traffic) and make sure they reach their destination without undue delay. As Figure 11.4 illustrates, the packets that make up a message may arrive at their destination after taking very different routes through the internetwork.

FIGURE 11.4

Datagram packet switching can send individual packets through different routes.

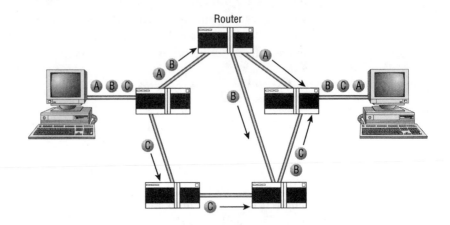

Because the datagram packets can follow different routes through the internetwork, they're likely to arrive at their destination out of order. The packet headers include a sequence number that the receiving device uses to reassemble the packets and reconstruct the original message.

Datagram packet switching lets you transmit large messages quickly and efficiently by using a smaller frame size. The network layer on the sending device divides the messages from upper layers into smaller datagrams that the data link layer can handle. Then the packets are transmitted through the internetwork. Finally, the network layer on the receiving machine reconstructs the messages from the data link layer frames into messages for the upper-layer protocols.

Virtual-Circuit Packet Switching

Virtual-circuit packet switching establishes a logical connection between the sending and receiving devices, called a virtual circuit. The sending device starts the conversation by communicating with the receiving device and agreeing on communication parameters, such as maximum message size and the network path to be taken. Once this virtual circuit is established, the two devices use it for the rest of the conversation, or for as long as the two devices are operational.

Virtual-circuit packet switching is radically different from datagram packet switching. In virtual-circuit packet switching, all the packets travel through the logical connection established between the sending device and the receiving device. In datagram packet switching, the packets travel different routes through the internetwork.

The logical connection that the sending and receiving machine establishes is termed virtual because there is no dedicated physical circuit between the machines, even though the machines are acting as though they have established one. A logical connection is established. Each node in the logical path can perform switching and error control.

One of the main areas where you'll see virtual circuits used frequently is connection-oriented services such as audio and video.

Advantages and Disadvantages of Packet Switching

Packet switching has a great advantage over circuit switching in that it improves the use of network bandwidth by enabling many devices to communicate through the same network channel. A switching node may concurrently route packets to several different destination devices and is able to adjust the routes as required by changing network conditions in order to get the packets through in good order.

Another advantage of packet switching is that it suffers far shorter transmission delays than does message switching because the switching nodes are handling the packets entirely in memory rather than committing them to disk before forwarding them.

When considering packet switching, take the following factors into account:

- **RAM versus hard disk space:** Switching nodes for packet switching will require large amounts of RAM to handle large quantities of packets successfully. By way of compensation, they won't need such large hard drives (because they won't be writing the messages to disk).

- **Processing power:** The packet-switching protocols are more complex than message-based protocols, so the switching nodes will need more processing power.

- **Lost packets:** Because the data is divided into a larger number of pieces, packets are more easily lost than entire messages. Packet-switching protocols need to be able to recognize which packets have been lost and to request that those packets be retransmitted. The sequence numbers play an important role in helping to identify missing packets.

Lines

 NALOG AND DIGITAL lines offer one of the most popular media for connection WANs. As you saw in Chapter 9, lines can be either dial-up or dedicated.

Dial-Up Lines

Dial-up lines provide connections across the PSTN. Dial-up lines open a new circuit with each call and may use different routing paths to the same destination.

The public switched telephone network is slow because it was originally designed for voice-grade analog communications.

Because the PSTN is a circuit-switched network, end-to-end circuit links between any two origin/destination points, as well as the line quality of those links, may vary from one call to the next. Consequently, transmission quality may vary from one call to the next. Over long distances, the variable circuit quality may show up as differences in modem connect speed, throughput, or loss of carrier (abnormal disconnect).

Analog Dedicated Lines

Dedicated, or leased, analog lines provide subscribers with direct end-to-end exclusive circuits that are always available. In contrast with a dial-up connection that opens a new circuit with each call and may use different routing paths to the same destination, dedicated circuits are more reliable and more costly because they are unswitched, always available, and dedicated to your exclusive use.

REAL WORLD PROBLEM

You need to set up a server on the Internet, and you need to establish a line to the server that will offer 24-hour access to the server.

■ Would you choose a dial-up or dedicated line? Why?

Digital Lines

For high-quality, continuous connections, *digital lines* are preferred over dedicated analog lines. For many non-critical network operations, dial-up or dedicated analog lines are adequate. However, analog signal quality is often degraded by voice frequency limitations. So-called "noisy" lines can corrupt data or even drop a carrier connection altogether. A poor-quality line will cause modems to fall back to the next highest mutually acceptable transmission rate until line quality improves or the connection is lost. After a connection is lost, bottlenecks can occur while a new connection is being established.

When a WAN carries the heavy traffic of critical operations, data corruption and bottlenecks quickly become expensive burdens. A solution to noisy analog lines is to switch to digital lines. Digital lines are more expensive, but if your need for a faster, more reliable, and more secure transmission environment justifies the cost, you might consider digital data service (DDS) lines. Figure 11.5 illustrates a DDS line.

FIGURE 11.5

Two remote networks
connected via a digital
data service (DDS) line

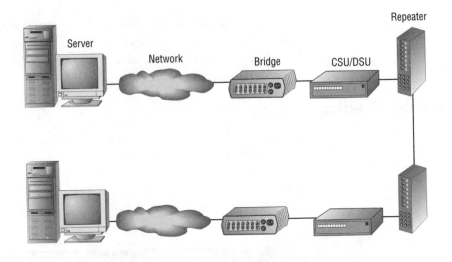

DDS lines are popular for several reasons:

- They provide nearly error-free synchronous transmission.

- Transmission speeds offered are 2400bps, 4800bps, 9600bps, and
  56Kbps.

- Connections are permanent, end-to-end, and full-duplex.

- Local phone companies typically offer the service.

T-Carrier

T-carriers are a type of high-speed leased telephone line used for voice and
data transmission. There are four main T-carrier service levels:

- T1 (1.544Mbps)

- T2 (6.312Mbps)

- T3 (44.736Mbps)

- T4 (274.176Mbps)

T-carrier service employs multiplexing to allow the bit streams of the smaller
carriers (such as T1) to be multiplexed into the larger ones, as illustrated in

Figure 11.6. The following table compares the number of T1 channels that are multiplexed into the other T-carrier services:

T-CARRIER	NUMBER OF T1 CHANNELS USED
T1	1
T2	4
T3	28
T4	168

FIGURE 11.6

T-carriers are multiplexed like "Chinese boxes."

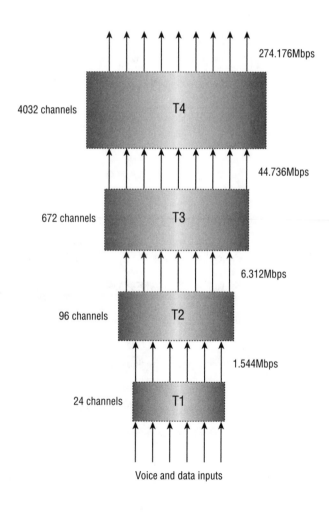

Because T-carrier service is too expensive for some purposes, service providers often allow you to lease subdivisions of a full T-carrier service. This less expensive service, based on the 64Kbps channels, is known as fractional T.

REAL WORLD PROBLEMS

You are responsible for designing a WAN that needs to communicate at a minimum speed of 1Mbps.

- What type of T-carrier service should you use?

You have three locations that you are going to connect using T-carrier service.

- How can you connect the locations so that, if a single link fails, communications can still continue between each of the three locations?

- How many T-carrier lines will you need?

Switched 56

Switched 56 is a version of DDS that is used on demand; it is not dedicated. Recall that DDS lines are the entry point into dedicated high-speed (56Kbps) point-to-point digital transmission. Switched 56, therefore, represents a way to reduce the full cost of a dedicated DDS line.

REAL WORLD PROBLEMS

Your boss asks you to set up a server on the Internet that offers a connection of at least 56Kbps.

- Which types of the lines listed above would you consider using?

Your boss contacts you again and says that the server will actually need to offer dedicated 512Kbps service. "Unfortunately," she says, "we don't have much of a budget."

- Which of the above services would you recommend? Why?

The X.25 Packet-Switching Protocol

X.25 PACKET SWITCHED networks allow remote devices to communicate with each other without the expense of individual leased lines.

One of the key design features of packet-switched networks is redundant error checking, which allows for the limitations of analog voice-grade lines when they are used for data communications. X.25 is a packet-switching protocol that defines the interface between a synchronous packet-switching host computer and analog dedicated circuits or dial-up switched virtual circuits in the voice-grade public data network. Therefore, it implements the original design objectives of packet switching. Its dominant features are:

- Virtual circuit switching and dynamic virtual routing to transport self-contained, self-addressed message packets

- Ability to use any available network channels or links

- Ability to use redundant error checking at every node

X.25 allows a variety of devices that are designated as data terminal equipment (DTE) to talk to the public data network (PDN). The PDN is designated as data communications equipment (DCE), as are devices such as modems, packet switches, and other ports. Hardware/software devices, such as terminals, hosts, and routers, that deliver data to or from a network I/O point are DTE. The X.25 protocol is a DTE-to-DCE synchronous interface.

To begin communication, one DTE device (for example, a router) calls another DTE to request a data exchange session. The DTE called can accept or refuse the connection. If the called DTE accepts the connection, the two systems begin full-duplex data transfer. Either side can terminate the connection at any time.

X.25 has been used since the mid 1970s, so it is pretty well debugged and stable. There are literally no data errors on modern X.25 networks.

X.25 does have some drawbacks. The store-and-forward mechanism causes delays. On most single networks the turn-around delay is about 0.6 seconds.

This does not affect large block transfers, but in transmissions that require extensive "back and forth" communication, the delay can be very noticeable.

Frame relay (also called fast packet switching) does not store and forward; it simply switches to a destination partway through the frame, considerably reducing the transmission delay.

Line speeds normally used with X.25 are too slow to provide most LAN application services on a WAN. Transmission speeds of up to 64kbps are typical.

Frame Relay

IKE X.25, frame relay is a packet-switching network service that uses variable-length packets to provide high-speed data transmission rates. Frame relay, however, is less robust than X.25. By eliminating some of the accounting and error-checking services that X.25 requires, frame relay achieves greater efficiency and higher throughput. Because it uses a permanent virtual circuit in a reliable environment, frame relay does not need as much overhead as X.25.

Frame Relay evolved from X.25. It can, however, provide speeds of up to 1.544 Mbps and can employ fiber-optic media.

Because it eliminates unnecessary overhead, frame relay outperforms other systems with its fast packet-switching technology. Frame relay uses permanent virtual circuits (PVCs) to establish stable end-to-end circuits. The system doesn't need to build and abandon circuits or instantaneously create temporary best-path routes, which occurs with traditional packet switching. The resulting transmission speeds account for its increasing popularity. Add to that a dynamically responsive bandwidth and you have a transmission medium that accommodates mixed and irregular demands. Frame relay is cost effective, mostly because the network buffering requirements are carefully optimized.

(ATM) Asynchronous Transfer Mode

ATM IS A descendant of packet-switching. Its high-speed advantage comes from transmitting uniform data packets that are subdivided into data frames, and each frame is enclosed within an addressable 53-byte cell and routed by hardware switching. The switching achieves very high-speed data transmission rates, between 155- and 622Mbps (and theoretically, up to 1.2 gigabits per second). ATM offers fast, real-time, demand-responsive switching for efficient use of network resources using broadband and baseband LANs or WANs.

ATM Methods

Unlike other switching technologies, which use frames that vary in length, ATM is based on 53-byte cells of fixed size. Each cell comprises 48 bytes of application information and a 5-byte ATM header. The consistent, standard-sized cells allow switching mechanisms to achieve faster switching rates.

ATM cells are compatible with both time-division multiplexing and packet-switching data schemes.

Instead of relying on slower software switching and error checking at every node, which is what occurs in traditional packet switching, ATM uses hardware switching at the data link medium access layer of the OSI model. Its high-quality, nearly noise-free dedicated digital lines do not require the burden of error checking associated with traditional analog packet-switching lines; the destination computer assumes that burden.

At each switching node, the ATM header identifies a virtual circuit that will route the cell's message to the destination computer. The cell header enables the switch to forward the cell and data to the next neighboring link in the total circuit. The virtual circuit is set up through the appropriate ATM switches when two endpoints wish to communicate. This scheme allows ATM switching to be implemented in hardware that is fast enough to support transmission rates to 1.0 gigabits per second.

ATM can provide for simultaneous data, video, and voice transmissions.

ATM Media Compatibility

ATM is compatible with current and widely used cable media such as twisted-pair, coaxial, and fiber-optic, as well as a great deal of LAN and WAN technology. However, some cable media lacks sufficient bandwidth to fully realize ATM's potential. The sticking point that slows ATM conversions is that ATM networks require consistent, compatible hardware throughout.

To date, there are ATM standards for transmitting at 25Mbps, 45Mbps, 52Mbps, 100Mbps, 155Mbps, and 622Mbps. ATM is compatible with other transmission methods: ATM cells can be encapsulated in other protocols, including those of FDDI, SONET, T3, OC3, and Fiber Channel.

(ISDN) Integrated Services Digital Network

ISDN IS A switched digital service that is typically sold on a time-and-distance rate schedule, just like ordinary phone calls. It is provided by local telephone service providers where telephone companies have converted from analog to digital switching systems.

ISDN channels are available in bandwidth increments of 56/64Kbps, 384Mbps, and 1.544Mbps. The most common service options are Basic Rate and Primary Rate. Basic Rate ISDN divides its available bandwidth into three data channels. Two channels are designated as B channels and transmit data at 64Kbps, and a third D channel, also known as a service channel, transmits signaling and link management data at 16Kbps. ISDN Basic Rate desktop service is called 2B+D.

A computer connected to an ISDN service can use both B channels together for a combined 128Kbps speed. When both the sending and receiving computers support compression, much higher throughput is possible. Optionally, one 64Kbps B channel can be used for data transmission while the other

B channel is simultaneously used for voice. When one B channel is being used for voice, the data transmission rate on the other B channel will drop back to 64Kbps. When the user stops using one channel for voice, the data rate will resume its 128Kbps speed.

ISDN has long been viewed as a replacement for the slower PSTN services.

Primary Rate ISDN or PRI (23B+D) uses the entire 1.544Mbps T1 bandwidth to provide 23 B channels at 64Kbps and one D channel at 64Kbps. The D channel is used for signaling and link management.

The billing method is both an advantage and a liability, depending on how many hours a month the ISDN channels are to be used. When used continuously, ISDN channels in the United States are substantially more expensive than using the bandwidth equivalents offered over dedicated leased lines (FT1/T1), which are based on fixed monthly charges, distance factors, and clock time. However, if ISDN channel usage is limited to only a few dial-up hours a month, it can be more cost effective than full-time leased lines.

(FDDI) Fiber Distributed Data Interface

FDDI (Fiber Distributed Data Interface) is a topology standard that transmits information packets using light produced by a laser or LED (light-emitting diode) and offers tremendous speed. FDDI uses fiber-optic cable and equipment to transmit data packets. Typical data rates are around 100Mbps. Cable lengths can easily be up to 100 kilometers (with repeaters at least every two kilometers).

TP-PMD (twisted pair–physical medium dependent) is a type of FDDI that uses copper cable for transmission over short distances.

This topology manages access to the network using IEEE 802.5, like Token Ring. It also has many improvements over Token Ring, including a system fault-tolerance strategy that employs two rings instead of one and a technique called *wrapping*.

How FDDI Works

With FDDI, a station must have a token before it can transmit frames. The size of FDDI frames can be between 17 and 4500 bytes. Stations on the network read the messages that travel around the ring from NIC to NIC. When a station reads a frame that matches its address, it copies the frame and creates an acknowledgment frame. Then it transfers the token to the next attached network node.

FDDI uses the primary ring to move data and a second ring to provide system fault tolerance and backup. The two rings rotate (send messages) in opposite directions, so they are called *dual counter-rotating rings*. The second ring is inactive until it is needed. Figure 11.7 shows the design of an FDDI topology.

Devices such as workstations, bridges, and routers can be attached to the rings. There are two types of stations: Class A and Class B. Class A stations are also called *dual-attached stations* (DASs) because they can be attached to both rings at the same time. Class A stations are extremely stable. They can survive a break in one or both rings. The only time a Class A station will be isolated from the network is if there are two breaks in both rings on both sides of one workstation.

Class B stations are called *single-attached stations* (SASs) because they attach to only one ring. Class B workstations are not as fault-tolerant as Class A workstations because they cannot use *wrapping*, the strategy that takes advantage of the dual-ring system if a break occurs in one or both of the rings. A break in the ring on which a Class B station is attached will probably isolate a Class B workstation.

Wiring concentrators can also be used to provide protection against breaking the rings. FDDI concentrators function much like Token Ring MSAUs, but they are more intelligent. FDDI concentrators can communicate with stations to verify the integrity of the station-to-concentrator connection, and they can reroute packets instantaneously.

Wrapping is the system fault-tolerance feature that takes effect when a break occurs on one or both of the rings. When a break occurs in a ring, the first step is the identification of a failure domain (the area affected by the break that cannot carry data). The failure domain includes the machine closest

FIGURE 11.7

FDDI topology design

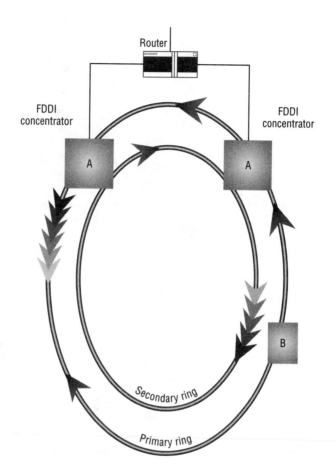

to the cable break and its nearest upstream neighbor. Wrapping reroutes the packets around the two workstations bordering that failure domain. Two Class A machines can then use the second ring to route packets around the failure domain. Class B workstations cannot take advantage of wrapping because they are connected to only one ring. During this time, FDDI concentrators play an important role and must be able to reroute information instantaneously. Figure 11.8 shows how FDDI wrapping works.

FIGURE 11.8

FDDI wrapping

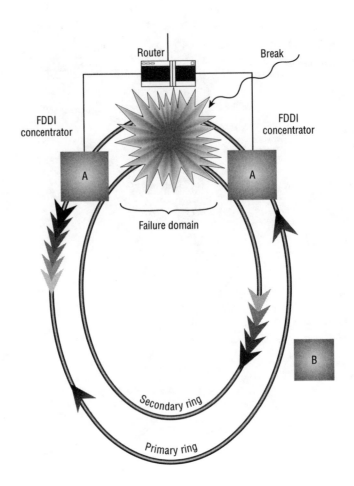

Advantages and Disadvantages of FDDI

FDDI has some strong advantages. Advantages resulting from the use of fiber-optic cable (described in the next section) include the following:

- **High bandwidth:** Using light provides enormous bandwidth, as high as nearly 250Gbps. High bandwidth allows for tremendous speed. As stated earlier, most FDDI implementations can handle data rates of 100Mbps.

- **Security:** It is difficult to eavesdrop on fiber-optic cable transmissions.

- **Physical durability:** Fiber-optic cable doesn't break as easily as do other kinds of cable.

- **Resistance to EMI:** Fiber-optic cable is not susceptible to EMI.

- **Cable distance:** Fiber-optic cables transmit signals over 2 kilometers. Under experimental conditions, distances of hundreds of kilometers are possible.

- **Weight:** Fiber-optic cable weighs a lot less than copper wire with similar bandwidth.

In addition to those resulting from the use of fiber-optic cable, FDDI has other advantages:

- **Use of multiple tokens:** FDDI uses multiple tokens to improve network speed.

- **Ability to prioritize workstations:** FDDI can designate some workstations as low-priority workstations. This allows FDDI to bypass low-priority workstations when necessary, providing faster service to high-priority stations.

- **System fault tolerance:** FDDI can isolate faulty nodes with the use of wiring concentrators for instantaneous rerouting. Wiring concentrators function as centralized cabling connection devices for workstations. The other big advantage is wrapping.

As you can see, there are a number of advantages to FDDI. As with all topologies and systems, there are also some disadvantages. FDDI is a complex technology. Installation and maintenance require a great deal of expertise. However, this is a new technology, and advancements should be coming.

The other disadvantage of FDDI is cost. Fiber-optic cable itself is becoming more inexpensive. However, other equipment, such as adapters and concentrators, can be very expensive. With some of this core equipment costing a great deal (a typical FDDI concentrator might run more than a thousand dollars per network node), costs for even a small network add up quickly.

Cabling for FDDI

Rings in FDDI are made of fiber-optic cables. Fiber-optic cable, which was discussed in Chapter 2, consists of optical fibers made from glass (or plastic). The fiber consists of an inner glass core surrounded by more glass, called cladding. Light is flashed at either end of the cabling by LEDs or ILDs (injection laser diodes). The signals are then sent through the core, and the cladding acts as a mirror, reflecting light back into the core. Fibers are often bundled together to allow multiple signals to be sent at one time. Each fiber can carry signals in only one direction.

Today, many fiber-optics manufacturers are working to improve fiber-optic cable to make it less expensive and easier to use. Some manufacturers have begun to offer cable with plastic rather than glass. Plastic, however, typically does not have the purity to allow long cable runs or high throughput.

A second improvement has been more successful: snap-in connectors. Formerly, fiber-optic termination included using epoxy preparation and polishing of the glass; it was an involved process. Snap-in connectors have simplified the connection process greatly.

Fiber-optic cable comes in various types and wavelengths. To make the best selection, choose a fiber-optic cable based on its intended use. Then be careful to match the cable to its appropriate connectors.

(SONET) Synchronous Optical Network

SONET IS A high-speed, fiber-optic data transmission system. It can move data at rates faster than 1 gigabit per second. SONET data rates begin at 51.84Mbps. Higher data rates come in multiples of the basic rate. Rates for SONET are calculated in terms of optical carrier (OC) speed.

SONET can easily surpass 1 gbps. 10Gbs SONET metropolitan area rings, supporting gigabit ATM applications, have been implemented.

Applications for SONET (as well as the other very high-speed transmission systems covered here) include

- High-speed, large-scale LAN interconnection

- Video-on-demand

- Full-motion catalogs, movies, and so on

- Professional services

- High-resolution imaging

- High-fidelity sound broadcast

REAL WORLD PROBLEMS

You are responsible for providing a high-speed link between two corporate offices. The company plans to use extensive video conferencing and large file transfers. The board of directors wants you to give a briefing on the different types of services. You do some research and determine that all the services described in this chapter are available in your area.

- Create a brief list with two- or three-sentence descriptions for each transmission technology that might serve the company.

- List pros and cons of each of the possible choices.

You are responsible for a network at a quickly growing company in Chicago. Your boss calls you into her office one day and says, "We've decided to open another office in Denver, and we'd like to know what you think we should do to connect the PCs we'll have there with the LAN we have here. The office in Denver will have a couple of peer-networked PCs that will occasionally need a direct connection with the LAN in Chicago."

- Of the technologies listed in this chapter, which ones look like possible solutions? Why?

- Which technologies would you choose if the connection needed to be relatively error-free? Why?

Review

THIS CHAPTER HAS presented an overview of major types of connections used to create wide area networks.

Different terms are used to describe networks in terms of their size: LAN, MAN, and WAN.

You can use existing networks to expand your network. The Internet and the Public Switched Telephone Network (PSTN) are existing networks widely used for network expansion.

SLIP and PPP are two protocols frequently used to make serial line or telephone connections to the Internet. PPP is slowly replacing SLIP.

The PSTN consists of the network across which telephone connections take place. It also offers several levels of internetwork connectivity, including services that involve routing and various types of switching. Circuit switching, message switching, and packet switching are the three major switching techniques.

Dial-up and dedicated lines provide connections across the PSTN. Dial-up lines open a new circuit with each call and may use varying routing paths, while dedicated, or leased, lines provide exclusive, direct circuits that are always available.

The chapter ended with a quick view of ATM, ISDN, and other technologies you can use to create high-speed internetwork connections.

Review Questions

1. Which of the following protocols available for Dial-Up Networking is most often used to connect to the Internet?

   A. PPTP

   B. ISDN

   C. PPP

   D. SLPP

2. Which of the following high-speed network types uses fixed- rather than variable-length cells to achieve higher speeds?

A. Fast Ethernet

B. Frame Relay

C. FDDI

D. ATM

3. Of the network types listed below, which will provide 100Mbps transmission over fiber-optic cable? Choose all that apply:

A. 100VG-AnyLAN

B. FDDI

C. 100BaseT4

D. ATM

4. Suppose the following situation exists: Your company is located in three offices in the Bay Area. Each office includes between 30 and 50 workstations, with 2 to 3 servers in each office. The offices are currently not connected.

Required result: Propose a wide-area networking solution to connect the three offices.

Optional desired results: Provide bandwidth over 1Mbps. Include redundancy in the specification.

Proposed solution: Install ATM in a mesh configuration between all three sites.

Which results does the proposed solution produce?

A. The proposed solution produces the required result and produces both of the optional desired results.

B. The proposed solution produces the required result and produces only one of the optional desired results.

C. The proposed solution produces the required result but does not produce any of the optional desired results.

D. The proposed solution does not produce the required result.

5. T-carriers are widely used to connect LANs to form WANs. Which of the following describes a feature of T1 circuits?

   A. 128 Kbps transmission

   B. 1.544 Mbps transmission

   C. Limited to half-duplex transmission

   D. Satellite based

6. Which of the wide-area networking technologies listed below provides the highest transmission speeds?

   A. Frame Relay

   B. T3

   C. ISDN

   D. ATM

7. Which of the following Dial-Up Networking protocols includes support for both IPX and TCP/IP?

   A. DLC

   B. PPP

   C. SLIP

   D. UDP

8. Certain packet-switched networks establish virtual circuits to facilitate communication. Which of the following protocols function in this way? Choose all that apply:

   A. Frame Relay

   B. Switched 56

   C. FDDI

   D. ATM

9. The specifications for ATM include encapsulation into other protocols. Which of the following can ATM be encapsulated in? Choose all that apply:

A. ARCNet

B. Token Ring

C. Fiber Channel

D. SONET

10. Which of the following protocols available for Dial-Up Networking does not support automatically assigned IP addresses?

A. SNMP

B. PPP

C. SMTP

D. SLIP

11. Which of the following describes some of the features of ATM? Choose all that apply:

A. ATM uses packet switching.

B. ATM has a maximum throughput of 56Mbps.

C. ATM can simultaneously transmit data and video.

D. ATM uses variable-length packets.

12. Which of the following protocols provides robust low-speed packet-switching with extensive error checking mechanisms over either dedicated or switched circuits?

A. FDDI

B. X.25

C. ATM

D. Frame Relay

13. Which of the following provides digital rather than analog dial-up service?

   A. DUN

   B. X.25

   C. ISDN

   D. POTS

14. Which of the following wide-area networking technologies will support transmission rates of 1 Gbps or higher?

   A. SONET

   B. X.25

   C. Ethernet

   D. T3

15. Suppose the following situation exists: Your company is located in three offices in the Bay Area. Each office includes between 30 and 50 workstations, with 2 to 3 servers in each office. The offices are currently not connected.

   Required result: Propose a wide-area networking solution to connect the three offices.

   Optional desired results: Provide dedicated support for video and voice traffic in addition to data. Provide redundancy in case of a failure.

   Proposed solution: Install three Switched 56 lines connecting all offices.

   Which results does the proposed solution produce?

   A. The proposed solution produces the required result and produces both of the optional desired results.

   B. The proposed solution produces the required result and produces only one of the optional desired results.

   C. The proposed solution produces the required result but does not produce any of the optional desired results.

   D. The proposed solution does not produce the required result.

16. Suppose the following situation exists: Your office has been instructed by corporate to establish a wide-area network connection with a client office across town. Both of the networks are using Windows 95 in a peer-to-peer environment. For ease of use, both offices are using NetBEUI.

Required result: Provide a solution to connect the two offices.

Optional desired results: Continue to use NetBEUI. Keeps costs low.

Proposed solution: Connect the two offices using a 56K leased-line and brouters.

What results does the proposed solution produce?

A. The proposed solution produces the required result and produces both of the optional desired results.

B. The proposed solution produces the required result and produces only one of the optional desired results.

C. The proposed solution produces the required result but does not produce any of the optional desired results.

D. The proposed solution does not produce the required result.

17. Frame Relay is a largely accepted wide-area networking technology. Which of the following statements are true of Frame Relay. Choose all that apply:

A. It was developed from the X.25 standard.

B. Is supports variable-length packets.

C. It incorporates redundant error-checking.

D. Because it is the most robust transmission method, it functions well on older, less reliable phone lines.

CHAPTER

12

The Basics of Network Troubleshooting

AS A NETWORK ADMINISTRATOR, one of your major tasks after the network is up and running is to keep it that way. The best way to keep the network productive is to avoid potential problems. An ounce of prevention is worth a pound of cure. You probably already know that preventing problems is a lot easier than troubleshooting them. With a little effort, you can minimize the number and kinds of problems that occur. No matter how diligent you are, though, something will happen. The information in this chapter should help you prevent some of the most common problems and develop a strategy for troubleshooting problems when they do happen.

Preventing Problems

THE FIRST STEP in problem prevention is to set up the network carefully. Viruses and electrical problems can wreak havoc on a network, but they are almost entirely preventable. You can minimize other risks by taking care of the physical environment of the network.

Your job is to protect the network from accidental or deliberate acts that threaten the security, reliability, and availability of data. You probably know that you need to take care of your hardware—the machines that make up the network. You probably also know that you must take care of your data if you don't want to lose it. However, you may not have given enough thought to a third component: the people. Remember that keeping your data safe means considering all threats.

Let's take a closer look at the things you can do to prevent problems. Network problems fall into four general categories:

- Physical environment
- Electrical problems
- Viruses, worms, and Trojan horses
- Security

Problems in the Physical Environment

Although computers are not especially sensitive to their environment, their physical surroundings do have an impact on them. A good rule of thumb is this: If you feel comfortable in a room, the computers probably do, too. However, the general areas where you can protect your network include temperature, air quality, and magnetism.

Microsoft ✓ *Exam Objective*

Identify and resolve network performance problems.

Temperature

Temperature has a definite effect on a computer. When components get hot, they expand; when they get cold, they contract. This can cause what is known as *chip creep,* which means that integrated circuits gradually lose contact with their sockets. This lack of contact can cause problems because the chip won't send or receive signals as necessary. It doesn't take a heat wave to make this happen, either. The temperature inside a working computer can be as much as 40 degrees higher than the temperature outside the computer. The extra heat is generated by the computer's components. Check your fans periodically to make sure they are working correctly.

You might also consider leaving your computers on. Shutting down and bringing up a computer affects the temperature of the chips. It may seem contrary to what you've always been taught about machinery, but it's true: leaving a computer on all the time makes it last longer. Tests have shown this.

One factor is the temperature change the CPU goes through when it is shut down and brought back up. Avoiding cold boots greatly increases the longevity and reliability of network components.

Whenever you receive new equipment, let it adjust to room temperature before using it. Remember, the equipment may have been somewhere cold while you were in a warm building. Taking a few minutes to let the equipment slowly warm to room temperature might increase the lifetime of your new, and probably expensive, equipment.

Air Quality

To cool the computer, a fan circulates air through its case. The question is, what is in the air that is circulating? Dust, smoke particles, thermal insulation, and hair can damage hard disks and other components inside the computer. All of these environmental pollutants can affect the workings of a computer. Don't underestimate these factors. A workstation's life can be cut in half by the kind of air found in some offices. You should use filtration devices to filter out pollutants in the air.

Magnetism

Magnetism poses a problem for computers. It can corrupt computer data on magnetic storage devices (such as tapes, floppy disks, and hard disks). You should ensure that magnetic objects are removed from proximity to devices or storage media they might affect. Phones that ring, stereo speakers, and anything with a magnet can affect computer data. Take care of the potential threats of magnetism before your network suffers data loss.

Electrical Problems

Most of the physical conditions that cause problems happen over an extended period of time. Electrical problems occur quickly and often without warning. Problem prevention here requires you to plan carefully and to take precautionary actions during installation and maintenance. These are the four main types of electrical problems:

- Crosstalk

- Noise

- Static

- Transients

These types are described in the following sections.

Crosstalk

When two wires are close to each other, the magnetic fields each wire generates can interfere with normal transmission, or create crosstalk. Crosstalk can result in data loss or corruption. There are two ways to combat crosstalk. The first is to add space. If one cable is affecting another cable, you can try to increase the distance between the cables. The second solution is shielding. Unshielded twisted-pair (UTP) cable is the medium most affected by crosstalk. It is better to use shielded twisted-pair (STP) cable, because the shielding provides some protection from interference. Fiber-optic cable is the best medium. Because it uses light rather than electricity, this medium is completely immune to crosstalk. A major problem with fiber-optic, however, is that it is very expensive.

Noise

For electrical environments, noise is defined as a low-voltage, low-current, high-frequency signal that interferes with normal network transmissions, often corrupting data. Noise normally occurs in observable patterns. You can use an oscilloscope to check for the presence of noise.

In terms of computer networks, there are two kinds of noise: *electromagnetic interference (EMI)* and *radio frequency interference (RFI)*. EMI is the most common type of computer noise. Possible sources of EMI include lights, engines, industrial tools, and radar. Possible RFI sources include microwaves, appliances, and furnaces.

Noise can distort signals to random fuzziness. This distortion prevents the system from detecting thresholds.

To minimize noise, you may want to take the following precautions:

- Properly ground equipment.

- Avoid placing cables close to possible EMI and RFI sources.

- Use shielding in cables whenever possible.

- Check the FCC noise emission rating of your equipment.

Static

The buildup of static electricity doesn't damage a computer system, but the sudden discharge does. Static discharge can build up to dangerous levels before discharging all at once.

Most people are familiar with static electricity. You've probably built up a charge by dragging your feet on a dry, brittle carpet, hoping to shock a friend, and you probably were disappointed when the friend didn't feel it. This discharge, called *electrostatic discharge (ESD)*, must be close to 3000 volts for a person to feel it. In contrast, computer components such as microchips can be damaged by charges of 20 to 30 volts. To make matters worse, about 90 percent of the time, ESD does not affect equipment immediately. Instead, components tend to degrade over time and fail later.

Here are a few ways to avoid ESD:

- Always ground yourself and any equipment you will be working on. Use matting and wrist straps. However, don't use a wrist strap when working on a monitor. The high voltage can be conducted into your body through the strap.

- Never let anyone touch you while you are working on sensitive equipment. It is silly to go to the effort of grounding yourself, just to let someone else deliver an ESD by touching you.

- Never directly touch electrical leads of components or integrated circuits.

- Always use anti-static bags to transport and store components with integrated circuits.

- Keep ambient humidity at 70 to 90 percent. Low humidity makes static problems worse.

Some materials carry static charges more easily than others. Styrofoam is one common material that carries static buildup. Make sure Styrofoam cups and packing materials are not left near devices with integrated circuits. Polyester ties and other types of synthetic clothing can also carry static buildup.

Transients

A *transient,* also commonly called a *spike,* is a high-voltage burst of current. Transients rise and decay quickly, usually lasting less than 1 second, and occur randomly. Their random nature means you usually cannot predict them. A transient can occur as a result of trouble somewhere down the power line, such as a blackout or lightning strike.

Transients can seriously damage network components. To protect your equipment from power spikes, consider taking the following precautions:

- Put the computer on its own circuit with a separate circuit breaker, and avoid placing too much equipment on that circuit.

- Ensure that the computer is properly grounded. Check that no one has put a two-prong adapter on a three-prong plug. This negates the ground.

- Use a surge suppressor.

The flip side of transients is a *brownout,* also called a *sag.* When lights flicker in a room, it is usually the result of a brownout, which is a temporary decrease in voltage level. Systems can crash and data can be corrupted as a result of a brownout. The best solution to this problem is to use an uninterruptible power supply (UPS).

Viruses, Worms, and Trojan Horses

A computer *virus* is a pernicious computer program that alters stored files or system configuration and copies itself onto external disks or other computers. Viruses cause problems by altering files and configurations or by growing exponentially, which interrupts the data flow.

Viruses require an action of some sort to activate them. To achieve this, they attach themselves to executable files. (Executable files have the file name extension .EXE, .BAT, or .COM.) Other opportunities are provided by overlays (OVL), file allocation tables (FATs), disk boot sectors, and memory. A virus can attack immediately or wait until a specific action, such as a warm boot, triggers it. Unlike some other threatening programs, such as worms, viruses cannot run independently, but rather require a "host" program to activate them.

Worms are another form of destructive or dangerous program. A worm can run by itself and can spawn a fully working version of itself to other machines. A worm may be set up, for example, to penetrate a database and transfer information to an unauthorized individual.

Although the distinction between a virus and a worm is not always clear, in general, if the spreading program is self-sufficient, you can call it a worm; if it embeds itself inside other programs or boot code, you can call it a virus. Worms are so-named because they move across a network without leaving detectable signs.

A *Trojan horse* is a program that is designed to disguise itself as something harmless, waiting for the right moment to do its deed. A Trojan horse might, for example, create a dialog box on your screen asking you to enter your network password. When you enter the password, the Trojan horse could then e-mail your password to another location (presumably, to the person who created the program).

Anyplace data enters a computer—a floppy drive, modem, network interface card, and so on—offers a point of entry for a virus, worm, or Trojan horse. These are the areas you must strive to control. For the most part, pernicious programs do not come with retail software from reputable dealers. Most of the time, viruses, worms, and Trojan horses come from software obtained in some other way, such as with programs that are pirated or downloaded. What can you do to protect against viruses? Here are some strategies:

- Teach network users about viruses and how to prevent them. Most users have at least one vulnerable point of entry. If they are aware of the threat of viruses, they can help combat it. If they must install any programs, teach them how to check the programs for viruses first. Tell them to avoid downloading untested programs from the Internet or bulletin board services if possible.

- Perform regular backups on servers and workstations, and check the backups.

- Always boot the server from the same source.

- Clean DOS workstations' Master Boot Records using FDISK /MBR.

- Regularly scan your workstations and servers with a reputable anti-virus package and install the scanning software on each machine. Some packages to consider are Dr. Solomon's Anti-Virus, IBM Anti-Virus, InocuLAN, Intel LANDesk, MacAfee Virus Scan, and Norton Anti-Virus.

- Control entry points on workstations and servers.

- Use your network operating system security features to limit access to susceptible files.

Security

True network security means protecting network data from both deliberate and accidental threats. A network is no good without the data it can send, manipulate, and receive.

Although Windows NT provides some powerful security features, it offers only a small portion of the defense needed for a truly secure network. One of the main causes of network problems, for example, is its users. Although some users may wish to deliberately harm the network and server, problems caused by users are usually accidental. Users can do damage simply by trying a command they don't understand or turning off something they shouldn't.

Threats to the network fall into these general categories:

- **Destruction:** Data and hardware can be destroyed by deliberate or negligent acts.

- **Corruption:** Data that has been corrupted is untrustworthy and often worthless.

- **Disclosure:** Data of a confidential nature can be intercepted. You must vigorously protect passwords and other confidential data.

- **Interruption:** If the network goes down, you can't use the resources you need. Downtime means unavailable data, which means loss of money.

Your Security Plan

Problems caused by negligence are bad enough, but if someone is actively and maliciously trying to cause problems, you have a greater threat. To deal with these possible threats, you need to come up with a security plan. Your plan should include these steps:

1. Examine and analyze each segment of the network for possible security breaches.

2. If you discover a possible threat to your network, consider various responses in terms of their cost and how important they are.

3. Make affordable changes as needed.

4. Check and maintain your controls to keep them working and protecting the network.

As a general rule, someone who can get to a server and spend a few minutes unnoticed can access the data. If you are concerned about security, keep servers locked away.

Security Controls

The proper use of controls minimizes threats to data, software, and hardware. The extent to which you decide to implement security precautions will depend on how sensitive your data is, how large your network is, and how susceptible it is to attack. Controls you might want to implement include the following:

- Require unique passwords with a minimum length.

- Require regular, frequent password changes.

- Restrict login times.

- Require adequate security on dial-up telephone lines (modems).

- Carefully limit guest accounts.

- Limit access to network resources to a need-to-know basis.

- Use software that employs encryption.

- Use data redundancy on the server (RAID or another backup system).

Develop contingency plans for vital services in case of natural disaster (earthquake, flood, fire, and so on).

REAL WORLD PROBLEMS

A customer calls you at your consulting office and asks for some advice. He is installing some unshielded twisted-pair cable in an office building.

■ Which possible types of possible electrical problems should you warn him about?

Troubleshooting the Network

P ROBLEM PREVENTION REDUCES the number and types of problems that occur, but things will still go wrong with the network. When they do, it's time to do some troubleshooting. Troubleshooting usually involves applying a combination of knowledge and experience.

To be able to recognize the source of network troubles, you should have some understanding of your network's baseline performance. Once a baseline is established, you will be able to identify performance problems and bottlenecks when they arise. Because many network problems are the result of a trend of increasing network usage, a baseline can help you decide when a new file server, new network adapters, or network partitioning might be appropriate.

**Microsoft
Exam
Objective**

Identify common errors associated with components required for communications.

Isolating the Problem

Troubleshooting requires the ability to separate a problem into smaller parts and see how all the parts relate to one another. Breaking down a problem allows you to test individual guesses at what went wrong. To help you isolate a problem, take these steps:

- Eliminate the possibility of user error.

- Check the physical site. Is everything that should be there present and connected correctly?

- Back up data if there is a question that storage media (hard drive or disk drives) may be the problem.

- Turn everything off and back on again. This solves a number of problems.

- Simplify the system. Remove unnecessary elements and isolate the problem by involving a minimum number of factors.

These steps can be useful for solving a number of network problems. However, for more complex and persistent problems, turn to the troubleshooting model described in the next section.

A Troubleshooting Model

Microsoft's troubleshooting model generally has five steps:

1. Set the problem's priority.

2. Collect information to identify the symptoms.

3. Develop a list of possible causes.

4. Test to isolate the cause.

5. Study the results of the test to identify a solution.

Let's look at these steps in detail.

Setting Your Priorities

Network problems always have different levels of priority. John and Frank's inability to play Doom across the network is probably not going to be as important as ensuring that the accounting server doesn't have a virus. For this reason, before you begin work on a network problem, you must assess its priority. At times you will need to let a problem wait while you deal with more urgent matters.

Sometimes you may even wish to replace equipment rather than repair it. If, for example, you're having repeated troubles with a 2400-baud modem that is scheduled to be replaced in the near future, you might want to replace it right away. Remember that if you are working for someone else, every minute you spend working on a problem costs your employer money.

Collecting Basic Information

The first step in collecting information is to discover what you can through communication with users and other sources of information. Find out the extent of the problem (what has been affected), what problems the end user is experiencing, and what the computer was doing when the problem occurred.

Ask network users experiencing a particular problem several questions as you begin the troubleshooting process. For example, the following questions may provide a wealth of information:

- **When was the last time it worked?** Have they used it recently or has it sat dormant for a period of time? This question is particularly pertinent to hardware problems. If the last time users used this modem was two years ago, it can make a difference in how you approach the problem.

- **What changes have been made since the last time it was used?** Have there been new hardware additions? Software additions? Has anything on the network been rearranged?

When you have talked to the users, check your documentation to find out how the network usually operates. When you know what is normal for the network, you can compare that performance with what is occurring now.

As you can see, communication with the user is a major part of this first step. You need to be calm and a good listener. The better you communicate with the people who use the network, the easier troubleshooting will be. Also, remember that users may be nervous about their deadlines and responsibilities; some may even feel their jobs are on the line. Be reassuring. At the same time, take what users tell you with a grain of salt—they may be providing inaccurate information.

Developing a List of Possible Causes

Once you have gathered some basic information, use that information and your own knowledge to formulate an idea about what the problem is most likely to be. Break the problem into smaller parts. Is the problem in the area of user error, application software, operating system software, or equipment? Then prioritize your hypotheses according to their chance of success and the cost of attempting the solution. Remember that cost involves more than hardware; you must factor in network downtime and technician time as well. This prioritization will help you decide which solution to work on first.

Approaching a network problem in this way is similar to the approach for repairing your car. When you take it to a mechanic, the mechanic asks what the problem is, looks at the car, and then tries to analyze probable causes. If you are having trouble starting the car, the mechanic may look at the battery, battery cables, starter, and ignition switch (breaking the problem into smaller parts). You want to start with the most likely and least expensive fix, of course. Taking a wrench to tighten battery cables might not cost you more than a few minutes of time. Replacing the starter motor will be more expensive.

If you are having a hard time determining the exact location of a network problem, try separating the network into parts and testing those parts individually. Try workstations on a stand-alone basis.

Because network protocols are designed to adapt to network problems by working around them, they tend to have the unfortunate side effect of hiding problems from network administrators. Sometimes the only immediately noticeable difference will be a slight performance lag.

Testing to Isolate the Cause

When you have a good idea of where the problem is, you are ready to test your hypotheses. First, determine which hypothesis is most likely to be successful and cost the least. Then test each part of your hypothesis, one element at a time.

To identify the problem as efficiently as possible, make only one change at a time. Making several at once won't help you determine the exact problem. (Would you want the mechanic in the car repair example to replace the starter motor and your battery before knowing which was faulty?)

Be sure to use reliable procedures, testing equipment, and software when you are testing. Otherwise, you may become confused trying to determine what the original problem was and what new problems have been introduced.

It may be best to begin testing your hypothesis using forward chaining, which is the technique of beginning with the source device and moving toward the destination device. Investigating in the reverse fashion, from the destination device to the source device, is called reverse chaining.

Studying the Results to Identify the Solution

After you have tested the system, you either will have a better idea of what the problem is or will have to go back a couple of steps or to the beginning and start again.

Now that we've looked at the five steps of the Microsoft troubleshooting model, let's consider some other important aspects of network troubleshooting.

Recovering from Disaster

Whether it's an earthquake, an attack from a pernicious program, hardware failure, or simply the janitor unplugging the file server in the middle of the night, disaster will eventually strike your network. When the moment hits and you find that your network data has been corrupted, there is nothing more comforting than knowing you have backed up your data on a reliable backup system. The necessity of having a secure backup system cannot be overemphasized.

Microsoft ✓ *Exam* *Objective*

Choose a disaster recovery plan for various situations.

Establishing a Dependable Backup System

To determine whether your backup system is reliable, consider the following:

- Can you successfully restore selected parts of your backups to a disk test area on your server (without overwriting current data, of course)?

- Does your backup software allow you to verify-after-write? This feature is crucial because it allows you to make sure data is actually being written to the backup medium.

- Do your backup logs indicate that all files backed up are actually stored on the backup medium?

- Do you rotate tapes rather than overwrite the most recent copy?

- Do you back up as often as you go home from work (lunch breaks excluded)?

These are minimum requirements. Alone, they will not ensure complete safety, but they are certainly procedures you need in a solid backup system.

Recovering Data

For those times when disaster does strike and your backup system fails to back you up, you have at least three options:

- The utilities provided by your network operating system

- Professional data-recovery services

- Third-party utilities

Documenting the Solution

After you have found a satisfactory resolution to your problem, there is another important step to take: documentation. Enough of the right kind of documentation will save hours in troubleshooting time for a network of any size. With detailed, up-to-date documentation, you can predict possible network problems and take precautionary measures. Also, if a similar problem occurred in the past, you may find the answer in the documentation without needing to go through the process again.

The kinds of records/databases that provide troubleshooting documentation include

- The LAN system

- History

- Technical reference resources

THE LAN SYSTEM Troubleshooting documentation starts with the LAN system. Your LAN system documentation should include a detailed map that identifies the locations of all users and user groups, as well as all hardware components: printers, workstations, cabling, routers, and so on. The documentation should include a diagram of all cabling layouts, equipment standards, and the capacity of the network. You should also have an inventory of all components on the system.

In addition to hardware information, your documentation should describe what is stored on the servers, software licensing details, and critical technical support and supplier telephone numbers.

Keep in mind that you may not be the only person who will use this documentation. If and when you move on to bigger and better things, the documentation you leave behind will prove invaluable to the person who inherits your network. For that reason, make sure it is clear and well organized.

A record of the jumper and DIP switch settings for network components can be very helpful. A good effort at standardization of equipment across the network can also be fruitful. If all your equipment is the same, you will be able to upgrade, manage, and repair it all in the same way.

HISTORY Network history documentation can help you with current problems and prevent even larger problems in the future. The history should include a description of the purpose the LAN serves for the organization that uses it, who the end users are, which workstations and other equipment each user employs, and the training backgrounds of end users. The LAN history should also include a detailed log of past problems so recurrent problems can be isolated and corrected.

Another part of LAN history is a record of normal LAN operation. Baseline statistics might include traffic, CPU usage, errors, bandwidth utilization, and other relevant information. When a problem occurs, you can compare the network's current operation with the records of its normal operation.

TECHNICAL REFERENCE SOURCES There are a number of resources that can help you find the solution you are looking for. Choose the one that is best for you. You probably won't want to call Microsoft's technical support division and pay an arm and a leg to find answers to technical questions. However, you may want to use tools such as the Micro House Technical Library and Microsoft's TechNet. The next section takes a look at some of the best tools available to you.

Reference Sources for Troubleshooting

FORTUNATELY, YOU AREN'T left alone in the troubleshooting battle. The references listed here can provide valuable data about hardware and software problems:

- **The Micro House Technical Library:** Available from Micro House Corporation, this library is an extensive CD-ROM database of network cards, motherboards, hard drives, and other hardware.

- **Microsoft's TechNet:** Contains Microsoft technical information, product details, and articles about the latest software releases, updates, and revisions.

- **Novell Support Encyclopedia (NSEPro):** A large database of information about NetWare and networking.

- **Novell NetWire:** Includes much the same information and features as the NSEPro, but in a constantly updated form, and it's actually cheaper than an NSEPro subscription. NetWire also allows you to post questions of your own and receive answers from other users.

- **Microsoft's World Wide Web site and download library:** Offer the latest information on Microsoft products.

- **Numerous periodicals and user groups:** Offer up-to-date information.

Each of these tools is discussed in detail in the following sections.

The Micro House and Novell products are not covered in the Networking Essentials exam, but they are excellent resources for network administrators.

The Micro House Technical Library

The Micro House Technical Library, or MTL, is the ultimate reference for hardware. It includes more than 500MB of data on a CD-ROM. The MTL has four main components:

- **Encyclopedia of Hard Drives:** Provides information about hard drives, such as jumper settings and BIOS parameters.

- **Encyclopedia of Main Boards:** Provides information about all aspects of PC operation and motherboards.

- **Encyclopedia of Network Cards:** Provides configuration information about network interface cards. It also includes driver software for a wide variety of cards.

- **Encyclopedia of I/O Cards:** Supplies information about other cards you might install in a PC: video cards, printer cards, modems, and disk controllers.

These encyclopedias don't just give you technical information about how things work. The database includes complete details for thousands of cards and hard drives, including jumper settings, configuration information, and even diagrams of how they look.

At this writing, the retail price for the MTL CD (subscription) is $595. New updates are released regularly.

The main MTL screen is shown in Figure 12.1. To use each section of the MTL, click the corresponding button on the main screen. The options are described in the following sections.

FIGURE 12.1

The MTL includes four main options.

The Encyclopedia of Hard Drives

When you select the Hard Drives option on the main screen, you see the screen shown in Figure 12.2.

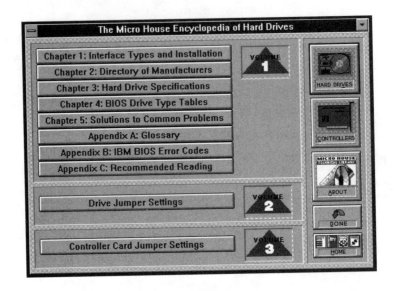

The Encyclopedia of Hard Drives is divided into three volumes. Volume 1 includes the following chapters and appendices:

- **Chapter 1, Interface Types and Installation:** Describes the types of hard drive interfaces and provides the information needed to install and use them.

- **Chapter 2, Directory of Manufacturers:** Provides contact information for all the common hard drive manufacturers.

- **Chapter 3, Hard Drive Specifications:** Lists specifications for hard drives. This includes the settings you must enter into your computer's BIOS to use the drive.

- **Chapter 4, BIOS Drive Type Tables:** Lists common BIOS drive type codes, which you may use instead of entering each parameter individually.

- **Chapter 5, Solutions to Common Problems:** Lists common problems with hard drives.

- **Appendix A, Glossary:** Provides definitions for many hard drive–related terms.

- **Appendix B, IBM BIOS Error Codes:** Lists the codes the IBM BIOS displays for errors. This is useful if you are diagnosing hardware and have access to a diagnostic card.

- **Appendix C, Recommended Reading:** Lists books that explain some of the concepts in more detail.

Volume 2 of the Encyclopedia of Hard Drives is one of the most useful. It includes jumper settings for hundreds of different hard drives, including diagrams of the jumper locations. Volume 3 contains jumper setting information for hard drive controller cards.

The Encyclopedia of Main Boards

The Encyclopedia of Main Boards includes several options relating to the motherboard in your PC. The menu for the Main Boards option is shown in Figure 12.3.

The sections of this encyclopedia offer information about all aspects of the board's operation. You can also search for boards by manufacturer or other specifications.

The Encyclopedia of Network Cards

The Encyclopedia of Network Cards includes two main options: the Network Interface Technical Guide, which includes information about the technical aspects of network cards and their operation, and the Network Cards listing, which includes specifications for hundreds of network cards. The main screen for the Technical Guide is shown in Figure 12.4.

The Encyclopedia of I/O Cards

The Encyclopedia of I/O Cards is the most recent addition to the MTL. It includes information about cards that are not hard drive or network cards.

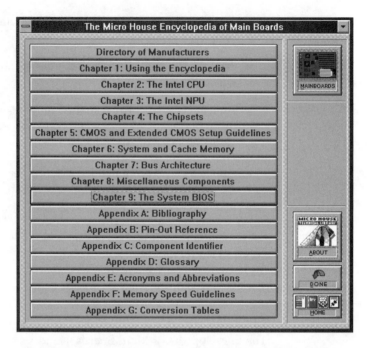

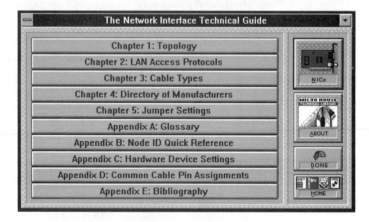

This category includes video cards, serial and parallel cards, and so on. The main screen for this encyclopedia is shown in Figure 12.5.

The many options on this screen may seem a bit overwhelming. It lists all the possible criteria for I/O cards. You can select a manufacturer, a type of card, and many other options. After you have selected options, click the Search button to list the cards that match your criteria.

Microsoft Technical Information Network (TechNet)

Microsoft TechNet is the standard database of Microsoft products. It comes on a CD and contains articles, service packs, utilities, technical notes, and other information that is useful for supporting Microsoft products. Figure 12.6 shows the main screen of TechNet.

FIGURE 12.6

The Microsoft TechNet
Entire Contents screen

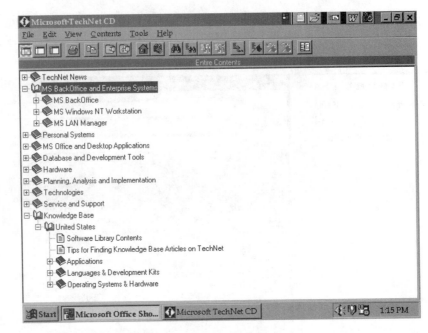

Microsoft TechNet is available from Microsoft for the relatively low price of $295 a year. Each month you receive CDs containing the full contents of the latest version of TechNet. You can subscribe to TechNet by calling Microsoft Corporation at (800) 344-2121.

The Network Support Encyclopedia

Novell's Network Support Encyclopedia, Professional Edition, or NSEPro, contains a huge database of information about NetWare and networking. It includes more than 170MB of text, graphics, and downloadable files (some with fixes and patches for NetWare versions).

The NSEPro is sold on a subscription basis and is quite expensive—about $1500 per year. However, you may be able to purchase a single copy from a NetWare reseller. Novell also gives a single copy of the latest version to candidates who complete CNE certification. Figure 12.7 shows the main screen for the NSEPro.

FIGURE 12.7

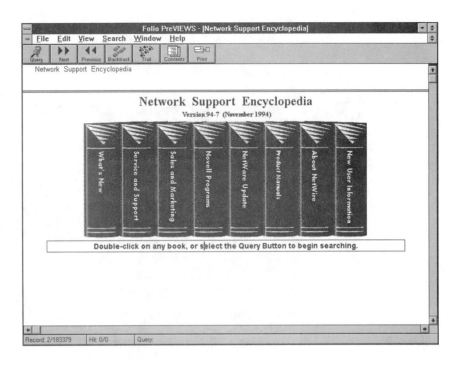

FIGURE 12.7

The NSEPro main screen includes eight options, each represented as a book.

NetWire on CompuServe

Another service provided by Novell is NetWire. You can access NetWire at:

http://netwire.novell.com

You can also access NetWire as a forum on CompuServe, the world's largest proprietary online service. To access NetWire, you can use WinCIM, the CompuServe Information Manager. Novell has its own version of WinCIM, called NOVCIM. The only difference is that the NetWire options are on the main menu. You can access NetWire equally well with either program. WinCIM is available for Microsoft Windows and will run in OS/2 Warp or Windows 95.

WinCIM isn't the only way to access CompuServe. You can do so from any operating system, although the interface may be just a simple text-based command line.

The main NetWire screen is shown in Figure 12.8. This screen includes several options as starting points. These options are similar to the options in the NSEPro (but they don't look like books).

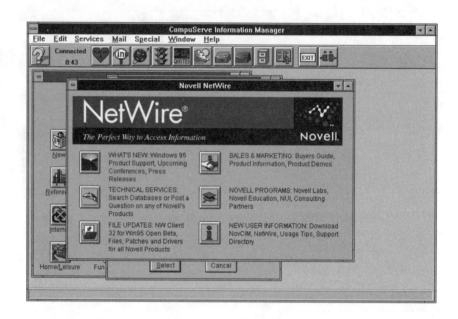

www.microsoft.com and the Download Library

If you'd like to access the latest Microsoft news and product information across the Internet, you can visit the Microsoft web site. It can be found at:

http://www.microsoft.com

To download the latest information about Microsoft networking products, as well as the latest drivers and other software, you can also visit the Microsoft Download Library (MSDL) by dialing (206) 936-6735.

Periodicals and User Groups

LAN Magazine, PC Week, NT Magazine, and other periodicals can help keep your knowledge current. Some periodicals also make news available on the

Internet. Try a web search (using your favorite search engine, such as Infoseek or Yahoo) to see what's out there.

User groups can also be a valuable tool. One benefit of user groups is that you can normally post questions and receive answers or suggestions from other networking professionals.

REAL WORLD PROBLEMS

Early one Monday morning you begin receiving reports from numerous network users that they cannot log on to the network or that there is some other problem. Since you are quitting your job soon and need to train a fellow employee to take over your role, you decide to outline a strategy for approaching the resolution of this problem.

- What strategies would you give this fellow employee for dealing with the problem?

- Create a master document that details the steps your fellow employee should go through.

- What are Microsoft's five steps of troubleshooting?

After resolving the problem, your fellow employee comes to you and says, "Phew! It wasn't too difficult. But I'm not sure it would go so easily if the problem were more of a disaster. What should I do to make sure this network, and a new network I'm responsible for installing, can recover from a disaster?"

- Explain the basics of a good disaster recovery plan.

- What types of reference sources might help during disaster recovery of a Windows NT and/or Novell network?

Diagnostic Tools

A S YOU GRAPPLE with more and more network problems, you'll probably discover that cabling, cable connectors, and network adapter cards are the home of most network hardware problems. Cable breaks, shorts, bad connectors, and faulty adapter cards are common.

To handle these problems, you might want to try some of the approaches described in the following sections.

Microsoft
Exam
Objective

Select the appropriate hardware and software tools to monitor trends in the network.

Microsoft
Exam
Objective

Diagnose and resolve common connectivity problems with cards, cables, and related hardware.

There are several important tools you can use to diagnose network problems. Many network engineers use these tools when they are not able to solve hardware problems otherwise. You may wish to purchase the tools for use, depending on how often you run into hardware problems. Keep in mind, however, that prices for this equipment range from $50 to $25,000.

Some of the most useful tools are

- Terminators

- Cable testers

- Time-domain reflectometers (TDRs)

- Digital volt meters (DVMs)

- Protocol analyzers

Terminators

If you suspect that there is a break in a cable, you can use a terminator to narrow down the problem. By dividing a piece of cable and putting a terminator in its place, you can see whether the problem is at that point in the cable or somewhere earlier. Once you find the general portion of the network where the problem resides, you can repeatedly divide the cable, using the terminator to further isolate the problem.

Cable Testers

A cable tester is an instrument for testing the integrity of a stretch of cable. Cable testers run tests to determine a cable's attenuation, resistance, and other characteristics.

If you're going to use a previously installed cable for your network, make sure all of it works properly before you begin. A cable tester can provide detailed information about the cable's physical and electrical properties. When you're dealing with a long cable system, the chances are good that at least parts of it will be faulty.

Cable testers can provide a wide range of networking services. While most cable testers only work at the physical layer of the OSI model, advanced cable testers work up to the network layer. Advanced cable testers can provide you with information about message frame counts, excess collisions, late collisions, error frame counts, congestion errors, and beaconing.

Knowledge of the various levels of resistance a cable tester shows for each type of media can be useful for determining the status of a cable segment. For example, when you connect a cable tester (or volt-ohm meter) to a Thinnet terminator or Thinnet coaxial cable you should get a reading of 50 ohms. However, if you connect the tester to the barrel connector or T-connector you should get a reading of 0 ohms. This is normal, and simply shows that the connector properly supplies no resistance between the two parts of the network it connects. If you connect the tester to the cable and read a resistance level of infinity, you have determined that there is a cable break on that cable.

Time-Domain Reflectometers

Time-domain reflectometers work by emitting short pulses of known amplitude that travel down a cable. A TDR analyzes the time delay associated with the resultant signal reflections. The TDR is then able to help you determine whether there are any shorts or open cable sections. TDRs are available for all LAN types. Optical TDRs provide a similar test capability for fiber cable. If the TDR you are using is good, it will be able to give you a pretty clear idea of where a cable problem is located.

Here is how a TDR is typically used—an end of a network cable is connected to a TDR device. The type of device must be selected on the TDR. For example, if you are testing a coaxial cable, you need to select "coaxial." If there is a problem with the cable, a message should indicate whether the cable is "open" or "short" and how far down the cable the problem resides.

To help ensure that your TDR works as effectively as possible, be sure to connect the TDR to the end of a segment. Also, turn off any repeaters and bridges you have connected to the local network before attaching the TDR to the cable.

TDRs typically use a positive electric pulse. Since transceivers do not have positive voltage protection, power down the network while doing a TDR test unless you are sure your TDR is specially designed for testing with the power on.

Digital Volt Meters (DVMs)

Digital volt meters can help you find a break or a short in a network cable by checking the voltage being carried across a network cable. A DVM is a handheld unit with which you can measure both the continuity of a cable and whether or not there is a short.

Protocol Analyzers

A protocol analyzer monitors and logs network activity and provides guidelines for optimizing performance. A very powerful tool for troubleshooting a network, a protocol analyzer can provide detailed network traffic analysis of the behavior of your network over time. They are very useful for analyzing the overall behavior of your network, but keep in mind that they alone do not serve the same functions as cable testers or time-domain reflectometers. For example, by themselves they cannot determine if there is a cable break on a certain segment and where that break might be. (However, most protocol analyzers are packaged with a time-domain reflectometer to deal with such issues.)

The most important function of the protocol analyzer itself is to work at the packet level. Doing so, a good protocol analyzer can indicate if a particular network adapter card is causing problems, where a network traffic bottleneck might be, what components of a network are malfunctioning, and the general performance level of your network.

Protocol analyzers can capture packets, decode them, and determine which components of a network are generating errors.

Another feature of some protocol analyzers is an alarm that alerts you if network traffic exceeds the limits you set.

Three of the most popular protocol analyzers are Novell's LANalyzer for Windows, Network General's Sniffer, and Hewlett-Packard's Network Advisor. Just to get a sense of how a network analyzer works, let's take a look at LANalyzer, the most popular analyzer for Novell networks.

LANalyzer runs on a Windows workstation attached anywhere in the network. To properly monitor and diagnose the performance of the network, you may want to run it on workstations at several different points on the network.

The main LANalyzer screen, called the Dashboard, is shown in Figure 12.9. The dashboard includes several useful indicators:

- **Packets:** Displays the actual number of packets traveling across the network. If the number is high, you probably have lots of network bandwidth and lots of traffic.

- **Utilization:** Displays the percentage of the network cable's bandwidth that is being used. If the percentage is above 50, you may need to add network segments to increase the available bandwidth.

- **Errors:** Displays a count of errors that have occurred—packets that have required resending. If this gauge shows any activity at all, something is wrong on the network: a disconnected cable, a bad network card, or a short.

- **Packet Capture:** Captures packets. Click the Start button to begin monitoring activity on the network for a period of time and then display statistics for that time. This makes it easy to determine peak usage times for the network and times when errors occur.

The Dashboard screen also shows the Server Monitor, which lists servers detected on the network and parameters for them. Another list you can view is called the Station Monitor, shown in Figure 12.10. It displays a list of

FIGURE 12.9

The LANalyzer
Dashboard includes
indications of network
performance.

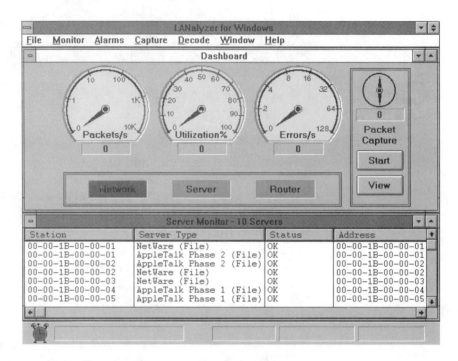

FIGURE 12.10

LANalyzer's Station
Monitor displays active
workstations on the
network.

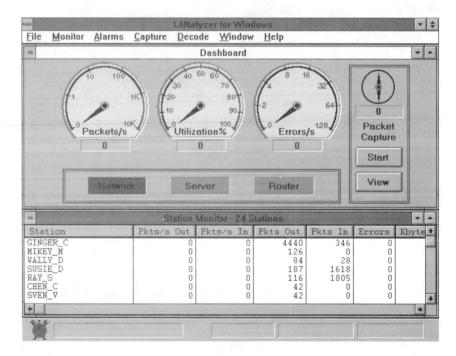

workstations (logged-in users) on the system. You can watch network traffic for each user and determine whether anyone is using a lot of bandwidth and slowing down the system. (This situation could be caused by a bad network card or cable on the workstation.)

The most important use of LANalyzer is to monitor trends on the network, such as ways in which the network is used and the times when the most usage happens. You can use the Packet Capture option to monitor the network for an extended amount of time and then display a graph showing trends as they develop. This can help you detect problems with the network and find the sources of errors.

REAL WORLD PROBLEMS

Your network apparently has a cable problem. You have a terminator.

■ How can you use the terminator to isolate your network problem?

You purchase several hundred meters of cabling but want to make sure of the integrity of the cabling before you pay for it and install it.

■ Without hooking up the network to a computer, would a protocol analyzer be of any use?

■ What can a protocol analyzer do? Why would one not work on cabling without a computer?

■ What device can emit pulses down a cable to determine whether there are any significant cabling problems?

Your network is performing very poorly but you are not sure what to do to get a picture of the problems. You have used Performance Monitor but suspect that you must look at the packet level to isolate a problem.

■ What tool can you use to optimize performance by monitoring network activity over time, at the packet level?

■ What are some popular models of this type of tool available in the market?

■ Can this tool help you determine which components of a network are generating errors?

Review

BY UNDERSTANDING THE techniques and services available for troubleshooting your network, you can solve most network problems. The best way to keep your network productive is to avoid potential problems, and the first step is to set up the network carefully.

The four general categories of network problems are physical, electrical, viruses (as well as worms and Trojan Horses), and security. You can use Microsoft's five-step troubleshooting model to isolate persistent network trouble spots.

1. Set the problem's priority

2. Collect information to identify the symptoms.

3. Develop a list of possible causes.

4. Test to isolate the cause.

5. Study the results of the test to identify a solution.

Numerous network troubleshooting resources are also available, ranging from information on the WWW to CD-ROMs to user groups. Other troubleshooting tools include time-domain reflectometers (TDRs), digital volt meters (DVMs), cable testers, and protocol analyzers.

Review Questions

1. Which of the following statements most accurately describes the network threat known as a worm?

   A. A small piece of code that writes itself to the boot sector of your hard disk drive

   B. A program that acts as a logon prompt to capture usernames and passwords

C. A small program that propagates itself from machine to machine and exploits the weaknesses of the operating system

D. A bit of code that attaches itself to other program files

2. There are many devices that are able to test the continuity of a network cable. Which of the following is also able to provide information on collisions and congestion?

    A. Time-domain reflectometers

    B. Oscilloscopes

    C. Volt-ohm meters

    D. Advanced cable testers

3. To successfully administer a network, you must include planning, monitoring, and troubleshooting. Which of the following is not true of network troubleshooting?

    A. Most problems occur at the Physical layer.

    B. Network monitors are used to check for congestion on the network.

    C. Protocol analyzers are able to determine if there is a break in the cable.

    D. TDRs and volt-ohm meters are able to identify breaks in the cable.

4. A time-domain reflectometer is used in network troubleshooting for which of the following tasks?

    A. To identify cable faults

    B. To provide protocol-level analysis

    C. To test network throughput

    D. To segment network traffic for analysis

5. When considering attacks on your network, which of the following executable code can be introduced onto the boot sector of a hard disk?

    A. A Bacterium

    B. An SST

    C. A Trojan Horse

    D. A Virus

6. You have recently noticed that network communication is slow. You fear that a faulty network adapter is sending bad packets. Which of the following troubleshooting tools could you use to determine which station has the faulty NIC?

    A. A protocol analyzer

    B. A volt-ohm meter

    C. An SNMP manager

    D. A transceiver

7. A protocol analyzer can be used to troubleshoot a network. Which of the following are available from a protocol analyzer? Choose all that apply:

    A. Capture of packets for analysis

    B. Cable break location

    C. Traffic alarm

    D. Resistance measurement

8. Network security can be increased by implementing which of the following? Choose all that apply:

    A. Standardize passwords to a consistent format.

    B. Require users to change their passwords every 60 days.

    C. Limit guest accounts.

    D. Store file servers in a locked room.

9. When using a volt-ohm meter to check the continuity of a twisted-pair cable, which of the following settings would you use?

   A. Voltage measure in volts

   B. Resistance measured in watts

   C. Resistance measured in ohms

   D. Resistance measured in volts

10. Although they are the easiest cables to work with, unshielded twisted-pair cables are prone to problems. Which of the following often affect UTP cables? Choose all that apply:

   A. Improper resistance between the conductor and the cladding

   B. Electromagnetic Interference

   C. Refraction

   D. Crosstalk

11. Your network administration plan should include equipment to ensure no data is lost. Which of the following will protect against data loss? Choose all that apply:

   A. Encryption

   B. UPS

   C. Compression

   D. Disk Duplexing

12. Which of the following network troubleshooting devices can best be used nonintrusively to verify network performance? Choose one:

   A. A time-domain reflectometer

   B. A protocol analyzer

   C. An advanced cable tester

   D. A volt-ohm meter

APPENDIX

A

Major Protocol Suites

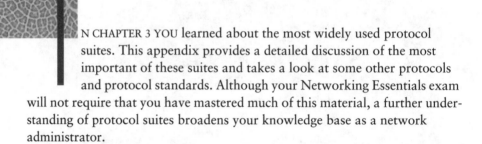

N CHAPTER 3 YOU learned about the most widely used protocol suites. This appendix provides a detailed discussion of the most important of these suites and takes a look at some other protocols and protocol standards. Although your Networking Essentials exam will not require that you have mastered much of this material, a further understanding of protocol suites broadens your knowledge base as a network administrator.

Microsoft
✓ *Exam*
Objective

Select the appropriate network and transport protocol or protocols for various token-ring and Ethernet networks. Protocol choices include:

- DLC
- AppleTalk
- IPX
- TCP/IP
- NFS
- SMB

These are the protocol suites examined in this appendix:

- NetWare IPX/SPX, Novell NetWare's proprietary protocol suite

- TCP/IP, the nonproprietary protocols that make up the Internet

- AppleTalk, Apple Computer's proprietary protocols, which began with the Macintosh

- DNA, Digital Equipment Corporation's proprietary suite of protocols, which has evolved from a mainframe-centric environment to OSI compliance. DECnet is an implementation of DNA.

- SNA, IBM's proprietary protocol suite, based on the Systems Network Architecture (SNA) model, the grandfather of data communications technology and the inspiration for the OSI model.

Review of Protocols, Models, and Implementations

A PROTOCOL IS A set of rules for communication. A simple example of a protocol from the realm of human communications is the different ways of greeting people: should you bow, shake hands, or kiss both cheeks of the person you're greeting? It depends on where you are and whom you are greeting. If you make a mistake, you could be misunderstood.

Although in the data communications world protocols are more complex and precise, the same idea holds true. For example, a protocol may define the shape of a packet that will be transmitted across the network, as well as all the fields within the packet and how they should be interpreted. Obviously, both the sender and receiver must agree on the exact way the packet should be formatted in order for communication to occur.

Any protocol product available on the market will necessarily be a protocol implementation, which means any one company's interpretation of the protocol definition or standard. Therefore, one company may interpret a standard in a different way than another, which can cause incompatibility.

A protocol suite is a group of protocols that evolved together, whether created by the same company, as in the case of IBM's SNA, or used in the same environment, such as the Internet protocol suite. Protocol suites have definitions for the interface between protocols that occur at adjacent layers of the OSI model, such as IPX and SPX in the NetWare suite.

NetWare IPX/SPX Protocols

THE NETWARE PROTOCOL suite takes its name from the two main protocols at the network and transport layers of the OSI model: IPX and SPX.

NetWare was first developed by Novell, Inc., in the early 1980s. Its design was based on a network developed by Xerox at its Palo Alto Research Center (PARC) called Xerox Network System (XNS).

The NetWare IPX/SPX protocol suite provides file, print, message, and application services. This architecture is server-centric because workstations make requests for file services or other services from the server. To the user at a workstation, all resources appear local to that workstation. For example, saving a file to a file server on the network is simply a matter of saving it to drive F (or another mapped drive) in the same way it would be saved to the user's C hard drive.

The NetWare protocols are modular; you can use them with many different hardware configurations. You can also use other protocols, such as TCP/IP and AppleTalk, with NetWare, making it very flexible. NetWare, therefore, is not limited to its proprietary protocols, IPX and SPX. Allowing additional protocols provides more interoperability with other computer systems.

The NetWare protocol suite can be mapped to the OSI model as shown in Figure A.1. The following sections discuss the NetWare protocols, organized by their function with respect to the OSI model.

FIGURE A.1

The NetWare protocol suite mapped to the OSI model

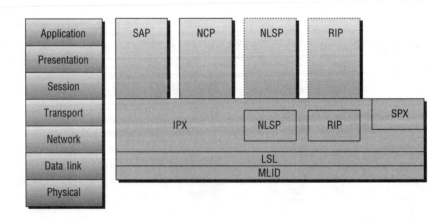

NetWare Lower-Layer Protocols

NetWare normally runs over standard lower-layer protocols, such as Ethernet (IEEE 802.3) and Token Ring (IEEE 802.5). The lower-layer protocol discussed here, MLID, is a proprietary standard for network interface card drivers.

MLID (Multiple Link Interface Driver)

THE MLID protocol operates at the MAC sublayer of the OSI model's data link layer. It is concerned with medium access and uses these methods:

- Contention

- Token passing

- Polling

The MLID is a standard for network drivers. Each type of network board has a unique MLID driver. The MLID is implemented in software. A common example is the DOS file called NE2000.COM, written for the Novell/Eagle NE2000 network card.

The MLID is also called the network driver or LAN driver. Its job is to communicate directly with the hardware network card. The MLID is independent of upper-layer protocols because of the LSL (link support layer) module at the LLC sublayer of the data link layer, which acts as an interface between the MLID and network layer protocols.

The interaction between the MLID, LSL, and other components is specified by the ODI (Open Data-link Interface) specification, a Novell standard for modular network communications. The ODI specification allows you to easily configure client software using the same programs, regardless of the type of network board used. With this architecture only the MLID changes; before ODI, you needed to create a customized version of the IPX driver for each network card.

NetWare Middle-Layer Protocols

NetWare's middle-layer protocols include the following:

- **IPX:** Used for transporting packets

- **RIP and NLSP:** Routing protocols

- **SPX:** Runs at the transport layer and adds connection-oriented service when added reliability is required

IPX (Internetwork Packet Exchange)

Novell's main network layer protocol is IPX. It deals with addressing (the logical network and service addresses), route selection, and connection services. IPX provides connectionless datagram service, which means that data is sent over the whole network segment rather than across a direct connection. IPX is based on the IDP (Internetwork Datagram Protocol) of XNS (Xerox Network System).

Because of its connectionless nature, IPX is not suitable for some types of network communications. Most of the communication on a network, including workstation connections and printing, uses the SPX protocol, described a little later in this appendix. Simple IPX is used for broadcast messages, such as error notifications and time synchronization.

IPX performs dynamic route selections based on tables of network reachability information compiled by RIP. In NetWare 4.1, IPX is usually implemented by the IPXODI.COM program, which follows the ODI specification. Earlier NetWare versions used a program called IPX.COM. As discussed in the section "MLID (Multiple Link Interface Driver)" earlier in this appendix, before ODI, a custom version of IPX was required for each type of network card and settings.

RIP (Routing Information Protocol)

RIP is the default protocol NetWare uses for routing. RIP uses the distance-vector route discovery method to determine hop counts. The hop count is the number of intermediate routers a packet must cross to reach a particular device.

RIP functions at the network layer of the OSI model, although it has a service address assigned to it. Because it is a distance-vector routing protocol, RIP periodically broadcasts routing table information across the internetwork. This can create a bottleneck when the information must be transmitted over wide area links. For WANs, you should use a link-state routing protocol instead, such as NLSP.

NLSP (Network Link Services Protocol)

NLSP is another routing protocol that functions at the network layer. NLSP uses the link-state route discovery method to build routing tables. It is based on an OSI routing protocol called IS-IS (Intermediate System-to-Intermediate System).

Link-state routing protocols do not broadcast routing tables periodically, as distance-vector routing protocols do. Instead, they broadcast only when a change occurs in the state of the network, such as when a link goes down or an additional router is installed. NLSP can support mesh and hybrid mesh networks for increased fault tolerance.

SPX (Sequenced Packet Exchange)

SPX is a transport layer protocol that adds reliability to IPX. This protocol is concerned with addressing, segment development (division and combination), and connection services (segment sequencing, error control, and end-to-end flow control).

SPX provides connection-oriented packet delivery and is used when IPX datagram packet delivery is not reliable enough, such as for a print server. It provides reliability through virtual circuits that are identified as connection IDs. Packets that arrive at their destination correctly are acknowledged. If the receiving system does not acknowledge the packet, that packet must be retransmitted. IPX is less reliable because it does not send acknowledgments.

A Xerox protocol called Sequenced Packet Protocol was the basis for SPX.

NetWare Upper-Layer Protocols

Novell's two upper-layer protocols, NCP and SAP, both cover multiple layers of the OSI model. NCP functions at the transport, session, presentation, and application layers. SAP functions at the session and application layers.

NCP (NetWare Core Protocols)

NCP functions at four layers of the OSI model:

- At the transport layer, it provides connection services, with segment sequencing, error control, and end-to-end flow control.

- At the session layer, NCP handles session administration for data transfer.

- At the presentation layer, NCP is responsible for translation (character code and file syntax).

- At the application layer at the top, this protocol deals with service use, providing an operating system (OS) redirector.

NCP provides a group of function calls that define the interchange between client and server. For example, a client might call on a server to open a file or write to a file. Other NCP functions support printing, name management, file services, synchronization, and file locking and unlocking. Because NCP functions at the transport layer (in addition to its functionality at the higher layers), it provides reliable, connection-oriented packet delivery and therefore makes SPX unnecessary in many cases.

SAP (Service Advertising Protocol)

At the session layer, SAP is concerned with session administration for file transfer. At the application layer, SAP provides active service advertisement.

Service providers, such as file servers and print servers, use SAP to advertise their services to the network. Each service provider broadcasts a SAP packet every 60 seconds. This packet lets clients know that that server is available and what its address is. Clients can also request service information, such as the location of the nearest file server, on the internetwork by transmitting a Service Query Packet.

On WANs, SAP can become a problem because of the quantity of broadcasts from multiple servers over sometimes slow links. In that case, network administrators can turn SAP off for particular servers.

Internet Protocols

T HE INTERNET PROTOCOL suite was developed along with its name-sake, the Internet. The Internet began as a project funded by the United States Department of Defense in the 1970s to interconnect educational institutions and government installations. At that time it was called ARPAnet (Advanced Research Projects Agency Network). Over time it has evolved into the huge, worldwide network known as the Internet. The protocols that make up the Internet protocol suite, the best known being TCP (Transmission Control Protocol) and IP (Internet Protocol), have become de facto standards because of the success of the Internet. The entire protocol suite is sometimes referred to as TCP/IP.

The Internet protocol suite is unique in that it is made up of nonproprietary protocols. This means that they do not belong to any one company and that the technology is available to anyone who wishes to use it. As a result, the Internet protocol suite is supported by the widest variety of vendors.

The Internet suite was developed about ten years before the OSI model was defined and can therefore be only roughly mapped to it. The Internet protocol suite was defined according to its own model, known as the Internet or DOD model. Figure A.2 illustrates the relationship between the Internet protocol suite and the OS reference model.

FIGURE A.2

The relationship between the Internet protocol suite and the OSI model

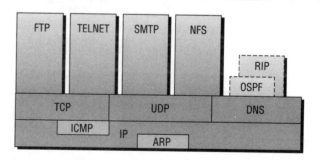

The four DOD model layers (shown in Figure A.3) and the OSI model layers they correspond to are as follows:

- The network access layer corresponds to the physical and data link layers of the OSI model.

- The Internet layer corresponds to the OSI network layer. Protocols at this layer are concerned with transporting packets through the internetwork. The main Internet layer protocol is IP.

- The host-to-host layer corresponds roughly to the OSI transport layer. Protocols at this layer communicate with peer processes in other hosts or networked devices. An example of a host-to-host protocol is TCP.

- The process/application layer corresponds to the OSI session, presentation, and application layers. Protocols at this layer provide application services on the network. Examples of protocols at this layer are Telnet (a terminal emulator) and FTP (a file transfer protocol).

FIGURE A.3

The Internet (DOD) model mapped to the OSI model

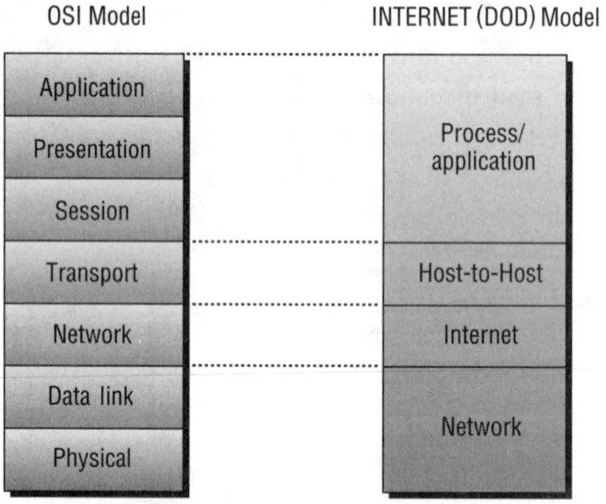

Figure A.3 shows the Internet (DOD) model mapped to the OSI model.

The Internet protocols do not cover the lower two layers of the OSI model. This is because the designers of TCP/IP used existing physical and data link standards, such as Ethernet and Token Ring, to make TCP/IP hardware independent. As a result, the protocols of the Internet suite are widely used to connect heterogeneous systems.

Since the Internet protocol suite does not include lower-layer protocols, we will begin our discussion of the individual protocols at the middle layers.

Internet Middle-Layer Protocols

As you have learned, the protocols at the OSI model's network and transport layers are concerned with transporting packets across the internetwork. TCP/IP and other Internet protocols use three types of addresses for network addressing:

- Hardware or physical addresses are used by the data link and physical layers. Physical addresses are usually hardcoded into the network cards at each device.

- IP addresses provide logical node IDs. IP addresses are unique addresses assigned by an administrator according to certain guidelines. They are expressed in four-part dotted-decimal notation—for example, 123.144.131.12.

- Logical node names, which an administrator can also assign, are easier to remember than an IP address—for example, BARNEY.COM.

IP (Internet Protocol)

IP works at the network layer. The functions it handles and methods it uses are as follows:

- For addressing, IP uses the logical network address.

- For switching purposes, it uses the packet-switching method.

- For route selection, it uses the dynamic method.

- For connection services, IP provides error control.

IP is a connectionless, datagram protocol. (IP packets are also referred to as IP datagrams.) IP uses packet switching and performs route selection by using dynamic routing tables that are referenced at each hop. The packets making up a message could be routed differently through the internetwork depending on the state of the network at each hop. For example, if a link were to go down or become congested, packets could take a different route.

Appended to each packet is an IP header, which includes source and destination information. IP uses sequence numbering if it is necessary to fragment a packet into smaller parts and reassemble it at its destination or at an intermediate point. IP performs error checking on the header information by way of a checksum.

A checksum is an error-checking method in which the data is submitted to an algorithm and the result is appended to the packet. When the packet arrives at its destination, the same calculation is performed on the data to see whether it matches the checksum value.

IP addresses are unique, 4-byte addresses that must be assigned to every addressable device or node on the internetwork. Depending on the class of IP address, a certain number of bytes specifies the network portion and a certain number of bytes specifies the host or node portion. If a connection to the Internet is desired, a unique IP network address must be requested from a governing body called the SRI Network Information Center. This ensures that the new network will have an address different from any other on the Internet. IP addresses are assigned according to three classes of networks:

- **Class A addresses:** Used for systems with a small number of networks and a large number of hosts. These addresses use the first byte to specify the network and the last three bytes to specify the host. The first byte of a Class A address can be in the range from 0–127—for example, 80.23.102.3. The available IP addresses for this class have already been assigned.

- **Class B addresses:** Provide for an equal number of networks and hosts by assigning the first two bytes to the network and the last two bytes to the host. The range of values for the first byte of a Class B address is 128–191—for example, 132.45.67.28. This class is most often assigned to universities and commercial organizations.

- **Class C addresses:** Use the first three bytes of the address to specify the network and the last byte to specify the host. Because there is only one byte available for host addresses, a Class C network will only support a small number of hosts (or nodes). The range of values for the first byte of a Class C address is 192–223—for example, 194.123.45.7.

ARP (Address Resolution Protocol)

ARP is a network layer protocol concerned with mapping node names to IP addresses. It equates logical and physical device addresses. ARP maintains tables of name-to-address mappings and can send out discovery packets if a desired name or address is not currently in its table. The discovery packet requests that the entity corresponding to the known name or address respond with the needed information.

A related protocol, RARP (Reverse Address Resolution Protocol) performs the same function in reverse; that is, given an IP address, it determines the corresponding node name.

ICMP (Internet Control Message Protocol)

ICMP is a protocol used with IP to augment error-handling and control procedures. It works at the network layer and is concerned with connection services. ICMP provides error control and network layer flow control.

ICMP detects error conditions such as internetwork congestion and downed links and notifies IP and upper-layer protocols so packets can be routed around problem areas.

RIP (Routing Information Protocol)

RIP is a network layer protocol. It is a distance-vector routing protocol, which means it periodically broadcasts routing tables across the internetwork. Similar to NetWare RIP, Internet RIP causes bottlenecks in WANs and is therefore being replaced by OSPF.

OSPF (Open Shortest Path First)

OSPF is another network layer protocol that addresses route discovery. It is a link-state routing protocol similar to NetWare's NLSP, described earlier in this appendix. It was developed to be more efficient and to create less overhead than RIP. It provides load balancing and routing based on class of service.

TCP (Transmission Control Protocol)

TCP is the Internet protocol suite's main transport layer protocol. It also provides addressing (with service addresses) services at the network layer.

TCP provides reliable, full-duplex, connection-oriented transport service to upper-layer protocols. TCP works in conjunction with IP to move packets through the internetwork. TCP assigns a connection ID (port) to each virtual circuit. It also provides message fragmentation and reassembly using sequence numbering. Error checking is enhanced through the use of TCP acknowledgments.

UDP (User Datagram Protocol)

UDP is a connectionless protocol that works at the transport layer. UDP transports datagrams but does not acknowledge their receipt. UDP also uses a port address to achieve datagram delivery, but this port address is simply a pointer to a process, not a connection identifier, as it is with TCP. The lack of overhead makes UDP more efficient than TCP.

DNS (Domain Name System)

DNS is a distributed database system that works at the transport layer to provide name-to-address mapping for client applications. DNS servers maintain databases that consist of hierarchical name structures of the various domains in order to use logical names for device identification. This type of address/name resolution is called service-provider initiated. The largest use of DNS is in the Internet. Name servers (DNS servers) are used to translate site names, such as SYBEX.COM, to actual network addresses.

Internet Upper-Layer Protocols

The upper-layer Internet protocols generally provide applications or services for use on the Internet, such as file transfer and electronic mail.

FTP (File Transfer Protocol)

As its name implies, FTP is used for file transfer between internetwork nodes. In addition, it allows users to initiate processes on the remote host. FTP enables users to log in to remote hosts. It functions at the top three layers of the OSI model, as follows:

- At the session layer, FTP provides session administration, handling connection establishment, file transfer, and connection release.

- At the presentation layer, FTP is concerned with translation, using a machine-independent file syntax.

- At the application layer, this protocol supplies network services, namely file services and collaborative service use.

FTP is a peer-to-peer protocol. FTP supports the ability to transfer files between dissimilar hosts because it uses a generic file structure that is operating-system independent.

Telnet

Telnet is used for remote terminal emulation. It enables users to access host-based applications by emulating one of the host's terminals. Telnet provides connectivity between dissimilar operating systems.

Telnet functions at the top three layers of the OSI model, as follows:

- At the session layer, it provides dialog control, using the half-duplex method. It also provides session administration, handling connection establishment, file transfer, and connection release.

- At the presentation layer, Telnet is concerned with translation, using the byte order and character codes.

- At the application layer, this protocol supplies the service use functions for remote operation.

SMTP (Simple Mail Transfer Protocol)

SMTP is a protocol for routing e-mail messages. It works at the application layer to provide message service.

SMTP does not provide a user interface for sending and receiving messages, but many Internet e-mail applications interface with it. SMTP uses TCP and IP to route the mail messages across the internetwork.

NFS (Network File System)

NFS is an application layer protocol that provides file services and remote operation service use. A major advantage of NFS is its transparency; it allows remote file systems to appear as though they were part of the local machine's file system.

NFS is a family of protocols developed by Sun Microsystems and is considered part of the Internet protocol suite. This group of protocols comprises Sun's ONC (Open Network Computing) platform. NFS is also the name of one of the protocols in Sun's family of protocols.

XDR (External Data Representation)

XDR is a presentation layer protocol that handles translation. It uses the methods of byte order, character codes, and file syntax.

XDR is used for the representation of data in a machine-independent format. It allows data descriptions and encoding through the use of a library of C routines that allow a programmer to create arbitrary data structures that can be ported between different machine environments.

RPC (Remote Procedure Call)

RPC is a session layer protocol concerned with session administration (connection establishment, file transfer, and connection release). With this protocol a software redirector determines whether a request can be satisfied locally or whether it requires network access. The redirector handles the packaging of the network request, and the interchange is transparent to the user.

RPC servers are usually specialized for the purpose of handling RPC requests. They tend to have large amounts of file storage and the ability to handle many procedure calls. The server executes the request and generates a reply packet to the originating host.

AppleTalk Protocols

PPLETALK IS THE name given to the protocol suite designed for the Apple Macintosh. Apple Computer began the development of AppleTalk in 1983. Phase 1 of AppleTalk was limited in scope. It did not provide support for internetworks because the addressing scheme did not include a network address. In 1989, Apple Computer expanded the capabilities of AppleTalk with the release of AppleTalk Phase 2. Phase 2 allows for internetworking by supporting network addresses. It allows multiple protocols to coexist with AppleTalk on large, complex networks.

Table A.1 summarizes the differences between AppleTalk Phase 1 and Phase 2.

TABLE A.1

Differences between AppleTalk Phases 1 and 2

CHARACTERISTIC	PHASE 1	PHASE 2
Maximum zones on a network segment	1	255
Maximum nodes per network	254	About 16 million
Dynamic addressing based on	Node ID	Network + Node ID
Link-access protocols supported	LocalTalk EtherTalk	LocalTalk IEEE 802.3 IEEE 802.5
Split-horizon routing	No	Yes

The protocols that make up AppleTalk can be mapped to the OSI model, as illustrated in Figure A.4.

FIGURE A.4

AppleTalk and the OSI model

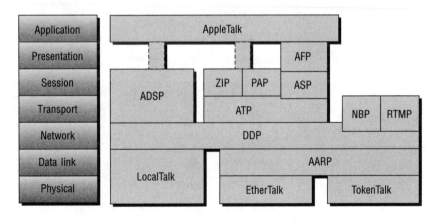

AppleTalk Lower-Layer Protocols

The lower-layer protocols of AppleTalk include Apple's original LocalTalk, as well as versions of Ethernet and Token Ring. Another protocol included here is the AppleTalk Address Resolution Protocol (AARP), which functions at the OSI model's data link and network layers.

LocalTalk (LLAP)

The LocalTalk Link Access Protocol, or LocalTalk, is Apple's original data link and physical layer protocol.

At the physical layer, LocalTalk handles the following:

Connection types:	Multipoint
Physical topology:	Bus
Digital signaling:	State-transition
Bit synchronization:	Synchronous
Bandwidth use:	Baseband

At the MAC sublayer of the data link layer, this protocol is concerned with the following:

Logical topology:	Bus
Media access:	Contention
Addressing:	Physical device

Finally, LocalTalk has these functions at the LLC sublayer of the data link layer:

Transmission synchronization:	Synchronous
Connection services:	LLC flow control and error control

LocalTalk was developed for small workgroups. It is slow, at 230.4Kbps, and is limited to 32 devices and 300-meter segment lengths. It is still useful for small offices, however. LocalTalk uses a dynamic addressing scheme, which allows each workstation to negotiate a unique node address with the other workstations at startup.

EtherTalk (ELAP)

EtherTalk (the EtherTalk Link Access Protocol) is an implementation of AppleTalk that uses the Ethernet protocol (contention access, collision detection, and star/bus topology).

TokenTalk (TLAP)

TokenTalk (the TokenTalk Link Access Protocol) is an adaptation of Apple-Talk at the physical and data link layers. It uses the Token Ring protocol (token-passing access and star/ring topology).

AARP (AppleTalk Address Resolution Protocol)

AARP maps AppleTalk addresses to Ethernet and Token Ring physical addresses. AARP allows upper-layer protocols to use data link layer protocols other than LocalTalk.

AppleTalk Middle-Layer Protocols

The AppleTalk protocols that run at the OSI middle layers include the following:

- **DDP:** For datagram packet delivery
- **RTMP:** A distance-vector routing protocol
- **NBP:** To map logical names to addresses
- **ATP:** A transport layer protocol that uses acknowledgments to keep track of transactions

Datagram Delivery Protocol (DDP)

DDP is the workhorse of AppleTalk's network layer protocols. It provides connectionless or datagram service.

DDP uses the concept of sockets or service addresses to specify the source and destination upper-layer protocol. DDP uses the complete address to route packets through the internetwork. The complete address consists of a logical network address, a node address, and a socket number. An address such as logical network 1002, node 1, socket 3, refers to an exact connection.

DDP works with the RTMP, NBP, and ZIP protocols to provide datagram packet delivery. It uses dynamic route selection and supports interoperability by providing network layer translation.

Routing Table Maintenance Protocol (RTMP)

RTMP is a distance-vector routing protocol, similar to RIP, that functions at the network layer. This protocol creates and maintains routing tables that DDP uses to make dynamic route selections.

Name Binding Protocol (NBP)

AppleTalk uses NBP at the transport layer to match a logical device name with its associated address. Because AppleTalk allows dynamic node addressing, NBP must obtain the current address for a given node name. This address resolution method is service-requester-initiated.

AppleTalk Transaction Protocol (ATP)

ATP is an acknowledged connectionless protocol that functions at the transport layer. It is based on transactions instead of connections. A transaction consists of a request followed by a response and is identified by a transaction ID. ATP acknowledges packet delivery and initiates retransmission if a packet remains unacknowledged for too long.

AppleTalk Upper-Layer Protocols

These AppleTalk protocols work at the upper layers of the OSI model:

- **ADSP:** Actually runs at both the transport and session layers

- **ASP:** Manages dialogs

- **PAP:** Mainly used for printing

- **ZIP:** For managing logical groups called zones

- **AFP:** For file sharing

- **AppleShare:** For application layer services

AppleTalk Data Stream Protocol (ADSP)

ADSP is categorized as a session layer protocol even though it also performs transport layer functions. The session layer functions it performs are establishing and releasing connections. The transport layer functions are segment sequencing and flow control. ADSP is an alternative to ATP as a transport protocol. ADSP does not keep track of transactions; it uses connection identifiers instead and transmits data in byte streams.

AppleTalk Session Protocol (ASP)

ASP provides session layer services by establishing, maintaining, and releasing connections. It works in conjunction with ATP to provide reliable packet delivery. ASP allows multiple sessions to be established with the same service provider, as long as requests are made individually by service requesters.

Printer Access Protocol (PAP)

You can use PAP for more than just printing, in spite of its name. It is a session layer protocol that permits sessions to be initiated by both service requesters and service providers. PAP allows connections between file servers and workstations, as well as between workstations and print servers.

Zone Information Protocol (ZIP)

ZIP allows devices to be organized into logical groups called zones. A zone can reduce the apparent complexity of an internetwork by limiting the number of service providers viewed to the subset the user needs to see. Routers and other network nodes use ZIP to map between zone and network names.

AppleTalk Filing Protocol (AFP)

AFP was developed to facilitate file sharing. It works at the session and presentation layers to translate local file system commands into a format that can be used for network file service. AFP provides file-syntax translation for other applications as well. It enhances security by verifying login names and passwords at connection establishment and by encrypting login information before sending it across the network.

AppleShare

AppleShare is a suite of three protocols or applications that provide AppleTalk's application layer services. The following protocols make up AppleShare:

- **AppleShare File Server:** The Macintosh's network operating system. It uses AFP to provide access to remote files. AppleShare File Server registers users and allows those users to log in and access resources.

- **AppleShare Print Server:** Uses lower-layer protocols (such as NBP and PAP) to provide printer sharing on the network. Similar to NetWare, AppleShare Print Server stores print jobs in a queue before sending them to the selected printer. AppleShare Print Server's utilization of NBP allows users to refer to a printer using a name of their choice; NBP maps that name to the printer's address.

- **AppleShare PC:** Allows DOS workstations to access AppleShare file services. An MS-DOS user running an AppleShare PC can read or write files to an AppleShare File Server and print to an AppleTalk printer.

AppleShare provides active service advertisement and collaborative service use.

DNA (Digital Network Architecture) Protocols

DNA WAS FIRST developed in 1974 by Digital Equipment Corporation as a network architecture. The implementation of DNA is known as DECnet. This architecture has gone through several changes since its inception; it is currently in Phase V. Digital developed Phase V along the lines of the OSI model, although certain older protocols are still supported.

DNA has become so OSI-compliant that it has actually adopted some of the OSI protocols. Some of the DNA protocols don't even have an acronym—they're referred to by number. Figure A.5 maps DNA to the OSI model.

FIGURE A.5

DNA mapped to the OSI model

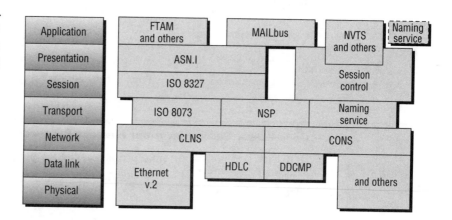

DNA Lower-Layer Protocols

The lower-layer protocols included here are Ethernet Version 2, DDCMP, and HDLC.

Ethernet Version 2

Digital, along with Intel and Xerox, developed the first version of Ethernet. Ethernet Version 2 is very similar to, and provided the design basis for, IEEE 802.3. Like IEEE 802.3, it uses the CSMA/CD (Carrier Sense Multiple Access with Collision Detection) media access method and Manchester digital encoding to achieve a 10Mbps data rate over coaxial cable. Ethernet Version 2 uses a slightly different frame format than IEEE 802.3, however.

At the physical layer, Ethernet Version 2 handles the following:

Connection types:	Multipoint
Physical topology:	Bus
Digital signaling:	State-transition
Bit synchronization:	Synchronous
Bandwidth use:	Baseband

At the MAC sublayer of the data link layer, this protocol is concerned with the following:

Logical topology:	Bus
Media access:	Contention
Addressing:	Physical device

Digital Data Communications Message Protocol (DDCMP)

DDCMP is one of the original proprietary DNA protocols. It functions at the physical layer and the LLC sublayer of the data link layer. Characteristics of DDCMP include

- Asynchronous or synchronous service

- Half-duplex or full-duplex mode

- Point-to-point or multipoint topologies

- Connection-oriented error control using commands and acknowledgments

- LLC-level flow control and message (frame) sequencing services

High-Level Data Link Control (HDLC)

HDLC is a data link level protocol modeled after SDLC (discussed in the section "Systems Network Architecture Protocols (SNA)" later in this appendix). It supports both asynchronous and synchronous transmission synchronization. HDLC defines a data-frame format and a command-frame format, as well as a set of control commands. Using these commands, HDLC can provide LLC-level flow control. At the physical layer, it provides point-to-point connections.

DNA Middle-Layer Protocols

The DNA middle-layer protocols include the following:

- **CLNS:** An ISO standard network layer protocol

- **CONS:** Another ISO standard protocol at the network layer

- **NSP:** A proprietary DNA protocol

- **ISO 8073:** A transport protocol that offers different classes of service

Connectionless-Mode Network Service (CLNS)

CLNS is a connectionless network layer protocol that is supported through the following ISO protocols:

- **ISO 8473:** Protocol for Providing the Connectionless-Mode Network Service. This protocol manages communication between two end systems (devices).

- **ISO 9542:** End System to Intermediate System Routing Exchange Protocol for Providing the Connectionless-Mode Network Service, also referred to as ES-IS. It performs simple routing functions that do not involve internetwork routing.

- **ISO 10589:** Intermediate System to Intermediate System Intra-Domain Routing Exchange Protocol for Use in Conjunction with the Protocol for Providing the Connectionless-Mode Network Service, referred to as IS-IS. This protocol determines routes through complex internetworks.

DNA Phase V typically uses CLNS at the network layer instead of the connection-oriented CONS protocol (see the next section). CLNS provides link-state route discovery and dynamic route selection.

Connection Oriented Network Service (CONS)

CONS is a network layer, connection-oriented service, comprising the following protocols:

- **ISO 8208:** X.25 Packet-Level Protocol for Data Terminal Equipment. The ISO version of X.25 (See the section "X.25" later in this appendix.)

- **ISO 8878:** Use of X.25 to Provide the OSI Connection-Mode Network Service. A protocol that enables X.25 to provide complete connection-oriented services

CONS provides link-state route discovery and dynamic route selection. It supplies network layer flow control, error control, and packet sequence control.

Network Services Protocol (NSP)

NSP, at the transport layer, is one of the original DNA protocols; it has been part of the suite since the 1970s. It is a connection-oriented, flow-controlled protocol that can utilize normal or expedited full-duplex channels.

Connection-Oriented Transport Protocol Specification (ISO 8073)

ISO 8073 is a transport layer protocol that provides different classes of service, allowing it to be tailored to specific implementation requirements. A service class can be selected based on desired levels of flow control, error control, and packet sequencing.

DNA Upper-Layer Protocols

The DNA upper-layer protocols include both DNA proprietary protocols and OSI standard protocols. We will look at the following protocols in this section:

- **Session control:** A proprietary DNA protocol

- **ISO 8327:** A session protocol specification

- **ASN.1 with BER:** Describes a generic file syntax to facilitate file exchange between disparate computer systems

- **FTAM:** A generic file transfer protocol

- **DAP:** Used with FTAM

- **NVTS:** A virtual terminal protocol

- **MAILbus and X.400 Message Handling System:** A service that provides messaging for remote clients

- **Naming Service and X.500 Directory:** Provides service addressing and OSI directory services

Session Control

The session control protocol is a proprietary DNA protocol that operates at the session and presentation layers of the OSI model. It provides an interface between application layer services and transport layer protocols. The functions provided by the Session Control protocol include

- Address/name resolution

- Transport connection management

- Protocol stack selection

- Connection identifier addressing

Session Protocol Specification (ISO 8327)

The ISO 8327 protocol is implemented according to the ISO definition of the session layer, as specified in the document ISO 8326, Session Service Definition. It provides the following services:

- Negotiated connection establishment and release

- Half-duplex data transfer

- Support for multiple transport layer connections for each session

- Packet-transfer synchronization

Packet transfer synchronization is achieved by using markers called synchronization tokens, which allow the dialog to be restarted at any synchronization point.

Abstract Syntax Notation One with Basic Encoding Rules (ASN.1 with BER)

ASN.1, a presentation layer protocol, describes a set of syntax rules designed to facilitate data exchange between different systems. It describes a standard character code set different entities can use as a mutually agreeable code. The rules themselves are listed in the BER. One of the rules is the character code type descriptions used to distinguish between two different floating-point number schemes.

File Transfer, Access, and Management (FTAM)

FTAM is a generic file transfer, access, and management protocol that operates at the application layer. It specifies that any FTAM implementation must include certain document types, such as text and binary, and service classes, such as file transfer and management. Vendors are permitted to create customized implementations of this protocol.

Data Access Protocol (DAP)

DNA provides the ability to transfer files by means of DAP. This application layer protocol enhances FTAM by providing file system operations such as file creation, deletion, storage, and retrieval. It also allows access to indexed files.

Network Virtual Terminal Service (NVTS)

NVTS is a service that provides virtual terminal access to hosts. It operates at the presentation and application layers. NVTS uses character-code translation to translate data from the local terminal format to the network format before it is transmitted to the host. This allows seamless communication between heterogeneous systems.

MAILbus and X.400 Message Handling System

MAILbus and X.400 are application layer protocols used for e-mail services. MAILbus provides DNA proprietary mail services. It also uses the X.400 standard to interface with other X.400-compatible systems on an internetwork. X.400 is a recommendation that specifies how messages are stored and forwarded between dissimilar devices.

Naming Service and X.500 Directory

The DNA Naming Service works at the transport and application layers to perform address/name resolution. This allows network devices to be described in human terms with logical, alphanumeric names. The Naming Service then translates these names into network addresses. The DNA Naming Service is not yet completely compatible with X.500, a recommendation for Directory Service implementations, but Digital has stated that future releases will be X.500 compatible.

Systems Network Architecture Protocols (SNA)

S NA IS IBM'S proprietary networking architecture. It was initially developed in 1974 according to the hierarchical model of networking used by IBM at that time. The devices in the hierarchy include hosts or mainframes, communication controllers, cluster controllers, and terminals.

In 1984, IBM added support for advanced features, such as distributed processing, internetworking, and network management. This extension is known as Advanced Peer-to-Peer Networking, or APPN.

IBM announced the Systems Application Architecture (SAA) in 1987. It promotes the more advanced features of SNA, such as LU 6.2 and PU 2.1. (See the section "The SNA Architecture and Its Components" later in this chapter.)

SNA was developed following a seven-layer model known as the SNA model, which predates the OSI reference model (and, in fact, was the basis for the OSI model). Figure A.6 compares the two models and maps various SNA products and protocols to the OSI model.

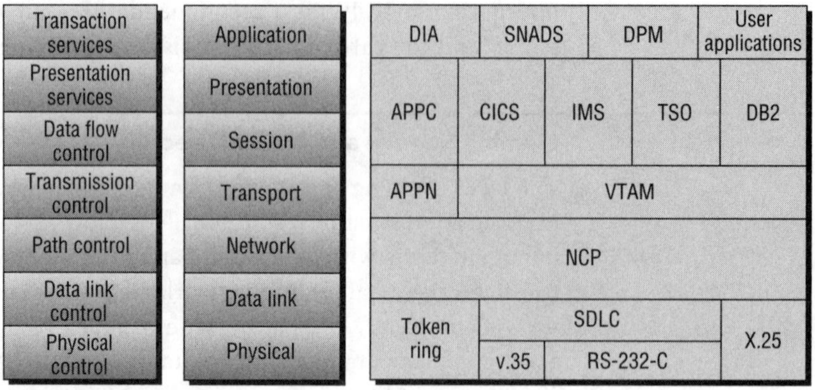

FIGURE A.6

SNA mapped to the OSI model

Transaction services	Application	DIA	SNADS		DPM	User applications
Presentation services	Presentation	APPC	CICS	IMS	TSO	DB2
Data flow control	Session					
Transmission control	Transport	APPN	VTAM			
Path control	Network	NCP				
Data link control	Data link	Token ring	SDLC			X.25
Physical control	Physical		v.35	RS-232-C		

Layers of the SNA Model

The SNA model, as Figure A.6 shows, is quite similar to the OSI model, except that the functionality is grouped slightly differently. The SNA model has the following layers:

- **Physical control:** The first layer of the SNA model is concerned with physical transmission characteristics. This layer defines electrical, mechanical, and procedural characteristics of the physical media and the interfaces to it. SNA does not define any physical control protocols. Instead, IBM has relied on international standards for physical layer implementations, with the exception of Token Ring, which began as a proprietary implementation and is now standardized as IEEE 802.5.

- **Data link control:** The next SNA layer is analogous to the OSI data link layer, where channel-access methods and data framing are specified. At the data link control layer, SNA defines the SDLC protocol for master-slave or primary-secondary communication links and the Token Ring standard for peer-to-peer networks.

- **Path control:** This layer defines functions that are primarily included in the OSI network layer, particularly routing and datagram fragmentation/

reassembly. The SNA path control layer also includes flow control, considered a data link layer function in the OSI model.

- **Transmission control:** This layer provides reliable end-to-end connection services, similar to the OSI transport layer. In addition, this layer handles data encryption services, a function the OSI model assigns to the presentation layer.

- **Data flow control:** The next SNA layer roughly corresponds to the OSI session layer. It manages dialogs, controls request and response processing, groups messages, and interrupts data flow on request.

- **Presentation services:** This layer includes services from the OSI presentation layer, mainly data-translation services, as well as OSI application layer services, such as coordinating resource sharing and synchronizing operations.

- **Transaction services:** The top SNA layer performs OSI application layer functions. It provides application services for distributed processing and network management. One example of an SNA transaction services layer product is SNA Distribution Services (SNADS), which provides a distribution system for SNA applications.

The SNA Architecture and Its Components

The SNA hierarchical architecture has its own terminology for the different types of hardware and software that make up the network. The devices that make up an SNA network are referred to as nodes, and they are categorized by type. Figure A.7 illustrates the different SNA node types.

Host nodes (type 5) are mainframes and midrange systems or minicomputers. A host node controls a domain, which encompasses physical units, logical units, links, and other associated resources. Domains include one or more subareas, which are divisions of SNA networks, consisting of a communication controller and associated physical and logical units.

Communications controller nodes (type 4) are devices that route and control the flow of information in a subarea of an SNA network. These nodes are also called front-end processors because they offload some of the processing

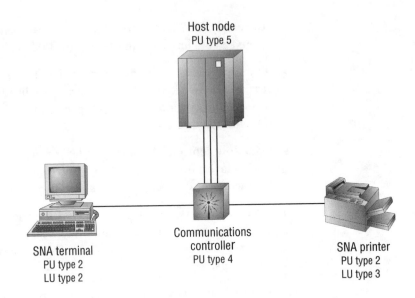

from the host nodes. They are normally attached via a high-speed channel to the host or communicate remotely through another communication controller. Peripheral nodes (type 2) include client devices such as cluster controllers, terminals, and printers.

To interconnect the different types of nodes, IBM has further classified network devices and software as follows:

- **Physical units (PU):** Combinations of hardware, firmware, and software that manage and monitor the resources of a node. The three node types described above are physical units.

- **Logical units (LU):** Combinations of software and hardware that provide connection points for communication between nodes. They enable people and applications to access the network.

- **Control points:** Software management tools that operate within type 5 and type 2.1 physical units to allow them to manage and control data flow on the network.

Tables A.2, A.3, and A.4 shows how these three categories and the device types they contain are classified.

TABLE A.2	TYPE	DESCRIPTION
SNA Physical Units	1	Terminal nodes
	2	Cluster controllers, terminals, and printers. These devices can communicate only with mainframes
	2.1	Minicomputers, cluster controllers, gateways, and workstations that can communicate with mainframes or any other type 2.1 device. Type 2.1 physical units are the physical foundation of the new APPN (Advanced Peer-to-Peer Networking) specification
	4	Communication controllers
	5	Host computers

TABLE A.3	TYPE	DESCRIPTION
SNA Logical Units	0	General-purpose logical units used for program-to-program communications. These logical units are being replaced by the more advanced LU type 6.2
	1	Batch terminals, card readers, and printers
	2	Terminals (such as 3270)
	3	Batch devices, similar to type 1
	4	Old peer-to-peer connections, such as 6670 to 6670
	6 and 6.1	CICS peer connections or IMS communication between mainframes
	6.2	Advanced Peer-to-Peer Networking (APPN)
	7	Display stations (such as 5270)

TABLE A.4	TYPE	DESCRIPTION
SNA Control Points	5	These physical units (hosts) run a centralized software program within an SNA network to manage configurations, coordinate requests, and provide session services to network users. This system is called System Services Control Point (SSCP). Multiple SSCPs can divide the network into hierarchical domains
	2.1	These physical units (minis, gateways, and so on) are capable of the same type of network management as type 5 devices, but on a smaller scale. Type 2.1 physical units provide control points in peer-to-peer systems

The following sections describe some key SNA protocols and products according to their function within the OSI model.

SNA Lower-Layer Protocols

The SNA lower-layer protocols are Token Ring, SDLC, and NCP, a protocol that includes both network and data link layer functionality.

Token Ring

Token Ring is IBM's LAN specification at the physical and data link (MAC sublayer) layers. It uses the token-passing media access method to transmit data at 4- or 16Mbps over a physical star, logical ring topology. It uses point-to-point connections, state-transition digital signaling, synchronous bit synchronization, and the baseband bandwidth.

Token Ring was the basis for the IEEE 802.5 standard. IBM's Token Ring specifies shielded twisted-pair (STP) cabling and uses proprietary IBM data connectors.

Synchronous Data Link Control (SDLC)

SDLC is a data link layer protocol that supports point-to-point or multipoint connections between SNA primaries and secondaries. SDLC uses the polling channel access method and synchronous frame synchronization. It can provide both half-duplex and full-duplex connections over dedicated leased or dial-up phone lines. SDLC generates specific control messages in addition to adding data link level headers to the packets it receives from the network layer protocol.

NCP (Network Control Program)

IBM's NCP was originally designed to control resources attached to communications controllers. Primarily, it handled data link layer functions. NCP has been expanded to include routing and SNA gateway services at the network layer. It uses the polling channel access method and performs both physical and logical addressing. In addition to flow control, it performs static route selection.

SNA Middle-Layer Protocols

The SNA protocols that function at the OSI model's middle layers include APPN and VTAM.

Advanced Peer-to-Peer Networking (APPN)

APPN works at the network and transport layers to provide peer-to-peer networking between multiple physical unit type 2.1 devices. APPN relies on APPC (Advanced Program-to-Program Communications) for logical connection points. APPN provides route discovery, window flow control, and directory services.

Virtual Telecommunications Access Method (VTAM)

VTAM is an IBM product that provides control of data communication and data flow in an SNA network. VTAM controls single and multiple domains. SSCP (System Services Control Point) is the main software component of VTAM.

At the transport layer, VTAM uses connection identifiers for addressing, uses division and combination for segment development, and provides end-to-end flow control. At the session layer, VTAM handles half-duplex dialog control and session administration (connection establishment, data transfer, and connection release).

SNA Upper-Layer Protocols

The following SNA protocols function at the upper layers of the OSI model:

- **CICS:** An environment for transaction-processing application programming

- **IMS:** A tool similar to CICS

- **APPC:** The extension to SNA that allows peer-to-peer communications

- **DDM:** Provides transparent remote file access

- **SNADS:** Controls the distribution of messages

- **DIA:** A standard for document exchange

Customer Information Control System (CICS)

CICS is a tool for building transaction-processing applications. It supplies a set of generic input and output commands for the SNA networking environment. CICS provides distributed file access, security, multitasking, terminal-to-application communication, storage management, transaction tracking, transaction recovery, and rollback.

At the session layer, CICS handles half-duplex dialog control and session administration (connection establishment, data transfer, and connection release. At the presentation layer, it is concerned with file syntax translation.

Information Management System (IMS)

IMS is another transaction-processing application programming environment similar to CICS. It consists of two parts: the IMS Transaction Manager and the IMS Database Manager. IMS allows multiple applications to share databases and schedule priority transactions.

Like CICS, IMS functions at the session and presentation layers, handling half-duplex dialog control, session administration, and file syntax translation.

Advanced Program-to-Program Communication (APPC)

APPC is the extension to SNA that defines LU type 6.2 and allows peer-to-peer communications between logical units. APPC provides transport and session layer functionality. At the transport layer, it uses connection identifiers for addressing and provides segment sequencing and end-to-end flow control. At the session layer, APPC handles half-duplex dialog control and session administration.

Distributed Data Management (DDM)

DDM is an application layer service that provides transparent remote access to files. It uses operating system call interception to achieve this transparency. DDM receives requests for file access from client processes and, depending on the location of the file, retrieves the files through the local operating system or packages requests to other DDM servers across the network.

SNA Distributed Services (SNADS)

SNADS is an application layer service that controls the distribution of messages and documents. It uses store-and-forward techniques to distribute files. SNADS provides an infrastructure for the distribution of e-mail.

Document Interchange Architecture (DIA)

DIA is an application layer protocol that defines a standard for exchanging documents between dissimilar computer systems. File transfer, document retrieval, and storage are coordinated by DIA.

Miscellaneous Protocols and Standards

THE REST OF this appendix covers some miscellaneous protocols and standards. Some are LAN protocols; others, including those used for public data networks, primarily make up WANs.

Microsoft ✓ *Exam Objective*

Distinguish whether SLIP or PPP is used as the communications protocol for various situations.

Serial Line Internet Protocol (SLIP)

The SLIP and PPP (discussed in the next section) protocols are used with dial-up connections to the Internet. If you connect to the Internet from your home computer, chances are you're using one or the other of these protocols. SLIP was the first of the two to be developed, and it is the simplest. It functions at the physical layer only and does not provide error control or security. Despite these drawbacks, SLIP is a popular protocol for Internet access. Most users don't need a secure connection, and most high-speed modems provide their own error control.

Although SLIP functions at the physical layer of the OSI model, it is frequently referred to as a data link communications protocol.

Point-to-Point Protocol (PPP)

PPP was developed as an improvement to SLIP, and the functions it provides encompass both the physical and data link layers. PPP's additional functions include error control, security, dynamic IP addressing, and support for multiple protocols. Both SLIP and PPP are point-to-point protocols. PPP provides physical device addressing at the MAC sublayer and LLC-level error control.

Figure A.8 shows SLIP and PPP mapped to the OSI model.

Fiber Distributed Data Interface (FDDI)

FDDI is a LAN and MAN standard based on the use of fiber-optic cable wired in a physical ring or star. Because the use of fiber-optic cable allows a network to span greater distances than the typical LAN, it is commonly used for campus-wide and even larger networks. FDDI uses a token-passing media

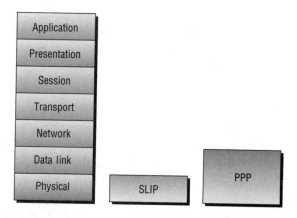

access method, similar to IEEE 802.5 Token Ring. Like IEEE 802.5, the FDDI standard covers the physical and MAC sublayers of the OSI model and uses the LLC defined by IEEE 802.2. Figure A.9 shows FDDI mapped to the OSI model.

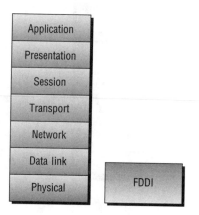

FDDI has a very high bandwidth at 100Mbps, which makes it suitable for applications such as multimedia and video. It is also designed with the potential for very effective fault tolerance. An FDDI ring can be cabled with dual counter-rotating rings (meaning that the token is passed in the opposite direction on each ring). Stations on an FDDI ring can be either single-attached stations, connected to one of the rings, or dual-attached stations, connected to both rings.

If there is a break in the ring and all the stations are single attached, the ring will fail because the token cannot arrive at the next station. However, if the stations are dual attached, the ring will automatically be reconfigured to route the token around the break.

X.25

The international standards organization CCITT (International Telegraph and Telephone Consultative Committee), since renamed to the International Telecommunications Union (ITU), developed X.25 in 1974 as a WAN standard using packet switching.

As you can see in Figure A.10, X.25 functions at the network layer. It normally interfaces with a protocol called LAPB (Link Access Procedures—Balanced) at the data link layer, which in turn runs over X.21, or another physical layer CCITT protocol, such as X.21bis or V.32.

FIGURE A.10

The X.25 protocol mapped to the OSI model

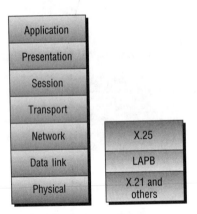

X.25 provides permanent or switched virtual circuits, which imply reliable service and end-to-end flow control. However, line speeds used with X.25 are too slow to provide LAN application services on a WAN.

At the physical layer, X.21 allows for a hybrid mesh topology and a point-to-point connection type.

LAPB is a data link layer protocol based on SDLC (see the section "Systems Network Architecture (SNA)" earlier in this appendix) that provides LLC-level flow control and error control.

At the network layer, X.25 uses a type of addressing called channel addressing, which is similar to logical network addressing except that the address is maintained for each connection.

Frame Relay

Frame relay is a newer packet-switching technology, similar to X.25, that uses virtual circuits. Like X.25, frame relay is used in WANs. Frame relay assumes that certain error-checking and monitoring tasks will be performed by higher-level protocols, and this allows it to be faster than X.25. Frame relay functions at the physical and data link layers of the OSI model, as illustrated in Figure A.11. Frame relay is defined by CCITT recommendations I.451/Q.931 and Q.922.

FIGURE A.11

Frame relay mapped to the OSI model

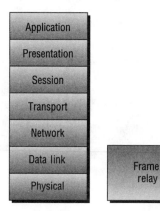

At the physical layer, frame relay handles point-to-point connections in mesh (hybrid) physical topologies. At the LLC sublayer of the data link layer, frame relay provides error detection but not error recovery.

Frame relay services generally allow customers to specify committed information rates according to their bandwidth requirements.

Integrated Services Digital Network (ISDN) and Broadband ISDN (B-ISDN)

ISDN is a set of standards designed to provide voice, video, and data transmission over a digital telephone network. B-ISDN provides greater bandwidth, which can be used for applications such as video, imaging, and multimedia. B-ISDN can be used with SONET and ATM, which are described in next two sections.

At the physical layer, ISDN provides time-division multiplexing (TDM). At the network layer, the ISDN standard is defined by CCITT recommendations I.450/Q.930 and I.451/Q.931. Figure A.12 shows ISDN mapped to the OSI model.

FIGURE A.12

ISDN mapped to the
OSI model

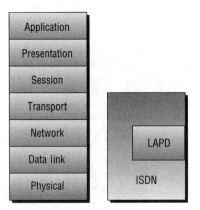

ISDN functions as a transmission media service only. The ISDN specification uses the LAPD (Link Access Procedure, D Channel) protocol at the data link layer to provide acknowledged, connectionless, full-duplex service. At the MAC sublayer, LAPD provides physical device addressing. At the LLC sublayer, it handles flow control and frame sequencing.

The ISDN standard for integrating analog and digital transmissions using digital telecommunications networks allows for circuit-switched or packet-switched connections. These connections are provided by means of digital communication channels, or bit pipes. Using the ISDN bit pipes, several standard rate multiplexed channels are available. These channels are classified as follows:

- **Channel A:** 4kHz analog channel

- **Channel B:** 64Kbps digital channel

- **Channel C:** 8- or 16Kbps digital channel (used for out-of-band signaling)

- **Channel D:** 16- or 64Kbps digital channel (used for out-of-band signaling). Includes three subchannels: *s* for signaling, *t* for telemetry, and *p* for low bandwidth packet data

- **Channel E:** 64Kbps digital channel (for internal ISDN signaling)

- **Channel H:** 384-, 1536-, or 1920Kbps digital channel

LAPD operates on the D channel.

The following three channel combinations have been standardized by CCITT as international service offerings:

- **Basic rate:** Includes 2 B channels (at 64Kbps) and 1 D channel (at 16Kbps)

- **Primary rate:** Includes 1 D channel (at 64Kbps), 23 B channels in the U.S. and Japan, or 30 B channels in Europe and Australia

- **Hybrid:** Includes 1 A channel (4Khz analog) and 1 C channel (8- or 16Kbps digital)

Synchronous Optical Network (SONET) and Synchronous Digital Hierarchy (SDH)

SONET was developed by Bell Communications Research. It is a physical layer protocol standardized by ANSI and generally used for WANs. ITU (formerly CCITT) created a similar standard called SDH. Regional variations, developed because of local differences in telecommunications, are SDH-Europe, SDH-SONET (North America), and SDH-Japan. Figure A.13 shows SONET and SDH mapped to the OSI model. SONET and SDH provide point-to-point connections, work with mesh or ring physical topologies, and use the TDM multiplexing method.

FIGURE A.13

SONET and SDH mapped
to the OSI model

Asynchronous Transfer Mode (ATM)

ATM is an emerging standard being developed by the ITU Telecommunications Standards Sector and the ATM Forum. It is most frequently considered for WANs, but it can be used for LANs and MANs as well. This protocol covers the OSI model's data link and network layer functionality and can operate over physical layer protocols such as FDDI and SONET/SDH. Figure A.14 maps ATM to the OSI model.

A distinguishing feature of ATM is that it uses cell switching. A cell is a 53-byte packet that follows a virtual circuit. Its other network layer function is static route selection.

FIGURE A.14

ATM mapped to the
OSI model

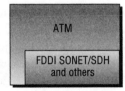

At the LLC sublayer of the data link layer, ATM provides isochronous transmission synchronization and error control.

Switched Megabit Data Service (SMRS)

SMDS is a cell-switching technology developed by Bell Communications Research. Like ATM, it uses small packets, called cells. It can be mapped to the data link and network layers of the OSI model, and it is normally used with physical layer protocols such as the DQDB standard for MANs (IEEE 802.6) and SONET/SDH. At the LLC sublayer of the data link layer, SMDS provides isochronous transmission synchronization. Figure A.15 shows SMDS mapped to the OSI model.

FIGURE A.15

SMDS mapped to the OSI model

APPENDIX

B

PC Fundamentals

ICROSOFT'S NETWORKING ESSENTIALS exam does not specifically cover PC fundamentals. However, as a network administrator, you must have a good understanding of them. This appendix provides a basic review of PC hardware. If you are an experienced computer professional, you may wish to skip this discussion.

Networks these days typically contain a variety of old and new technologies. Workstations may range from 12-year-old systems that boot from floppies to top-of-the-line Pentium multimedia workstations. As you might have guessed, not all organizations have upgraded to the most recent line of hardware. It is important to be informed about older technologies.

The Motherboard

HE LARGE, PRINTED circuit board known as the motherboard is the foundation upon which many of the most critical components of a PC rest. The motherboard also serves as the backbone into which peripheral hardware is connected and contains these components:

- The central processing unit (CPU)

- Memory

- Interrupts, addresses, ports, and DMA channels

- The data bus

The Microprocessor (CPU)

The microprocessor, or CPU, is the brain of the PC. Most PC-compatible machines use CPUs manufactured by Intel Corp. These processors range from the early 8086 and 8088 to the latest Pentium, Pentium Pro, and Pentium II. Without the CPU, your computer would not be able to execute programs.

Other manufacturers, including AMD and Cyrix, sell Intel clone processors. They typically offer similar performance and a better price, but they may not be 100 percent compatible with all software and devices.

To effectively execute programs, a CPU must be able to quickly perform these functions:

- Read and write information into the computer's memory
- Recognize and carry out the series of commands or instructions supplied by the programs
- Direct the operation of the other parts of the computer

CPU speed is measured in terms of megahertz (MHz). Because 1MHz is equal to 1,000,000 cycles per second, we're talking about a lot of processing in the CPU. Typical speeds range from 16MHz for the older 386 computers to 300MHz and beyond for the latest Pentiums.

These speeds are called clock speeds and are controlled by an internal timing source, or clock, on the CPU. However, some instructions—basic actions the CPU performs—can take more than one clock cycle to complete. For this reason, the actual work a processor can perform is measured in MIPS—Millions of Instructions Per Second.

Intel has built upon a successful design to create a series of CPUs, called the X86 family, which reside in the majority of PCs. Each new design has maintained 100 percent compatibility with previous versions, allowing new designs to execute software written for previous designs.

Although it is called the X86 family, the first Intel CPU to be widely accepted was called the 8088.

To the end user, the most noticeable difference among Intel CPUs is speed. Table B.1 presents the chronological order of Intel CPUs, along with their processing speeds (measured in MIPS):

	CPU	PROCESSING SPEED
TABLE B.1 Intel CPUs and Processing Speeds, in Chronological Order	8086	0.33MIPS
	8088	0.33MIPS
	80286	3MIPS
	80386	11MIPS
	80486	41MIPS
	Pentium	Over 100MIPS
	Pentium Pro and Pentium II	Over 300MIPS

The 8088 was implemented with 29,000 transistors. Pentium-class processors have transistors numbering in the millions!

What Do You Really Need?

Although the Pentium processor and its successor, the Pentium Pro or P6, are the most powerful processors, not everyone uses them—or needs them. Practically speaking, a 486 DX-33 or higher processor can be used for just about any application, and even a 386 is usable for DOS-based applications. Nevertheless, you'll find that many companies still try to do the nearly impossible—run Windows applications from the network using a 386, or even a 286. Even if the system works, it will be very slow.

Statistically, 486 machines are the most popular workstations, but a great many 386 (and lower) machines are still out there. Some applications don't need anything better, and some organizations aren't willing to spend the money to upgrade. Keep in mind, however, that Windows 95 and Windows NT demand a lot of system resources. A 386 with 4MB of RAM simply won't do.

Bits and Bytes

All of the information traveling across the motherboard of a computer is represented digitally as either a 1 or a 0. For example, the instruction that tells an Intel X86-family CPU to subtract is 0010110. This method of using 1's and 0's to represent information is called the binary system. The 1's and 0's are called binary digits, or, more simply, bits. When a computer processes 1's and 0's, however, it does so in bytes, which are groups of 8 bits.

Computer circuitry is capable of reacting to two states in the flow of the electric current that runs through it: high current and low current. These states of high and low current are what is represented by the 1's and 0's. One of the primary factors contributing to the development of computers as we know them is that it is relatively easy and inexpensive to create a circuit that can recognize the difference between high and low current (with an extremely low error ratio).

Because today's typical machine has over 8 million bytes of memory, several metric terms are used to describe quantities of memory storage. Here are the most common ones:

- A byte is 8 bits.

- A kilobyte (K or KB) equals 1024 bytes.

- A megabyte (M or MB) equals 1,048,576 bytes.

- A gigabyte (G or GB) equals 1,073,741,824 bytes.

These aren't the nice round numbers the metric system is famous for. This is because of the binary system that computers use to address memory. While 1000 is a round number to humans, it's not round to a computer—in binary, it's 1111101000. For this reason, memory is measured in amounts convenient to the computer. Thus, a kilobyte (1024 bytes) is a nice, round 10000000000 in binary. A megabyte is 1024 kilobytes, or 1024 x 1024 bytes, and so on.

Memory

Memory is crucial to the CPU's operation. It provides a quickly accessible temporary storage place for all the instructions the CPU processes. Memory resides on the motherboard in close contact with the CPU.

There are two main types of memory:

- Random-access memory (RAM)

- Read-only memory (ROM)

Random-Access Memory (RAM)

Because PC CPUs operate at such high speeds, they need quick access to the raw data that needs to be processed, and they must be able to quickly store the results of what has been processed. The CPU itself can hold only a few bytes at a time, so memory must be able to hold enough bytes to support complex programs. Disks and tapes can store large quantities of information, but they are simply too slow for the CPU. The solution is random access memory (RAM).

RAM has several characteristics that make it appropriate for working with the CPU. One of these characteristics is that the CPU can access programs and data that are stored in RAM directly, or randomly. This access method is similar to the way you use office mailboxes: you can retrieve mail directly from any one box without needing to go through the others.

The terms memory *and* RAM *are often used interchangeably.*

RAM is volatile, which means it requires a constant supply of electricity to maintain its data; if electricity is shut off, RAM loses its data. Volatility is the reason you can lose data that has not been saved to a disk or tape if the power to your PC goes down. Disks and tapes are examples of non-volatile storage.

Newer PC motherboards often have two kinds of RAM:

- Dynamic RAM (DRAM)

- Static RAM (SRAM)

DRAM is typically found in the main memory. For example, a typical Pentium PC has 8 or 16 megabytes of this type of RAM. DRAM is relatively inexpensive. It is, however, much slower than SRAM.

Although SRAM and DRAM are both volatile, SRAM is able to maintain data as long as the power is on. DRAM, on the other hand, requires that each byte of memory be accessed several times per second in order to keep it. This constant cycle, called memory refresh, is the reason DRAM is slower.

SRAM often appears on a motherboard in small banks of chips that are used as data caches. Because SRAM is much faster than DRAM, it can help boost system performance.

Most PCs also have another type of RAM, called a complementary metal oxide semiconductor (CMOS). CMOS stores system information including information about the floppy and hard disks, the amount of installed memory, and the type of display. CMOS memory is also volatile, but it is powered by a small battery to hold this information after you shut off your PC. Your system uses this information when it boots up again.

Read-Only Memory (ROM)

Read-only memory (ROM) is a type of permanent memory. It does not disappear when you shut off the PC, and it does not require a battery to keep it running. The data in ROM is usually placed on the chips by the manufacturer and cannot be changed.

The information stored in ROM is frequently called firmware.

An important piece of ROM on a PC is called the Basic Input/Output System, or BIOS. The BIOS is responsible for some fundamental functions in a PC, such as displaying text on a monitor and allowing keyboard input. When a PC boots up, the BIOS programs perform an elemental system test and then use information supplied by the CMOS to identify the disk drives attached to the system, which are then searched for the operating system.

How a DOS-Based PC Uses Memory

Today's DOS-based PC typically includes 8- to 32MB of memory, well over ten times the original 640K. However, because of the limitations of the 8086 architecture—still present in today's Intel processors—memory must be accessed in several ways. These are the types of memory you can access in a PC:

- **Conventional memory:** This is the same 640K that the original IBM PC used. This area stores programs; many programs can use only this area of memory.

- **Upper memory:** This is the memory just above the 640KB area, which includes a total of 384K. Your video card, NIC, and other hardware components use a sizable amount of this space. Conventional 640K and the upper 384K add up to the first 1024K—the first megabyte of RAM.

- **Expanded memory:** This memory uses a 64K block of memory to swap memory to and from the higher areas of memory. This system is rarely used in today's PCs but remains as a standard.

- **Extended memory:** This is memory above 1MB; a computer with 16MB of RAM has only 15MB of extended memory. Today's PCs can access this memory without swapping, but use of extended memory still requires a different method of access.

Although the use of extended memory has overcome the 640KB barrier, the limit still applies to many programs, which use only conventional memory. Thus, you may even get out-of-memory errors when you have 8- or 16MB of RAM. Most likely, it's the 640KB conventional memory that is running out.

- **High memory:** This is a 64K area that begins at the 1MB boundary (an area that otherwise would be considered extended memory). It is addressed by HIMEM.SYS, which is shipped with recent versions of DOS and Windows. The most common use of high memory is for part of the COMMAND.COM file in DOS 5 and 6.*x* products from Microsoft. This allocation scheme allows DOS to take a much smaller portion of the precious 640KB area.

The IBM XT's 8086 could address a maximum of 1MB of RAM. The 286 addressed 16MB of RAM. The 80386 and later processors can address as much as 4GB. However, a computer with an 80386 processor will not always address more than 16MB. The computer's motherboard must also support the addressing. For example, the IBM PS/2 Model 80 is an 80386 machine that was commonly used as file server. System administrators who installed more RAM were disappointed to find that the IBM PS/2 Model 80 supported a maximum of 16MB, even though the Intel 80386 processor in the IBM is capable of addressing up to 4GB.

A PC operates in two modes when accessing memory: real mode and protected mode. Real mode is a backward-compatible technology developed for *x*86 processors. When a 286, 386, 486, 586, or 686 is running in real mode, it is running like an 8086 processor. This feature means that programs created for the original IBM-XT will still run on your Pentium Pro chip (and just a bit more quickly).

Protected mode was developed for 286 chips and higher. Many programmers writing for the original 8086 chip's memory walked over each other's memory, causing conflicts and instability. Protected mode helps solve this conflict by making programs request memory from the operating system.

The theory is that memory a program is using is protected by the operating system. Another program running on the PC is required to request memory from the operating system. The operating system will give access only to memory that is not used.

This section on DOS memory does not apply to the Windows NT and Windows 95 operating systems, which do not suffer the limitations of the DOS memory model.

Optimizing Memory

In its DOS 6.*x* versions, Microsoft ships two utilities to optimize memory: MEM.EXE and MEMMAKER.EXE. MEM.EXE shows current memory usage file by file, and MEMMAKER.EXE optimizes the memory settings. You can also purchase third-party memory optimization programs, such as Quarter Deck's QEMM Optimize program. IBM DOS and Novell DOS also sell memory optimization utilities.

Although MEMMAKER will almost always give you an automated configuration that is superior to manual optimization, you can sometimes outdo it. If MEMMAKER doesn't give you the results you need, try loading programs in a different order as a last resort. Because memory is filled on a first-come, first-served basis, this may allow for a more efficient arrangement.

Interrupts, Addresses, Ports, and DMA Channels

Hardware devices installed in the PC, such as modems and network cards, use interrupts, addresses, and ports to communicate with the computer.

Interrupts (IRQs)

The CPU in a PC has several inputs that allow devices to get its attention—to interrupt it—if it is performing another task. These are called interrupt requests (IRQs). Interrupts are numbered from 0 to 15. Some are used for specific purposes, and others are available for new devices you may install. Table B.2 summarizes the IRQs and their typical uses.

TABLE B.2 IRQs and Their Uses	INTERRUPT NUMBER	STANDARD USE	NOTES
	0	System timer	Reserved by system
	1	Keyboard	Standard for all machines
	2	System I/O	Reserved by system
	3	COM2/4 (serial port)	Standard for most machines
	4	COM1/3 (serial port)	Standard for most machines
	5	LPT2 (printer)	Available on most machines
	6	Floppy disk	Standard for all machines
	7	LPT1 (printer)	May be shared with some devices
	8	Real-time clock	Reserved by system
	9	Redirected IRQ2	Available in some cases
	10	Unused	Available on most machines
	11	Unused	Available on most machines
	12	Unused	Available on some machines
	13	Math coprocessor	Reserved by system if math coprocessor is installed
	14	Hard disk	Standard for most machines
	15	Unused	Available on some machines; sometimes used for hard disks

An interrupt can typically be used by one device. When you install a new device, such as a network card, in the computer, you must choose an unused interrupt. You usually specify an interrupt by setting a jumper or switch on the device or by running a special configuration program.

The interrupts listed here are for 386 and later CPUs. Although the list is similar for older systems, they do not allow the use of interrupt numbers above 9.

When two devices use the same interrupt, a conflict occurs. This conflict may cause the computer to immediately crash (refuse to function at all), or it may allow things to work normally and then crash when one or both of the devices are used. In any case, you should resolve the conflict quickly. It can seriously affect the operation of your computer, and you may lose precious data.

Ports (I/O Addresses)

Along with an interrupt, most devices use a small part of the upper memory area to send data back and forth to the CPU. This area is called a port address or an I/O address. These addresses are used in small blocks—usually 16 bytes or fewer. Addresses are specified using a hexadecimal number and typically range from 300 to 360.

As with interrupts, multiple devices using the same address can cause a conflict. The use of addresses is not as standardized as interrupts, so you will probably need to consult a device's manual to see which port address it is using.

Memory Addresses

Some devices, particularly video cards and high-speed network cards, use another area of memory as a larger buffer. These areas are specified with a hexadecimal number and usually range from C000 to E000.

DMA Channels

Another resource a device may use is a direct memory access (DMA) channel. These are high-speed interfaces to the bus that allow a device to access memory directly. DMA channels are numbered from 0 to 2 and are typically used only by time-critical devices, such as sound cards and high-speed disk controllers.

The Data Bus

A CPU by itself is useless. It can process data but can't read it from a disk or display it on your screen. For the CPU to communicate with the memory and output devices, there must be a medium through which data is transmitted. On a PC motherboard, this medium is known as the bus. The bus serves as a channel through which data is transmitted. The bus that connects the CPU to the memory on a motherboard is known as the data bus. It is made of printed-circuit wiring on the motherboard. This bus also connects to the expansion bus, which carries data to and from the bus slots that accept the adapters that allow you to add capabilities to your computer—video cards and network cards, for example.

A PC motherboard normally has several bus slots. These slots are attached to the expansion bus and are used to connect adapter cards to the motherboard. Adapter cards give a computer the ability to have serial, parallel, and game ports; to communicate across modems; to produce video output on a monitor and audio output to external speakers; and to connect to a network. Typical adapter cards include network interface cards, video cards, disk controller cards, input/output (I/O) cards, sound cards, and modems.

Controller cards may include the following:

- A disk controller, which allows the PC to communicate with disk drives

- An I/O (input/output) controller, which provides one or more serial ports, used for communications, and parallel ports, usually used for printers

- A NIC (Network Interface Card), which allows the PC to communicate with servers on the network

Internal Data Bus

Within the circuitry of the CPU is another bus, called the internal data bus. This bus carries data among the different parts of the CPU itself. A bus is measured in terms of how many bits it can carry at one time. Internal data buses of the first popular Intel CPU, the 8088, carried 8 bits at a time. Pentium 586s have 64-bit internal data buses. Apple Macintosh machines are also popular in many companies, particularly those involved with graphics design or art. The Macintosh architecture uses a 68000-series CPU developed by Motorola and an operating system created by Apple. The latest Mac operating system is System 7.5, although System 8 is in the works. New Macintosh machines called Power Macs use the PowerPC processor, a new processor line from Motorola and IBM. The PowerPC is as fast as a Pentium, and in some cases faster. The PowerPC can also run Windows NT, and a version of Novell NetWare for the PowerPC is in the works.

Hard Drives

I N MANY RESPECTS the hard drive is the most crucial component on your network. It is the basis of the file server because the network operating system resides on it. It also holds the most current files on the network. As a network administrator, you must be able to maintain this foundation for the entire network. You must carefully plan fault tolerance and frequently back up the data stored on the hard drive.

Nearly all PCs (except some notebooks and palmtop computers) support a floppy drive in addition to the hard drive. A floppy drive shares some common features with a hard drive. The main differences are that the medium used in a floppy drive is flexible ("floppy") and easily removed and that the speed at which data is read is considerably different. Since floppies are much slower than hard drives, they cannot replace hard drives for most functions.

A storage system using hard drives consists of two major components:

- The hard drive itself
- The disk controller

The hard drive is composed of fixed disks (as opposed to removable floppy disks) that are contained in a vacuum-sealed casing. These disks, often referred to as platters, are made of aluminum coated with magnetic recording material on which data is stored.

Opening the vacuum-sealed hard drive casing of a fixed disk exposes the platters to dust. This dust can scratch the platters and destroy data.

The disk controller provides the interface between the hard drive and the motherboard of the server. The disk controller communicates commands from the CPU to seek, read, or write data to the hard drive. Disk controllers commonly use one of the following interface methods:

- ST-506 (MFM or RLL)
- IDE or EIDE
- ESDI
- SCSI

How Hard Drives Work

Most hard drives contain a number of two-sided platters on which data is stored. Data is read from, and written to, the platters by what is called the read/write head. Read/write heads reside on the head arms, which move the heads across the platters. As a head is drawn across a platter surface, the data stored on that surface is read.

Within the drive casing is a small spindle motor that rotates the platters inside the drive casing at speeds of 3600 to 7200 revolutions per minute (rpm). The read/write heads are held above the platters by a head carriage. Figure B.1 illustrates the components of a hard drive.

FIGURE 2.1

Parts of a hard drive

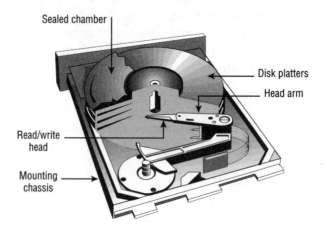

Sealed chamber

Disk platters

Head arm

Read/write head

Mounting chassis

Read/write heads normally never actually touch the platter. When a read/write head does touch the platter, destroying data, you have what is called a head crash.

A new hard disk must be partitioned and formatted before it can store files. Partitioning prepares platters for formatting, which is the process of setting up the disk for the use of the operating system.

Data is stored on the disk under a system with three main divisions:

- Tracks
- Sectors
- Cylinders

Tracks are concentric rings into which platters are divided when the hard disk is formatted. The platter is also divided into sectors, which resemble the slices of a pie (see Figure B.2). The multiple platters of a hard drive, stacked on top of each other, create cross-sections called cylinders. Within these cross-sections are minimum units of data storage.

FIGURE 2.2

Segmentation of a platter

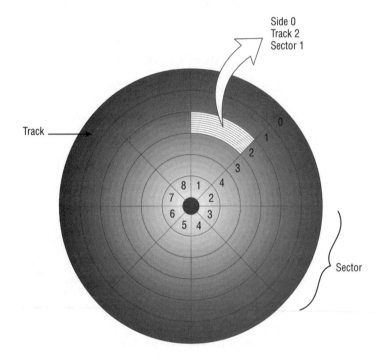

After the CPU requests data, it takes a short time for the read/write head to reach the track on which the data is stored. This is called the seek time. Once the track is reached, the platter must be rotated until the correct data is under the read/write head. The time it takes for this to happen is called drive latency. The combination of drive latency and seek time is called access time.

When the read/write head reaches the correct position on the platter, it reads the magnetically encoded data stored on the disk surface, which the disk controller interface transfers back to the CPU. The rate at which this data is transferred is called the data transfer rate. It is measured in megabytes per second.

Hard Drive Interface Types

Hard drive interfaces are the means by which hard disk controllers transfer data between the hard drive and the data bus. The interface is the method that determines how data is transferred in terms of speed, which components are utilized, and compatibility with different operating systems.

The four most common hard drive interfaces are

- ST-506

- Integrated Drive Electronics (IDE)

- Enhanced Small Device Interface (ESDI)

- Small Computer Systems Interface (SCSI)

Because familiarity with these hard drive interfaces can come in handy on occasion, let's examine them in detail.

ST-506

The ST-506 interface was built by Seagate Corporation in the 1970s to deal with 5MB hard drives. It uses a coding system called modified frequency modulation (MFM). MFM was created to fit more information on hard disks.

Run-length limited (RLL) is an encoding scheme that provides improvements over MFM. It increases data density and supports a data throughput that is 50 percent higher than the MFM encoding scheme. Both schemes are used with ST-506 drives; in fact, an MFM drive can be formatted as an RLL drive with the right controller. RLL typically fits 50 percent more data on the same drive.

Today, ST-506 drives are a part of history; no current models are available. However, you may find it on some older workstations, especially those with hard drives smaller than 80MB. You can easily recognize an ST-506 drive and controller because it uses two cables between the controller and the drive. ST-506 controllers typically support only one drive. A separate cable is usually included for one or two floppy drives.

Integrated Drive Electronics (IDE)

Western Digital Corporation developed the IDE interface in the mid-1980s, using a variation of the RLL encoding scheme. What was new with this interface was that more intelligence was built into the hard drive. With IDE, the intelligence of the interface is centered on the drive itself, instead of on the controller interface. (Although it does still require a controller, IDE controllers are simple devices.) This produces a shorter data path and protects the communication from external electrical noise.

IDE has replaced ST-506 in most of today's PCs. Drive sizes range from 340MB to 1.6GB. The IDE interface has several limitations:

- It provides a maximum drive capacity of 540MB using a standard BIOS. Newer BIOS versions support drives larger than 1GB.

- It does not support optical or tape drives. However, CD-ROM drives using the IDE interface have recently become available at low cost.

- Because IDE controllers do not support multitasking, they can slow the speed at which the network operating system issues commands to other types of drives. The IDE drive must finish its current operation before another drive can be accessed.

A new version of the IDE standard, EIDE (Enhanced IDE) is beginning to become popular. EIDE removes many of the disadvantages of IDE drives and supports higher capacities and multitasking. It also supports optical drives. Finally, EIDE drives are much faster than SCSI. To use EIDE, both the drive and the controller must support it.

Enhanced Small Device Interface (ESDI)

ESDI is an enhanced, more powerful version of the ST-506 standard. It uses the same cabling system as the ST-506 (one cable for floppy control, one for hard drive control, and one for data), but the two are not interchangeable.

ESDI can transfer data up to twice as quickly as the ST-506 and has a larger storage capacity. ESDI can also work with tape systems. Because the ESDI technology resides on the controller instead of the drive, it consumes more of the CPU's power than IDE drives. Although this interface was a popular solution for high-performance, large-capacity drives, it has now joined ST-506 as part of history. The SCSI drive system is now the preferred interface on network servers.

Small Computer Systems Interface (SCSI)

The SCSI interface is known for more than its peculiar name (pronounced "scuzzy"). Beyond being a disk interface, SCSI provides a complete expansion bus capable of connecting other SCSI-type devices, such as tape backup drives, CD-ROMs, and magneto-optical devices.

SCSI allows up to eight devices to be connected to the SCSI bus, including one host bus adapter and up to seven drive controllers. Usually, this means seven drives, but it's possible to control two drives using a single SCSI address. You must assign an address, or LUN (logical unit number), to each device. Typically the controller uses ID 7, and the drives are assigned from 0 to 6. The first drive is usually ID 0, but you can actually use any number as long as it is unique.

You can use devices that are all the same type, use different combinations of devices, or use only one device on one bus slot. A cable attaches the devices in a chain to the SCSI controller card installed in a server or client. Internally installed devices, those within the CPU, are attached with ribbon cables designed for SCSI. External devices are attached with cables that have the appropriate connectors for that type of device.

SCSI data rates are faster than IDE and ESDI because SCSI uses a parallel data communication system. SCSI supports a total of nine data lines and nine control lines.

A SCSI controller usually has a built-in BIOS. This BIOS loads into the upper memory area of the PC and controls all operations on the SCSI bus. The SCSI controller uses a DMA channel, a hardware port address, and a memory address. You must be careful to assign unique numbers to avoid a conflict with other devices in the system.

SCSI controllers usually include floppy disk controllers. If your system uses a separate floppy controller, you should disable floppy support on the SCSI controller. Many new SCSI controllers also include serial and parallel ports; the same warning applies.

A terminating resistor, or terminator, is used at each end of the SCSI bus. The terminator absorbs the signal and prevents it from reflecting back through the bus. Terminators are usually small devices that you plug into sockets near the SCSI connector on the controller and on the last drive in the chain. Many SCSI controllers and drives have built-in control over termination, and you simply have to change a jumper setting to turn termination on or off.

SCSI uses an advanced SCSI programming interface (ASPI) device driver, provided by the manufacturer.

Because drives, CPUs, and data buses are getting faster, there has recently been a need for faster versions of the SCSI standard. Several new standards have been created, with enhanced features.

Standards for the SCSI interface are set by the American National Standards Institute (ANSI) X3T9.2 committee. The committee has created a new version of the SCSI standard, simply called SCSI-2. SCSI-2 goes beyond running hard drives by defining the protocols, hardware, and command set to run other devices. Most modern drives and controllers now support the SCSI-2 standard.

Mixing SCSI-1 and SCSI-2 on the same host is not recommended unless the SCSI adapter has a method of handling both standards.

SCSI-2 has improved data rates of up to 4Mbps. Another improved standard, FAST SCSI-2, supports data rates as high as 10Mbps. For FAST SCSI-2 to operate efficiently, you need to use the appropriate SCSI interface card with the MCA, EISA, VESA, or PCI bus. The speed of SCSI-2 requires a high-speed bus.

WIDE SCSI-2 goes even further, making speeds of 20- to 40Mbps theoretically possible. WIDE SCSI-2 is a new technology, not yet as widely used as FAST SCSI-2. WIDE SCSI-2 increases speed by providing a second data path. Standard SCSI devices use a single-ended signaling process and a 50-pin cable. WIDE SCSI-2 uses a differential signaling process and 68-pin cable. Some newer SCSI host adapters include connectors for both the regular and WIDE SCSI formats.

Because they are electronically incompatible, you cannot mix differential and single-ended signaling on the same SCSI bus. If you must support both regular and WIDE SCSI, you need two controllers.

APPENDIX

C

Glossary

Microsoft ✓ *Exam Objective*

Define common networking terms for LANs and WANs.

10BASE5 A standard for transmitting Ethernet over Thicknet (1/2 inch round, 50-ohm coaxial) cable.

10BASE2 A standard for transmitting Ethernet over Thinnet (RG58) cable.

10BASET A standard for transmitting Ethernet over twisted-pair cable.

10BASEFL A standard for transmitting Ethernet over fiber-optic cable.

ACCESS PERMISSIONS A network security model in which rights to access network resources are determined on the basis of security policies stored in a user-access database on a server. A user logs on to a network. After that user has been allowed onto the network, the network security system determines access privileges in accordance with the security policies stored in the user-access database.

ACTIVE HUB A hub that amplifies transmission signals and sends them to all the computers connected to it. This type of hub is often called a *multiport repeater*.

ACTIVE MONITOR A device on a Token Ring network (usually the device that has been operating on the network for the longest time) that periodically checks the status of the network and monitors for network errors.

AMPLIFIER A type of repeater that simply amplifies the entire incoming signal. Unfortunately, it amplifies both the signal and the noise.

AMPLITUDE In communications, the distance between the highest and lowest points in a wave. The amplitude controls the strength, or volume, of the signal.

ANALOG DATA Data that has an infinite number of possible states, rather than the simple 1's and 0's of a digital signal. Audio, video, and voice telephone signals, for example, can all be represented using analog signals.

APPLETALK A networking system developed by Apple for use with Macintosh computers. The software for AppleTalk connectivity is built in to the Macintosh operating system (MacOS and System 7).

ARCNET A network topology, created by Datapoint Corporation in 1977, that can connect up to 255 nodes on coaxial, twisted-pair, or fiber-optic. ARCnet uses a token-passing scheme and typically reaches speeds up to 2.5Mbps. Some newer generations of ARCnet can reach a speed of 100Mbps.

ASYNCHRONOUS A type of communication that sends data using flow control rather than a clock to synchronize data between the source and destination.

ASYNCHRONOUS TRANSFER MODE (ATM) A network transfer method that transmits data in 53-byte packets, called *cells*. ATM is most frequently used on WANs but is sometimes used for LANs and MANs. ATM can reach speeds of up to 2.488 gigabits per second. ATM is frequently called *cell relay*.

ATTACHMENT USER INTERFACE (AUI) AUI specifies how a transceiver is attached to an Ethernet device.

ATTENUATION A communications term referring to a signal decreasing in volume (and amplitude) over a distance. The length of the cable and its resistance can affect the amount of attenuation.

BACK END The server component of a client-server system. It provides services to the front end (the client component).

BANDWIDTH In network communications, the amount of data that can be sent across a wire in a given time. Each communication that passes along the wire decreases the amount of available bandwidth.

BASEBAND A transmission technique in which the signal uses the entire bandwidth of a transmission medium. Computers can transmit across the medium only when the channel is not busy.

BAUD RATE The per-second rate of state transitions (that is, from 1 to 0 and vice versa) of a signal. Baud rates of modems define the speed at which they make state transitions. Because state transitions can represent more than a single bit each, this rate is different from the BPS rate.

BEACONING The process on a Token Ring network by which a device, in the event of a cable fault, determines the state of the network and the location of the fault.

BINARY The numbering system used in computer memory and in digital communication. All characters are represented as a series of 1's and 0's. For example, the letter *A* might be represented in a translation code as 01000001.

BINDING The process of linking a protocol to a network interface card or device driver.

BITS In binary data, each unit of data is a bit. Each bit is represented by either 0 or 1 and is stored in memory as an on or off state.

BITS PER SECOND (BPS) The amount of data transferred in a second.

BOTTLENECK A condition in which network data transfer is slowed significantly because of a problem with a network device.

BRIDGE A network interconnectivity device that selectively determines the appropriate segment to which it should pass a signal. Through address filtering, bridges can divide busy networks into segments and reduce network traffic.

BROADBAND A network transmission method in which a single transmission medium is divided and shared simultaneously.

BROADCAST STORM A network condition in which a malfunctioning network card or some other problem overwhelms a network with message broadcasts. You can use routers to limit broadcast storms.

BROUTER A network interconnectivity device that can provide both bridge and router services.

BROWNOUT A temporary decrease in the voltage level of power supplied to network devices. Brownouts are frequently called *sags*.

BUFFER In communications, an area of memory used as temporary storage for data being sent or received. The term *buffer* can refer to any area of memory in a computer.

BUS (LINEAR BUS) A network topology in which all computers are connected by a single length of cabling with a terminator at each end. The bus is the simplest and most widely used network design.

BYTE The unit of data storage and communication in computers. In PC systems a byte is usually 8 bits, or an 8-digit binary number. A single byte can represent numbers between 0 and 255.

CARRIER SENSE MULTIPLE ACCESS WITH COLLISION DETECTION (CSMA/CD)
This is the protocol by which Ethernet devices share access to an Ethernet network.

CELLS The data blocks used by ATM. Cells are exactly 53 octets long.

CHANNEL SERVICE UNITS/DIGITAL SERVICE UNITS (CSUS/DSUS)
Network interconnectivity devices that connect a network to the public telephone network. CSUs/DSUs translate signals and shield networks from noise and high voltage on the public network.

CHIP CREEP A situation in which integrated circuits gradually lose contact with their sockets because of temperature changes.

CIRCUIT A communications channel established between two network devices.

CIRCUIT SWITCHING A type of data transmission in which a circuit is established between endpoints and data is sent in a stream through a network.

CLADDING In fiber-optic cabling, a layer of glass that surrounds the inner core and reflects light back into the core.

CLIENT-SERVER ARCHITECTURE A network architecture in which clients request data, programs, and services from servers. The servers then provide the data, programs, and services to the clients. Applications written for the client-server architecture typically have different components for the server and for the client. Client-server architecture allows clients to exploit the processing power of the server.

CLIENT-SERVER NETWORK A server-centric network in which some network resources are stored on a file server, while processing power is distributed among workstations and the file server.

COAXIAL CABLE One type of cable used in network wiring. Typical coax types include RG-58 and RG-62. The 10base2 system of Ethernet networking uses coaxial cable. Coaxial cable is usually shielded. The thicknet system uses a thicker coaxial cable.

COLLISION A situation that occurs when two or more network devices transmit at the same time, through the same channel. The two signals transmitted meet and cause data to be destroyed.

CONCENTRATOR See *hub*.

CONGESTION A condition in which a network transmission medium is overwhelmed with network traffic, causing network performance to decline.

CROSSTALK Interference, or noise, created on a network transmission medium by another physically adjacent medium. This interference can corrupt data.

DATAGRAM PACKET-SWITCHED NETWORK A type of network on which messages are divided into a stream of separately addressed packets. Each packet is routed independently. The packets are reassembled at the destination address.

DECODING The process of translating a message from a transmittable standard form to the native form of the recipient.

DECRYPTION The opposite of *encryption*.

DEDICATED LINE A transmission medium that is used exclusively between two locations. Dedicated lines are also known as leased lines or private lines.

DEDICATED SERVER A computer that functions only as a server and is not used as a client or workstation.

DEMARCATION POINT The point inside your building (or on the campus premises) at which the phone company (or other service provider) is no longer responsible for network cabling or service.

DIGITAL DATA Data that uses 1's and 0's to store information.

DIGITAL INTEL XEROX (DIX) Another term for the AUI connector.

DIGITAL LINE A data or voice network interconnectivity medium that supports digital signaling.

DIGITAL SIGNALING Data transmission in the form of discrete units (on or off, 1 or 0, and so on).

DISTANCE-VECTOR ROUTING A method of route discovery in which each router on the network broadcasts the information contained in its routing table. The other routers then update their routing tables with the broadcast information they receive.

DOMAIN In Windows NT Server, a group of computers that share the same security and logon authentication database.

DUPLEXING A method of using a second hard drive with a second hard drive controller to provide fault tolerance.

DYNAMIC ROUTE SELECTION Uses the cost information that is continually being generated by routing algorithms and placed in routing tables to select the best route for each packet. As network conditions change, the router can select the best path.

ELECTROMAGNETIC INTERFERENCE (EMI) A type of low-voltage, low-current, high-frequency signal that interferes with normal network transmission. EMI is typically caused by improper insulation or insufficient grounding.

ELECTROSTATIC DISCHARGE (ESD) An electric shock created by a buildup of static electricity. ESD frequently damages computer components.

ENCODING The process of translating a message from the native form of the sender to a transmittable standard form.

ENCRYPTION The encoding of messages for security reasons. Also called *ciphering*.

ETHERNET The most popular network specification. Developed by Xerox in 1976, Ethernet offers a transfer rate of 10Mbps. Ethernet uses a bus topology and thick or thin coaxial, fiber-optic, or twisted-pair cabling.

FIBER DISTRIBUTED DATA INTERFACE (FDDI) A network specification that defines the transmission of information packets using light produced by a laser or light-emitting diode (LED). FDDI uses fiber-optic cable and equipment to transmit data packets. It has a data rate of up to 100Mbps and allows very long cable distances.

FIBER-OPTICS One medium type used for network communications. Fiber-optics uses a tiny glass or plastic fiber and sends a light signal through it.

FILE TRANSFER PROTOCOL (FTP) A TCP/IP protocol that permits the transferring of files between computer systems. Because FTP has been implemented on numerous types of computer systems, file transfers can be done between different computer systems (for example, a personal computer and a minicomputer).

FRAME A unit of data, often called a *packet* or *block,* that can be transmitted across a network or internetwork. The term *frame* is most frequently used regarding Ethernet networks.

FREQUENCY The repetition rate, usually of a signal, usually reported in cycles per second, or Hz.

FRONT END The client component of a client-server system. A front-end application works with a back-end component stored on a server.

GATEWAY A network interconnectivity device that translates communications protocols.

GROUPWARE Applications that involve group interaction across a network (excepting simple e-mail). Lotus Notes and Microsoft Exchange are two popular groupware packages.

GUARANTEED STATE CHANGES A type of synchronous timing coordination, used by synchronous modems, in which the clock information is embedded in the data signal.

HANDSHAKING The exchange of codes between two devices in order to negotiate the transmission and reception of data.

HOP In routing, a server or router that is counted in a hop count.

HOP COUNT The number of routers a message must pass through to reach its destination. You use hop counts to determine the most efficient network route.

HUB A network connectivity device that brings media segments together in a central location. The hub is the central controlling device in some star networks. The two main types are active hubs and passive hubs. See also *active hub, intelligent hub,* and *passive hub.*

INTEGRATED SERVICES DIGITAL NETWORK (ISDN) A CCITT standard for digital communications. ISDN lines allow voice, video, and data transfer all on the same line.

INTELLIGENT HUB A hub that provides network management and intelligent path selection in addition to signal regeneration.

INTERCONNECTIVITY DEVICES Devices that connect independent networks. They include routers, brouters, gateways, and CSUs/DSUs.

INTERNETWORK Two or more independent networks that are connected and yet maintain independent identities. Internetworks are joined by interconnectivity devices.

INTERRUPTS Inputs to the CPU in a PC that allow devices to get its attention—to interrupt it— if it is performing another task. Interrupts are also called *IRQs* (for interrupt requests).

ISDN MODEM An interconnectivity device that connects a computer to an ISDN line.

LEASED LINE A communications circuit permanently established for a single customer. Also called a *private line*.

LINK-STATE ROUTING A type of routing in which routers broadcast their complete routing tables only at startup and infrequent intervals.

LOCAL AREA NETWORK (LAN) A number of computers in close proximity linked together through network media.

MEDIA ACCESS PROTOCOL A specification for arbitrating access to physical network media among all devices that wish to transmit on the network. CSMA/CD is a media access protocol.

MESSAGE SWITCHING The process of transmitting messages over a network, where each message is routed through the network independently.

METROPOLITAN AREA NETWORK (MAN) A network larger than a local area network (LAN) but smaller than a wide area network (WAN) MANs span a single city or metropolitan area.

MICROWAVES A type of unbounded network transmission medium. Microwaves are most often used to transmit data across satellite links and between earth-based equipment, such as telephone relay towers. Microwave transmission is commonly used to transmit signals when bounded media, such as cable, cannot be used.

MIRRORING The process of keeping a constant backup of server hard drive data on a second hard drive (or, in some cases, on another drive partition on the same drive). Every change made to the data on the primary hard drive is also immediately made on the second hard drive, so that if the first hard drive fails, the second can take over. This is similar to disk duplexing, but doesn't require separate hard drive controllers.

MODEM A device that converts the digital communications of a computer into analog signals that can be carried over a regular telephone line.

MODULATION The process of modifying a carrier signal to transmit information.

MULTIPLEXER A device that multiplexes signals for transmission over a segment and reverses this process for multiplexed signals coming in from the segment. Frequently shortened to *mux*.

MULTIPLE STATION ACCESS UNIT (MSAU) The hub in a Token Ring network.

MULTIPLEXING A method of sharing a single medium segment by combining several channels for transmission over that segment using a multiplexer. Multiplexed signals are later separated at the receiving end in a process called *demultiplexing*.

MULTIPORT REPEATER See *active hub*.

MUX See *multiplexer*.

NETWORK A group of computers and various devices (such as printers and routers) that are joined together on a common network transmission medium.

NETWORK ADDRESS A unique address that identifies each node, or device, on the network. The network address is generally hardcoded into the network card on both the workstation and server. Some network cards allow you to change this address, but there is seldom a reason to do so.

NETWORK CONNECTIVITY Linking of segments of a single network.

NODE Any network device (such as a server, workstation, or router) that can communicate across the network.

NOISE A low-voltage, low-current, high-frequency signal that interferes with normal network transmissions, often corrupting data.

OCTET Exactly 8 bits of data. Bytes are usually, but not always, 8 bits. Octets are always 8 bits.

OPEN SYSTEM INTERCONNECTION (OSI) A model defined by the International Standards Organization (ISO) to conceptually organize the process of communication between computers in terms of seven layers, called *protocol stacks*. The seven layers of the OSI model provide a way for you to understand how communications across various protocols take place.

OPTICAL FIBER Glass filament cable that conveys signals using light rather than electricity.

OVERSAMPLING A type of synchronous communication in which the receiver samples the signal at ten times the data rate. One of the ten samples provides the data; the other nine provide clocking information.

PACKET The basic division of data sent over a network. Each packet contains a set amount of data along with a header containing information about the type of packet and the network address to which it is being sent. The size and format of a packet depend on the protocol and frame types used.

PACKET SWITCHING A type of data transmission in which data is divided into packets, each of which has a destination address. Each packet is then routed optimally across a network. An addressed packet may travel a different route than packets related to it. Packet sequence numbers are used at the destination node to reassemble related packets.

PARITY CHECKING A simple form of error checking employed by asynchronous modems. Extra bits added to data words can indicate when data transmission has been flawed.

PASSIVE HUB A hub that simply combines the signals of network segments, with no signal processing or regeneration.

PASSWORD-PROTECTED SHARES A network security model in which passwords are required for gaining access to each shared resource on a network.

PEER-TO-PEER NETWORK A local area network in which network resources are shared among workstations, without a file server.

PHASE The amplitude of a cyclic signal at a specific point in time.

PLANT The wires that connect computers together in a LAN.

PLENUM The space between the ceiling of an office and the floor above. Usually, fire codes require that only special, plenum-grade cable be used in this space.

POINT-TO-POINT Network communication in which two devices have exclusive access to a network medium. For example, a printer connected to only one workstation would be using a point-to-point connection.

POINT-TO-POINT PROTOCOL (PPP) Allows the sending of IP packets on a dial-up (serial) connection. It supports compression and IP address negotiation.

PROPRIETARY Describes a system that is defined by one vendor and typically not supported by others. ARCnet started as a proprietary protocol, as did Token Ring.

PROTOCOL ANALYZER A device that monitors network activity, providing statistics you can use in determining baseline and optimum performance.

PROTOCOLS The specifications that define procedures used by computers when they transmit and receive data. In other words, the rules by which computers communicate.

PROTOCOL STACK (SUITE) A collection of protocols that are associated with and implement a particular communication model (such as the DOD Networking Model or the OSI Reference Model).

PUBLIC SWITCHED TELEPHONE NETWORK (PSTN) A term that includes the network used to make ordinary telephone calls and modem communications, as well as dedicated lines that are leased by customers for private, exclusive use. Commercial service providers offer numerous services that facilitate computer communication across PSTN.

RADIO FREQUENCY INTERFERENCE (RFI) Noise created in the radio-frequency range.

REDIRECTOR Software loaded onto a workstation that can forward or redirect requests away from the local bus of the computer onto a network. These requests are then handled by a server. This type of software is often called a *shell, requester,* or *client.*

REDUNDANT ARRAYS OF INEXPENSIVE DISKS (RAID) A technique for achieving fault tolerance on a network by using several hard disks. If one or more drives fail, network data can be saved.

RELATIVE EXPENSE A measure of the actual monetary cost when a given link is used during routing.

REPEATER A network connectivity device that amplifies network signals to extend the distance they can travel.

REQUESTER See *redirector*.

RING A network topology in which computers are arranged in a circle. Data travels around the ring in one direction, with each device on the ring acting as a repeater. Ring networks typically use a token-passing protocol.

ROUTABLE PROTOCOLS Protocols that support internetwork communication.

ROUTE DISCOVERY The process a router uses to find the possible routes through the internetwork and then build routing tables to store that information.

ROUTER An intelligent internetwork connectivity device that routes using logical and physical addressing to connect two or more logically separate networks. Routers use algorithms to determine the best path by which to send a packet.

RS-232 The most common serial communications system in use.

SAG See *brownout*.

SEGMENTATION The process of splitting a larger network into two or more segments linked by bridges or routers.

SEPARATE CLOCK SIGNAL A method of synchronous communication in which a separate channel carries clocking information.

SERIAL LINE INTERNET PROTOCOL (SLIP) A protocol that permits the sending of IP packets on a dial-up (serial) connection. It does not by itself provide support for compression or for IP address negotiation.

SHIELDED TWISTED-PAIR A type of wiring that includes a pair of conductors inside a metal or foil shield. This type of medium can support faster speeds than non-shielded wiring. See also *twisted-pair*.

SIGNALING The process of sending information over media.

SIGNAL-REGENERATING REPEATERS A type of repeater that eliminates noise by creating an exact duplicate of incoming data, identifying it amidst the noise, reconstructing it, and retransmitting only the desired information.

SOURCE-ROUTING BRIDGE A type of bridge that requires a predefined route to be included with the addresses of signals it receives. IBM Token Ring networks use this type of bridge.

SPIKE See *transient*.

SPOOLER A software program that stores documents until they can be printed and coordinates how print jobs are sent to a printer.

STAND-ALONE ENVIRONMENT Computers operating without connection to a network.

STANDBY MONITOR A device on a Token Ring network that monitors the network status and may become the active monitor in the case of failure of the active monitor.

STAR A network topology in which all the cables run from the computers to a central location, where they are connected by a hub.

START BIT A bit that is sent as part of a serial communication stream to signal the beginning of a byte or packet.

STATIC ROUTE SELECTION A type of routing in which the data path is determined in advance rather than on the fly by the router.

STOP BIT A bit that is sent as part of a serial communications stream to signal the end of a byte or packet.

SUBNETS (SUBNETWORKS) Routers organize networks in logical network segments, known as subnets or subnetworks, to facilitate internetwork packet transmission. Each subnet or subnetwork is given a logical address.

SWITCHING In a LAN environment, switching provides each network transmission with an independent path through the network free of collisions with other network transmissions.

SYNCHRONOUS MODEM A connectivity device that uses careful timing and coordination between modems to send large blocks of data without start and stop bits.

SYNCHRONOUS TRANSMISSION A type of transmission that uses a clock to control the timing of bits being sent.

T-CARRIER A type of multiplexed, high-speed, leased line. T-carrier service levels include T1, T2, T3, and T4. T-carriers offer transmission rates of up to 274Mbps.

TCP/IP Transmission Control Protocol/Internet Protocol. Generally used as shorthand for the phrase *TCP/IP protocol suite.*

TERMINATOR A device at the end of a cable segment that indicates that the last node has been reached. In the case of Ethernet cable, a 50-ohm resistor (a terminator) at both ends of the cable prevents signals from reflecting back through the cable.

THROUGHPUT The amount of data that has been sent over a given time. For example, 10baseT Ethernet has a theoretical maximum throughput of 10Mbps. In practice, the throughput depends on the quality and length of wiring and is usually slightly less than 10Mbps.

TICK COUNT A term used to quantify routing costs. A tick count refers to the amount of time required for a message to reach its destination.

TIME-DIVISION MULTIPLEXING (TDM) A type of multiplexing in which a channel is divided into time slots that are allocated to each communicating device.

TOKEN PASSING A network access method used by FDDI, Token Ring, and Token Bus networks. A short message (token) is passed around the ring. To transmit, a node must be in possession of a token. This prevents multiple nodes from transmitting simultaneously and creating collisions.

TOKEN RING A network that uses a token-passing protocol in a logical ring. A token is a small frame with a special format that designates that its holder (a network device) may transmit. When a node needs to transmit, it captures a token and attaches a message to it, along with addressing information. Token Ring transmits at 4- or 16Mbps.

TOPOLOGY A type of network connection or cabling system. Networks are usually configured in bus, ring, star, or mesh topology.

TRANSCEIVER The device that performs both the transmission and reception of signals on a given medium.

TRANSIENT A high-voltage burst of electric current, usually lasting less than 1 second, occurring randomly. Transients are often referred to as *spikes.*

TRANSPARENT BRIDGE A type of bridge that determines where to send data based on a table of addresses stored in memory.

TROJAN HORSE A dangerous or destructive program that is designed to disguise itself as something harmless.

TWISTED-PAIR A type of wiring used for network communications that uses copper wires twisted into pairs.

UNSHIELDED TWISTED-PAIR A type of cable usually containing four pairs of wire, each pair twisted to reduce interference. Commonly used in telephone and LAN cabling.

VAMPIRE TAP A specific type of Ethernet transceiver on a Thicknet network. The vampire tap does not break the Thicknet cable, but instead pierces the jacket of the cable to contact the center conductor.

VIRTUAL CIRCUIT A logical connection made between two devices across a shared communications path. There is no dedicated physical circuit between the devices, even though they are acting as though there is one.

VIRTUAL CIRCUIT PACKET SWITCHING An internetwork transmission technique in which all packets travel through a logical connection established between the sending device and the receiving device.

VIRUS A dangerous or destructive program that alters stored files or system configuration and copies itself onto external disks or other computers.

WIDE AREA NETWORK (WAN) A network typically spanning multiple cities.

WORD The standard unit of data manipulated by a computer. A word typically consists of 8, 16, 32, or 64 bits.

WORKGROUP A group of computers linked together to share resources. A workgroup is less sophisticated than a domain in that workgroups lack the central administrative capacities of a domain.

WORLD WIDE WEB (WWW) The collection of computers on the Internet running HTTP (hypertext transfer protocol) servers. The WWW allows for text and graphics to have hyperlinks connecting users to other servers. By using a Web browser, such as Netscape or Internet Explorer, a user can cross-link from one server to another at the click of a button.

WORM A destructive or dangerous program that can spawn another fully working version of itself.

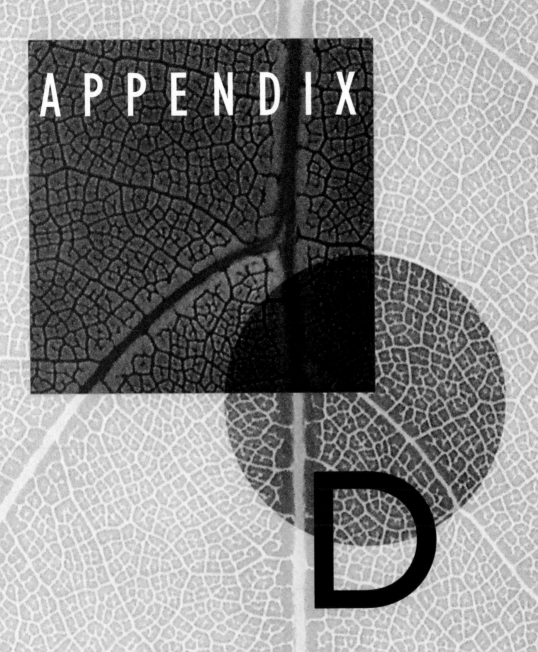

APPENDIX

D

Answers

Chapter 1 Answers

1. You are installing a new network for a company that is growing rapidly. The current design calls for 40 computers, with expansion to 100 in the next six months. Because of the speed at which the network is expected to grow, you want to make sure that troubleshooting will be as easy as possible. Considering these factors, which of the following topologies should be used in the new network?

   A. Star

   B. Ring

   C. Mesh

   D. Bus

   Answer: A

2. The Windows NT operating system provides many features that take advantage of advanced server hardware. Which of the following features are supported by Windows NT? Choose all that apply:

   A. Extremely large file size

   B. Intel and RISC microprocessors

   C. Symmetric Multiprocessing

   D. Plug-and-Play

   Answer: A, B, C

3. You manage a small engineering firm that has 10 employees, all with their own computers. Sharing resources has become a necessity, but cost is an issue. You trust each of your employees to handle their computers responsibly. Which of the following network types would be best to install in your situation?

   A. Hybrid

   B. Mainframe/terminal

   C. Peer-to-peer

   D. Server-based

   Answer: C

4. Which of the following network topologies degrades most gracefully in high network load situations?

A. Star

B. Ring

C. Mesh

D. Bus

Answer: B

5. The network that you support includes 14 separate offices nationwide, connected via T-1 lines. What kind of network do you have?

A. Campus Area Network

B. LAN

C. MAN

D. WAN

Answer: D

6. You are planning a network installation for a small design firm. The majority of the staff is not terribly computer savvy, so centralized administration and backups are important. However, the CAD/CAM team is very experienced and is able to handle much of their own networking needs. Which of the following network types is best suited to your situation?

A. Hybrid

B. Mainframe/terminal

C. Peer-to-peer

D. Server-based

Answer: A

7. You need to connect two buildings on your corporate campus with a high-speed link. Due to security concerns, it must be immune to electro-magnetic interference and highly secure. Which of the following media types should you choose?

   A. Air (wireless infra-red)

   B. Copper

   C. Glass

   D. Radio

   Answer: C

8. Which of the following best describes a network that connects computers in the same building?

   A. Campus Area Network

   B. LAN

   C. MAN

   D. WAN

   Answer: B

9. Suppose the following situation exists: Your company has decided to network some of its existing computers. The manager would like to get the operations staff networked together first, then, if all goes well, move on to the rest of the company. There are 22 computers in operations, and 45 computers in the rest of the company.

   Required result: You must have a highly reliable topology that tolerates problems with individual computers.

   Optional desired results: The lowest setup costs of any topology. The network should be relatively easy to expand.

   Proposed solution: Implement a ring topology network.

Which result does the proposed solution produce?

A. The proposed solution produces the required result and produces both of the optional desired results.

B. The proposed solution produces the required result and produces only one of the optional desired results.

C. The proposed solution produces the required result but does not produce any of the optional desired results.

D. The proposed solution does not produce the required result.

Answer: D

10. You have been asked to wire a conference room with six computers for a demonstration tomorrow. It needs be done quickly and with the lowest possible expense. What network topology is best suited to this situation?

A. Star

B. Ring

C. Mesh

D. Bus

Answer: D

11. You have been asked to put together a proposal for a new computer network for your company. Your boss has asked you to specifically list the advantages to networking. Of the following equipment your company owns, which devices can be shared on a network? Choose all that apply:

A. Keyboards

B. Scanners

C. CD-ROM drives

D. Printers

Answer: B, C, D

12. Your computer network must be fairly secure, but as transparent as possible. It is very important that you are able to control access to resources by user account. What type of security should you implement?

    A. Physical

    B. Peer-based

    C. Server-based

    D. Hybrid

    Answer: C

13. Your company has asked you to provide a plan to network an auditorium for a large presentation. Speed is not an issue, nor is cost. However, the presentation manager is concerned that attendees will trip over cables and take the whole network down. Which of the following media would be appropriate to implement this network? Choose all that apply:

    A. Air (wireless infra-red)

    B. Copper

    C. Glass

    D. Radio

    Answer: A, D

14. As a consultant, you have been asked to design a network for a mid-sized accounting firm. Because of the data handled by the company, security is extremely important. The network must support 80 computers with easy expandability to more than 100 in the next few months. What type of network would be best for you to install at your client's office?

    A. Internet

    B. Mainframe/terminal

    C. Peer-to-peer

    D. Server-based

    Answer: D

15. The Internet is a collection of redundant high-speed wide-area links. Which network topology does the Internet use?

    A. Star

    B. Ring

    C. Mesh

    D. Bus

    Answer: C

16. You want to implement a network with the most readily available and widely supported media. Which of the following media types would you choose?

    A. Air (wireless infra-red)

    B. Copper

    C. Glass

    D. Radio

    Answer: B

17. You are planning a small server-based network with requirements for file, print, e-mail, and database services. You are leaning toward using Windows NT as your server operating system. What is the minimum number of servers you will need?

    A. One

    B. Two

    C. Three

    D. Four

    Answer: A

18. Your boss is considering implementing a bus topology network. Which of the following arguments could you use to dissuade him from this decision? Choose all that apply:

    A. A loose connector can interfere with network communication.

    B. Heavy network traffic can slow a bus network considerably.

    C. Failure of one computer in the network interrupts communication throughout the network.

    D. A cable break disrupts communication on the network

    Answer: A, B, D

19. In a client/server networking environment, the processing (choose all that apply):

    A. Takes place only on the client side.

    B. Is shared between the client and the server.

    C. Of requests by the client is handled by the server.

    D. Takes place only on the server side.

    Answer: B, C

20. Which of the following statements describe benefits of a ring topology network? Choose all that apply:

    A. It requires fiber-optic cable.

    B. It gracefully handles increased numbers of computers.

    C. A single computer failure does not affect network communication.

    D. It ensures equal access to the media for all computers.

    Answer: B, D

21. A series of star networks connected together (hubs linked, but not in a loop) is what?

    A. A hybrid ring

    B. A hybrid mesh

    C. A star bus

    D. A hybrid star

    Answer: C

22. What kind of topology is Token Ring? Choose the most correct answer:

    A. Star Ring

    B. Star Bus

    C. Hybrid Star

    D. Mesh

    Answer: A

Chapter 2 Answers

1. One cable run in your UTP network is nearly 100 meters long. Which of the following should first be considered if this run experiences communication problems?

    A. EMI

    B. Crosstalk

    C. Attenuation

    D. Dispersion

    Answer: C

2. The cabling in your new building must be run through walls and drop ceilings. To meet the fire codes, what type of cable must be used?

   A. Fire-retardant

   B. Gel-filled

   C. Plenum

   D. PVC

   Answer: C

3. Which of the following cable types supports the highest bandwidth?

   A. Coaxial

   B. Fiber-optic

   C. STP

   D. UTP

   Answer: B

4. Which of the following cable types would be used to transmit at speeds of 1.2 Gbps and higher?

   A. Coaxial

   B. Fiber-optic

   C. STP

   D. UTP

   Answer: B

5. You have recently installed a new network adapter card in your computer and connected it to the twisted-pair network. However, when you try to communicate on the network, you get no response. The NIC is

configured with IRQ 7 and port address 320h. Which of the following is most likely the problem?

A. The network has another adapter with the same Ethernet MAC address.

B. The network cable is improperly terminated.

C. LPT 1 is conflicting with the adapter's interrupt setting.

D. COM 2 is conflicting with the adapter's interrupt setting.

Answer: C

6. What is the standard cable type used with IBM's Token Ring network specification?

A. Coaxial

B. Fiber-optic

C. STP

D. UTP

Answer: C

7. By nature, fiber-optic cables are less susceptible to outside factors than are other types of cable. Which of the following do not significantly affect fiber-optic LAN cables? Choose all that apply:

A. EMI

B. Crosstalk

C. Attenuation

D. Dispersion

Answer: A, B, C

8. The four buildings on your campus form a rough square, approximately 250 meters on a side. You have been asked to provide your boss with cable specifications that will provide connectivity between the buildings.

Which of the following cable types could you easily use without additional equipment? Choose all that apply:

A. Coaxial

B. Fiber-optic

C. STP

D. UTP

Answer: A, B

9. Which of the following cable types is the least expensive that can support 100 Mbps?

A. Coaxial

B. Fiber-optic

C. STP

D. UTP

Answer: D

10. Your production facility has a new inventory program that requires access to the network. However, as with most production environments, EMI is a concern. Because of the layout of the building, additional cables cannot be run. Which of the following radio technologies is least susceptible to EMI?

A. AM

B. Low power, single frequency

C. High power, single frequency

D. Spread spectrum

Answer: D

11. Which type of cabling is considered "Category 5" by the Electrical Industries Association (EIA)?

    A. STP

    B. unshielded twisted-pair

    C. token ring

    D. coaxial

    Answer: B

12. Which type of network card offers the best performance?

    A. An EISA card with I/O memory transfer

    B. An EISA card with shared memory transfer

    C. An ISA card with I/O memory transfer

    D. An ISA card with shared memory transfer

    Answer: B

13. The design for the network you are implementing calls for numerous cable runs in a production plant. The plant makes silicon molds and uses many machines that are powered by electricity. What should your primary concern be for these cables?

    A. EMI

    B. Crosstalk

    C. Attenuation

    D. Dispersion

    Answer: A

Chapter 3 Answers

1. Historically, telegraph operators translated the Morse code they received into language their bosses understood. Which layer of the OSI model performs a similar function, translating binary data into language the application layer understands?

    A. 1 - Network

    B. 6 - Presentation layer

    C. 5 - Session layer

    D. 4 - Transport layer

    Answer: B

2. Which layer of the OSI model is responsible for translating the data format?

    A. Application layer

    B. Network layer

    C. Presentation layer

    D. Data Link layer

    Answer: C

3. Your MAN encompasses two offices on opposite sides of town that are connected via a leased 56K line. However, computers in each office are not able to communicate with computers in the other office. You believe there is a router configuration problem. At which layer of the OSI model does this problem reside?

    A. 4 - Transport

    B. 3 - Network

    C. 2 - Logical link

    D. 1 - Physical

    Answer: B

4. Your network includes both NetWare 3.*x* and Windows NT servers. You prefer to use only one protocol. Which of the following protocols would best suit your situation?

    A. NWLink

    B. RFC

    C. AppleTalk

    D. NetBEUI

    Answer: A

5. Which of the following connectivity devices typically work at the Physical layer of the OSI model?

    A. routers

    B. bridges

    C. repeaters

    D. gateways

    Answer: C

6. Compression is often used to increase the speed on a network. Which of the following layers of the OSI model is responsible for compression and decompression of data?

    A. Application

    B. Presentation

    C. Session

    D. Transport

    Answer: B

7. The IEEE 802 project divides the Data Link layer into two sublayers. Which sublayer of the Data Link layer communicates directly with the network interface card?

   A. Logical Link Control sublayer

   B. Logical Access Control sublayer

   C. Media Access Control sublayer

   D. Data Access Control sublayer

   Answer: C

8. Which TCP/IP Transport layer protocol is the fastest?

   A. ICMP because it is connection-oriented

   B. TCP because it is connection-oriented

   C. IP because it is connectionless

   D. UDP because it is connectionless

   Answer: D

9. At which layer of the OSI model would a communication problem due to an improperly terminated cable reside?

   A. 5 - Session

   B. 4 - Transport

   C. 2 - Data link

   D. 1 - Physical

   Answer: D

10. Connection-oriented network communication is best described by which of the following statements?

   A. It is only used in Ethernet networks.

   B. It provides fast but unreliable delivery.

   C. It provides guaranteed delivery.

   D. All network communications are connection-oriented.

   Answer: C

11. Which of the following network protocols do not contain Network layer information and thus cannot be routed? Choose all that apply:

    A. IPX/SPX (NWLink)

    B. NDS

    C. NetBEUI

    D. TCP/IP

    Answer: C

12. Which layer of the OSI model packages raw data bits into data frames?

    A. Physical layer

    B. Network layer

    C. Presentation layer

    D. Data Link layer

    Answer: D

13. If, through an error in manufacturing, two network cards were created with the same MAC address, which layer of the OSI model would discover the problem?

    A. 4 - Topological

    B. 3 - Application

    C. 2 - Data link

    D. 1 - Physical

    Answer: C

14. Which layers of the OSI model are specified by IEEE 802?

    A. The Data Link and Network layers

    B. The Physical and Data Link layers

    C. The Transport and Session layers

    D. The Network and Transport layers

    Answer: B

15. The speed of a protocol often depends on the amount of overhead information it carries. Which of the following protocols doesn't have routing overhead, and therefore is fairly fast?

A. DLC

B. NWLink

C. NetBEUI

D. TCP/IP

Answer: C

16. Part of IEEE Project 802 defined the sublayer (of the Data Link layer) at which bridges communicate. What is the name of this sublayer?

A. the Physical layer

B. the Transport layer

C. the Media Access Control layer

D. the Network layer

Answer: C

17. The IEEE 802 group has developed many networking standards. Which specification defines the rules for using Ethernet over fiber-optic cable?

A. 802.2

B. 802.3

C. 802.5

D. 802.8

Answer: D

18. Several companies in the computer network industry have developed driver interfaces that allow multiple cards to be bound to multiple transport protocols. There are two widely used driver interfaces; one developed by Microsoft, one developed by Apple, Novell and other networking companies. What are they? Choose two:

A. ATM

B. ODI

C. OSI

D. NDIS

Answer: B, D

Chapter 4 Answers

1. When installing an Ethernet 10BaseT network, what type of cable is used?

    A. Fiber-optic cable

    B. None

    C. Thinnet coaxial

    D. Twisted-pair cable

    Answer: D

2. You have been asked to implement a new high-speed network for your server connections. Because you are currently running Ethernet, you would like to remain within its standards. Which of the following will provide you with the highest possible speed?

    A. 10baseFL

    B. 10baseT

    C. 100VG-AnyLAN

    D. 10base5

    Answer: C

3. In an Ethernet network, what method is used to access the media?

   A. Demand Priority

   B. CSMA/CD

   C. Polling

   D. CSMA/CA

   Answer: B

4. To prevent signal attenuation, what is the maximum number of repeaters that can be placed on one 10Base5 or 10Base2 network?

   A. Three

   B. Four

   C. Five

   D. Any number

   Answer: B

5. A Macintosh computer using LocalTalk for network communications ensures that data is successfully transmitted by using which of the following media access methods?

   A. Token Passing

   B. Polling

   C. CSMA/CD

   D. CSMA/CA

   Answer: D

6. Which of the following are true of 10BaseT networks? Choose all that apply:

   A. They use fiber-optic cable.

   B. They use hubs as the central point of connection.

   C. They must be terminated at each end.

   D. They utilize Category 3 UTP.

   Answer: B, D

7. Which of the following thicknet Ethernet components is used to make new connections?

   A. NCB T connector

   B. A Terminating Resistor

   C. A Vampire Tap

   D. A DIX connector

   Answer: C

8. Fiber-optic cable is used in which of the following Ethernet networks?

   A. 10BaseFL

   B. 10Base5

   C. 10BaseT

   D. 10Base2

   Answer: A

9. The building your company occupies has been pre-wired with Category 3 UTP. Which of the following fast Ethernet standards could you possibly implement without rewiring the building?

   A. 100baseT5

   B. 100baseFX

   C. 100baseT4

   D. 100baseTX

   Answer: C

10. A BNC terminator is used in which of the following Ethernet networks? Choose all that apply:

   A. 10base5

   B. 10base2

   C. 10baseT

   D. 10baseFL

   Answer: A, B

11. Through extensive testing you have learned that network utilization has steadily increased over the last year to over 66 percent. Your four file servers have increased utilization commensurate with the increase in network traffic. You are currently serving 153 clients on a 10BaseT Ethernet network.

    Required result: Reduce network utilization to below 50 percent.

    Optional desired results: The network is Ethernet. The new network must be easily expandable.

    Proposed solution: Upgrade network to 100BaseTX by replacing all hubs, NICs, and any wiring necessary.

    Which result does the proposed solution produce?

    A. The proposed solution produces the required result and produces both of the optional desired results.

    B. The proposed solution produces the required result and produces only one of the optional desired results.

    C. The proposed solution produces the required result but does not produce any of the optional desired results.

    D. The proposed solution does not produce the required result.

    Answer: A

12. In some types of networks, a special packet called the token is used to guarantee access to the network media. Which of the following networks use this method? Choose all that apply:

    A. ARCnet

    B. FDDI

    C. ATM

    D. Token Ring

    Answer: A, B, D

13. The IEEE 10Base5 Ethernet standard specifies what type of cable?

   A. Fiber-optic cable

   B. Thicknet coaxial

   C. Twisted-pair cable

   D. None

   Answer: B

14. A terminator prevents the electronic signal sent by a computer from bouncing across the network. Which of the following Ethernet implementations require terminators? Choose all that apply:

   A. 100base5

   B. 10base5

   C. 10baseF

   D. 10base2

   Answer: B, D

15. In planning your Token Ring network, you have chosen to use STP cable. What is the maximum distance a client workstation can be from the MAU using STP?

   A. 50 feet

   B. 100 feet

   C. 50 meters

   D. 100 meters

   Answer: D

16. A 10Base2 Ethernet network uses what type of cable?

   A. None

   B. Twisted-pair cable

   C. Thicknet coaxial

   D. Thinnet coaxial

   Answer: D

17. In your new network design, there is a requirement to place a workstation at the far end of the building. You are going to be installing a 10BaseT Ethernet network, but are worried that this run might be too long. What is the maximum length of a 10BaseT cable?

A. 25 meters

B. 50 meters

C. 75 meters

D. 100 meters

Answer: D

18. Your company is expanding to include offices in the building next door. The buildings are approximately 400 meters apart. Which of the following Ethernet cable types could you use? Choose all that apply:

A. 10base2

B. 10base5

C. 10baseT

D. 10baseFL

Answer: B, D

19. The network design calls for one MAU to be placed on the south side of the first floor and another MAU to be placed on the north side of the second floor. The design also specifies that STP cable be used. What is the maximum distance allowable between the MAUs?

A. 100 meters

B. 200 meters

C. 400 meters

D. 800 meters

Answer: B

Chapter 5 Answers

1. Suppose the following situation exists: Your company occupies three building on a campus. Each of these buildings has a 10BaseT network running to all floors. The buildings form a rough triangle, 1,500 meters on each side. Each are within sight of the others. You must choose a network type to connect the buildings.

   Required result: The network must support 100Mbps transfer speeds.

   Optional desired result: The network must be easy to install and maintain. The network should be immune to EMI.

   Proposed solution: Implement a fiber-optic network between buildings.

   Which results does the proposed solution produce? Choose one:

   A. The proposed solution produces the required result and produces both of the optional desired results.

   B. The proposed solution produces the required result and produces only one of the optional desired results.

   C. The proposed solution produces the required result but does not produce any of the optional desired results.

   D. The proposed solution does not produce the required result.

   Answer: B

2. You have just been hired to manage the network for a law firm. Currently, no network is installed, but each of the 42 employees has a computer. Because of the type of data being processed, security is very important, and centralized backups are required. However, speed is not of the utmost importance. Which of the following network types is best suited to your environment?

   A. Multi-Server with a high-speed backbone

   B. Enterprise

   C. Hybrid

   D. Single Server

   Answer: D

3. Suppose the following situation exists: Your company is installing five new computer kiosks for general employee information. The wiring closet is centrally located in the building. However, the cable runs range anywhere from 200 to 600 feet.

   Required result: Select a single type of cable that will enable all computers on the network to communicate with each other.

   Optional desired results: Keep costs to a minimum. The cable must be resistant to EMI.

   Proposed solution: Select fiber-optic cable as the standard.

   Which results does the proposed solution produce? Choose one:

   A. The proposed solution produces the required result and produces both of the optional desired results.

   B. The proposed solution produces the required result and produces only one of the optional desired results.

   C. The proposed solution produces the required result but does not produce any of the optional desired results.

   D. The proposed solution does not produce the required result.

   Answer: B

4. As a consultant, you have been hired by an advertising firm to optimize their network performance. They currently have 180 computers and printers connected to the network. They use centralized file storage and backups, and have groupware applications, Internet access, and a database of client information. Which of the following network types is best suited to their company?

   A. Multi-Server

   B. Enterprise

   C. Peer

   D. Mesh

   Answer: A

5. Suppose the following situation exists: Your company occupies three building on a campus. Each of these buildings has a 10BaseT network running to all floors. The buildings form a rough triangle, 1,500 meters on each side. Each are within sight of the others. You must choose a network type to connect the buildings.

> **Required result:** The network must support 100Mbps transfer speeds.

> **Optional desired result:** The network must be Ethernet. The network should be immune to EMI.

> **Proposed solution:** Implement a fiber-optic network between buildings.

Which results does the proposed solution produce? Choose one:

A. The proposed solution produces the required result and produces both of the optional desired results.

B. The proposed solution produces the required result and produces only one of the optional desired results.

C. The proposed solution produces the required result but does not produce any of the optional desired results.

D. The proposed solution does not produce the required result.

Answer: A

Chapter 6 Answers

1. Historically, computing installations used a single, very powerful computer for processing. What type of computing model does this situation represent?

A. Client/Server computing

B. Standalone computing

C. Distributed computing

D. Centralized computing

Answer: D

2. You are expanding your Windows NT network to include a second server. To ensure that the new server will act as a Domain Controller if the Primary Domain Controller fails, how should you install Windows NT?

A. As a Standby Domain Controller

B. As a Standalone Server

C. As a Backup Domain Controller

D. As a Primary Domain Controller

Answer: C

3. Suppose the following situation exists: You administer the network for a large, multinational corporation. You must design a naming system that will scale easily across the wide-area network as it is implemented. The total network covers 56 offices in 14 countries, with a total of 15,000 clients and 75 servers.

Required result: Design a naming system which uniquely identifies each of the clients and servers.

Optional desired results: The naming system for clients should include the primary user's logon name. The naming system for servers should describe their function as well as their location.

Proposed solution: Assign each client and server a 12-character random, unique, alphanumeric name. Track the list of computers and names via a Microsoft Access database.

What result does the proposed solution provide?

A. The proposed solution produces the required result and produces all of the optional desired results.

B. The proposed solution produces the required result but produces only one of the optional desired results.

C. The proposed solution produces the required result but does not produce any of the optional desired results.

D. The proposed solution does not produce the required result.

Answer: C

4. Your database, which was originally created in Microsoft Access, is stored on the Windows NT file server so that multiple people have access. However, as the database has grown and more people have required access, you've noticed that performance has suffered. Which of the following steps can you take to increase the performance of your database?

A. Import the database into SQL and run MS-SQL Server on the file server.

B. Install a faster network card in the server.

C. Increase the memory in the client computers.

D. Buy copies of Access for workstations. Import the database into each workstation and keep the master database on the server.

Answer: A

5. For computers to communicate on a network using TCP/IP, which of the following settings must be unique for each computer?

A. IP Address

B. Subnet Mask

C. Default Gateway

D. WINS Server Address

Answer: A

6. It is possible to automatically configure TCP/IP settings on computers running Microsoft operating systems. Which of the following protocols perform this function?

A. ICMP

B. SMTP

C. RARP

D. DHCP

Answer: D

7. Suppose the following situation exists: Your company has recently merged with another company of approximately the same size. Both companies have been running peer-to-peer networks, but are looking for new ideas. The companies are located in different cities and must have access to each other's files. In addition, a database has been created merging the client information for both companies that must be accessed by all employees.

   Required result: Recommend a centralized network model for the new company.

   Optional desired results: The network needs to accommodate extensive security. The network must have room for growth.

   Proposed solution: Implement a Windows NT domain multi-server network using user- and group-level security.

   Which result does the proposed solution produce? Choose one:

   A. The proposed solution produces the required result and produces both of the optional desired results.

   B. The proposed solution produces the required result and produces only one of the optional desired results.

   C. The proposed solution produces the required result but does not produce any of the optional desired results.

   D. The proposed solution does not produce the required result.

   Answer: A

8. Which of the following network printing components hold a print job until it can be processed by the printer?

   A. Spooler

   B. Print Server

   C. Redirector

   D. Printer Share

   Answer: A

9. One of the benefits to networking is the ability to share devices. Which of the two following devices can be shared as a print job destination?

A. A Cannon Color Laser printer

B. A Hayes 56K fax modem

C. A Hewlett-Packard CD-R drive

D. A Hewlett-Packard Scanjet attached to LPT1

Answer: A, B

10. You have just purchased an Ethernet card for your Windows NT Server. Which of the following can you reference to verify your new card will work in your server? Choose all that apply:

A. TechNet

B. MSDL

C. WinMSD

D. HCL

Answer: D

11. Your network includes the following printers: three HP Laserjet 860s, one Okidata dot-matrix, and two Tektronix color laser. In addition, you have an HP Laserjet 860 connected directly to the back of your computer. How many printer drivers need to be installed on your computer for you to utilize all printers available to you?

A. Seven

B. Four

C. Three

D. Two

Answer: C

12. You are planning a new Windows NT Server implementation and would like to ensure that the system files have enough room to operate and are not overrun by user and application files. Which of the following partition configurations best suits your situation?

    A. Create a single partition and install all files there.

    B. Create multiple partitions; one containing the system files, one the applications, and one the user data.

    C. Create a mirrored partition utilizing one disk set for system files, and one for other files.

    D. Use a RAID5 array to ensure no files are lost.

    Answer: B

13. Your PC utilizes the file storage and backup facilities on the file server, but runs all applications locally. Which of the following computing models does this represent?

    A. Client computing with Central File Storage

    B. Centralized computing

    C. Standalone computing

    D. Peer-to-peer computing

    Answer: A

14. In an effort to centralize management of applications, your boss has recommended that all programs be installed on the server, rather than on each individual client. Which of the arguments can be made for storing applications on the server? Choose all that apply:

    A. Software upgrades are easier because the files are centrally located.

    B. The server handles fewer requests.

    C. Software licensing is often easier to manage because you pay for the number of concurrent users.

    D. Access to the software can be controlled through user and group permissions.

    Answer: A, C, D

15. Suppose the following situation exists: You have been hired to design and manage a mid-size network for a law firm. The firm occupies three offices in the metropolitan area. Because the computers contain confidential client information, file access control is of the utmost importance. The firm is planning to implement a database and an internal e-mail system once the network is up and running.

Required result: Implement a centralized network design that will suit the firm's needs.

Optional desired results: The network design must handle the plans for expansion. The network design must prevent unauthorized access to files.

Proposed solution: Implement a Windows NT server-based network with user-level security. As more servers become necessary, add dedicated e-mail and/or database servers.

What results does the proposed solution produce?

A. The proposed solution produces the required result and both of the optional desired results.

B. The proposed solution produces the required result and only one of the optional desired results.

C. The proposed solution produces the required result but does not produce any of the optional desired results.

D. The proposed solution does not produce the required result.

Answer: A

Chapter 7 Answers

1. Which of the following operating systems will allow you to run Windows programs, but still use device drivers developed for MS-DOS?

A. MS-DOS

B. MacOS 8

C. Windows NT Server

D. Windows 95

Answer: D

2. In a networked computing environment, which of the following software components provides the means for computers to establish communications sessions over the network?

   A. The network interface card

   B. The network device driver

   C. The client software

   D. The protocol stack

   Answer: D

3. What is the maximum size a computer's name may be in a Microsoft network?

   A. 12

   B. 8+3

   C. 8

   D. 15

   Answer: D

4. You have begun to notice communications problems on your thinnet network. You use a volt-ohm meter to test the resistance between the conductor and the shield. It registers a resistance of 50-ohms. Which of the following is most likely the problem on your network?

   A. Your network is using the incorrect cable type.

   B. The resistance setting is incorrect on a network adapter card on your network.

   C. There is a defective network card interrupting communication.

   D. There is a faulty terminator on your network.

   Answer: D

5. When configuring a new computer for a Token Ring network, which of the following must be considered?

A. The IP address of the new computer should match the IP addresses of the other computers.

B. The MAC address of the new computer should match the MAC address of the other computers.

C. The NIC should be configured to operate at the same speed as the NICs on other computers.

D. The node address of the new computer should be the next highest available address to preserve the continuity of the ring.

Answer: C

6. You must implement a new operating system for the client computers on your network. Which of the following operating systems will support both DOS and Windows applications? Choose all that apply:

A. Windows 95

B. LINUX

C. MS-DOS

D. Windows NT Workstation

Answer: A, D

7. The NDIS and ODI specifications define the rules for communication between the protocol stack and the network interface adapter. Which of the following components should be NDIS or ODI compliant to operate in a Windows 95 computer?

A. The client software

B. The operating system

C. The network device driver

D. The network interface adapter

Answer: C

8. Which of the following is used by Microsoft to describe a server-based network?

   A. Domain

   B. Session

   C. Workgroup

   D. LAN

   Answer: A

9. If two computers running NWLink are unable to communicate, which of these situations is the most likely problem?

   A. The computers share the same MAC address.

   B. The IPX default gateway is set incorrectly on one of the computers.

   C. The IPX frame type is not the same on both computers.

   D. The network does not support NWLink.

   Answer: C

10. The development staff for your company needs a desktop operating system that can gracefully handle a program crash without taking down the entire computer. In addition, certain developers need the power of multiple processors. Choose one operating system from the following list to install on all of your developer's computers.

   A. Windows NT Workstation

   B. DR-DOS

   C. Windows for Workgroups

   D. Windows 95

   Answer: A

11. In a network that is using Windows 95 clients and Windows NT servers, which of the following protocols can be used for communication? Choose all that apply:

    A. AppleTalk

    B. DLC

    C. IPX/SPX

    D. NetBEUI

    Answer: C, D

12. You have noticed recently that network performance is suffering. By using a protocol analyzer to capture network traffic, you find that one workstation on your network is consistently sending packets with CRC errors. You suspect this may be the problem with network performance. Which of the following can you do to correct the problem?

    A. Increase network speed to 100Mbps.

    B. Replace the network card because it has failed.

    C. Configure the network card to use a different MAC address.

    D. Change the protocols being used on the network.

    Answer: B

13. You have decided to install a second Ethernet adapter in your server. To ensure that it works properly, you configured it with the same IRQ and port settings as the adapter already in the machine. Each card works independently, but when both are installed, neither works. Which of the following is the cause of the problem?

    A. The adapters must have unique settings, including IRQ and port.

    B. The server's BIOS must be configured to support multiple network adapters.

    C. The server does not support more than one Ethernet adapter.

    D. The adapters must be configured to recognize each other.

    Answer: A

14. Which of the following operating systems includes support for both Intel and Digital Alpha architectures? Choose all that apply:

    A. Windows for Workgroups

    B. Windows NT Workstation

    C. OS/2

    D. Windows 95

    Answer: B

15. What is the term Microsoft uses to describe a peer-to-peer Windows network?

    A. Domain

    B. Session

    C. Workgroup

    D. LAN

    Answer: C

16. Your network consists of two LANs, one 10BaseT and one 10Base2. Your server is connected to both networks to allow easy communication. Each of your client workstations has a combo network adapter card with both RJ-45 and BNC connectors. You are in the process of moving a workstation from the Thinnet LAN to the UTP LAN. Which of the following must you do before the workstation will be able to communicate?

    A. The computer name must be changed to reflect the new network.

    B. The network adapter card must be assigned a new node address.

    C. The network adapter must be configured to use the transceiver for the RJ-45 port.

    D. The network adapter must be configured to use a new IRQ and port address.

    Answer: C

17. One of the keys to troubleshooting a 10Base2 network is the ability to identify how far down the network segment the cable is broken. Which of the following troubleshooting devices will help you determine a cable break's location?

A. Time-domain reflectometer

B. SNMP manager

C. Volt-ohm meter

D. Sniffer

Answer: A

18. Which of the following Ethernet components is unique for each card created?

A. Frame type

B. CRC address

C. IRQ

D. MAC address

Answer: D

Chapter 8 Answers

1. The manager of the accounting department has decided not to return from maternity leave. Her replacement has been hired from outside the company. Which of the following is the best way to ensure that her replacement has the same access to the network she had?

A. Change the password on the old manager's account and let the new manager use the same account.

B. Disable the old manager's account. Create a new account with the same settings as the old account.

C. Delete the old account. Create a new account for the new manager.

D. Rename the account to the new manager's username and assign a new password.

Answer: D

2. When designing a disaster recovery and prevention plan, it is always a good idea to include a UPS. When connected to your server, what will a UPS do?

   A. Ensure that the server is protected from virus attacks.

   B. Ensure that the server is protected from unauthorized access.

   C. Ensure that the server is protected from power failure.

   D. Ensure that the server is protected from fire.

   Answer: C

3. You are planning the installation of a new Windows NT server. You would like to provide some hard disk fault-tolerance. Which of the following could you use in your new server to provide fault tolerance? Choose all that apply:

   A. UPS

   B. Disk striping with parity

   C. Disk duplexing

   D. Disk striping

   Answer: B, C

4. What is the maximum length a username can be when using Microsoft products such as Windows NT?

   A. 15 characters

   B. 12 characters

   C. 16 characters

   D. 20 characters

   Answer: D

5. A number of user groups are automatically created when Windows NT Server is installed on a computer. Which of the following groups provides no special privileges to its members?

   A. Users

   B. Server Operators

   C. Replicator

   D. Administrators

   Answer: A

6. You manage a rather large 100BaseTX network. It encompasses 20 servers and 900 client computers. You have been tasked with implementing a security plan that will withstand audits by clients.

   Required result: Provide a security plan that will ensure solid security and provide centralized control of resources.

   Optional desired results: Your plan should include a mechanism to track failed logon attempts as well as other network events. Include plans to protect your network from password discovery programs.

   Proposed solution: Implement Windows NT user-level security on NTFS partitions including access-control security to shared resources. Set password restrictions to require users to change their passwords every 30 days and limit the number of failed attempts before an account is locked.

What results does the proposed solution provide?

   A. The proposed solution produces the required result and produces all of the optional desired results.

   B. The proposed solution produces the required result but produces only one of the optional desired results.

   C. The proposed solution produces the required result but does not produce any of the optional desired results.

   D. The proposed solution does not produce the required result.

   Answer: B

7. When the Windows NT operating system, either Workstation or Server, is installed on a computer, two accounts are created. Which of the accounts in the following list are created when the operating system is installed? Choose two:

A. Manager

B. Guest

C. Administrator

D. Supervisor

Answer: B, C

8. The manager of the accounting department is going on maternity leave. When she returns she will need to maintain the access level she has now. However, you are concerned about someone else using her logon while she is gone. Which of the following can you do to ensure this doesn't happen?

A. Delete her account and re-create it when she returns.

B. Change the password on her account so that no one knows it.

C. Disable her account and re-enable it when she returns.

D. Enable password protection on her computer so that no one can access it.

Answer: C

9. When implementing a virus-protection system for your network, which of the following will provide reliable protection? Choose all that apply:

A. Remove floppy drives from client computers.

B. Install virus scanning software on all client and server computers.

C. Update virus protection software regularly.

D. Restrict physical access to the servers.

Answer: A, B, C

10. You have been asked to develop a naming system for the users on your Windows NT network. Which of the following statements apply to user-names on Microsoft networks? Choose all that apply:

A. Must be unique among domain members

B. Must coincide with the computer name.

C. Can include /, \, and ?

D. Can use mixed case, but are not case sensitive.

Answer: A, D

11. When Windows NT Server is installed on a computer, a number of global and local groups are created. Which of the following groups provides its members with the ability to administer any computer in the domain?

A. Domain Guests

B. Domain Users

C. Domain Operators

D. Domain Admins

Answer: D

12. Which of the following RAID levels provides the fastest reads and best fault tolerance?

A. RAID Level X

B. RAID Level 5

C. RAID Level 1

D. RAID Level 0

Answer: B

13. Suppose the following situation exists: In an audit of your network security you learn that more than 100 of your 500 users have been granted

Administrator privileges. This is too large a security risk to accept on your network.

Required result: Implement a new security structure that restricts user access.

Optional desired results: The new structure must ensure that only specific personnel are granted Administrator privileges. The new security structure should include auditing of logon events.

Proposed solution: Create departmental groups encompassing the entire company structure. Include an Administrators group for yourself and other network administrators. Remove all Administrator and equivalent privileges from all users.

Which result does the proposed solution produce?

A. The proposed solution produces the required result and produces both of the optional desired results.

B. The proposed solution produces the required result and produces only one of the optional desired results.

C. The proposed solution produces the required result but does not produce any of the optional desired results.

D. The proposed solution does not produce the required result.

Answer: B

Chapter 9 Answers

1. Which of the following statements describe dedicated leased lines? Choose all that apply:

A. Utilize CSU/DSUs

B. Can provide data transfer rates between 56Kbps and 45Mbps

C. Provide only a temporary connection between two sites

D. Use packet switching technology

Answer: A, B

2. Most modems employ a number of functions that improve performance and reliability. Which of the following increases the reliability of a modem?

A. Error detection

B. Demodulation

C. Encryption

D. Compression

Answer: A

3. It is essential that communication between two devices be synchronized. Which of the following methods maintains synchronization without a clocking signal?

A. Time division multiplexing

B. Asynchronous data transmission

C. Synchronous data transmission

D. Asynchronous transfer mode

Answer: B

4. Which of the following cable types can be used to connect an analog modem to your computer?

A. Parallel

B. SCSI

C. 10BaseT

D. RS-232

Answer: D

5. When RAS is installed on a Windows NT server, what is the maximum number of concurrent dial-in connections?

   A. 144

   B. 256

   C. 64

   D. 128

   Answer: B

6. To improve performance over a dial-up line, a modem can employ any number of functions. Which of the following increases the data rate of a modem?

   A. Error correction

   B. Asynchronous transfer

   C. Compression

   D. Encryption

   Answer: C

7. When configuring an ISDN device, a single B channel can be set to what speed on a BRI (basic rate interface)?

   A. 28.8 Kbps

   B. 1.44 Mbps

   C. 64 Kbps or 56Kbps

   D. 128Kbps

   Answer: C

8. For all intents and purposes, a RAS connection is an extension of the network. Which of the following is not possible over a RAS connection?

   A. Read and manipulate files

   B. Administer users and groups

   C. Execute programs

   D. None of the above. RAS will allow all network functions.

   Answer: D

9. Which of the following Windows NT services could you install to allow remote Windows computers access to your network via modem?

   A. CDS

   B. SLIP

   C. PPP

   D. RAS

   Answer: D

Chapter 10 Answers

1. Which of the following would most effectively segment traffic on a network using NWLink? Choose the most correct answer:

   A. Repeater

   B. Router

   C. Modem

   D. Bridge

   Answer: B

2. Of the devices listed below, which is capable of operating at all of the upper layers of the OSI model?

   A. Gateway

   B. Brouter

   C. Router

   D. Bridge

   Answer: A

3. Some networking devices regenerate the signals they receive, effectively increasing the distance the signal can travel before succumbing to attenuation. Which of the following devices does not have this ability?

   A. Multiplexer

   B. Active hub

   C. Bridge

   D. Passive hub

   Answer: D

4. Which of the following networking devices will allow you to transmit Ethernet, Token Ring, and voice over a single cable?

   A. Router

   B. Multiplexer

   C. Repeater

   D. Bridge

   Answer: B

5. Which of the following steps can you take to control broadcast storms on a network?

   A. Segment the network with a router.

   B. Use a network analyzer to track which computers are sending the most broadcasts.

   C. Convert the network to 10BaseT.

   D. Segment the network with a bridge.

   Answer: A

6. Your network consists solely of Windows 95 clients and Windows NT servers. You have recently acquired a smaller company that is using NetWare servers. You would like to provide access to the NetWare servers for your Windows 95 clients, but you do not want to install a new redirector on each client computer. Which of the following could you install to provide Windows 95 clients access to NetWare servers?

   A. Gateway

   B. Bridge

   C. Router

   D. Brouter

   Answer: A

7. An excessive number of broadcasts on a network will cause the network media to be flooded, effectively halting network communication. What is this phenomenon called?

   A. A broadcast flood

   B. A broadcast storm

   C. A collision storm

   D. EMI

   Answer: B

8. Which of the following networking devices operate below the network layer of the OSI model? Choose all that apply:

   A. Bridges

   B. Gateways

   C. Repeaters

   D. Routers

   Answer: A, C

9. Suppose the following situation exists: Your Windows NT Workstation workgroup consists of 15 computers spread over 175 meters on a 10Base2 network. A repeater has been installed near the middle of the network, effectively creating two network segments. You notice, however, that because of high network traffic, performance is not as high as you would like.

   Required result: Increase network performance.

   Optional desired result: Continue to use NetBEUI as the transport protocol. Keep upgrade costs to a minimum.

   Proposed solution: Replace the repeater with a bridge between the two network segments.

   What result does the proposed solution produce?

   A. The proposed solution produces the required result and produces both of the optional desired results.

   B. The proposed solution produces the required result and produces only one of the optional desired results.

   C. The proposed solution produces the required result but does not produce any of the optional desired results.

   D. The proposed solution does not produce the required result.

   Answer: A

10. Which of the following devices is able to increase the network segment length by increasing signal strength?

    A. BNC barrel connector

    B. Repeater

    C. Transceiver

    D. Passive hub

    Answer: B

11. If your network requires a multiplexer to support the assignment of priorities to particular devices, which of the following forms of multiplexing would be used?

    A. Statistical Time Division Multiplexing

    B. Statistical Frequency Division Multiplexing

    C. Frequency Division Multiplexing

    D. Time Division Multiplexing

    Answer: A

12. Broadcast storms are often a problem on networks. With which of the following protocols can broadcast storms not be controlled by installing a router?

    A. IPX/SPX

    B. NetBEUI

    C. DLC

    D. TCP/IP

    Answer: B

13. Which of the following route-discovery techniques uses frequent broadcasts that can increase network traffic?

    A. Broadcast routing

    B. Distance-vector routing

    C. Comprehensive routing

    D. Link-state routing

    Answer: B

14. Suppose the following situation exists: Your 10Base2 network is expanding rapidly as more and more computers are added. You are very concerned about attenuation and are beginning to notice inconsistent network behavior. Your network consists of 2 NT servers and 35 workstations, all using NetBEUI for transport.

    Required result: Install a networking device that will eliminate the effects of attenuation.

    Optional desired results: Ensure that broadcast storms do not incapacitate the network. Filter traffic based on MAC addresses.

    Proposed solution: Install a repeater at a central point of the network.

    Which result does the proposed solution produce?

    A. The proposed solution produces the required result and produces both of the optional desired results.

    B. The proposed solution produces the required result and produces only one of the optional desired results.

    C. The proposed solution produces the required result but does not produce any of the optional desired results.

    D. The proposed solution does not produce the required result.

    Answer: C

15. Generally, the more advanced a product is, the more expensive it is. Which of the following devices operates highest on the OSI model and is more expensive?

    A. Repeater

    B. Transceiver

    C. Router

    D. Bridge

    Answer: C

16. A brouter generally provides greater functionality than a router. Which of the following statements accurately describes the differences?

    A. A brouter works at all layers of the OSI model.

    B. A brouter chooses the best path to a destination.

    C. A brouter filters traffic according to network address.

    D. A brouter is able to bridge those protocols that are not routable.

    Answer: D

17. Which of the following terms describes the process employed by routers to determine possible routes through a network?

    A. Segment discovery

    B. Network discovery

    C. Route discovery

    D. Path discovery

    Answer: C

18. There are two types of gateways in networking, one of which provides the next hop for TCP/IP packets whose destination is outside the local network. Which of the following describes the other type of gateway?

A. It provides connectivity for computers to the Internet.

B. It provides connectivity between physically dissimilar networks.

C. It provides protocol translation.

D. It provides a mechanism for sending data and voice over the same phone line.

Answer: C

19. Suppose the following situation exists: Your 10Base2 network is expanding rapidly as more and more computers are added. You are very concerned about attenuation and are beginning to notice inconsistent network behavior. Your network consists of 2 NT servers and 35 workstations, all using NetBEUI for transport.

Required result: Install a networking device that will eliminate the effects of attenuation.

Optional desired results: Ensure that broadcast storms do not incapacitate the network. Filter traffic based on MAC addresses.

Proposed solution: Install a typical bridge at a central point of the network.

Which result does the proposed solution produce?

A. The proposed solution produces the required result and produces both of the optional desired results.

B. The proposed solution produces the required result and produces only one of the optional desired results.

C. The proposed solution produces the required result but does not produce any of the optional desired results.

D. The proposed solution does not produce the required result.

Answer: B

20. What type of multiplexing would a device use if it transmits each signal at a different frequency?

A. Time Division Multiplexing

B. Statistical Time Division Multiplexing

C. Statistical Frequency Division Multiplexing

D. Frequency Division Multiplexing

Answer: D

Chapter 11 Answers

1. Which of the following protocols available for Dial-Up Networking is most often used to connect to the Internet?

A. PPTP

B. ISDN

C. PPP

D. SLPP

Answer: C

2. Which of the following high-speed network types uses fixed- rather than variable-length cells to achieve higher speeds?

A. Fast Ethernet

B. Frame Relay

C. FDDI

D. ATM

Answer: D

3. Of the network types listed below, which will provide 100Mbps transmission over fiber-optic cable? Choose all that apply:

   A. 100VG-AnyLAN

   B. FDDI

   C. 100BaseT4

   D. ATM

   Answer: A, B, D

4. Suppose the following situation exists: Your company is located in three offices in the Bay Area. Each office includes between 30 and 50 workstations, with 2 to 3 servers in each office. The offices are currently not connected.

   Required result: Propose a wide-area networking solution to connect the three offices.

   Optional desired results: Provide bandwidth over 1Mbps. Include redundancy in the specification.

   Proposed solution: Install ATM in a mesh configuration between all three sites.

   Which results does the proposed solution produce?

   A. The proposed solution produces the required result and produces both of the optional desired results.

   B. The proposed solution produces the required result and produces only one of the optional desired results.

   C. The proposed solution produces the required result but does not produce any of the optional desired results.

   D. The proposed solution does not produce the required result.

   Answer: A

5. T-carriers are widely used to connect LANs to form WANs. Which of the following describes a feature of T1 circuits?

   A. 128 Kbps transmission

   B. 1.544 Mbps transmission

   C. Limited to half-duplex transmission

   D. Satellite based

   Answer: B

6. Which of the wide-area networking technologies listed below provides the highest transmission speeds?

   A. Frame Relay

   B. T3

   C. ISDN

   D. ATM

   Answer: D

7. Which of the following Dial-Up Networking protocols includes support for both IPX and TCP/IP?

   A. DLC

   B. PPP

   C. SLIP

   D. UDP

   Answer: B

8. Certain packet-switched networks establish virtual circuits to facilitate communication. Which of the following protocols function in this way? Choose all that apply:

   A. Frame Relay

   B. Switched 56

   C. FDDI

   D. ATM

   Answer: A, D

9. The specifications for ATM include encapsulation into other protocols. Which of the following can ATM be encapsulated in? Choose all that apply:

   A. ARCNet

   B. Token Ring

   C. Fiber Channel

   D. SONET

   Answer: C, D

10. Which of the following protocols available for Dial-Up Networking does not support automatically assigned IP addresses?

    A. SNMP

    B. PPP

    C. SMTP

    D. SLIP

    Answer: D

11. Which of the following describes some of the features of ATM? Choose all that apply:

    A. ATM uses packet switching.

    B. ATM has a maximum throughput of 56Mbps.

    C. ATM can simultaneously transmit data and video.

    D. ATM uses variable-length packets.

    Answer: A, C

12. Which of the following protocols provides robust low-speed packet-switching with extensive error checking mechanisms over either dedicated or switched circuits?

    A. FDDI

    B. X.25

    C. ATM

    D. Frame Relay

    Answer: B

13. Which of the following provides digital rather than analog dial-up service?

   A. DUN

   B. X.25

   C. ISDN

   D. POTS

   Answer: C

14. Which of the following wide-area networking technologies will support transmission rates of 1 Gbps or higher?

   A. SONET

   B. X.25

   C. Ethernet

   D. T3

   Answer: A

15. Suppose the following situation exists: Your company is located in three offices in the Bay Area. Each office includes between 30 and 50 workstations, with 2 to 3 servers in each office. The offices are currently not connected.

   Required result: Propose a wide-area networking solution to connect the three offices.

   Optional desired results: Provide dedicated support for video and voice traffic in addition to data. Provide redundancy in case of a failure.

   Proposed solution: Install three Switched 56 lines connecting all offices.

Which results does the proposed solution produce?

A. The proposed solution produces the required result and produces both of the optional desired results.

B. The proposed solution produces the required result and produces only one of the optional desired results.

C. The proposed solution produces the required result but does not produce any of the optional desired results.

D. The proposed solution does not produce the required result.

Answer: D

16. Suppose the following situation exists: Your office has been instructed by corporate to establish a wide-area network connection with a client office across town. Both of the networks are using Windows 95 in a peer-to-peer environment. For ease of use, both offices are using NetBEUI.

Required result: Provide a solution to connect the two offices.

Optional desired results: Continue to use NetBEUI. Keeps costs low.

Proposed solution: Connect the two offices using a 56K leased-line and brouters.

What results does the proposed solution produce?

A. The proposed solution produces the required result and produces both of the optional desired results.

B. The proposed solution produces the required result and produces only one of the optional desired results.

C. The proposed solution produces the required result but does not produce any of the optional desired results.

D. The proposed solution does not produce the required result.

Answer: B

17. Frame Relay is a largely accepted wide-area networking technology. Which of the following statements are true of Frame Relay. Choose all that apply:

A. It was developed from the X.25 standard.

B. Is supports variable-length packets.

C. It incorporates redundant error-checking.

D. Because it is the most robust transmission method, it functions well on older, less reliable phone lines.

Answer: A, B

Chapter 12 Answers

1. Which of the following statements most accurately describes the network threat known as a worm?

A. A small piece of code that writes itself to the boot sector of your hard disk drive

B. A program that acts as a logon prompt to capture usernames and passwords

C. A small program that propagates itself from machine to machine and exploits the weaknesses of the operating system

D. A bit of code that attaches itself to other program files

Answer: C

2. There are many devices that are able to test the continuity of a network cable. Which of the following is also able to provide information on collisions and congestion?

A. Time-domain reflectometers

B. Oscilloscopes

C. Volt-ohm meters

D. Advanced cable testers

Answer: D

3. To successfully administer a network, you must include planning, monitoring, and troubleshooting. Which of the following is not true of network troubleshooting?

A. Most problems occur at the Physical layer.

B. Network monitors are used to check for congestion on the network.

C. Protocol analyzers are able to determine if there is a break in the cable.

D. TDRs and volt-ohm meters are able to identify breaks in the cable.

Answer: C

4. A time-domain reflectometer is used in network troubleshooting for which of the following tasks?

A. To identify cable faults

B. To provide protocol-level analysis

C. To test network throughput

D. To segment network traffic for analysis

Answer: A

5. When considering attacks on your network, which of the following executable code can be introduced onto the boot sector of a hard disk?

A. A Bacterium

B. An SST

C. A Trojan Horse

D. A Virus

Answer: D

6. You have recently noticed that network communication is slow. You fear that a faulty network adapter is sending bad packets. Which of the following troubleshooting tools could you use to determine which station has the faulty NIC?

A. A protocol analyzer

B. A volt-ohm meter

C. An SNMP manager

D. A transceiver

Answer: A

7. A protocol analyzer can be used to troubleshoot a network. Which of the following are available from a protocol analyzer? Choose all that apply:

A. Capture of packets for analysis

B. Cable break location

C. Traffic alarm

D. Resistance measurement

Answer: A, C

8. Network security can be increased by implementing which of the following? Choose all that apply:

A. Standardize passwords to a consistent format.

B. Require users to change their passwords every 60 days.

C. Limit guest accounts.

D. Store file servers in a locked room.

Answer: B, C, D

9. When using a volt-ohm meter to check the continuity of a twisted-pair cable, which of the following settings would you use?

A. Voltage measure in volts

B. Resistance measured in watts

C. Resistance measured in ohms

D. Resistance measured in volts

Answer: C

10. Although they are the easiest cables to work with, unshielded twisted-pair cables are prone to problems. Which of the following often affect UTP cables? Choose all that apply:

    A. Improper resistance between the conductor and the cladding

    B. Electromagnetic Interference

    C. Refraction

    D. Crosstalk

    Answer: B, D

11. Your network administration plan should include equipment to ensure no data is lost. Which of the following will protect against data loss? Choose all that apply:

    A. Encryption

    B. UPS

    C. Compression

    D. Disk Duplexing

    Answer: B, D

12. Which of the following network troubleshooting devices can best be used nonintrusively to verify network performance? Choose one:

    A. A time-domain reflectometer

    B. A protocol analyzer

    C. An advanced cable tester

    D. A volt-ohm meter

    Answer: B

Index

Note to the Reader:

Main level entries are in **boldface**. **Boldface** page numbers indicate primary discussions of a topic. *Italic* page numbers indicate illustrations.

Take the
interactive
MULTIMEDIA COMPUTER-BASED TRAINING
Challenge

Installation

Installation for Win95, NT 3.51 and NT 4.0

1. Start MS Windows 95, NT 3.51 or NT 4.0
2. Insert the CD into the CD-ROM drive
3. Choose "Run" from the Start button
4. Type D:\setup.exe (If necessary, substitute D with correct letter for your CD-ROM drive)
5. Follow the instructions that are found on the screen.
6. After the installation is complete, MS Video for Windows will launch. Installing the program is not necessary, simply select "Exit".

n this CD-ROM?

arnKey training CD-ROM contained in this book is only the first course of a com-
ded as a sample of what LearnKey's interactive training can do for you while
s relative to the content of this book. Each LearnKey
xpert instruction with interactive exercises. Our
ners help perfect your MCSE skills, and our intuitive
apply the techniques you've learned.

egins with instruction from our Microsoft Certified
vie window. Instructors demonstrate how to install
networking software.

allows you to perform procedures learned in the
gh interactive task simulations. Two "Help" features
u through specific tasks.

ne your network administration abilities. Each test
rmance-based progress report that pinpoints your areas of strength and weak-
E training program is an ideal way to enhance your networking skills and pre-
certification exams.

In order for more than one user to use this CD, you must purchase additional site licenses. For more information regarding site licenses, or to purchase the remaining volumes in this set, call 800-865-0165.

Technical Support & FAQ

LearnKey provides comprehensive technical support online. Please refer any installation or troubleshooting questions to our technical support team at www.learnkey.com.

MCSE: Networking Essentials Study Guide, Third Edition

Exam 70-058: Objectives